THE GOLDEN BOOK OF TAGORE

THE GOLDEN BOOK OF TAGORE

A HOMAGE TO RABINDRANATH TAGORE FROM INDIA AND THE WORLD IN CELEBRATION OF HIS SEVENTIETH BIRTHDAY

RAMANANDA CHATTERJEE

GYAN

Published by

Gyan Publishing House
5, Ansari Road
Daryaganj, New Delhi-110002
Phone: 011-47034999, 9811692060
E-mail: books@gyanbooks.com

Distribution Network
gyanbooks.com
India, USA, Canada, UK, Australia

ISBN: 978-93-7316-412-0 (HB)

First Published, 1931

2nd Impression 2025

Printed at: Gyan Press, Delhi.

THE GOLDEN BOOK OF TAGORE
Author: RAMANANDA CHATTERJEE

THE GOLDEN BOOK OF TAGORE

A HOMAGE TO RABINDRANATH TAGORE
FROM INDIA AND THE WORLD
IN CELEBRATION OF HIS SEVENTIETH BIRTHDAY

EDITED BY RAMANANDA CHATTERJEE

PUBLISHED BY THE GOLDEN BOOK COMMITTEE

CALCUTTA 1931

THE GOLDEN BOOK OF TAGORE

FOREWORD

ALONG with the readers of this volume and the members of the Golden Book of Tagore Committee, I am grateful to and cordially thank the ladies and gentlemen who have contributed to it, as they have enabled all of us thereby to have some idea of the genius, personality and achievement of Rabindranath Tagore. But these are so great and many-sided that a complete appraisal of them is hardly practicable within any manageable compass. Nevertheless, I, too, on whom has been conferred the honour of editing this book, must venture to write briefly what I know of the Poet—if only in obedience to a natural public desire.

Rabindranath Tagore is our greatest poet and prose-writer. Son of a *Maharshi* (a "great seer"), and himself a seer and sage, he belongs to a family the most gifted in Bengal in the realms of religion, philosophy, literature, music, painting, and the histrionic art. There is no department of Bengali literature that he has touched which he has not adorned, elevated, and filled with inspiration and lighted up by the lustre of his genius. Difficult as it undoubtedly would be to give an exhaustive list of his multifarious achievements from early youth upwards—for his is a many-sided and towering personality, even the departments of literature and knowledge which he has touched and adorned would make a pretty long list. The late Mahamahopadhyaya Haraprasad Sastri, M.A., D.LITT., C.I.E., said of the Poet in the course of his presidential address at the preparatory meeting for the Tagore Septuagenary Celebrations:

> He has tried all phases of literature—couplets, stanzas, short poems, longer pieces, short stories, longer stories, fables, novels and prose romances, dramas, farces, comedies and tragedies, songs, operas, *kirtans, pālās,* and, last but not least, lyric poems. He has succeeded in every phase of literature he has touched, but he has succeeded in the last phase of literature beyond measure. His essays are illuminating, his sarcasms biting, his satires piercing. His estimate of old poets is deeply appreciative, and his grammatical and lexicographical speculations go further inward than those of most of us.

Tennyson, in his poem addressed to Victor Hugo, called that great French author "Victor in Drama, Victor in Romance, Cloud-weaver of phantasmal hopes and fears," "Lord of human tears," "Child-lover," and "Weird Titan by thy winter weight of years as yet unbroken. . . ." All these epithets and many more can be rightly applied to Rabindranath Tagore.

Many works and some kinds of works of Rabindranath in Bengali have not yet been translated into English or thence into other Western and Eastern languages. In the translations, moreover, much, if not all, of the music, the suggestiveness, the undefinable associations clustering round Bengali words and phrases, and the aroma, racy of Bengal and India, of the original has been lost. No doubt, the translations of the poems and dramas—particularly when done by the Poet himself, have often gained in directness, in the beauty and sublimity of simplicity, and in the music and strength belonging to the English or other language of the translations. But admitting all this, one is still constrained to observe that, for a correct estimate and full appreciation of Rabindranath's intellectual and literary powers, his gifts and genius, it is necessary to study both his original works in Bengali and their English translations as well as his original works in English like *Personality, Sadhana,* and *The Religion of Man.* What high estimates of Tagore as an author many competent judges have formed without the advantage of reading his Bengali works, will appear from their contributions to this volume.

The music of his verse, and often of his prose as well, which fills the outer ear, is but an echo of the inner harmony of humanity and the universe—"the music of the spheres"—which exists at the heart of things and which he has caught and made manifest by his writings. How wonderfully full of real life and colour and motion and variety they are! His hymns and sermons and some of his other writings let us unconsciously into the secret of his access to the court of the King of kings, nay to His very presence, and of his communion with Him. His hymns and other writings in a spiritual vein have, therefore, brought healing to many a troubled soul.

Insight and imagination are his magic wands, by whose power he roams where he will and leads his readers thither, too. In his works Bengali literature has outgrown its provincial character and has become fit to fraternize with world literature. Universal currents of thought and spirituality have flowed into Bengal through his writings.

In philosophy he is not a system-builder. He is of the line of our ancient religio-philosophical teachers whose religion and philosophy are fused components of one whole. Both his poetry and prose embody his philosophy—the latest prose-work in English being *The Religion of Man.*

But he is not simply a literary man, though his eminence as an author is such that for a foreigner the Bengali language would be worth learning for his writings alone.

It does not in the least detract from his work as a musician to admit that he is not an *ustad* or "expert" in music, as that term is understood in common parlance. He has such a sensitive ear that he appears to live in two worlds—one, the world of visible forms and colours, and another, which one may call the world of sound-forms and sound-colours. His musical genius and instinct are such that his achievement in that art has extorted the admiration of many "experts." This is said not with reference only to his numerous hymns and patriotic and other songs and the tunes to which he has himself set them, or to his thrilling, sweet, soulful and rapt singing in different periods of his life, but also in connection with what he has done for absolute music. He is not only the author of the words of his songs, possessed of rare depth of meaning and suggestiveness and power of inspiration, but is also the creator of what may be called new airs and tunes.

Six years ago, I had the good fortune to be present at some of the meetings in Germany and Czechoslovakia where he recited some of his poems. His recitations were such that even when the poems recited were in a language not understood by the vast majority of the audience, he had to repeat them several times at the earnest request of the hearers. Those who have heard him read his addresses and deliver his extempore speeches and sermons in Bengali know how eloquent he could be as a speaker, though his delivery in years past was often so rapid and his sentences branched out in such bewildering luxuriance as to make him the despair of reporters.

He is a master and a consummate teacher of the histrionic art. Those who have seen him appear in leading rôles in many of his plays have experienced how natural and elevating acting can be. From the prime of his manhood upwards he has been in the habit of reading out his new poems, discourses, short stories, plays and novels to select circles. On such occasions, too, his elocution and histrionic talents come into play.

If it is true that the credit of reviving music in public for respectable women goes to the Brahma Samaj, that credit belongs in great part to the Tagore family and Rabindranath Tagore. They have also made it possible for girls and women of respectable classes to act in public. The poet has also rehabilitated in Bengal dancing by respectable girls and women as a means of self-expression and innocent amusement and play.

Tagore's patriotic songs are characteristic. They are refined and restrained, and free from bluff, bravado, bluster and boasting. Some of them twine their tendrils round the tenderest chords of our hearts, some enthrone the Motherland as the Adored in the shrine of our souls, some sound as a clarion call to our drooping spirits filling us with hope and the will to do and dare and suffer, some call on us to have the lofty courage to be in the minority of one; but in none are heard the clashing of interests, the warring passions of races, or the echoes of old, unhappy, far-off historic strifes and conflicts. In many of those written during the stirring times of the *Swadeshi* agitation in Bengal more than a couple of decades ago, the Poet spoke out with a directness which is missed in many of his writings, though not in the *Katha-O-Kahini* ballads which make the heart beat thick and fast and the blood tingle and leap and course swiftly in our veins.

To Andrews Fletcher of Salton, a famous Scottish patriot, is attributed the authorship of the observation that "if a man were permitted to make all the ballads, he need not care who should make the laws of a nation." He is generally quoted, however, as having said so with respect to songs. Both ballads and songs have much to do with the making of nations. Rabindranath's songs and ballads—the former to a greater extent than the latter, have been making Bengal to no small extent and will continue to mould the character of Bengalis, literate and illiterate, town-dwellers and village folk, and their culture and civilization. But it is not merely as a maker of songs that he has taken part in the *Swadeshi* movement. His socio-political addresses, the annual fairs suggested or organized by him, are part of the same national service. He has worked earnestly for the revival of weaving and other arts and crafts of the country—particularly village arts and crafts, and contributed his full share to making education in India Indian as well as human and humane in the broadest sense, and to the sanitation, reconstruction, reorganization and rejuvenation of villages. Even official reports have praised him as a model landlord for his activities in these directions in his estate.

His scheme of Constructive Non-co-operation, as outlined in some of his writings and addresses about a quarter of a century ago, was part of his *Swadeshi* movement politics. The "no-tax" campaign adumbrated in his play *Paritran* ("Deliverance") and the joyful acceptance of suffering and chains by its hero, Dhananjay Bairagi, are his idea of what political leaders should do on such occasions.

As he has denounced Nationalism in his book of that name, taking the word to mean that organized form of a people which is meant for its selfish aggrandizement, even at the expense of other peoples by foul, cruel and unrighteous means, and as he is among the chief protagonists of what is, not quite appropriately, called Internationalism, his profound and all-sided love of the Motherland, both as expressed in words and as manifested in action, has sometimes not been evident perhaps to superficial observers. But those who know him and his work and the literature he has created, know that he loves his land

> "with love far-brought
> From out the storied Past, and used
> Within the Present, but transfused
> Thro' future time by power of thought."

His penetrating study of and insight into the history of India and Greater India have strengthened this love.

The origin of what is called his Internationalism has sometimes been traced to his revealing and disappointing experiences during the Anti-partition and *Swadeshi* movement of Bengal of the first decade of this century. Such experiences are not denied. But his love and interest in the affairs of the whole of humanity are traceable even in his writings of his boyhood in his teens. And in maturer life, this feature of his character found distinct expression in a poem, named *Prabasi,* written thirty-one years ago, in which he says that his home is in all lands, his country in all countries, his close kindred in all homes, and that he is resolved to win this country, this home and these kindred.

In his patriotism there is no narrowness, no chauvinism, no hatred or contempt of the foreigner. He believes that India has a message and a mission, a special work entrusted to her by Providence. But he has never denied that other countries, too, may have their own special messages and missions. He does not dismiss the West with a supercilious sneer, but respects it for its science, its strength and will to face martyrdom in the cause of truth, freedom and justice and its activities for human welfare, and wishes the East to take what it should and can from the West, not like a beggar without patrimony or as an adopted child, but as a strong and healthy man may take wholesome food from all quarters and assimilate it. This taking on the part of the East from the West, moreover, is the reception of stimulus and impetus, more than or rather than learning, borrowing or imitation. The West, too, can derive advantage from contact with the East, different from the material gain of the plunderer and the exploiter. The study of his writings and utterances leaves us with the impression that the West can cease to dominate in the East only when the latter, fully awake, self-knowing, self-possessed and self-respecting, no longer requires any blister or whip and leaves no department of life and thought largely unoccupied by its own citizens.

His hands reach out to the West and the East, to all humanity, not as those of a suppliant, but for friendly grasp and salute. He is among the foremost reconcilers and uniters of races and continents. He has renewed India's cultural connection with Japan, China, Siam and Islands-India by his visits to those lands.

In spite of the cruel wrongs inflicted on India by the British *nation,* and whilst condemning such wrong-doing unsparingly, he has never refrained from being just and even generous in his estimate of the British *people.*

His politics are concerned more with the moulding of society and character-building than with the more vocal manifestations of that crowded department of national activity. Freedom he prizes as highly and ardently as the most radical politician, but his conception of freedom is full and fundamental. To him the chains of inertness, cowardice and ignorance, of selfishness and pleasure-seeking, of superstition and lifeless custom, of the authority of priestcraft and letter of scripture, constitute our bondage no less than the yoke of the stranger, which is largely a consequence and a symptom. He prizes and insists upon the absence of external restraints. But this does not constitute the whole of his idea of freedom. There should be inner freedom also, born of self-sacrifice, enlightenment, self-purification and self-control. This point of view has largely moulded his conception of the Indian political problem and the best method of tackling it. He wishes to set the spirit free, to give it wings to soar, so that it may have largeness of vision and a boundless sphere of activity. He desires that fear should be cast out. Hence his politics and his spiritual ministrations merge in each other.

Age and bodily infirmities have not made him a reactionary and obscurantist. His spirit is ever open to new light. He continues to be a progressive social reformer. His intellectual powers are still at their height. His latest poetic creations of the month—perhaps one may safely say, of the week or the day—do not betray any dimness of vision, any lack of inspiration or fertility, nor are there in them any signs of repetition. He continues to be among our most active writers. This is for the joy of creation and self-expression and fraternal giving, as he loves his kind, and human intercourse is dear to his soul. His ceaseless and extensive reading in very many diverse subjects, including some out-of-the way sciences and crafts, and his travels in many continents enable him to establish ever new intellectual and spiritual contacts, to be abreast of contemporary thought, to keep pace with its advance and with the efforts of man to plant the flag of the conscious master in the realms of the unknown—himself being one of the most sanguine and dauntless of intellectual and spiritual prospectors and explorers.

When Curzon partitioned Bengal against the protests of her people, he threw himself heart and soul into the movement for the self-realization and self-expression of the people in all possible ways. But when popular resentment and despair led to the outbreak of terrorism, he was the first to utter the clearest note of warning, to assert that Indian nationalism should not stultify and frustrate itself by recourse to violence, though with him abstention from the use of force under all circumstances is not a religious principle. He has been equally unsparing in his condemnation of the predatory instincts and activities of nations, whether of the military or of the economic variety. He has never believed that war can ever be ended by the pacts of robber nations so long as they do not repent and give up their wicked ways and the spoils thereof. The remedy lies in the giving up of greed and the promotion of neighbourly feelings between nation and nation as between individual men. Hence the poet-seer has repeatedly given in various discourses and contexts his exposition of the ancient text of the *Ishopanishad*:

ईशावास्यमिदंसर्व्वं यत्किञ्च जगत्यां जगत्।
तेन त्यक्तेन भुञ्जीथा मा गृधः कस्यस्विद्धनम्॥

"All this whatsoever that moves in Nature is indwelt by the Lord. Enjoy thou what hath been allotted by Him. Do not covet anybody's wealth."

In pursuance of this line of thought, while the poet has expressed himself in unambiguous language against the use of violence by the party in power in Russia, and while he still holds that private property has its legitimate uses for the maintenance and promotion of individual freedom and individual self-creation and self-expression and for social welfare, he sees and states clearly the advantages of Russian collectivism, as will be evident from his following cabled reply to a query of Professor Petrov, of V. O. K. S., Moscow:

"Your success is due to turning the tide of wealth from the individual to collective humanity."

As an educationist, he has preserved in his ideal of Visva-bharati, the international university, the spirit of the ancient ideal of the *tapovanas* or forest retreats of the Teachers of India—its simplicity, its avoidance of softness and luxury, its insistence on purity and chastity, its spirituality, its practical touch with nature, and the free play that it gave to all normal activities of body and soul. While the ancient spirit has been thus sought to be kept up, there is in this open-air institution at Santiniketan no cringing to mere forms, however hoary with antiquity. The Poet's mental outlook is universal. He claims for his people all knowledge and culture, whatever its origin, as their province. Hence, while he wants the youth of India of both sexes to be rooted in India's past and to draw sustenance therefrom, while he has been practically promoting the culture of the principal religious communities of India as far as the resources of the institution permits, he has also extended a friendly invitation and welcome to the exponents of foreign cultures as well. This has made it possible, for any who may so desire, to pursue the study of comparative religion at Santiniketan. He wants that there should be no racialism, no sectarian and caste and colour prejudice in his institution.

Visva-bharati stands neither for merely literary, nor for merely vocational education, but for both and more. Tagore wants both man the knower and man the maker. He wants an intellectual as well as an artistic and aesthetic education. He wants the growth of a personality equal to meeting the demands of society and solitude alike. Santiniketan now comprises a primary and a high school, a college, a school of graduate research, a school of painting and modelling and of some crafts, a music school, a school of agriculture and village welfare work, a co-operative bank with branches and a public health institute. Here students of both sexes have their games and physical exercises, including jiujitsu as taught by a leading Japanese expert and other arts of defence. The poet's idea of a village is that it should combine all its beautiful and healthy rural characteristics with the amenities of town life necessary for fullness of life and efficiency. Some such amenities have already been provided in his schools. There is co-education in all stages. It is one of the cherished desires of the poet to give girl students complete education in a Woman's University based on scientific methods, some of which are the fruits of his own insight and mature experience.

When he is spoken of as the founder of Visva-bharati, it is not to be understood that he has merely given it a local habitation and a name and buildings and funds and ideals. That he has, no doubt, done. To provide funds, he had, in the earlier years of the school, sometimes to sell the copyright of some of his books and even temporarily to part with some of Mrs. Tagore's jewellery. In the earlier years of the institution, he took classes in many subjects, lived with the boys in their rooms, entertained them in the evenings by story-telling, recitations of his poems, games of his own invention, methods of sense-training of his own devising, etc. Even recently he has been known to take some classes. And he continues to keep himself in touch with the institution in various ways.

Rabindranath has been a journalist from his teens. He has often written with terrible truthfulness—I can bear witness to the fact from personal knowledge. In years past the Poet successfully edited several monthlies and contributed, and still contributes, to numerous more. He has written for many weeklies, too. He is the only man in Bengal I know who was and still is capable of filling a magazine from the first page to the last with excellent reading in prose and verse of every description required.

I have been privileged to publish perhaps a larger number of poems, stories, novels, articles, etc., from Rabindranath's pen, in Bengali and English, than any other editor. It has been a privilege without any penalty attached to it, as he is regular, punctual and methodical, and as it is easy and pleasant to read his beautiful handwriting. As an editor, he was the making of many authors, who subsequently became well known, by the thorough revision to which he subjected their work.

His beautiful handwriting has been copied by so many persons in Bengal that even I who have had occasion to see it so often cannot always distinguish the genuine thing from the imitation.

There is an impression abroad that no English translation by Rabindranath of any of his Bengali poems was published anywhere before the *Gitanjali* poems. That is a mistake. As far as I can now trace, the first English translations by himself of his poems appeared in the February, April and September numbers of *The Modern Review* in 1912. So far as my knowledge goes, this is how he came to write in English for publication. Sometime in 1911 I suggested that his Bengali poems should appear in English garb. So he gave me translations of two of his poems by the late Mr. Lokendranath Palit. Of these *Fruitless Cry* appeared in May and *The Death of the Star* in September, 1911, in *The Modern Review*. When I asked him by letter to do some translations himself, he expressed diffidence and unwillingness and tried to put me off by playfully reproducing two lines from one of his poems of which the purport was, 'On what pretext shall I now call back her to whom I bade adieu in tears?', the humorous reference being to the fact that he did not, as a schoolboy, take kindly to school education and its concomitant exercises. But his genius and the English muse would not let him off so easily. So a short while afterwards, he showed me some of his translations, asking me playfully whether as a quondam school-master I would pass them. These appeared in my *Review*. These are, to my knowledge, his earliest published English compositions. Their manuscripts are with me now.

I have referred to his beautiful hand. All calligraphists cannot and do not become painters ; though, as Rabindranath burst into fame as a painter when almost seventy, the passage from calligraphy to painting might seem natural. I do not intend, nor am I competent, to discourse on his paintings. They are neither what is known as Indian art, nor are they any mere imitation of any ancient or modern European paintings. One thing which may perhaps stand in the way of the commonalty understanding and appreciating them is that they tell no story. They express in line and colour what even the rich vocabulary and consummate literary art and craftsmanship of Rabindranath could not or did not say. He never went to any school of art or took lessons from any artist at home. Nor did he want to imitate anybody. So, he is literally an original artist. If there be any resemblance in his style to that of any other schools of painters, it is entirely accidental and unintentional. Over seventy now, he has often expressed a desire to practise the plastic arts. He may have begun already. In this connection I call to mind one interesting fact. In the Bengali *Santiniketan Patra* ("Santiniketan Magazine") of Jyaistha, 1333 B.E., published more than five years ago, Dr. Abanindranath Tagore, the famous artist, describes (pp. 100-101) how his uncle Rabindranath was instrumental in leading him to evolve his own style of indigenous art. Summing up, Abanindranath writes:

"বাংগলার কবি আর্টের সূত্রপাত কল্লেন, বাংগলার আর্টিষ্ট সেই সূত্র ধরে একলা একলা কাজ করে চল্লো কত দিন—"

"Bengal's poet suggested the lines of art, Bengal's artist (*i.e.*, Abanindranath himself) continued to work alone along those lines for many a day—"

It has been my happy privilege to live at Santiniketan as the poet-seer's neighbour for long periods at a stretch. During one such period, my working room and sleeping room combined commanded an uninterrupted view of the small two-storied cottage in which he then lived—only a field intervened between. During that period I could never catch the poet going to sleep earlier than myself. And when early in the morning I used to go out for a stroll, if by chance it was *very* early I found him engaged in his daily devotions in the open upper storey verandah facing the East, but usually I found that his devotions were already over and he was busy with some of his usual work. At midday, far from enjoying a nap, he did not even recline. During the whole day and night, he spent only a few hours in sleep and bath and meals, and devoted all the remaining hours to work. During that period, I never found that he used a hand-fan or allowed anybody to fan him in summer. And the sultry summer days of Santiniketan are unforgettable.

The infirmities of age may have now necessitated slight changes in his habits. But even now he works harder than most young workers.

I have all along looked upon him as an earnest *Sadhak*. He is not, however, an ascetic, as his ideal of life is different.

"বৈরাগ্য সাধনে মুক্তি সে আমার নয়,"

"Liberation by detachment from the world is not mine,"

he has said in one of his poems.

One object of the *sadhana* of all believers in God, is to be somewhat godlike. As God's universe, which is both His garment and self-expression, is not a dreary desert, the life and externals of godlike men need not always be imitations of a desert. As bare deserts are, however, a phase of God's creation, asceticism may be a stage, a phase, of God-seeking and self-realization, but not the whole of it. Genuine asceticism for finding one's own soul and the Oversoul and for the good of man is worthy of reverence. Equally worthy of reverence, if not more, is the treading of the fuller and more difficult path of *sadhana* of those who are in the world without being of it.

CALCUTTA

RAMANANDA CHATTERJEE

CONTRIBUTORS

SPONSORS

MOHANDAS KARAMCHAND GANDHI.
ROMAIN ROLLAND.
ALBERT EINSTEIN.
KOSTES PALAMAS.
JAGADIS CHANDRA BOSE.

EDITOR

RAMANANDA CHATTERJEE, Editor, the *Modern Review* and *Prabasi*, Calcutta.

JANE ADDAMS, Chicago (Nobel Peace Prize).
H. G. ALEXANDER, Society of Friends, Selly Oak, Birmingham.
C. F. ANDREWS, Santiniketan, India.
M. ANESAKI, Imperial University, Tokyo.

A. A. BAKE, Santiniketan, India.
PRAMATHANATH BANERJEA, Professor, President of Council of Post-Graduate Studies in Arts, Calcutta University.
JAMES BARRIE, Dramatist, London.
COUNT R. BASSEWITZ, Consul-General for Germany, Calcutta.
ROYAL ACADEMY OF FRENCH LANGUAGE AND LITERATURE, Belgium.
ANTONIO OLIVER BELMAS, Poet, Cartagena, Spain.
S. K. BELVALKAR, Professor, Deccan College, Poona, India.
EDWYN BEVAN, Author, London.
BHAGAVAN-DAS, Kasi Vidyapitha, Benares.
D. R. BHANDARKAR, Professor, the University, Calcutta.
VIDHUSEKHAR BHATTACHARYYA, Principal, Vidya-Bhavana, Visva-Bharati.
LAURENCE BINYON, British Museum, London.
JOHAN BOJER, Hvalstad, Norway (Nobel Prize for Literature).
SUDHINDRA BOSE, Professor, State University, Iowa, U.S.A.
BERNARD BOUVIER, Author, Geneva.
FRU ANDREA BUTENSCHON, Oslo, Norway.

R. J. CAMPBELL, Dean of Chichester, Chichester, England.
AMIYA C. CHAKRAVARTY, Santiniketan, India.
RAMAPRASAD CHANDA, late of the Archæological Survey of India, Calcutta.
L. CHARLES-BAUDOUIN, Poet and Author, Geneva, Switzerland.
SIR ATUL CHANDRA CHATTERJEE, India Office, London.
BIJAY C. CHATTERJEE, Bar-at-Law, Calcutta.
SUNITI KUMAR CHATTERJI, Professor, the University, Calcutta.
PRAMATHA CHAUDHURI, Author, Calcutta.
CARMEN CONDE, Authoress, Cartagena, Spain.
ANANDA K. COOMARASWAMY, Museum of Fine Arts, Boston, Mass., U.S.A.
J. H. COUSINS, Poet and Author, Theosophical Society, Adyar, Madras.

SIR JAHANGIR C. COYAJEE, formerly Principal, Presidency College, Calcutta.
BENEDETTO CROCE, Naples, Italy.

RAJANI KANTA DAS, International Labour Office, Geneva, Switzerland.
SONYA RUTH DAS, Geneva.
SURENDRA NATH DAS GUPTA, Principal, Sanskrit College, Calcutta.
TARAKNATH DAS, Author and Journalist, Munich, Germany.
SRI DEVAMITRA DHARMAPALA, the Mahabodhi Society, Calcutta.
G. LOWES DICKINSON, Author, the University, Cambridge, England.
THEODORE DREISER, Poet and Novelist, New York, U.S.A.
W. E. BURGHARDT DU BOIS, African Writer and Journalist.
WILL DURANT, Author, New York, U.S.A.

MARY VAN EEGHEN-BOISREVAIN, Naarden, Holland.
HAVELOCK ELLIS, London.
MARC ELMER, Journalist, Paris.
GERTRUDE EMERSON, Joint-Editor, *Asia*, New York, U.S.A.

ERNESTINE FITZMAURICE, Philadelphia, Pa., U.S.A.
CARLO FORMICHI, Vice-President, Royal Academy of Italy, Rome.
A. FOUCHER, Professor of Indology, University of Paris.
HEINRICH FRICK, Marburg, Germany.

JOHN GALSWORTHY, Author and Dramatist, London.
PATRICK GEDDES, Founder-Director, Indian College, Montpellier, France.
PAUL GEHEEB, Director, Odenwaldschule, Germany.
AUROBINDO GHOSH, Pondicherry, India.
ANDRE GIDE, Poet and Novelist, *Nouvelle Revue Française*, Paris.
O. P. GILBERT, Poet, Brussels, Belgium.
EMIL GOTSCHLICH, Professor, the University, Heidelberg, Germany.
SIR HARI SINGH GOUR, Member, Legislative Assembly, Delhi.
RICHARD B. GREGG, Boston, Mass., U.S.A.
BEATRICE GREIG, Trinidad, British West Indies.
NAGENDRANATH GUPTA, Author and Journalist, Bandra, Bombay.

H. DUNCAN HALL, Author, Sydney, Australia.
KNUT HAMSUN, Norholm, Norway (Nobel Prize for Literature).
RENDEL HARRIS, Society of Friends, Woodbrooke, Birmingham.
E. B. HAVELL, Artist and Author, Oxford.
SVEN HEDIN, Explorer and Author, Stockholm, Sweden.
H. HERAS, S.J., St. Xavier's College, Bombay.
FERENC HERCZEG, Author, Buda-Pest, Hungary.
HERMANN HESSE, Poet and Novelist, Montagnola, Switzerland.
WILLIAM E. HOCKING, Professor Harvard University, Cambridge, Mass., U.S.A.
JOHN HAYNES HOLMES, Community Church, New York.
LIU YEN HON, Poet, Peiping (Peking).
LAURENCE HOUSMAN, Poet, Somerset, England.
JOHN S. HOYLAND, Society of Friends, Woodbrooke, Birmingham.
DR. HUJER, Dean of the Faculty of Philosophy, Charles University, Prague.

JULIAN S. HUXLEY, Author, London.

TETSUJIRO INOUE, Professor, Tokyo.
D. J. IRANI, Solicitor and Author, Bombay.

RAJA JAIPRITHVI, Bangalore, India.
JOSEPH JANKOWSKI, Poet and Author, Warsaw, Poland.
GANGANATHA JHA, Vice-Chancellor, the University, Allahabad.
K. M. JHAVERI, Author, late of the Judicial Service, Bombay.
C. JINARAJADASA, Adyar, Madras.

ANDREE KARPELES, Artist and Authoress, Paris.
TOSHIHIKO KATAYAMA, Tokyo.
HELLEN KELLER, New York, U.S.A.
LIM BOON KENG, President, University of Amoy, Amoy, China.
HERMANN KEYSERLING, Darmstadt, Germany.
WILLIAM H. KILPATRICK, Professor and Educationist, Columbia University, New York, U.S.A.
P. S. KOGAN, Professor, College of Music, Moscow.
KAETHE KOLLWITZ, Artist, Bad Tolz, Bavaria, Germany.
STEN KONOW, Orientalist, Ethnographic Museum, Oslo, Norway.
STELLA KRAMRISCH, the University, Calcutta.
JAGADISAN C. KUMARAPPA, Economist and Journalist, Sabarmati, Ahmedabad.
J. KUNZ, Professor, University of Illionois, U.S.A.

SELMA LAGERLOF, Stockholm (Nobel Prize for Literature).
HAROLD J. LASKI, Economist and Author, Professor, University of London.
V. LESNY, Professor, Czech University, Prague, Czechoslovakia.
MURIEL LESTER, Kingsley Hall, East End, London.
SYLVAN LEVI, President, Société Asiatique and Professer, Collège de France, Paris.
EDWIN HERBERT LEWIS, Lewis Institute, Chicago, U.S.A.
SINCLAIR LEWIS, New York (Nobel Prize for Literature).
ALMA L. LISSBERGER, New York, U.S.A.

PRASANTA CHANDRA MAHALANOBIS, Presidency College, Calcutta.
SISIR KUMAR MAITRA, Professor, Hindu University, Benares.
H. H. PANGERAN ARIYO ADHIPATI MANGKOENEGORO VII, Soerakarta, Java.
THOMAS MANN, Novelist, Berlin (Nobel Prize for Literature).
JOHN MASEFIELD, Poet-Laureate of England, Boar's Hill, Oxford.
MAURICE MAETERLINCK, Brussels (Nobel Prize for Literature).
NANALAL C. MEHTA, Indian Civil Service, Naini Tal, U.P., India.
BRUNO & HERTHA MENDEL, Berlin.
INA METAXA, Poetess, Tokyo.
HEINRICH MEYER-BENFEY, Professor, Hamburg University.
HELENE MEYER-FRANCK, Author, Wandsbek, Germany.
SIR BRAJENDRA LAL MITTER, Law Member, India Government, Delhi.
H. E. CHANG MING, Consul-General for China, Calcutta.
SIR JIVANJI JAMSHEDJI MODI, Zoroastrian Scholar, Bombay.

HARRIET MONROE, Editor, *Poetry Magazine*, Chicago, U.S.A.
RADHA KUMUD MOOKERJI, Professor, the University, Lucknow.
T. STURGE MOORE, Poet, London.
H. W. B. MORENO, Calcutta.
DHURJATI PRASAD MUKERJI, the University, Lucknow.
RADHA KAMAL MUKHERJEE, Professor, the University, Lucknow.
SIR GILBERT MURRAY, REGIUS Professor of Greek, Oxford, President, International Intellectual Co-operation, League of Nations.
J. MUSHAKOJI, Poet and Author, Tokyo.
DR. MRS. MUTHULAKSHMI AMMAL REDDI, formerly Deputy President, Madras Legislative Council, Madras.

KALIDAS NAG, the University, Calcutta.
SIR VENKATARATNAM NAIDU, late Vice-Chancellor, Madras University.
JAWAHARLAL NEHRU, formerly President, Indian National Congress, Allahabad.
HENRY W. NEVINSON, Journalist and Poet, London.
YONE NOGUCHI, Poet and Author, Tokyo.
RADEN MAS NOTO-SOEROTO, Javanese Poet and Author, The Hague, Holland.

BARON OKURA, Tokyo.
BHIKKHU OTTAMA, Religious and Nationalist Leader, Burma.
RUDOLF OTTO, Professor, University of Marburg, Germany.
KIHACHI OZAKI, Poet, Tokyo.

ALFONS PACQUET, Frankfort-on-Main, Germany.
BIPIN CHANDRA PAL, Journalist and Author, Calcutta.
RAFAEL PALMA, President, University of the Philippines, Manila.
K. M. PANIKKAR, Secretary, Chamber of Princes, Bhopal.
MANILAL C. PATEL, Ahmedabad.
H. M. THE SHAH OF PERSIA, through H. E. FOROUGHI, Minister of Foreign Affairs.
R. MENENDEZ PIDAL, President, Spanish Academy, Madrid.
ALBERT E. PINKEVITCH, Professor, the University, Moscow.
H. A. POPLEY, General Secretary, Y.M.C.A. for India, Calcutta.
JAMES BISSETT PRATT, Professor, Williamstown, Mass., U.S.A.

SIR SARVAPALLI RADHAKRISHNAN, Vice-Chancellor, Andhra University, Waltair.
PRINCE DAMRONG RAJANUBHAB, Bangkok, Siam.
SIR CHANDSEKHARA VENKATA RAMAN, Professor, Calcutta University (Nobel Prize for Physics).
SIR PRAPHULLA CHANDRA RAY, Professor, University College of Science, Calcutta.
C. R. REDDY, late Vice-Chancellor, Andhra University, India.
ERNEST RENAULD, Journalist, Paris.
J. N. REUTER, Professor of Sanskrit, the University, Helsingfors, Finland.
ERNEST RHYS, Author and Editor, *Everyman's Library*, London.
EDWIN ARLINGTON ROBINSON, Poet and Author, Boston, U.S.A.
NICHOLAS ROERICH, Artist and Author, Roerich Museum, New York.
MADELEINE ROLLAND, Villeneuve, Switzerland.

Sir William Rothenstein, Principal, Royal College of Arts, London.
Mrs. Kamini Roy, Poetess and Author, Calcutta.
Sarat C. Roy, Anthropologist, Ranchi, Chota Nagpur, India.
Arnold Rubin, Poet and Author, London.
Bertrand Russell, Author, Harting, Petersfield, England.
George Russell, Poet and Author, Dublin.

R. S. Pant Sachiv, Chief of Bhor State, India.
Mufti Mohammad Sadiq, Qadian, Panjab, India.
Sir Michael E. Sadler, the University, Oxford.
Rahimzadeh Safavi, Ministry of Justice, Tehran, Persia.
Meghnad Saha, F.R.S., Professor, the University, Allahabad.
Har Bilas Sarda, Author, Member of the Legislative Assembly, Delhi.
Binay Kumar Sarkar, Author and Journalist, the University, Calcutta.
C. P. Scott, Editor, the *Manchester Guardian*, Manchester, England.
Vida D. Scudder, Authoress, Wellesley, Mass., U.S.A.
Sir Brajendranath Seal, formerly Vice-Chancellor, Mysore University.
P. Seshadri, Secretary, Inter-University Board, India.
H. M. the King of Siam, through Prince Dhani, Minister of Education, Siam.
A. T. Silcock, Society of Friends, London.
F. E. Sillanpaa, Helsingfors, Finland.
Upton Sinclair, Author and Novelist, Pasadena, California, U.S.A.
Jogendra Singh, Author, Member of the Legislative Assembly, Delhi.
St. Nihal Singh, Journalist and Author, Lahore.
Sir Nil Ratan Sircar, President of the Council of Post-Graduate Studies in Science, Calcutta University.
J. C. Smuts, Member, House of Assembly, Cape Town, South Africa.
Arnold Sommerfield, Professor, University of Munich, Munich.
Joseph Southall, Art-Critic, Birmingham, England.
Harold E. B. Speight, Author, and Professor, Dartmouth College, U.S.A.
J. A. Spender, late Editor, *Westminster Gazette*, Marden, Kent, England.
Hasan Suhrawardy, Vice-Chancellor, Calcutta University.
Jabez T. Sunderland, Unitarian Minister and Author, New York, U.S.A.

Edward Thompson, Author, Lecturer in Bengali, the University, Oxford.
Sybil Thorndike, London.
R. C. Trevelyan, Poet and Author, Dorking, England.
Hsu Tse-Mou, Poet and Author, Nanking, China.

Evelyn Underhill, Authoress, London.
Louis Untermeyer, Poet, New York.
Mrs. Margaret M. Urquhart, Calcutta.
W. S. Urquhart, Principal, Scottish Church College, Calcutta (formerly Vice-Chancellor, Calcutta University).

Paul Valery, Member of the French Academy, Paris.
Sergey Vassilenko, Composer, Moscow.

Sir R. Venkataratnam Nayudu, late Vice-Chancellor, University of Madras.
C. Vijiaraghavachariar, formerly President, Indian National Congress, Salem, Madras.
J. Ph. Vogel, Orientalist, Rector, University of Leyden, Holland.

Margaret Widdemer, Poet and Authoress, New York.
M. Winternitz, Professor, German University, Prague.
Theodor Von Winterstein, President, Deutsche Akademie, Munich.

W. B. Yeats, Poet and Author, Dublin (Nobel Prize for Literature).
F. Yeats Brown, Author, late of the Indian Army, Rye, Sussex, England.

Stefan Zweig, Poet and Author, Salzburg, Austria.

[The contributions have not been printed in the sequence given above—only a rough alphabetical order has been followed in the two sections—*Greetings and Appreciations* and *Offerings*. The Editor begs to apologise for this. Some of the contributions arrived late, after a considerable part of the book was in print.]

LIST OF PLATES

IN common with thousands of his countrymen I owe much to one who by his poetic genius and singular purity of life has raised India in the estimation of the world. But I owe also more. Did he not harbour in Santiniketan the inmates of my *Ashram* who had proceeded from South Africa? The other ties and memories are too sacred to bear mention in a public tribute.

M K Gandhi

SABARMATI, AHMEDABAD.

NIOBÉ.

(Trois fragments d'une œuvre de jeunesse)

Premier Fragment.

Campagne de Thèbes. Aux portes de la ville. Soir d'automne. Peu avant le coucher du soleil. Des chants au loin. Paraissent les Niobides,—Jeunes garçons et jeunes filles,—se tenant par la main.

NIOBIDES

O campagne de Thèbes, terre de la patrie, air embaumé qui me caresse, qu'il est doux de sentir votre souffle amoureux! Et vous, saintes montagnes, Cithéron, combien j'aime tes hauteurs rocailleuses, quand je suis à la course sur les pierres aigues les biches bondissantes, où qu'en la pureté solitaire des cimes je mire mes yeux bleus dans le ciel d'azur sombre, et regarde couler les nuages dorés, tandis qu'autour de moi soupirent tendrement leur langoureuse plainte les rossignols cachés. . . .

Puis, le soir, je descends, tandis que l'ombre monte, de la terre qui s'endort. Les cloches de troupeaux tintent dans la vallée. Les grillons font vibrer leur crécelle obstinée. L'air mystérieux s'allume d'une pluie d'étincelles, yeux d'or au vol tranquille, au doux battement d'ailes. J'orne mes cheveux blonds de lucioles, 'fleurs des nuits,' et vers les hautes ombres des murailles de Thèbes, qui se dressent au fond sur l'horizon rosé, nous revenons gaiment, nous tenant par la main, formant de nobles danses au travers des prairies, et baignant nos pieds blancs aux ruisseaux argentés.

NIOBE

O mes enfants, vos voix ont la fraîcheur des sources; vos bouches et vos bras ont le parfum des bois. Deioneus, Jolè, Hyacinthe, mes âmes, que vous avez tardé, ce soir! Dès que vous paraissez, je sens que j'étais sans vie, lorsque j'étais sans vous. . . . Et toi, Déidamie, rêveuse au pas languissant, pourquoi viens-tu, ma fille, seule, en arrière des autres? Tes cheveux fins et pâles voilent ton front de lait ; qu'as-tu fait aujourd'hui, loin de moi? Viens, dis-moi. . . . . .

DEIDAMIE

Sous le tremble au mouvant feuillage, le long du pur ruisseau,—au bruissement de l'eau qui coule entre les pierres, sans voix et les yeux clos,—sans mouvement, comme en dormant,—j'entendais les soupirs du vent dans les roseaux ; et du zéphyr la vive haleine—rafraîchissait mon front, mais sans calmer ma peine.

NIOBE

Qu'as-tu?

DEIDAMIE

Je ne sais pas. Ja crois que mon coeur bat trop vite. Je crois, . . . passent en moi tous les frissons du vent ; et ma poitrine est trop petite pour sentir tout ce que je sens.

NIOBE

Sur mes genoux, appuie ton front. Ton mal n'est pas un mal, O ma Déidamie, c'est l'approche d'un bien délicieux! . . . . (Enivrante douceur de sentir l'éclosion de ces fleurs de mon sang, chastes et voluptueuses!) . . . . . Et toi, Callirhoé, petit faon bondissant, tu n'es pas triste toi? Tu n'as pas de tournments, O la plus jeune des Niobides? . . . . Comme tu as couru! Sur tes mollets bruns, les ronces ont marqué leur griffe. Ta nuque s'est hâlée. Et de la chair des fraises tes lèvres sont rougies. Que t'importe? Sais-tu seulment que tu es jolie? Tu ris. . . . . Ah! Quand l'amour voudra s'en emparer, comme elle s'enfuira, ma petite hirondelle! . . .

Mon coeur set pénétré d'une tendresse fière. Mes enfants!

Olympiens, regardez-nous! Apollon, océan de lumiére, Artémis, lac paisible où se mire le jour,—qui de vous, immortels, est plus beau que mes fils? Qui de vous, O déesses, est plus heureuse que moi?

Le PEUPLE

Niobé, ne crains-tu pas la jalousie des dieux?

NIOBE

Mieux vaut exciter l'envie que la pitié!

Le PEUPLE

O ma fille, souvent l'une est bien près de l'autre.

(La nuit tombe tout d'un coup. Des nuages lourds couvrent le cied)

Second Fragment

La scène suivante voit passer dans la unit d'une tempête ; Atrée, roi d'Argos et frère de Niobé, que poursuit la vengeance des Olympiens. Le réseau noir du ciel s'est detendu lentement. La lumiere renaît. Jour crépusculaire, triste et doux. Le soleil descend derrière les montagnes.

Le PEUPLE

La nuit s'éclaire doucement. Ses longs voiles retombent avec une paisible majesté. O jour, je reverrai ton beau corps resplendir! Ami, mes yeux te baisent tres amoureusement.

NIOBE

O Dieux, que tout s'efface,—et tout ce que j'ai dit! . . . . .—Oui, la tendre lumière. . . . . . Un souffle frais baigne mon front brulant. Zeus sourit. Zeus pardonne. . . . (*Chant de flûtes lointaines*) Quel est ce chant plaintif?

Le PEUPLE

C'est le cortège de la Grande Déesse. Déméter a perdu sa fille, la blonde Proserpine. Elle erre par les champs, et l'appelle à grands cris. La nature est en deuil ; elle dort sous la terre, la blonde Proserpine, et durant de longs mois, Déméter gémira.

NIOBE

Infortunée! . . . . Mon coeur est ému de pitié! Ah! combien je le sens, le poids de tes douleurs!

Les NIOBIDES

Le doux automne est terminé. La lumière languissante sourit avec mélancolie. Les bois d'or rougissant éteignent leur splendeur. Du long sommeil d'hiver la nature s'endort. . . . . . . O fleurs, fermez les yeux! La terre avide vous dévore. En son sein, dans la nuit, vous allez disparaître, et pour les pieds charmants de la jeune déesse, vous irez tapisser les prairies de l'Hadès, tandis que notre coeur soupirera pour vous. . . . . Petites âmes parfumées, vous irez consoler le front pâle des ombres qui n'ont pas oublié. . . . Leurs lèvres épuisées, qui boiront votre haleine, chercheront sur vos lèvres la trace des baisers du jour évanoui. . . . . . .

Mais nous vous reverrons, chères petites fleurs! Et vous aussi, oiseaux qui chantez le printemps! Nous fêterons ensemble le retour du soleil, les jeunes pousses qui percent la prison de l'écorce, le frisson amoureux de la vie qui s'éveille, le souffle

NIOBE

Mon coeur est pénétré d'une douceur profonde. La musique de vos voix, O mes enfants, efface le rêve qui m'oppressait. Je respire. . . . La lumière s'étend. L'or de vos cheveux blonds s'allume à ses reflets. Je vois auprès de moi vos innocents visages. Parmi la rose des nuages, le ciel bleu refleurit, Et, déchirant les derniers voiles avec ses flèches reparaît Apollon.

Tandis que Niobé parle, la lumiére grandit en effet, prend un éclat intense. Et, quand Niobé prononce le nom d'Apollon, l'horizon s'embrase de l'apothéose du soleil couchant. Sur ce ciel rouge parait Apollon marmoréen, éblouissant, impassible, bras tendu, l'arc à la main.

Le PEUPLE

(*saisi d'effroi*).

Apollon!

(*Niobé se retourne, pousse un cri étouffé, ne peut ni parler ni bouger.*)

Les NIOBIDES

(*S'enfuient en désordre, comme une volée d'oiseaux.*)
Ah! . . . . *

Troisième Fragment.

Le soleil a disparu derriére la montague. Il a laissé au ciel de larges trainées de poussiere d'or, et des reflets oranges, qui s'éteignent graduellement, pendant la scène qui suit.

NIOBE

Bien-aimés! Bien-aimés!

119

*La scène qui suit le second fragment décrit la chasse des Niobides par l'Archer Divin.

Pleure pour m…

Je pleure, tu le vois. j'arrache mes cheveux.

NIOBE

Mes enfants! Mon amour, mon orgueil et ma vie!

Le PEUPLE

Ils dorment parmi les fleurs, qu'ils chantaient tout à l'heure.

NIOBE

Ah! Ta pitié est cruelle! . . . . "Tout à l'heure". . . . Mais toi, qu'as—tu fait, traître, pour les défendre? Ne devais-tu pas les couvrir de ton corps? Tu n'as pensé qu'à toi, à sauver honteusement ta misérable vie!

Le PEUPLE

Niobé, la vie est douce, même au peuple qui souffre.

NIOBE

Lâche, prends-la donc, ma vie, mon horrible vie! . . . . Ah! prends-la, meurtrier, dieu sanglant, aux féroces yeux clairs, Apollon! Justicier, qui te charges de châtier les crimes, qui châtiera les tiens? Que t'avaient fait ces innocents? Moi seule, je te méprisai, et je te méprise encore! Bourreau, je te méprise! Dieu qui tue des enfants, frappe-moi! As-tu peur?

Le PEUPLE

Tais-toi, je t'en supplie!

NIOBE

Quoi! je ne haïrais pas les monstres qui me déchirent?

Le PEUPLE

Hélas! ils sont des dieux ; ils peuvent tout sur nous. . . . .

NIOBE

C'est parce qu'ils peuvent Tout, que je veux les haïr. Contre leur force atroce, je n'ai que mon mépris ; mais mon mépris est, seul, au dessus de leurs coups.

Le PEUPLE

Prends garde que leur vengeance ne soit pas épuisée!

NIOBE

Que me fait leur vengeance? Il n'est plus rien que j'aime!

Le PEUPLE

La douleur est pareille à l'Océan immense. Qui connaît tous ses flots? La douleur est pareille à l'insondable ciel. Qui en à vu le fond?

NIOBE

La douleur a pour bornes celles de notre vie. Je puis mourir. Je ne crains donc plus rien.

Le PEUPLE

Malheureuse, ne parle point de la pire infortune!

NIOBE

J'ai touché le fond de l'abîme. Mon âme est descendue dans la nuit infinie. Jamais elle ne reverra la lumière perdue. Le vide m'enveloppe. Je tombe. Rien n'est plus. . . . .

La nuit vient doucement, la belle nuit lumineuse. Le ciel vert pâle est tendre comme une fleur. Au loin, reprend le chant des flûtes.

Le PEUPLE

Dans l'ombre des forêts, l'errante Déméter promène éternellement son chant inconsolé.

NIOBE

Hélas!

Le PEUPLE

(*Regardant Niobé.*)

La bienfaisante musique a fait jaillir les larmes de son coeur oppressé.

NIOBE

O douce et triste plainte, qui te mêles à la mienne! . . . Déméter, aie pitié! Tu connais ma douleur, je souffre comme toi!

Le PEUPLE

Tu vois, ma fille, les dieux sont soumis à l'universelle peine.

NIOBE

Crois-tu que mon coeur soit assez vil pour trouver une consolation dans le malheur des autres? Laisse-moi! Va-t-en! . . . . . . (*Plus doucement*) Ami, je te remercie. Ton âme est simple et bonne. Mais laisse-moi. Seule, je veux pleurer.

Le peuple se retire en silence. Le chant des flûtes continue trés document au loin.

NIOBE

Assise, appuyée à un tertre de *gazon au milieu de la scène.*

Déméter, que de maux nous souffrons toutes deux! . . . . . . Immortelle, tu portes une douleur immortelle, et sans cesse ta peine fleurit, renouvelée. Malheureuse! tu ne peux pas mourir! . . . . Mais toi, tu reverras ta fille! Et moi, jamais ils ne reviendront, les bien aimés. . . . . . O Déméter, tu ne sais pas l'horreur de "Jamais." Ton coeur est rêsigné et ta calme tristesse s'exhale en graves plaintes, pénétrées de pitié! . . . . Mais tu ne sais pas ce que c'est que: "Jamais". . . . . . Delivre-moi! Je ne te demande pas la vie de mes enfants. Hélas! Tu pleures le tien! . . . . . Mais la mort,—Déesse, accorde moi la mort! Seule grâce qui me reste, et que le dernier des misérables a le droit d'espérer! . . . . Tes pleurs tombent sur moi dans la rosse nocturne. Je sens flotter dans l'air ta compassion tendre. . . . . . Quelle soudaine paix! Voici la vie cruelle qui m'abandonne enfin! . . . . . . Lumière, tu es si belle! . . . . . . Et pourtant, au malheureux qui souffre, qu'il est doux de te perdre!

HERMES

(*Paraît derrière Niobé.*)

Niobé, Hermès je suis, messager de la mort. Ma main est secourable. Elle guide les âmes désolées à l'immortel oubli. Viens, appuie-toi sur elle! N'accuse point les dieux. Les dieux ont pitié de tes pleurs.

NIOBE

(*Soupire douloureusement.*)

Hélas! ne pouvaient-ils les laisser vivre encore? . . . . O mes fils bien aimés!

HERMES

(*A mesure qu'il parle, on voit sur les traits de Niobé succéder à la douleur la résignation, le calme, une paix mélancolique, enfin un sourire las—mourante, la tête renversée en arrière et regardant le ciel.*)*

Zeus les a délivrés. Il a sauvé leurs âmes du Destin de ta race. L'héritage d'orgueil et de folle puissance, leurs bras furent brisés avant de s'en souiller. N'accuse point les dieux, fille de Tantale! Pense à l'impie foudroyé! Pense à ton frère Atrée, l'insensé qu'emporte l'ouragan, loup hurlant, et légaunt à sa race ses tourments et ses crimes! . . . . Dans le divin sourire de la nature, tes fils sont endormis. L'inaltérable paix de l'Infini les remplit. Leur souffle s'est fondu dans le torrent serein de la lumière. Leur âme s'est unie à notre âme immortelle. Qui, une fois, a goûté à la source éternelle ne saurait approcher encore sa lèvre de l'eau trouble où se mêlent vos larmes. Femme, ne pleure plus! Les divins Olympiens sourient très doucement, quand ils vous voient répandre tant de larmes pour vivre. . . . . Apaise ton cœur blessé! Ta douleur est finie. Je verse sur ton front le long sommeil sans rêves. Sous son baume indulgent la peine se dissipe ; ce qu'on souffrit n'est plus. Endors-toi, Niobé, dans les bras affectueux de la Bonne Nourrice. L'auguste Déméter te berce tendrement. Voici le soir parfumé. Comme un fleuve de pourpre la lumière s'épanche. L'âme qu'un dur labeur, tout le jour, a lassé, voit venir avec joie la grande nuit paisible. L'haleine fraternelle de la terre profonde monte et baise ta tête pesante qui s'incline. Le soleil tout-puissant éteint son regard d'or. La sage mélancolie de la musique meurt dans l'air immobile. Tout se tait. Tout s'arrête. Tout rêve. . . . . . Tout est rêve. . . . . . .

**Niobé est vue de face. À l'apparition d'Hermès, elle ne s'est point tournée, elle n'a fait aucun mouvement pour le voir; elle regarde devant elle et le voit, pour ainsi dire, en elle.*

La musique très douce accompagne sa voix.—et s'efface, à la fin. C'est la lumière sans rayonnement d'après le jour et d'avant la nuit. La lune n'est pas encore levée. Dans le ciel vert-pâle fleurissent des étoiles. A la fin, l'une d'elles se détache. Elle trace sur la voûte un lumineux sillage, et s'éteint. . . . . .

[Cette tragédie, de Romain Rolland fut écrite, vers sa vingtième année, a Rome, où il était à l'École Française du Palazzo Farnese.]

ÜEBER DEN FREIEN WILLEN

von Albert Einstein für Rabindranath Tagore

WENN der Mond bei der Zurücklegung seines ewigen Weges um die Erde mit Bewusstsein begabt wäre, so würde er wohl überzeugt sein, dass er seinen Weg freiwillig, auf Grund eines ein für allemal gefassten Entschlusses, ausführen würde.

So würde ein mit höherer Einsicht und mit vollkommenerm Wahrnehmungsvermögen ausgestattetes Wesen den Menschen und sein Tun sehen und über dessen Illusion lächeln, nach freiem Willen zu handeln.

Dies glaube ich, wohl wissend, dass es nicht völlig beweisbar ist. Bei konsequentem Zuendedenken dessen, was wir genau kennen und wissen, würde sich wohl kaum ein Mensch dieser Auffassung verschliessen, wenn sich die Eigenliebe nicht dagegen sträubte. Der Mensch wehrt sich dagegen, sich im Ablauf des Weltganzen als machtloses Objekt anzusehen. Sollte die Gesetzmässigkeit des Geschehens, wie sie sich uns bei der anorganischen Natur mehr oder minder klar entschleiert bei den Vorgängen in unserm Gehirn haltmachen?

Abgesehen von der Inkonsequenz einer solchen Meinung spricht die Einwirkung des Alkohols sowie anderer scharf kontrollierbarer Faktoren auf unsere Gedanken, Gefühle und Handlungen sehr deutlich dafür, dass der Determinismus vor unserer Majestät nicht Halt macht.

Mögen wir und mag die menschliche Gesellschaft die Illusion der Freiheit der menschlichen Handlungen nötig haben!

Die Überzeugung von der Notwendigkeit des menschlichen Tuns bringt in unsere Auffassung den Menschen und dem Leben gegenüber eine Milde, Ergebenheit und Überlegenheit, welche ohne diese Überzeugung unerreichbar wäre.

Du sahest den wilden Kampf der Geschöpfe, der aus Not und dunklem Begehren hervorquillt. Du sahest Rettung in stiller Betrachtung und in den Werken der Schönheit. Diese pflegend hast Du den Menschen gedient durch ein langes fruchtbares Leben, überall milden and freien Sinn verbreitend, wie es die Weisen Deines Volkes als Ideal verkündet haben.

BERLIN

A. Einstein.

[TRANSLATION]

ABOUT FREE WILL

IF the moon, in the act of completing its eternal way round the earth, were gifted with self-consciousness, it would feel thoroughly convinced, that it would travel its way of its own accord on the strength of a resolution taken once for all.

So would a Being, endowed with higher insight and more perfect intelligence, watching man and his doings, smile about the illusion of his, that he was acting according to his own free will.

This is my conviction, although I know well that it is not fully demonstrable. If one thinks out to the very last consequence what one exactly knows and understands, there would hardly be any human being who would be impervious to this view, provided his self-love did not ruffle up against it. Man defends himself from being regarded as an impotent object in the course of the Universe. But should the lawfulness of happenings, such as unveils itself more or less clearly in inorganic nature, cease to function in front of the activities in our brain?

Leaving aside the inconsistency of such a view, the influence of alcohol and other sharply controllable factors on our thoughts, feelings, and activities, should show very distinctly that determinism does not stop before the majesty of our human will.

May be, that we and the human society require the illusion of the freedom of human activities!

The conviction about the law of necessity in human activities introduces into our conception of man and life a mildness, a reverence, and an excellence, such as would be unattainable without this conviction.

■■ ■■

Thou sawest the fierce strife of creatures, a strife that wells forth from need and dark desire. Thou sawest the escape in calm meditation and in creations of beauty. Cherishing these, thou hast served mankind all through a long and fruitful life, spreading everywhere a gentle and a free thought in a manner such as the Seers of thy people have proclaimed as the ideal.

Σὲ ὁμιλία μου γιὰ τὸν «ποιητή, γενικώτατα, καὶ τὸ ἔργο του» τὸ Δεκέμβριο τοῦ 1922 στὴ Θεσσαλονίκη τῆς Μακεδονίας ὅπου εἶχα προσκληθῆ ἀπὸ φίλους μου γιὰ νὰ γιορτάσουν τὴν πεντηκονταετηρίδα τῆς φιλολογικῆς μου ζωῆς, ἔλεγα: «Ποιητὴς παγκόσμιας φήμης ὁ Ἰνδὸς Rabindranath Tagore εἶναι τὸ ἐξαίσιο κομμάτι ποὺ μᾶς τὸ μελέτησε ὁ Romain Rolland στὸ βιβλίο του τὸ ἐπιγραφόμενο «Mahatma Gandhi», ὁ Ταγκὸρ μᾶς ἐτόνισε τί ἀξίζει ὁ κλεισμὸς τοῦ ποιητῆ στὰ φυσικά του σύνορα, ἕνας ἐνεργὸς πάντα ἀσκητισμός· τί ἀξίζει ἡ «γωνιά του ποιητῆ» εἶναι ὁ ἴδιος του λόγος. Τὸ τραγούδι τοῦ ποιητῆ, σὰν τὸ τραγούδι τοῦ πουλιοῦ. Καὶ τί εἶναι τὸ πουλί, ὅταν ἡ αὐγὴ τὸ ξυπνάει; «Τὸ ξύπνημά του, μᾶς λέει, δὲν τὸ ἀπορροφᾶ ἡ ἀναζήτηση τῆς τροφῆς. Τὰ φτερά του ἀπομένοντας ἀκούραστα στὸ κάλεσμα τῶν οὐρανῶν. Ὁ λάρυγγάς του χύνει τραγούδια χαρᾶς πρὸς τὸ νέο φῶς τὸ πρωινό.» Τὸ μάθημα μᾶς τὸ δίνει ὁ πολυταξίδευτος μεγαλοφυὴς Ἰνδός, «πνευματικὸς πρεσβευτὴς τῆς Ἀσίας στὴν Εὐρώπη», καθὼς τὸν εἶπαν. Μακαρισμένος ὁ ποιητὴς ποὺ τοῦ φτάνει ἡ γωνιά του. Εἶναι ἡ γαλήνη ποὺ γεννιέται ἐκεῖ, ἐνσαρκωμένη ἀνθρωπιστικά, ἡ Ποίηση.» Εἶπα τότε.

Καὶ τώρα προσθέτω: Ὁ ποιητής, ἕνας κόσμος χαρᾶς καθὼς εἶναι, καὶ ὅλα ἀφίνει σὲ γωνιὰ τοῦ κεφαλαίου του γιὰ κάποιο κήρυγμα, καὶ τότε, ὅπως σταθῇ, σκορπᾷ τὴ χάρη τῆς γωνιᾶς του, καὶ εἶναι σὰ νὰ κεφαλαιώσῃ καὶ ὅλο αναβλύζει. Ὁ Ραβιντρανὰθ Ταγκόρ, εἴτε τραγουδιστὴς τρυφερός, τὰ τραγούδια του, εἴτε παρουσιάζει τὸ διάγγελμά του, ἀπόστολος τῆς Ποίησης Μητέρας στὴν καμαριέρα σὰ θυγατέρα, εἶναι πάντα ὁ «Κηπουρὸς τῶν λουλουδιῶν τῆς Βασίλισσας.» Ὁ λόγος του περιέχει τὴν ἐσωτερικὴ μυστικότητα τῆς προσευχῆς καὶ τὴ δροσερὴ περιφάνεια τοῦ εἰδυλλίου. Καὶ ὁ λόγος του ὅμοια γνωρίζει νὰ γυρίσῃ καὶ ν' ἀνθολογήσῃ ἀπὸ τοὺς δρυμοὺς τοῦ Kalidasa καὶ τοῦ Valmiki στοὺς λειμῶνες τοῦ Shakespeare καὶ τοῦ Shelley.

Ἄξια στὰ ἑβδομῆντα πέντε χρόνια του μιὰ Χρυσῆ Βίβλος νὰ τοῦ ἀφιερωθῇ ποὺ νὰ θυμίσῃ κάτι ἀπὸ τὸ πολυτελικὸ Μανουσκρίπτο ποὺ τοῦ χρωστοῦμε. Ταπεινὰ τὸν χαιρετῶ μὲ τὸ θεῖο φῶς ποὺ μοῦ προσχύνει ὁ ἑλληνικὸς οὐρανός, καὶ ἡ ψυχή μου φτάνοντάς τον ἀπὸ μακρυὰ τὸ χέρι, θαρρῶ πὼς εἶναι κάποιο ἐλάφι ἀπὸ ἐκεῖνα ποὺ, καθὼς ὁ ἴδιος ἀναφέρει στὴν «Θυσία τοῦ δάσους», τρέχανε στὸ δάσος καὶ φιλήσανε τὰ χέρια τῶν ἐρημιτῶν.

28 Φεβρουαρίου 1931 Ἀθῆναι

Κωστῆς Παλαμᾶς

[TRANSLATION]

THE POET'S CORNER

IN December 1927 at Salonica, where I was invited to celebrate my literary jubilee, I said: 'A world-famous poet, Rabindranath Tagore, in one of his splendid utterances (transmitted to us by Romain Rolland in his book *Mahatma Gandhi*) tells us what a great thing is the poet's seclusion within his natural precincts, and his ever-active asceticism. What a great thing indeed is the "poet's corner," to use his own words. The poet's song is like the song of a bird. And the bird—what does it do when the rosy-fingered dawn puts life into it? "Its awakening," he tells us, "is not disturbed by the necessity of finding its food. Its wings never fail to respond to the call of heaven. Songs of joy it sings to the new morning light." A great lesson, from this great Wanderer from India, the spiritual ambassador whom Asia has accredited to Europe, as he has been happily described. Blessed be the poet who is satisfied in his own little corner. It is the crib where Poetry made flesh is born.' Thus did I speak then.

And I add now: The poet, who embraces within his inner being a world of joy, no matter wherever he stands, diffuses over the whole universe the charm of his little corner, and his message is like a song. Rabindranath Tagore whether he sings a lyric or delivers a message, like another apostle of the venerable Mother to her far-away daughter, he is always the Gardener who attends to the flowers which grow in the garden of the Queen. His words breathe forth the imperious mysticism of prophecy and the cool softness of an idyl, nay, he knows well how to loiter and pick up the best of flowers from the forests of Kalidasa and Valmiki and the flower-gardens of Shakespeare and Shelley.

The dedication to Rabindranath Tagore of a *Golden Book,* on the occasion of his Seventieth Birthday Anniversary, is but a very modest token of our gratitude to him. It would only remind us of the Temple of Spirit which we owe to his divine genius. I very humbly offer him my respects under the canopy of light poured out upon me by the sky of Attica; and my soul, in its flight to imprint a kiss of love and homage upon his venerable hand, reminds me of one of those stags which, as he himself depicts in his *Religion of the Forest,* "runs about in the wilds to kiss the hands of hermits."

ATHENS KOSTES PALAMAS

IT is more than a third of a century that the Poet Tagore and I have been drawn together in closest bonds of sympathy. His friendship has been unfailing through years of my ceaseless efforts during which I gained step by step a wider and more sympathetic view of continuity of life and its diverse manifestations. It was in following this quest that I succeeded in making the dumb plant the most eloquent chronicler of its inner life and experiences by making it write down its own history. The self-made records, thus made, prove that there is no life-reaction in even the highest animal which has not been foreshadowed in the life of the plant. The barrier which seemed to separate kindred phenomena was found to have vanished, the plant and the animal appearing as a multiform unity in a single ocean of being. In this vision of truth the final mystery of things will by no means be lessened, but greatly deepened. It is no less a miracle that man, circumscribed on all sides by the imperfection of his senses, should yet build himself a raft of thought to make daring adventures in unchartered seas. And in his voyage of discovery he catches an occasional glimpse of the ineffable wonder that was hidden from his view. That vision crushes out of him all self-sufficiency, all that kept him unconscious of the great pulse that beats through the universe.

The same cosmic unity has unfolded itself to Tagore's poetic vision and has found expression in his philosophic outlook and in his incomparable poems. May his vision expand every day and may his message reach every corner of the earth!

CALCUTTA

J. C. Bose

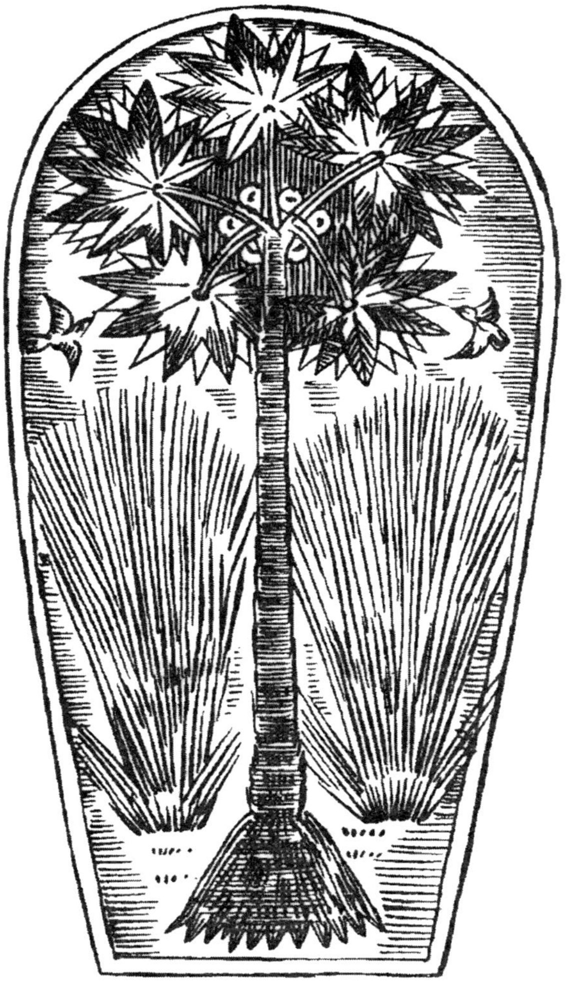

GREETINGS AND APPRECIATIONS

PERHAPS the most valuable contribution which can be made to our perplexing age is a revelation of the essential unity and validity of all human experiences, that our intellectual and emotional understanding may approach our commercial and political arrangements. Inspite of the magnificent methods of communication modern science has placed at our disposal, such a revelation can be made only in the age-old way—through the spirit of a genius. His message to be natural and inevitable must be varied as well as profound, romantic as well as classical, delightful as well as poignant ; above all it must be clothed in Beauty sufficient to carry it over the gulfs lying between different peoples, especially those who live in the East and those who live in the West.

Rabindranath Tagore has met all these requirements of genius combined in a man who is at once a poet, a philosopher, a humanitarian, an educator.

We therefore salute him on his birthday with gratitude, with admiration, with fellowship and affection.

He has once more made clear to us the saying we so often used in the early days of the University Settlement—the things that make us alike are finer and deeper than the things that make us different.

HULL HOUSE,
CHICAGO, U.S.A.

JANE ADDAMS

A GATHANJALI

DEDICATED TO RABINDRANATH

らびんだら翁あとに
さゝぐる和歌二首　正治

ひまらや此峯のはそむる
日のひかり末はがんぢ此
野をてらすべく

朝日子にきそはれひらく
ぷんだりけ色香に
みそらの存やどして

RABINDRANATH

NI SASAGURU WAKA NISHU

Himalaya no
Mine no ha somuru
Hi no hikari,
Sue wa Ganga no
No wo terasubeku.

Asahiko ni
Sasoware hiraku
Fundarike,
Iro-ka ni mi-sora no
Inochi yadoshite.

[TRANSLATION]

Lo! A glitter of light, the purple gleaming at the apex of the Himalaya! Who doubts that it shall finally pervade the plains of the Ganga?

Quickened by the first touch of the rising Sun, the *Pundarika* lotus opens its petals, harbouring the life of heaven in its lustre and scent.

IMPERIAL UNIVERSITY,
TOKYO

M. ANESAKI

TAGORE AT WOODBROOKE

It was a Red-Letter Day in Woodbrooke's history when first Rabindranath Tagore visited us. Woodbrooke believes that its method and ideal—the free study of the great movements of thought and life in the world to-day, rooted in a belief in man's divine brotherhood, in the conviction that we are all sons of God, sharing a common life—this religious conviction and this free method of study seem to us akin to what we have seen and heard of the educational method and ideal of Santiniketan.

Rabindranath Tagore arrived here in May, 1930. We felt at home with him, and we believe he was at home with us, for he came back for two further visits.

And in those days, few as they were, he revealed the richness of his nature. Do you think of him as a venerable, white-bearded patriarch? Yes: but listen to him reading from the *Crescent Moon,* and you know at once that he is the child of his own dreams—the wilful child, too! You say he is a wise man, a seer or mystic. Listen to his discourse on the nature of true civilisation, hear his profound utterances coming out of the depth of our silent meditations, and you know these things are true indeed. But watch him as he walks round the Art Gallery, looking at his pictures, and see the playful smile that lights up his face as he recalls the mood of fantastic creation that caught him one day, moving him to draw beasts and no-beasts, that have no other existence. Or see the pictures themselves; the delicate grace of one, the grotesque weirdness of another, the frightful force of one, the quiet of another, the minute detail, the bold line, the harmony of hue or colour, the strength—surely these creations are not all the work of one man.

Thus did he open before our eyes, as a flower of several hues, like a sweet-pea with no symmetry of equal petals, but none the less a flower of rare beauty, unique in its own way. And we loved him.

SELLY OAK,
BIRMINGHAM

HORACE G. ALEXANDER

THE POET

I

THE call to write this birthday greeting to the Poet, whom I love, came to me when I was in Cape Town in the very midst of the Indian struggle. We were incessantly engaged in resisting the encroachment of Colour Bar legislation, which was impending in the Transvaal. Every moment of my own time was occupied with the work in hand. Memories at once came thronging to my mind of all I owed to the Poet in the past, and I will recall one of them.

Nearly twenty years ago the poet himself had sent me out to South Africa, along with Willie Pearson, in order to help Mahatma Gandhi in his great Passive Resistance campaign, which had then reached its most critical stage. The summons had come to go there just after the glorious news had reached India that the Nobel Prize for World Literature had been awarded to Rabindranath Tagore. We went out with intense happiness at the Poet's literary triumph still echoing and ringing in our hearts.

Thus he himself sent us out on a great adventure of faith at a propitious moment with his own blessing. He told us to convey to Mahatma Gandhi, and to his noble band of followers, his deep love for them and his admiration for the heroic fight in which they were involved. He called it in one of his letters to me "the battle of India's freedom."

After a very stormy voyage across the Indian Ocean, we had disembarked at last, and had met Mahatma Gandhi on the wharf when the ship arrived safe in Durban harbour. The message we carried from Rabindranath Tagore to the Indian patriot formed a really important link in the Passive Resistance struggle in Natal. For it heartened the Indian community and its leader when they received from us direct this gift of love which came with the Poet's message. A bond of spiritual kinship was thus established between the Indians in South Africa and Santiniketan. This bond has never been broken. So strong was it that when Mahatma Gandhi left South Africa for England he placed his own boys, eighteen in number, who had lived with him for many years at Phoenix, under the care of Rabindranath Tagore, who kept them for many months in his own *Asram* at Santiniketan. Maganlal Gandhi was then in charge of these "Phoenix" boys, and a very deep affection sprang up between him and the Poet.

Let me dwell for a moment longer on these early days when Willie Pearson and I had just left Santiniketan, and had landed in South Africa. During that period of new spiritual vision and illumination thoughts of the Poet and his *Asram* would come clearly before us in all our conversations. It was the first full flush of our common enthusiasm and love for him and it coloured all our existence with its own bright hues. The very sky itself seemed more glorious as we spoke about him and shared our thoughts together.

This was also for us both the happy moment of discovery of a new friendship with Mahatma Gandhi. These two affections were blended into one in a very intimate manner. Often under the stars at night we would sit in the silence and then speak to one another in quiet accents of the wonderful evenings we had spent with our *Gurudev* on the terrace outside his little upper room at Santiniketan. Those were golden moments and Mahatma Gandhi realised with deep sympathy our own hearts' devotion to the Poet. He often spoke to us of his own great longing to meet him. Thus we were all drawn together into a single circle of affection.

II

I turn back again from this earlier recollection to last April, when the call came to me in Capetown, as I have related, to write this birthday greeting for the *Golden Book of Tagore*. The mail for India, *via* Lorenzo Marques, was just on the point of departure, and there would be no further steamer sailing from South Africa to India for many days. It seemed necessary for me, therefore, if I would be in time for the Poet's birthday, to sit down at once where I was in order to try to write out in full some of the thoughts which rose up from the depth of my heart, when I remembered all that the Poet had meant in my own life and what devotion and reverence I owed to him for all his goodness.

What I then thought out was written down in a home for destitute coloured children called "The House of St. Francis of Assisi." This home for the poor had been built on the Cape Flats for the sake of the orphans and waifs and strays among the African population. While I wrote they were all playing around me at their own games, and their merry laughter carried me back in thought to Santiniketan itself. I could easily picture the Poet, like another St. Francis of Assisi, in the midst of his own merry children in his *Asram* in Bengal, where the beauty of Nature is loved by the youngest boys and girls alike. The thought that came uppermost to my mind as I sat there watching the little children at play was to remember with deep affection how the Poet had been, in every sense of the word, my "Gurudev" for nearly twenty years. Let me explain in this Birthday Number how all this began.

III

The night when I first met the Poet was at W. Rothenstein's house, on the Hill near Hampstead Heath. H. W. Nevinson had taken me there. He had met me by accident in the street and had told me casually that Rabindranath Tagore had arrived in London. He mentioned also that W. B. Yeats was that very night reading aloud some of Tagore's poems in Rothenstein's house. It was in the summer of 1912, and my eagerness was so great that I hurried along almost too excited to talk to Nevinson as we walked up the Hill to meet the Poet.

The readings given by W. B. Yeats were taken from *Gitanjali*, and as I listened I was spell-bound. It is quite impossible for me to describe in words what had happened. The music of the poems took possession of me, and their beauty enthralled me. The Poet himself was there, in the background, shrinking from observation, and I can well recollect how my one great longing at that moment was to touch his feet. From the lighted room and the Poet's presence, and the sound of the music of his poems, I went out at last into the late evening twilight and walked in solitude on Hampstead Heath. The moon had just begun to rise and the air was full of enchantment. Darkness was slowly creeping over the earth, and a beautiful afterglow of light was still visible in the West. The glamour of it all was upon me, and I wandered across the Heath, up and down, hardly knowing where I was going. At that hour I was literally oblivious of time and space and things external. There was an inner vision of beauty that I saw with the eye of the spirit. It went far beyond the bounds of this temporal and material world.

The joy of this illumination has never altogether passed away. Whenever I return into the Poet's presence after a long absence, the memory of it unfailingly comes back to me. He has introduced me into the secret of this new spirit of beauty in the universe. Since that first time of vision I have tried to see this beauty with his eyes, both as he describes it in his own songs and also as he builds up its living fabric in his *Asram*.

Any one who knew my life before I met the Poet can appreciate how the dividing line came actually here. What followed that first meeting with the Poet has brought with it something new and different which has changed my whole outlook. He broke through the dull routine of outward form that had imprisoned me up to that time, and thus set me free. How it all happened I cannot explain or describe, but the effect has been obvious. Therefore, in human ways, I feel that I owe the change which I then experienced to him, and it is always a supreme joy to me whenever I am able to acknowledge this debt of love which I owe to him more than to any other human being.

IV

If I were asked to analyse the outstanding things in the Poet's own character that have drawn me to him most of all, I should mention in the first place the fearless love of freedom and passionate devotion to truth, which make him, even in his late declining years, the most daring adventurer of our own times, both in his thoughts and his actions. He has learnt the secret of perpetual youth. He has always retained the heart of a child, and has also kept the eager outlook of a new-comer upon the future. He is filled with admiration, hope and love. Suffering may come to him in incredible forms of pain. No one has suffered more acutely and sensitively than he has done. But as long as the ideal is set before him and a fresh adventure of faith and hope is in sight, he will go through torture, almost intolerable, to one of his supremely refined nature, in order to reach his goal. Even to-day in his failing years he is ready at a moment's notice without a single consideration of the hardships that must be undergone.

The goal itself with him is always high, always glorious, always noble. He has the poet's deep love for the colour and music, the song and drama of life. But all the time, there is an austerity of refinement that is fastidious in its purity, lest the ideal itself should become debased and the aim low. He cannot bear for a single moment that the beauty of the end in view should be tarnished by any meanness in the process. At the same time his moral idealism is never formal or conventional. It rests upon an unerring aesthetic instinct, which is like a strain of music played upon a perfect instrument by a master-hand. The slightest discord mars for him the whole song. It jars upon his inner spirit, creating an agony which less sensitive natures could not for a moment understand.

V

One incident is vividly recalled to my mind, which I personally witnessed in Japan. When he was in that country, he was asked on one occasion to write a short poem concerning a deed of violence which had been committed by two chiefs of rival clans. They had fought from dawn till evening on a grassy plateau, high up in the hills near Hakone. A great rock overshadowed the place. When the sun had set on that day of battle both the warriors had fallen dead, smitten with many wounds, and the ground had been covered with their blood. The leaders of the Japanese people, who had come to the spot with the Poet, asked him to write an epigram in a few words commemorating this heroic occasion.

I could see, at that moment, the strained anguish of the Poet's face as he quickly grasped the incident just as it had occurred and shrank back from it in his own mind in horror. In a moment, with a quick gesture, he wrote these words:—

"They hated and fought and killed each other:
And God in shame covered their blood with His own grass."

The beauty of the thought was only equalled by its daring. It is his spirit, ever new, ever young, ever fresh with the fullness of new life, and tender with the wisdom of sorrow, that has continually won my heart and quickened my inner spirit.

VI

There is a sentence in the Book of the Psalms of David that I have often remembered when Rabindranath Tagore's personality has come before me in some unexpected aspect of greatness. The Psalmist speaking to the Divine Lord says:

"Thy humility hath made me great."

That verse is true of the Poet. The divine humility in him has made him great. He is humble as a little child. The immortal spirit within him, keeping him thus childlike, has wrought this sovereign inspiration of true genius.

There is one more significant passage, this time taken from the Sermon on the Mount, which seems more than any other to complete for me the whole picture. It runs thus:—

"Blessed are the pure in heart; for they shall see God."

In the untarnished mirror of his own innocent and childlike heart the vision of God is reflected.

C. F. ANDREWS

I do not know Tagore personally, but I do ardently admire his works. Please send him my warm admiration and regards.

LONDON

JAMES BARRIE

It gives me great pleasure to express on behalf of my Government to Rabindranath Tagore on the occasion of the publication of the *Golden Book of Tagore* the best wishes for the future. The general admiration felt for him has found a beautiful expression in the *Golden Book*. Many thousands of my fellow-countrymen join the great poet's Indian followers in gratitude for his donations to mankind and wish that for many years to come Rabindranath Tagore will continue to be to the German people the outstanding interpreter of Indian philosophy, poetry and wisdom.

GERMAN CONSULATE,
CALCUTTA

COUNT R. BASSEWITZ

A TAGORE, DESDE EL MEDITÉRRANEO

I.

Pirámide truncada,
Talado acento.
Bosque sin auras.

Paletadas de niebla,
húmeda tierra,
sobre la barca negra.

Adolescentes quiero
para el cortado árbol!
Canten desnudas, duras,
la sumergida isla.

Huya la sombra y arda
frente a los soles vivos.
Desnudas, duras, firmes
canten en corro verde.

II.

La luz sobre la sombra cauta.
! Prado en Aries!
En zodiacos de yerba
pastan soles de naipe.

Entre margenes
vienen cielos y nubes,
llegan árboles.

Las ramas iza, amante.
! Las ramas y las aves!
Entra conmigo en este
bosque de claridades.

III.

Vuelven los dias tetradinamos,
los dias de precipitados azules,
los dias que cristalizan en rombos.

Tienen más luz los campos,
más luz las viejas torres,
más luz el mar y las distancias.

Bajo el solsticio de verano
miro a la tarde y siento:
es este cielo el mio,
es este cielo el que me eleva;
este cielo, tan puro,
que no cobija ofertas ni demandas.

Los árboles halágenos,
los huertos y las aves,
los muros de sal viva
lo alaban en sus cantos.

Es este cielo el que me eleva,
este cielo tan puro
donde mis ojos desembocan.

CARTAGENA

ANTONIO OLIVER BELMAS

TAGORE AND TUKARAM

FROM the Known to the Unknown is the accepted Language of Science. But here is the Language of the Heart hailing from the Unknown to the Known.

During the two years of my stay at Harvard (1912-14) I was fortunate in passing most of my time in the company of a few Bengali friends and colleagues, one of whom—a Doctor of Philosophy now, and Professor in one of the younger Indian Universities—I discovered one morning with a Bengali book under his pillow, which turned out to be a volume of Rabindranath Tagore's Poems. And my friend was so enthusiastic over the work that he prevailed upon me to learn Bengali and so help him to augment his own happiness in reading the Poems by getting me to share it with him. I did so: but unfamiliarity with the Bengali script came in the way of my making much progress in reading "Rabi Babu's" Poems in the original. How earnestly I wished it then—as I do even to-day—that at least a selection of the Poet's masterpieces is made available in Devanagari characters!

I had later the good fortune to meet the Poet himself during his visit to America in 1913. We then naturally wanted the Harvard University to arrange a course of lectures by Rabindranath. These American lectures of the Poet have been published since under the title of *Sadhana;* but would it be believed that before arranging these lectures at the University the officials there wanted to know whether the Poet (who had just then been awarded the Nobel Prize) could speak English! The disillusion soon followed when the whole audience stood enthralled by the rhythmic cadence and the bafflingly mystic suggestiveness of the periods as they flowed forth from one of the most musical of male voices that I have ever heard. And an American lady who was amongst the audience a few seats in front of me, unwilling perhaps to believe that such mellifluous English could be spoken by one who did not claim it as his mother-tongue, observed to her neighbour: "Don't you think that his face is so wonderfully like that of Christ?"—to which the other replied: "But even Christ was an Asiatic, you know!"

My Bengali friends prevailed upon Rabindranath to give a musical recitation of some of his poems in the original Bengali. Amongst the recitations given on the occasion was the Rigvedic Sukta (VII. 89) with the refrain—

मृळा सुक्षत्र मृळय ॥

—and I can never forget the thrill that went through me as I heard the Poet's voice rising and falling with surging inward emotion as the penitent Vedic Sage plaintively cried:

"Save me, my Sov'ran Lord, Save me!"

Amongst the mystic poets of Maharashtra Tukaram comes nearest to Tagore in directness of diction and the pathetic grandeur of the appeal, and I cannot conclude this humble tribute of mine better than by quoting one of the well-known *Abhangas* of Tukaram that one can hear to this day in Maharashtra from the mouth of some "Kathaka," or "Kirtana-kara" as we call him:

> **आपुलें मरण, पाहिलें म्यां डोळां । तो जाला सोहोळा । अनूपम्य ॥ १ ॥**
> **आनंदें दाटलीं, तीन्ही त्रीभुवनें । सर्वात्मकपणें । भोग जाला ॥ २ ॥**
> **येकदेसी होतों, अहंकारें अथीला । त्याच्या त्यागें जाला । सुकाळ हा ॥ ३ ॥**
> **फीटलें सुतक, जन्ममरणाचें । मी-माझ्या-संकोचें । दूरी जालों ॥ ४ ॥**
> **नारायेणें दिल्हा, वसतीचा ठाव । ठेउनीयां भाव । ठेलों पायीं ॥ ५ ॥**
> **तुका म्हणे दील्हें, उमटूनि जगीं । घेतलें तें अंगीं । लाउनीयां ॥ ६ ॥**

—Induprakash Edition, 2668.

[Translation: My death I witnessed with my (own) eyes; it turned out a festivity without compare. (1) With joy the three worlds got crowded: there ensued experience of the oneness-of-Self-in-all. (2) I had lived in the Particular, swayed by Egoism: By renouncing that has arrived this happy time. (3) Ended is the impurity-period of birth and death: I have remained apart from the limitations of the "I" and "Mine." (4) Narayana has afforded me an abode to reside: Reposing faith I have resorted to His Feet. (5) Says Tuka: What has been imprinted upon the whole world, that to my own person I have applied.]

POONA

S. K. BELVALKAR

THE POET AS UNITER

SOME lines of an English poet have been quoted till no self-respecting person can quote them any more, lines asserting that East is East, and West is West, and that "never the twain shall meet." But the quotation, stopping there, is really unfair to the poet in question; for the poem goes on to reverse the sentiment, to assert that when two brave men meet, coming from opposite ends of the earth, all difference of race is done away: "there is neither East nor West, border nor breed nor birth." The object, that is to say, of the Poet in this particular passage is not to insist upon difference, but to point to something which unites in spite of difference. There is a value, he says, which all men who are fully men recognize, to whatever part of the earth they belong, the value of manly strength of spirit: that recognition makes them one. But what Rudyard Kipling says here of one particular kind of value is true of many other kinds of value, recognized by the spirit of man universally, apprehensions of spiritual and moral worth, apprehensions of beauty; in their case too, men, in spite of abiding differences, meet in a communion in which "border and breed and birth" cease to count. Poetry is one of these uniting values; it is not the English only who understand the significance of Wordsworth, nor the Indians only who understand that of Rabindranath Tagore. In days therefore when antagonisms between race and race, between nation and nation, between one element in a country and another element, are perplexing and grieving all those who would like to see the human family advance by co-operation in the great tasks set before it, the poet who gives the world some new beauty in enjoying which men may forget their differences, is doing a work of great practical importance. It is certain that the only way by which the antagonisms of men can be overcome is by the growth of common interests. It is little use exhorting the different hostile groups to be at one; but if they discover some great interest which they have in common, the antagonisms fade away. Interest in literature is, of course, only one of the interests which transcend differences of race and nation, and it would be absurd to suppose that literary interest alone could cure the divisions of to-day. But literary interest may be one strand in a web of interests which draw men together, and the poet who weaves that strand may be doing his part in a great work of uniting. He may seem to live retired and to make his songs only for his own delight or a little group round about him, yet going abroad through the wide world those songs may help to make the world a kindlier world than it is to-day.

LONDON

EDWYN BEVAN

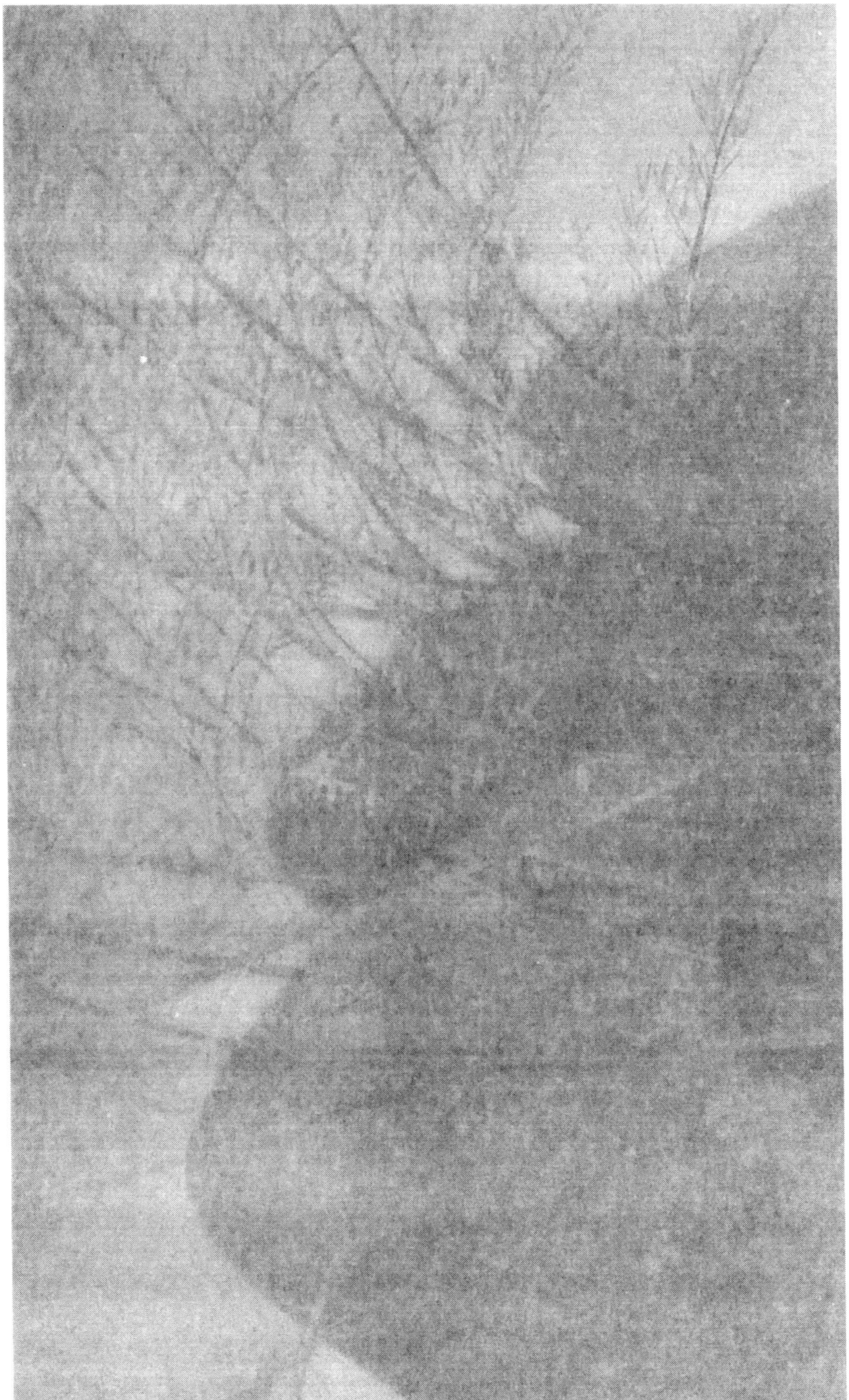

'SHOW US THE RIGHT PATH'

'Whom the Gods wish to foster, him they endow with Right Intelligence and Righteous Will'—so declares the great scriptural Epic of India:

यं तु रक्षितुमिच्छंति न देवा पशुपालवत् ।
दंडमादाय रक्षंति सद्बुद्ध्या योजयंति तम् ॥

He who has this *Sad-Buddhi* will unfailingly achieve everything that is worth having. Therefore has the heart of man, in every time and clime, prayed for it, prayed for the Intelligence that shows the Right Path, prayed to be kept away from the wrong path, in the Aryan Gayatri, the Muslim Namaz, the Lord's Prayer of the Christian.

When a nation has been chastened sufficiently, and prays, in the deeps of its heart, sincerely, passionately, compassionately, then Right Intelligence is given to it by the Oversoul, Vishv-atma, Ruh-i-Kull, Anima Mundi, the World-pervading, Unconscious and supremely Supra-conscious, in the shape of great leaders. When a nation begins to produce great leaders—that is a sign that happier days are returning to it.

India has been producing such in recent years: a spiritual leader unrivalled, who has, by his *tapas,* performed the miracle of converting a vast heterogeneous crowd into an organised army, has shown it the Right Path, and given it the determined will to walk upon it, who has transformed the sordid face of political struggle into a thing of ascetic beauty and riveted upon it the astonished, sympathetic, respectful and expectant gaze of the nations of the earth; an orator-poetess whose eloquent plea for the Mother-land has been heard with attention in four continents; scientists of international fame, one of whom has been presented by the scientific world with a world-mark of honor; speakers, writers, jurists, equal to those of any land. Even in aviation, and games and sports, sons of India have been taking their place side by side with the foremost of other countries, in skill, in daring, in endurance.

Seniormost, among her living sons, of the uplifters of the head of our Mother India from the tear-wet dust in which it had lain for long, leader of thought whose name is known most widely on the surface of the earth, with the one exception of him whom we lovingly and reverently call Bapu and Mahatmaji, is our World-Poet, whom we affectionately speak of as 'Thakur Dada'. He has re-interpreted for us the ancient teachings of the Upanishads and the Bhaktas, embodied them in wonderful language which makes them newly alive and invests them with fresh beauty, not only for us, the children of India, but also for the children of other lands, and thereby helps to bring the hearts of all nearer to one another.

The best, the highest, in his song, is the same as the song of the Upanishads, the song of the Bhaktas. It is the song of that Higher Self, which, pervading all life, appears as Love, as Sympathy, as Fellow-feeling, as that sense of Universal Brotherhood which shall prevail some day, however much the forces of Hate, of Evil, of the lower self, the inverted false reflection of the Higher—*Dæmon est Deus Inversus*—may try to thwart it.

Where the Higher Self reigns, in cottage or in palace, in village or in town, in home or in market-place, in place of business or in place of recreation, in journalist's room or in judge's court, in *panchayat* or in army, in hall of education or hall of legislation—wherever the Higher Self reigns, there is the Kingdom of Heaven, there are love and trust, there are selflessness and philanthropy, there are eager co-operation and strong organisation for the good and the happiness of all. Where the Higher Self is ignored and flouted, where the lower self reigns, there is the Kingdom of Satan, there are mutual jealousy and hate, selfishness and cruelty, pride and fear, lust and greed, perpetual struggle between all for the private profit and power and pleasure of each, and therefore the good and the happiness of none.

To Thakur Dada, for reminding the nations of the earth, by the power of his beautiful words, of that Higher Self which is the only source of the Light that illumines the Righteous Path of Life, which is the One and Only Basis of true Self-government, without the recognition of which such Self-government is impossible, I offer my tribute of homage, on his completing seventy years of a life devoted to the worship of inner and outer Beauty.

BENARES

BHAGAVAN-DAS

MY IMPRESSIONS ABOUT THE POET

TAGORE has become a household word in the Bombay Presidency, especially is Maharashtra. Years ago some of the hymns of Maharshi Devendranath Tagore were translated into Marathi. They are still sung and highly appreciated, as much for their poetic expression as for their spiritual import.

In the monsoon of 1905 I was in Calcutta acting for the late Dr. Bloch of the Archæological Department. The political agitation against the partition of Bengal was then in full swing. I was new to Bengal, but had made many Bengali friends. Even so early as 1905 everywhere among the elite of the society I found the songs of Rabi Babu far more frequently sung than those of other Bengali poets. The most favourite tunes of that time which we constantly heard were *Ekla chalo re, Bidhir bidhan katbe tumi emni saktiman,* the meaning and the music of which was much relished by me. But, strange to say, I had no occasion of meeting the Poet that year.

Many things happened after my return to Poona in the cold season of 1905. Rabi Babu was fast becoming a world celebrity. Some of his poems were translated into English and attracted the attention of not only Europe and America but also of parts of India outside Bengal, where Bengali was not understood. One of his books, the *Gitanjali,* so much engrossed the mind of the late Sir Narayan Chandavarkar that he made it a text-book of the Students' Brotherhood in Bombay and delivered many discourses on the message of the Poet. When the poems of Tagore were once known to the Western World, it was but natural that he should be a recipient not only of the Nobel Prize but also of the Knighthood that was conferred upon him by the Government of India.

In 1917 I came to Calcutta as Carmichael Professor of the Calcutta University. I came now here with a more reverent attitude towards Rabi Babu. The discourses delivered by the late Sir Narayan on the *Gitanjali* not only had made Tagore popular among the intelligentsia of the Bombay Presidency but also held him up as a seer, a poet with some definite message to give to the world. This admiration and reverence for the Poet was very much enhanced when I came to Calcutta in 1917 and heard about what was being done by him at Santiniketan to bring the East and the West together. Many Indologists, such as Prof. Sten Konow, Dr. Sylvain Lévi, Prof. Winternitz, later on came to India in that connection, and we cannot but be grateful to the Poet for inviting western savants into Bengal. In 1917 I certainly was far more fortunate than in 1905, because I actually saw the Poet not once but several times. When I met him first at Jorasanko, he struck me as the handsomest man of the age. His eyes were certainly most enchanting, although the Poet was then on the wrong side of fifty-five. But there was something deeper in his eyes. Every time I met him, I tried to study him, to obtain an insight into his inner soul through the expression of his face. Although I have seen him many a time, I confess my study has not yet been completed, though each time it is becoming more and more engrossing. It is not quite clear to me why they have not yet made a portrait of the Poet that would do him justice. Bengal is noted for painters. But it is inexplicable why none of them has made the Poet's face an object of special study. I wonder why no Bengali painter has yet come forward and done for him what Lenbach, for instance, has done for Bismarck. It is true that Lenbach has made Bismarck, but Bismarck has thereby made Lenbach also. I am sure if any young Bengali painter does such a portrait of the Poet, he will thereby immortalise himself.

Having come to Calcutta and stayed here almost for good, it was impossible not to study his works first hand. Curiously enough, his longer works never appealed to me so much as his smaller. And I cannot help saying that his *Galpaguchchha* and *Katha-o-Kahini* are unrivalled. Most of his songs especially are beautiful, not only in their import but also in their melody. He is not only a word painter but also a musician. Everywhere in his poems and songs you see sunshine, storm, floods, still night, and various other aspects of nature. Whenever he went from Bombay to Poona, as he told me once, the mountainous scenery of the Bore Ghaut enthralled his mind, not only by its beauty, but also by its sublimity. Rabi Babu is thus not a detached idealist, not a detached symbolist, not a detached psychologist, but he is everything that is based on the real. His is a mind most responsive to nature, and he sees the invisible always through the visible. A better tribute to the Poet and Seer of this description I cannot offer than by translating the following hymn of the Maharashtra poet-saint Tukaram, because the mentality of Tukaram reflected in it seems to be that of the Poet also:

> "Trees, creepers, and denizens of the wilds are my companions.
> The birds also are pleasing through their sweet notes.
> The sky is the canopy, and the earth the seat. My mind revels there.
> The breezes make me feel (the passing of) time. A quilt and water-pot alone are for bodily needs.
> Songs about Hari form my sustenance. This variety I enjoy with zest.
> On account of this felicity I appreciate residence in solitude. No blemish, no vice, can touch me there.
> Says Tuka—there is converse with my own mind. And I hold discourse with my own self."

UNIVERSITY OF CALCUTTA

D. R. BHANDARKAR

RABINDRANATH AND VISVA-BHARATI

LIFE expresses itself through the medium of the body, ideas seek forms for self-manifestation. Idea is the inner soul, form is external. Without content there can be no form—it would be dead matter, being devoid of rhythmic vibration; neither is content without form possible, as it would be mere vacuity, eternally homeless. Therefore, ideas seek embodiment, while forms seek ideas.

Many are those who perceive the mere body, being unable to apprehend the indwelling life, the soul. They consider the lines of a picture to be final, they cannot pierce through them to the majesty of the idea. Their realization must ever remain untrue, their knowledge incomplete.

We must also note that the external body, the form, may not have attained beauty, attractive to the eye, yet the soul, the idea within may be very great.

In appraising the truth about Visva-bharati let us bear all this in mind. Visva-bharati is an idea, of course it has also a form, but we must not identify its apparent form with the idea. Its form that we see now is small, but that does not as well indicate a corresponding narrowness of idea. The form that we see of it to-day may change to-morrow; again, inspite of the change of form, the idea may not change at all. From birth onward the body passess through a series of changes, but the soul remains the same; so that if we fix our mind on the changing form its substance too may appear to us to be naught.

When the body is in bondage it is painful, but when the soul is in fetters it is still more painful. Because in the former condition our manhood does not suffer, while slavery of the spirit reduces us to the level of the beast. It is not that external bonds are negligible but lack of spiritual freedom is fatal for us and must be relentlessly fought against.

In our intensive effort to solve our political problems we found new and newer manacles being forged for us, instead of our being able to cut through them once for all. Hemmed in from all sides by oppressive party-walls, our country was fast losing its power to recognize man as man. We were still proud of those ancient days of India when *Bharata* gave its eternal message to the *Visva,* but we could not hearken to its call with our hearts burdened by anger, hate and contending illusions. In those dark days of our country, in the *Asrama* of Santiniketan the vision of the *Visva-Bharati* slowly dawned in the heart of Rabindranath. That great realisation of the ancient *Rishis* came to Rabindranath: *yatra visvam bhavaty eka-nidam*—'There Where the Whole World unites in a Nest.' We have to spread an *Asana* of pure friendliness on which can gather all in unity; where man can meet man in a free relationship of joy; where country, politics, dogma, religious faiths and sectarian names can create no barrier; where the path for both accepting and bestowing the worthiest contributions of the world will ever be open; where all thoughts will unite *Bharata* with *Visva,* and not separate them; where all actions will be towards the welfare of the whole, and not against it; where good will be world's good, love will embrace the world-humanity; and peace will be peace of the world.

This is the ideal image of *Visva-Bharati;* it is gracious, it is beautiful, it is beneficial. It has to be established by each one of us, nobody can merely receive it from another. It awaits individual realization, not borrowed display.

Through Rabindranath, in this very *Asrama* this great idea has manifested itself, but it has no limitation in space, no termination in time, it is not bound in its expression to Santiniketan, or to any particular locality. Any attempt to monopolise it will be fatal to its truth, obscuring the eternal radiance of its purity. This thought-image of *Visva-Bharati* is in each thinker's heart; in this country, in other countries near and far. The bodily manifestation of *Visva-Bharati* we now find in Santiniketan; in the future it may be in another place: let it be so.

This particular manifestation of *Visva-Bharati* is naturally vitally connected with India, the land of its birth. In one of its aspects it is concerned with the exploration of the different avenues of Indian thought and culture; in the other, it seeks to gather knowledge about the contributions of countries beyond the confines of India. For knowledge, which is the generator of welfare, deserves respectful study as knowledge itself, whether its birth has been in India or outside of it. On this great truth rests the foundation of *Visva-Bharati.* In its Research Departments, diverse branches of knowledge which flourished in the past in countries other than India, cultures that are dimmed or almost lost by the passage of time, engage the closest attention of its scholars. *Visva-Bharati* needs co-operation with the outside world in order fully to know humanity, to remove its barriers of ignorance in its progressive attainment of truth.

On the 8th of Paush, Bengali Year 1325, during the annual festival in Santiniketan the idea of the *Visva-Bharati* was first formulated; in the next year, on the 18th of Ashadh, *Visva-Bharati* was formally established. The words with which Rabindranath closed his inspiring address on that occasion may be remembered now:

'*Visva-Bharati* is a great idea, though it has appeared in our midst in a material shape which is small. The arrival of the Great in the disguise of the very little, however, happens everyday in life. Let us therefore rejoice in the fact of its coming, let the auspicious music be sounded. Let us earnestly hope that this infant is the messenger bringing *Amrita* from the gods, that this nectar of divine life will make it live from within, make it grow, and also make us live and grow into fulness.'

Has not time given any justification of this prophecy?

SANTINIKETAN — VIDUSEKHAR BHATTACHARYYA

For Mercy, Courage, Kindness, Mirth,
There is no measure upon earth:
Nay, they wither, root and stem,
If an end be set to them.

Overbrim and overflow,
If your own soul you would know,
For the spirit, born to bless,
Lives but in its own excess.

BRITISH MUSEUM,
LONDON

LAURENCE BINYON

HE is India bringing to Europe a new divine symbol, not the Cross, but the Lotus. His wisdom knows no age, it is old as the rivers of India and younger than even childhood, for there shimmers in it something in-born, which will not be revealed until the Morrow. His poetry belongs to no school—the flowers of Bengal were created by sun and rain.

His love for his fellowmen is not the love of the Samaritan, but of the Song of Songs. He knows that just as the dew drop in the grass may mirror the Heavens, so the human mind may reflect God.

His religion knows neither hope nor fear. It dwells in the calm of the Spiritual Universe which nothing but the human heart can comprehend.

HVALSTAD, NORWAY

JOHAN BOJER

H. F. AMIEL, JOURNAL INTIME

Juillet 20, 1876

Au Poète et sage Rabindranath Tagore, qui a sondé la profondeur d'âme, et exploré les richesses de pensée d'H.F. Amiel, je presente, en respectueux hommage, ces pages inédites de son Journal Intime.

GENEVE BERNARD BOUVIER

L'IMAGINATION agrandit tout. Il est probablement moins difficile de mourir qu'on ne le croit. Quand on n'a plus la force de vivre, on meurt ; et la mort a tout l'air d'être le repos. . . . . .

Ce n'est pas le néant qui me fait frissonner, c'est l'impuissance de la longue douleur, c'est la souffrance sans consolations et sans espoir. J'éprouve aussi une vague anxiété de la conscience, et qui sait si cette solitude qui est un supplice n'est pas aussi un péché.

Cette défiance incurable de la destinée, qui se refuse aux conditions de la vie humaine, parce qu'elle a pénétré le redoutable secret de l'illusion, c'est le Pessimisme. Mais le Pessimisme est peut-être le péché contre le St Ésprit, car il maudit froidement la Création. Tu ne maudis pas, toi, mais c'est par douceuer, inconséquence et peut-être faiblesse.

Scepticisme, apathie, désespérance. Tu n'as plus la force d'espérer, ni celle de vouloir. C'est pourquoi tu n'es plus de ce monde, où tout repose sur l'âpre amour de la vie et sur l'impétueux désir. Tu n'es plus qu'une pensée qui a conscience de sa prochaine disparition, une bulle d'iris qui assiste à son éclosion fugitive et aux métamorphoses de sa coloration éphémère, le rien qui se sait rien et admire le quelque chose. L'âme n'est peut-être qu'un phénomène de phosporence du second degré ; c'est la forme d'une forme, le diagramme fantastique du MYSTÈRE universal, un dessin dans le vide, un éclair symbolique de la création, une miniature du feu d'artifice que Maia se tire depuis l'éternité.

L'intellectualisme est une philosophie ; le moralisme en est une autre, l'esthétisme une troisième. Comprendre le monde, tendre à la sainteté, créer la beauté, voilà trois types d'existence ; et que d'autres encore : viser à la volupté, exploiter les choses et les gens, poursuivre la gloire ne ressemblent nullement aux trois premiers ; et il me semble que le cœur a encore une autre philosophie et que vivre pour l'amour est une septième manière d'entendre la vie, celle que goûtent particulièrement les femmes.

Les différentes manières d'entendre la vie et d'expliquer le monde, ce sont les divers morales pratiques et les divers systèmes de philosophie. Notre instinct dominant tend à nous emprisonner dans l'une de ces cases ; la culture spirituelle se propose de nous les faire parcourir toutes ; la liberté critique consiste à rester au-dessus de ces geôles et à les envisager dans leur liaison, comme parties d'un plus vaste ensemble.

TO THE GURU,

RABINDRANATH TAGORE

One foggy spring eve in Sweden it seemed to me as if a string of light were all of a sudden lit through the mist, and I wondered what it might mean.

The same eve I heard your name uttered for the first time.

As Marconi's pressing of a button on the Eletta in the Mediterranean caused all the lights in Melbourne to glow, so your message to the world in beautiful song suddenly burst on thousands and thousands of yearning hearts in the West, shedding a new light over man's destiny. Once such a flame is lit, it always goes on burning, like lamps in sacred places.

You opened vistas to the Western world, that it might see what has been the glory of India from time immemorial—the spirit which goaded on her saints and her heroes in epic and in history to holy greatness.

Who has like you mingled the strains of joy and sorrow into one song, where "mirth spreads from leaf to leaf and gladness without measure," enabling us to realize "the joy that sits still with its tears on the red lotus of pain, and the joy that throws everything it has upon the dust and knows not a word"?

To those who have understood your message there shall be no fear left on earth.

Therefore to-day the flower of undying gratitude is planted in your courtyard.

OSLO, NORWAY

ANDREA BUTENSCHON

A GREETING

IT has been said that a man can live three days without water, but not a day without poetry. The thoughts of Rabindranath Tagore have that awareness, truth, and beauty which are of the very substance of life. I salute the great poet of India, who is to all the world a fount of life and a healer of souls.

STATE UNIVERSITY OF IOW[illegible]S.A.

SUDHINDRA BOSE

RABINDRANATH TAGORE

IT was my privilege to meet Rabindranath Tagore when he visited England in 1912. We spent an evening together with a small company at the house of a mutual friend, the late Sir Richard Stapley. It was an experience which ever since has lived vividly in my memory and to which I have recurred in thought again and again. The poet's personal appearance one could never forget, even had there been nothing more in regard to the influence emanating from him to fix and retain the attention of those present. I have never seen anyone before or since who came so near to one's ideal of what Jesus of Nazareth must have looked like in the days of His flesh. Nor was I alone in thinking so ; our host spoke of the fact to me privately as did several others. Mr. Tagore at that time was in the prime of life, spare, erect, with pale slightly olive-tinted complexion, luminous eyes, long, wavy, light brown hair and beard. His expression was gentle and winning, and his whole personality combined in a remarkable way high intelligence with benevolence and unself-conscious dignity. His demeanour is more patriarchal now ; the light brown hair has become white ; but in other respects, as his portraits evince, he has not changed. Of no man living can it be more truly said that a glorious spirit animates and dominates a mortal frame.

His conversation on that evening, I remember, was charming and courteous but restrained. He was not voluble, rather the contrary, though entirely at ease with his fellow guests. He seemed to be at home with them and to like them, as is perhaps easy to understand when it is noted that one of the most distinguished was Evelyn Underhill, author of important works on Mysticism and mystical writers. Another was Edmond Holmes, author of *The Creed of Buddha*, a book to which happy allusion was made by Mr. Tagore. The poet read to us in his quiet silvery voice his then unpublished mystical play, *The King of the Dark Chamber*. It was a revelation to us of the power and freshness of a great creative mind uttering itself in lucid, nervous, beautiful English. Later in the evening the reader told me that until he was nineteen he knew no English. A marvel indeed, that one of the greatest forces in the Renaissance of his own native Bengali Literature should also have become one of the greatest masters of contemporary English prose! I am told that he did not begin to write in English until he was fifty. I have all his books on my shelves now, and whenever I open one of them I can still hear that quiet musical voice repeating the words as I heard it to the muffled accompaniment of the London traffic outside on that memorable evening nearly twenty years ago.

Rabindranath Tagore's own spiritual evolution has made him one of the mightiest prophets of the coming unity of mankind of whom history will preserve the record. His ardent nationalism of earlier days has long been sublimated into a passion for the welding together of all peoples into a God-conscious whole. That is why he has dedicated his life not only to the East but to the W[illegible] and not simply in song but in service. Perhaps *Gitanjali* gives us the acme of his attainment of this vision ; at least it has not been surpassed.

> "Thou hast made me known to friends whom I knew not. Thou hast given me seats in homes not my own. Thou hast brought the distant near and made a brother of the stranger.
>
> When one knows thee, then alien there is none, then no door is shut. Oh, grant me my prayer that I may never lose the bliss of the touch of the One in the play of the many."

But the product of the poet's soul which I love best and which contains the ripest fruit of his meditations was not written for publication at all. It is the collection of his letters to his friend C. F. Andrews, recording his reflections during his tour of Europe and America in 1920-21. The moral insight displayed is unerring and pierces to the very quick of our habitudes and conventional assumptions. Herein is enshrined a new gospel of the East to the West, for it is nothing less, and we shall forbear to learn it at our peril. The East is teaching us through the voice of Rabindranath Tagore and those who think and act with him that there is no salvation in pelf and material might, that strength is made perfect in weakness and lordship in love. Faithful as is the diagnosis of our conditions, no less faithful to the promise of the religion that the West professes to revere is the following, mailed from New York:

> Those who are in posession of material resources have become slaves of their own instruments. Fortunately for us, in India, these resources are beyond all immediate possibility of realization. We are disarmed, and therefore we have no option but to seek for other and higher sources of power. The men who believe in the reality of brute force have made enormous sacrifices in order to maintain it. Let us, in India, have faith in the moral power in man and be ready to sacrifice for it all we have. Let us do our best to prove that Man has not been the greatest mistake in Creation. Let it not be said that, for the sake of peace and happiness in the world, the physical brutes were preferable to the intellectual brutes who boast of their factory-made teeth and nails and poison fangs.
>
> * * * * * * *
>
> The truth that moral force is a higher power than brute force will be proved by the people who are unarmed. Life, in its higher development, has thrown off its tremendous burden of armour and a prodigious quantity of flesh, till man has become the conqueror of the brute world. The day is sure to come when the frail man of spirit, completely unhampered by air-fleets and dreadnoughts, will prove that the meek are to inherit the earth.

This is the authentic note. This is the specific message that the pain-racked, unhappy, violence-riven world most needs to hear at the present critical hour. But will it listen? Once more the eternal has found an instrument in a singer who sings of heaven amid the clamorous noises of earth. We thank God for the *avatar*, and await its fulfilment.

CHICHESTER CATHEDRAL
CHICHESTER, SUSSEX, ENGLAND

R. J. CAMPBELL

THE POET AT WORK

RABINDRANATH has spoken of self-creation as the religion of man. This process subsumes the countless drives of human effort and aspiration in a deep continuous flow of personality which outgrows its limits in a progressive manifestation of being.

As a self-creative artist Rabindranath's evolving personality on its path of fulfilment has opened up realms of expression in a varied response to life. These creations of Art,—poems, songs, dramas and painting, represent an individuality revealing itself in the universal context of being, in the background of a wide world of humanity.

There are other aspects of the Poet's self-creation unknown to the public, which perhaps those who have been near to him in daily life may have viewed in a correct perspective of significance.

But Rabindranath is alive, indeed more profoundly alive than others, because of an intense energy of spirit which is the special prerogative of genius. We cannot detach the unfolding story of his living moments from their condensations into Art. Yet we shall knock at some backdoors in the Poet's mental workshop—may be glimpses will be vouchsafed to us into the character of his creative activities.

It is said that a man's library betrays the intimacies of his mind. Certainly the Poet's peregrinations in the world of printed matter have left their mark in the Visvabharati Library, which largely consists of his personal collections. Browsing in its cool chambers, loitering in the lanes of books vibrant with the silent thoroughfare of thoughts, we have stumbled upon strange data of which these inconsequential pages is the result.

We have discovered, to mention only a few items, that the Poet in his tendencies is not only a farmer but a philologist; historian as well as physician; a keen student of astro-physics, geology, bio-chemistry, entomology. We find him actively engaged in co-operative banking, experimenting with sericulture, indoor decoration, production of hides, manures, sugar-cane and oil; organizing local pottery, weaving-looms, lacquer-work; introducing tractors, formulating new schemes of village economies, and new recipes for cooking. Books on lighting and drainage system, calligraphy, plant-grafting and meteorology show unmistakable signs of pencilled perusal ; synthetic dyes, parlour games, not to speak of whole encyclopædias and comparative dictionaries have been probed by his lance-like intellect. Egyptology, road-making, incubators, wood-blocks, elocution and Jiu-jitsu have competed with printing presses and stall-feeding for equal claims on his attention.

Incongruously netted, this represents but one day's haul of facts. We could have added more; but lest a casual reader unacquainted with local lore be perplexed by these seemingly unpoetical acquisitions of the Poet's mind, we would refer him to Santiniketan and Sriniketan for proof positive of actual and systematic application of all the branches of knowledge mentioned above, and more. Few people outside know that he has been all through his life a pioneer of indigenous industries and enterprises, sparing neither his personal resources nor his right to leisure for raising the efficiency level of his people and their sinking reserves of self-assurance. Truant all his life from the fenced grooves of professional education, no one has surrendered himself more readily or completely than the Poet, to the harness of strenuous civic works of practical utility. Even in the days of his youthful isolation on the Ganges, while engrossed in literary work, he was one with the children of the soil, whose sorrows and sufferings found his active response in remedial measures, in far-sighted agrarian policies. He played his role as landlord and a friend of the people with consummate sagacity. Official records and cherished traditions in the Tagore estate in Bengal prove his remarkable organising capacity and aptitude for entering into and throwing illuminative practical suggestions upon complex details of village life, involving economic, religious and psychological issues. Students of his social and political writings know something of his pioneer ideas of co-operative enterprise, collective farming, village *panchayets* and the revival of arts and crafts and indigenous manufactured goods through organized annual fairs. An adequate chronicle of his constructive efforts, made at a time when such ideas were not only unknown to our own people but unappreciated in other countries, waits to be penned.

The utter helplessness of our people called him forth into yet closer co-operation with them in the arena of public affairs. The Swadeshi movement in Bengal claimed him as its hero. Not only in stirring poems and songs, and innumerable socio-political lectures and addresses but in original schemes of rural reconstruction, social reform, and revival of indigenous industries he laid the foundation of the National Renaissance of Bengal. The re-awakening and gradual self-assertion of India as a whole owes its direct inspiration to the cultural revival of Bengal. May it be noted in passing that even in the stormy Swadeshi days the Poet never for a moment swerved from his prophetic faith that the welfare of India involved the emancipation of total humanity in a mutual interdependence of freedom shared by the commonwealth of man? He never failed to remind his countrymen that barriers of national greed and exploitation have to be heroically demolished, not because a country can ever afford to indulge in suicidal isolation, but to provide a basis of equality and justice on which alone, freed from the shadow of parasitism, the peoples of the world now cruelly separated by the organised racial animosity of Nations can meet in a healthy commerce of goodwill.

We know the genesis of Santiniketan, and something of the history of its growth through the unrelenting self-sacrifice of one practical idealist who refused to yield to the hostile indifference of sceptical compatriots and the inherent obstacles of an unnatural political situation. That he triumphed will be evident to any one who visits to-day the different departments of Santiniketan and of its sister institution, the Rural Reconstruction centre at Sriniketan. Will it strike the visitor's realization that the various departments, with their multifarious activities, are but the projections of a poet's personality whose constant guidance and inspiration explain their existence?

The wide range of the Poet's perusal of books will now take on an added significance. Quick to reach at the basic values of new ideas and efforts he has gathered suggestions from all quarters and readily invited expert opinion and trained workers in launching practical enterprises and in establishing them. Much remains to be done, in fact, whole vistas of development lie ahead of us, but the beginning has been made. It required the impetus of a tremendous personality to break through the inertia of inclement circumstance, and an impoverished will-power which clogs all progress in our country. The Poet in his pilgrimage through life has taken up the challenge of the many-sided urges of his personality, moulding at the same time, through vital experiences of growth, the destiny of our nation itself.

This is how he has educated himself and his countrymen. In this attempt to deal completely with life in an intimately comprehensive manner will be found a clue to his principle of education. The human child is born to this world of life with a native self-creative impulse which seeks the direct stimulus of life itself. The aim of education is to equip man to face the totality of life, eliminating obstacles of ignorance and improper adjustment, developing resourcefulness, training the senses and the intellectual mind. The educator is there to inspire man with creative energy, by surrounding him with the atmosphere of living, growing thoughts and actions. In this educational colony of Santiniketan the Poet looks to the trees, and birds, the wide expanses of meadow and sky to join hands with the elder companions of the pupils, the educators, who would bring their gatherings of life to the open-air classes, in teaching the children how to live. It is his desire that the artists at work, the musicians improvising on their instruments, the scholars engrossed at their desks shall constantly radiate their influence into the receptive minds of children, who thus would feel drawn to experiment with their own creative persuasions. The various technical departments are there to challenge their curiosity, their inherent craft-making instincts compelling them to seek the directing guidance of their teachers in the exciting game of giving shape to things. With a wide-awake sense of wonder the children roam through the pathways of life, knowing, feeling, possessing, ceaselessly growing and outgrowing themselves in an expanding fulness of being. The allurement of books grows upon them, enlivening their study-periods with the surprises of unexpected riches. Guests come from distant lands to remind and assure them of the claims of common humanity in an idiom which can be translated into their own.

In his education scheme the Poet cherishes the hope that a sympathetic interest in their neighbours will be awakened in the minds of the students and some day they will be fully trained to organize medical relief work, sports, fairs as well as recitations, musical performances and dramas, and carry them to the heart of surrounding villages where life is cheerless, unhealthy and uncreative. Pioneer girls practise Jiu-jitsu, sword-play, and outdoor games, taking equal part with the boys in managing the civic affairs of the miniature metropolis of Santiniketan. The class hours of study are but an integral part of the whole life of education built up by the self-expressive activities of students and teachers alike, growing up together in an atmosphere of human aspiration harmoniously adjusted with the cyclic pilgrimage of seasons, the pageantry of the cosmic life of the Universe.

Santiniketan and Sriniketan are the consummation of the Poet's idea of education. Education to him is commensurate with the entire process of our living, of becoming, of directing our personality along widening intensities of growth. The painful memory of his own boyhood's contact with school-life, his constant dealings with the victims and perpetrators of a borrowed paraphernalia of imperial education, and his wide-travelled experiences of some of the modern pedagogic cults dragooning human personality into standardised grooves of respectability had been preying on his mind, suggesting to him the idea of launching an educational project in which he could concretise his ideas of creative education for children.

The Poet's ideal of a complete life of education emanated from the tradition of our country, as it persists in Sanskrit literature and history, in which Masters who had attained perfection in their lives blended their daily existence with those of youthful devotees of knowledge, initiating them into a life of truth through constant personal contact. In his sensitive recoil from the swift-spreading blight of a prim and supercilious modernity, fostered by pseudo-scientific education, hardening ingrained prejudices into callously unquestioning cants of civilization, and putting the premium on half-truths, fragmentary self-assertion, and one-eyed professionalism, the Poet's anguished soul first found its sanctuary in the vision of the ancient *Tapovanas* of India, serene abodes of culture in the forest retreats where human personality was given its spiritual food in a pervasive atmosphere of harmony with life, a harmony achieved through work and meditation, through exploration of all living avenues of knowledge, of the natural universe as well as of its indwelling spirit. Communion with the supreme source of realization based itself on a large awareness of the significance of the Many in creation, a consciousness which vitalizes our richly diverse human nature with the urgency of a unifying purpose. Students of the hermitages tended cattle, brought fire-wood for cooking, cultivated pasture land, devoting themselves no less keenly to the service of the community than to the acquirement of wisdom from their Masters, round whom they gathered in search of Truth. The home, the school, the life of civic responsibility were thus welded in one; teachers and the taught participated in a corporate life detached from the vicissitudes of uncontrolled urban excitement, yet preserving in full the chromatic elements of struggle and effort, of varied pursuits and diversions which compose the normal day of human life. It is not possible fully to recreate this atmosphere in our days, but the Poet has attempted with inevitable adjustment to make this ideal dynamic in a modern setting, harmonising its comprehensive simplicity with the amenities of scientific progress.

The library shelves point out that in this supremely difficult achievement of organizing available knowledge from past and present, West and East, into a luminous vision of the perfect, the Poet nourished his native synthetizing genius with assiduous garnering from wide areas of study. His representation of India is not built of idyllic concepts of a visionary golden age but of actualisations of a living past, a growing present, silhouetted against the background of historic truth. Sanskrit literature, sociology and abstruse philosophical texts have disclosed their inner truths to his exacting imagination. Erudite commentaries, modern and classical, have not been spared. From the eddying transience of current affairs, the obscurity of the obvious in the kaleidoscopic panorama of surrounding events, he has discovered the intangible continuity of India's spiritual life flowing in myriad channels through the heart of our repressed humanity. Different strata of progress and retrogression have revealed to him the unique mind of India which is perennially self-renewing in its precious gift to the commonwealth of Man. In folk-lore, artistic traditions, festivals and religious fairs, in the tree-shaded, river-skirted usual life of Indian villages the Poet's comprehension has found evidence of this undying India waiting to be redeemed from the etiolation of neglectful centuries. This India he has made known to the world, seeking to establish a confluence of cultures in which will mingle India's spiritual waters with those of other lands. Rabindranath's internationalism is the self-creative harmonisation of fully awakened national humanities. As an educator of nations he shows us that the elusive links of a common destiny hold humanity together in its progressive manifestation of the world-mind of Man.

The Poet is at work. Visitors pour into his study corner, autograph books pile up high on the desk, letters and cables gather from four quarters of the globe, urgent messages seek advice, confer patronships, invite presidential lectures, claim articles, subscriptions, names for the new-born, medicines for the sick, help for foreign travel, tips for out-manœuvring the Nobel Prize Committee. Our college, school, the art-and-craft rural-work centres, local meetings, afternoon gatherings, financial committees tackle his mind with an interminable procession of problems. Children, seniors, diverse local officials, correspondents, interviewers, and press-agents annihilate all available margin of his working day. Photographers, tourists, authors, hunters, baronets, struggling artists, round-the-world-cyclists, visionary poets, women aviators, political readers and misleaders parade on the narrow arena of his door step, each considerately assuring to take up only a few minutes of his time. Books hurry through the post, proof-copies for introductions, first copies for review, pamphlets for immediate attention. Books with blazing covers, fancy letterings ; ordinary, extra-ordinary, sensation-of-the-year books ; books with oriental atmosphere, raw modern flavour, archæological, pathological, ethereal and underworldly books speaking in a babel of tongues. Magazines, newspapers, American tabloids and news-digests, documents and Blue Books speed through continents and seas to his desk. You would consider one's daily share of two dimensions hardly enough to accommodate so much. Yet, there is time for each letter, space for visitors; problems are quietly faced, meetings attended. We have not spoken of the regular classes, evening readings, participation in informal discussions and debates with groups of students through which he keeps an intimate touch with the heart of our educational commune, inspiring its members with his generous approachability, his irresistible friendliness. And if, once more, you turn to a particular section of the Library, you will find books steadily growing, books of poems, stories, essays, drama, products of his untiring pen. And, Paintings. By the score they wing their way through the blue of his mind, to be netted in a magic web of colours and contours unprecedented in technique and imagining. Of his self-creative *lila* this is the latest phase.

The Poet is incessantly at work. Far-reaching schemes crowd into his brain, just now, the resolve to found a Women's University darkens his brows with a concentrated urgency of expectation. Having all his life given voice in poignant literature to their inmost travail and fulfilment, roused our women to self-assertion, inaugurated brightening reforms, he has pioneered co-education in his school till it has spread successfully all over the country. He must yet establish for them a full-fledged University to give complete scope to their self-expression. Original schemes for civic training for women, co-ordinated methods to help forward their manual and intellectual self-liberation moulding individual latencies into character, and diverse technical, vital innovations in education have matured in the Poet's mind through a life-time of experience and thought ready to be utilised. He waits while he works, strives to create clement circumstance to materialize his dream, knowing too that in the purity of truth's appeal lies its conscriptive power.

In the Poet's unhurried accomplishment of daily work, in the serenity of his self-possessed detachment which guides his intense gift of absorption into every detail of life will be found his harmonising principle of conduct. Through congregated distractions his mind hearkens back each day to the primal notes of creation, tuning itself to the pure music of life which is resonant in the Earth and Air, in green blades of grass, in flower and leaves. Hardly able to walk, early in the dawn he must yet visit the nursery of growing trees in front of his house in *Uttarayana*, to wish them a good day. He is ever an eager student in the school of life, with insatiable wonder in his heart for what is to come, for all the amazing things that are. In appraising a personality of such rare and complete self-creation, we must realize that its significance is not only a challenge for the present, but a prophecy of the future of Man.

SANTINIKETAN — AMIYA C. CHAKRAVARTY

HOMENAJE A TAGORE DESDE ESPANA

I

[Retorno.

He vuelto por el camino sin yerba.
Voy al rio en busca de mi sombra.
Qué soledad sellada, de luna fria.
Qué soledad de agua sin sirenas rojas.
Qué soledad de pinos ácidos, errantes.
Voy a recojer mis ojos
abandonados en la orilla.

II

[Acércate.

Mira qué junto a la noche te espero.
Cómo su corazón y el mio,
emiten radiaciones luminosas.
Nádame.
Fuentes profundas y frias
avivan mi corriente.
Mira qué puras son mis charcas,
qué gozo el de mi yelo.

III

Guardaré mi voz en un pozo de lumbre
y será crepúsculo toda la vida.
Ya girarán más leves los cuchillos
porque no encontrarán dónde herirme.
(Erguida de rocios negros,
para ti, cantaré.)
Que no me busquen los sin vista,
que no me llamen los ahogados,
que no me sientan los que huyo.
A mi soledad de reflejos,
Amor, sólo tú.

CARTAGENA

CARMEN CONDE

FROM CHINA

Greetings and Best Wishes.

NATIONAL UNIVERSITY
PEIPING

PRESIDENT

RABINDRANATH Tagore's place in the hierarchy of poets and writers of all ages will be assessed by those who follow us, but we who are his contemporaries know well the great power he has wielded and the influence he has exercised over life and thought during the last half century. Rabindranath and Bankim Chandra Chatterjee were the apostles of the renaissance, which, taking its rise in Bengal, spread through the length and breadth of India. Nor has his influence been confined to the purely cultural sphere. He has won renown as an educational reformer, a keen protagonist of social reform and a political thinker of wide sympathy and understanding. Not only has his creative genius been universally recognised but it has given our country a high place for intellectual achievement among the nations. His influence has been one of the primary factors of the day which are welding together in harmony and concord the peoples of the world.

LONDON

ATUL C. CHATTERJEE

LE PROPHÈTE D'ASIE

Il était assis dans sa robe aux larges manches sacerdotales,
Nous formions un cercle attentif et incliné autour de lui.
Il parlait : Sa voix caressante et mélodieusement égale
Coulait en eau surnaturelle dans le silence du salon recueilli.
Ses gestes languides et souples avaient des noblesses félines,
Sa barbe de soie argentée filait très bas sur la poitrine,
Et il gardait volontiers en parlant ses paupières très long baissées,
Comme pour contenir et goûter la modulation des pensées.
Puis il découvrait tout à coup dans un éclair sombre et serein
Le regard ardent et voilé des yeux dont le blanc même est brun.
Le mage d'un Orient d'amour et le poète au mystère de brahmane,
Celui-là dont la voix lointaine nous avait pris dès longtemps par un charme,
(Le charme d'un parfum troublant dans une lumière diaphane)
Etait là aujourd'hui parmi nous.

Son sourire insistant et doux
Paraissait entr'ouvrir des ciels. Sa voix de liquide lumière
Etait belle comme la voix de miel des vieillards harmonieux d'Homère.
Son esprit lucide et lustral purifiait le monde en le pensant..
Il reflétait ce pauvre monde tavelé de macules de sang.
Il voulait l'Europe et l'Asie accordés comme un chant d'hymen
D'où naîtrait enfin l'âme humaine.
Et nous laissions fluer en nous la simple présence d'un prophète.
"La seule existence d'un tel homme, avait dit l'un de nous, est un bienfait."

Je me rappellerai toujours le regard de joie sérieuse, le souffle contenu
De deux jeunes filles presque enfants qui le contemplaient suspendues.
Les peintres ont semé de ces visages extatiques de beauté sévère
Et de plénitude silencieuse le long de la voie du Calvaire.

Quand nous sommes sortis à sa suite, il pleuvait sur le vieux domaine
En de lentes gouttes pensives, comme dans certains des ses poèmes
Le soir respirait sous le tiède malaise d'un orage printanier
Et les gouttes s'étalaient clapotantes sur le feuillage plat des marronniers
Comme elles doivent s'écraser là-bas sur les feuilles sonores des bambous.
Les pelouses luisaient et le sable mouillé des allées était roux.
La pluie brassait l'odeur de vie des fleurs de mai,
Et de la terre montait bienfaisante une humide fraîcheur embaumée.
Dans le parc un oiseau isolé modulait des notes si profondes
Qu'on eût dit la pensée du monde

GENEVE

L. CHARLES-BAUDOUIN

TAGORE AND THE REBIRTH OF BENGAL'S SOUL

I.

TO the present hour, we Bengalis thrill at our remembrance of the new light that suffused our eastern skies, the new life that came pouring into the depths of our being in the opening years of the century. *Swadeshi* had dawned on Bengal. The qualities that lie on the Godward side of man reappeared in the Bengali one by one—faith, courage, hope, aspiration, defiance of death. The sureness of accent with which he pronounced his faith in his country and its future took India by storm, and soon began to make itself heard across the seas. The Bengali stepped right out of his dead self—a miracle of resurrection! Art, science, music and the spirit of research burst synchronously into life. A new protestantism was abroad against wrong. Men consecrated their lives to the service of fellowmen ; a new chivalry revealed itself towards women, who began building a new freedom on it ; missions of mercy sprang up to lessen suffering and pain. The call for brotherhood that had immemorially gone up from India's submerged children awakened a new response in the conscience of the twice-born. National industries raised their head. Institutions of national education were founded to revive and keep alive the philosophy of self-realisation and the ethics of *Ahimsa,* which were re-discovered by the Bengali as constituting India's abiding contribution to culture. And the political life of Bengal transformed itself beyond recognition.

II.

This passage of Bengal from darkness to dawn, the immersion of the Bengali, body and spirit, in the holy waters of a resurgent life, the maddening ecstasy born of his soul's vision of its lost self, was transparently not the freak of an hour, no momentary flashing of a fugitive hope, no illusion. For the Bengali has gone on ever since growing from more to more. Have we not been the privileged witnesses of one of those visitations of Divinity in man in the hour of his soul's flagging and failing, the light of which illumines the story of man?

All great movements of human renewal have had their prophets. Who was the prophet of the one of which we are speaking? Bengal will answer with one voice—Rabindranath Tagore. Was he not of the great company of Bengal's chosen few—the eldest of her sons whose ears, more finely attuned, had been filled with the cry of the Indian earth, whose souls had flown across the night of time to commune with the spirits of those aristocrats of humanity who had up-built the indestructible foundations of India's civilisation? Tagore, who came after Ram Mohun Roy, Debendranath Tagore, Keshub Chunder Sen, Ramakrishna and Bankim Chandra Chatterjee, was the soul-mate of every one of them and gathered up into his personality the essence of what they had thought and taught. And the reality strikes us to-day with the force of a revelation that a full score of years before the bursting of *Swadeshi* on Bengal, he wrote and sang with intuition and passion of all the great and the small things that marked the Bengali's re-entry into the life everlasting.

It was Tagore's words of fire, uttered in poetry and prose, that compelled his educated countrymen to the realisation that they were making priceless clowns of themselves by wrapping the imitation of Englishmen's clothes round their persons. Was he not the one distinguished son of Bengal who always appeared in immaculate *dhoti* in the midst of the Anglo-maniacs of the last century? The memory abides with us of how the one has since become many. It was Tagore, again, who rid his fellow-Bengalis of the nightmare under the seizure of which they had been disgracing their little ones by labelling them with English names. It was he, too, who righted the perversion of the Bengali mentality that had led Bengalis to import as many English words as they could into their daily converse with fellow-men, and even women. Tagore deliberately introduced the vogue of expressing oneself in unadulterated Bengali in conversation with one's countrymen ; and he won through, thanks to the time-spirit asserting itself through him. And what of the Bengali language itself? Bankim, indeed, had given it its modernity, and brought it up into conterminous rank with the tongues that were swaying the minds of men. But is it not Tagore who forced the secrets out of its heart, invested the very soul of it with the luminous garment of a divine potency that has since enabled it to catch the reflexions of the universe, to register the smallest ticking of the human heart no less distinctly than the thunder of high heaven, reveal and make real the infinitude of nuances of tones and colours inside the souls of man and woman with no less clarity and definition than the sights and sounds of the outer earth and heaven?

The plastic stress of Tagore's genius was making itself felt, as time went on, in the deeper strata of the Bengali's soul. The Bengali, who is a born mystic and lover of beauty, had felt his soul being ravished by the entrancing mysticism and beauty of English romantic poetry with which his "English education" had brought him into intimate contact. And cut off from all vitalising intimacy with Sanskrit or old Bengali Vaishnavic literature—thanks to the aforesaid education—and finding nothing in the contemporary literature of Bengal to match the music and the inspiration of the English Muse, the educated Bengali confessed himself a scorner of his mother-tongue, and a worshipper of England's literature and language. And then—about forty years back from to-day—he experienced the shock of a real surprise, intellectual and spiritual, as he read through a poem, christened *Sonar Tari,* by Rabindranath Tagore. For, here was a singer who seemed to incarnate the very spirit of romantic poetry. *Sonar Tari* revealed all the nature-love of Wordsworth, the sensitiveness of Keats to the beauty that caresses us from the face of things sensed and the equal glory of Shelley's music. And overlying it all, persistently playing over it, was the shadow (or was it a rarefied, ethereal light?) that the unseen but not unfelt soul of the universe throws over the human soul. Other poems followed in quick succession, each bearing a fresh revelation of Tagore the poet, and of the unsuspected richness and music hidden so long in the heart of the Bengali language.

Tagore completed the poetic conversion of the Bengali before *Sonar Tari* had gone round three summers. And his love of nature was equalled by his love of man. All the unshed tears of man and woman were falling like dew-drops from his pen ; all the human wistfulness, all the longing for what is not that has stirred in the bosom of humanity cried out to one from the lines of *Paras Pathar ;* and all the dream of beauty that has visited men, ever since the early dawning of it in the primæval founders of the race who scratched the reindeer on bones and sang and danced to an unbidden ecstasy in their souls, found its one adequate, heart-wrung utterance in *Urvasi.* In this last-named marvel of poetic creation Tagore used words as chisels—to the accompaniment of a ravishing music coming out of each of his strokes—to carve out before his reader's mind's eye that perfect figure of ideal beauty which entered into art's immortality from the moment of its birth. The same sense of delight and discovery surprised his countrymen poring over his prose works, his short stories, and his contributions to art, religion and sociology. Apart from their setting of abundant poetry and astonishing beauty, Tagore's utterances appealed to the educated Bengali by reason of the essential reality underlying them. There was no note discernible in his writings and sayings—he often spoke at public gatherings—of what some critics of our literature have implied by the phrase "Oriental Exaggeration." He led no revolt against the ascertained facts of science regarding man and nature. Even in his tensest moments of ecstatic utterance, in poetry or prose, Tagore and truth were one. He was also bringing out his earlier dramas—each one of them a string of lyrical moments. And he was writing novels too. And for the first time they eased the hidden ache in his countrymen who had long been reading Bengali novels in vain for a sight of the new Bengali, man and woman, specially the latter, whom the impinging of the West upon the East would be bound to bring into existence. Tagore's novels gave Bengal pre-visions of the coming being in most fascinatingly differing stages of readjustment between the old and the new.

Just think of the heart-clutching figure of Binodini in *Chokher Bali!* And this brings one to the Tagorean apotheosis of woman which has redeemed the men of Bengal. The chivalry into which the modern Bengali has been reinitiated by him makes all the difference between the Bengal of the last century and of the twentieth. And it is Tagore, once again, in whose creative brain were reflected the prototypes of the growing variety of Bengal's new women. Do not the living pictures of some of them step out of his later novels and his dramas with their highly modern problems?

How and where is one to end the story of Tagore and New Bengal? The roots of the former's being have so intertwined themselves in and about the latter's heartstrings that the two are become one. Take the wonderful religious literature that Tagore has given us, not only the hymns that he has written from his boyhood up, but also all his utterances in prose on the topic of God and man. Where is the Bengali whose being has not brimmed over with his thoughts on that elemental issue of life? And let us just think how his hymns have gone deep down into us, become part of our soul-substance, how they interpenetrate and inform the Bengali's daily thinking and doing. What about Tagore's songs of death? Who but he has opened the eyes of Bengal to the new vision of death as life's crowning consummation, as the bearer of the soul of man along the stairway to immortality?

Allied to his attitude towards death is Tagore's interpretation of sorrow. He has taught us to look on suffering as the discipline enforced on us by a Higher Power, interested in us, which hurts the human soul the better to heal it. He indeed has brought us healing such as none have since the age of Chaitanya.

And lastly, what is the history of Bengali patriotism?

Every Bengali knows that Bankim had built the temple of *Anandamath,* and put the image of the Mother in it, and also composed the *Mantra* which held the secret of life in its heart. But who was it that walked up the steps of the temple, entered its holy of holies, and wrested the secret out of its heart, and breathed it into the image so that it became a thing of life? Rabindranath Tagore. The vision that had filled the eyes of Bankim alone during his life-time found itself translated into the revelation of Mother India incarnate before the enraptured gaze of all Bengal, only after the Bengali had been touched by the spiritual alchemy of Tagore's transfiguring pen. Not that he was for a moment identifying India's existing conditions with perfection—the besetting error of the mass of his contemporary patriotic prattlers and pen-men. Far from it. Tagore insisted in words of burning eloquence that India must be purged of all the putrescent accretions of her Dark Age. The deep pathos of his impassionate pleading for the submerged, for the untouchable, moved his countrymen to tears. He would have India impress science into her service at every stage. But he called upon his countrymen in deep earnestness to abandon their ungodly attempt to turn India into Anglo-India. In permitting themselves to think of it, were they not flying in the face of the very science and history which Europe had taught them? No nation with a history behind it, such as the people of India had, could grow away from it, any more than it could grow out of its skin. And what do we find as we examine into her past? The formulation by the makers of her history and civilisation of a higher ideal of human perfection than any other known to humanity ; a philosophy and an ethic that alone can, and shall, on a glorious day of God's ordaining yet to be, lift mankind on to that shining tableland of the spirit whereon all mankind shall kneel together to worship the sun of truth. He based his great prophecy on a luminous study of the achievements of India's culture between the ages of the Upanishads and of Gautama Buddha, and found confirmations of the one great purpose of her history in all the later manifestations of her spirit in poetry, philosophy or religious ecstasy.

So Tagore gave Bengal a great ideal to transfer her allegiance to—one that soon struck music out of the chords so long silent in her race-consciousness, and started an upheaval of her national spirit. How that spirit grew and gathered invincible strength within the span of a decade was demonstrated by the way it reacted to Lord Curzon's unwitting effort to drive the point of his sword into it. How one's memory rushes back to the stupendous Town Hall gathering, vibrant and quickening with a new hope, hungrily drinking in Tagore's singing of *Sonar Bangla,* and joining in the chorus with him! How the wonderful songs of freedom flowed from his pen one after another to intensify the new-found patriotism of the Bengali, to nerve him for the struggle in which he would be inevitably involved in seeking and ensuring his new freedom! And the speeches that he delivered in quick succession in the same year appeared to be the direct revelations of his seer's madness. Bengal bowed to Tagore. And his soul seemed to be floating in among Bengal's men and women, like his *Sonar Tari,* with Beauty in the prow and Truth at the helm, and its precious load of golden corn, his gathered and garnered love for the motherland.

Not an avenue of our reawakened life but reaches back to Tagore. And on this auspicious and spacious morning that marks the 70th year of his sonship of Bengal, our hearts go out in salutation to him—thinker, singer, dreamer, poet, prophet, creator of *Sonar Bangla.*

Tagore—A Praise without End.

CALCUTTA — B. C. CHATTERJEE

VAK-PATI

Śaṁ Śabdāiḥ—'With Words, Welfare.'

With the above aphorism a mediæval Sanskrit grammarian begins his work, after his salutation to God in the time-honoured formula—

Oṁ Namaḥ Śivāya.

The benediction invoked by Bopadeva embodies the romance, the mystery, and the truth of speech. Speech is wonderful, one marvels at its power. Speech gives expression to that which is, and to the Idea. Speech sped man on his path in life. Ever since he began his quest for well-being and joy, for welfare and happiness, Speech has been a strong staff for him.

kaì phthégma kaì anemóen phrónēma edidáksato:

Man's greatest achievement, which raised him from the mere animal, was when he taught himself Speech, the symbol of his Thought, swift as the wind.

Bṛ́haspate prathamáṁ vācó ágraṁ yát prāírata nāma-dhéyaṁ dádhānāḥ,
yád eṣāṁ śréṣṭhaṁ yád aripráṁ āsīt preṇā́ tád eṣāṁ níhitaṁ gúhāviḥ.

'When men, O Brihaspati, giving names to objects, sent out Vak's first and earliest utterances,
All that was excellent and spotless, treasured within them, was disclosed through their affection.'

sáktum iva títaünā punánto yátra dhī́rā mánasā vā́cam ákrata,
átrā sákhāyaḥ sákhyā́ni jānate ; bhadrâíṣām lakṣmī́r níhitā́dhi vācí.

'Where, like men cleansing corn-flour in a cribble, the wise in spirit have created language,
Friends see and recognize the marks of friendship: their speech retains the blessèd sign imprinted.'

The goal and end of man's existence and life we wish to comprehend and to attain through speech. Sages, Saints and Poets have used speech with this aim.

yajñéna vācáḥ padavī́yam āyan, tā́m ánv avindann ṛ́ṣiṣu právíṣṭām:
tā́m ābhṛ́tyā ví adadhuḥ purutrā́, tā́ṁ saptá rebhā́ abhí sáṁ navante.

'With sacrifice the trace of Vak they followed, and found her harbouring within the Rishis:
They brought her, dealt her forth in many places: seven singers make her tones resound in concert.'

Many are the Rishis—the Sages and Poets—but only to few has Vak, the Goddess of Speech, manifested Herself.

utá tvaḥ páśyan ná dadarśa vā́cam ; utá tvaḥ śṛṇván ná śṛṇoti enām:
utó tuasmāi tanúam ví sasre—jāyé'va pátya uśatī́ su-vā́sāḥ.

'One man hath ne'er seen Vak, and yet he seeth: one man hath hearing, but hath never heard her.

But to another hath she shown her beauty, as a fond well-dressed wife to her husband.'

Rabindranath is one of those to whom the Goddess of Speech has given Her special blessing. Where else do we find Her manifesting herself with such power and such grace as in Rabindranath?

káś chándasāṁ yógam ā́ veda dhī́raḥ, kó dhiṣṇiā̄m práti vā́cam papāda?

'What sage hath learned the metre's application? Who hath gained Vak, the spirit's aim and object?'

He is not only the Poet, the Master Music-maker, at whose playing the words come and dance in a ring ; not only the Wizard, who works magic with words: he is also the Sage, the first of our sages in these latter days, who saw and pondered over words, and made them reveal to him the secrets of their form and meaning.

For he is also first among our students of language, who both read the past of his mother-tongue and drew out its hidden powers. With clear vision, born of the wise man's observation, he indicated, in his essays, which are of permanent value for the study of his mother-tongue Bengali, the right lines of enquiry and deliberation regarding the nature and history of our language. A great creator, with divine power behind him, the power of his genius, he is also the patient analyser.

Nullum tetigit, quod non ornavit: nothing did he touch, which he did not adorn. In him we have the greatest writer of Bengali, and at the same time one of its foremost philologists.

From one who is seeking to read the mysterious ways of words and of Speech in India, and who has been blessed in his quest by the approbation of the Master, this Homage and this Prayer on the present auspicious occasion:

Homage to Rabindranath, the Poet and Seer, the *Vak-pati,* Lord and Master of Speech:

Homage to the *Princeps,* the Inaugurator, of Speech-research in his Mother-tongue ;

Homage to the *Pathi-krt,* the Path-maker in the domain of Speech.

mahó árṇaḥ Sárasvatī prá cetayati ketúnā:
dhíyo víśvā ví rājati.

'Sarasvati, the mighty flood,—She, with her light, illuminates:
She brightens every thought.'

codayitrī́ sūnṛ́tānāṁ cétantī su-matīnā́m:
yajñáṁ dadhe Sárasvatī.

'Inciter of all pleasant songs, Inspirer of all gracious thought,
Sarasvati accept our rite.'

mā́ naḥ pári khyad ákṣarā cárantī:

'Let not the Deity of Speech, the swift-moving, the imperishable, neglect us.'

THE UNIVERSITY,
CALCUTTA

SUNITI KUMAR CHATTERJI

THE CHOICE

If choose I must a resting-place
  What time my feet begin to fail,
By God's most hospitable grace
  I choose a brook-side in a vale.

I ask not ocean's trumpetings,
  Or hills that hearken to the skies;
For one is loud with questionings,
  And one is silent with replies.

But by my brooklet's lyric leap
  My heart may contemplate at ease,
Life's deep desirings for the deep
  Mingled with mountain memories;

And mine own rivulet of rhyme
  May run from summit unto sea,
Singing between the banks of Time
  The music of Eternity.

SANTA BARBARA, CALIFORNIA

JAMES H. COUSINS

PROSA E POESIA

I

PROSA e poesia. Nella prima, lo studio e' a trattare la parola in modo che non si faccia valere per se', ma quasi sparisca nel pensiero, e sia un' acqua cosi' limpida e transparente che non si avverta come acqua. Nella seconda, la parola spicca in primo piano, e come immagine e canto ci riempie dei suoi colori e suoni. Qui' e' tutta la differenza tra pensiero e fantasia, tra logica ed estetica. Cattivo prosatore chi lavora la prosa (dico la prosa dottrinale e ragionante) come poesia. Cattivo poeta chi riduce la poesia a prosastica esposizione di sentimenti e di riflessioni.

II

Perche' la votazione di "impressioni" non da' poesia? Perche' quelle votazioni sono come tante parole smozzicate, nessuna intera. Affinche' risuoni intera, bisogna, nell' impressione come nella parola, mettere tutta l'anima; e allora l'impressione si approfondisce, si arricchisce, raccoglie intorno a se' l'intero Mondo, e si amplia a poesia. Altrimenti, si rimane in un trastullarsi pratico e voluttuario.

NAPOLI, ITALIA — BENEDETTO CROCE

PROSE AND POETRY

I

Prose and Poetry: In the first, the study consists in treating the word in such a way that the word ceases to have any value as a mere word and almost loses itself in Thought and emerges limpid and transparent, like a flow of water that could not even be noticed as water.

In the second, the word assumes the first place and like Imagination and Song, fills us up with colour and sound. Herein lies the difference between Thought and Fancy, Logic and Aesthetic. He is a bad prose-writer who labours at prose—I mean the dogmatic and conscious prose—leaning towards poetry. He is a bad poet who reduces poetry to a prosaic exhibition of sentiments and reflections.

II

Why does any offering of "impressions" as such, not give us Poetry? Because such offerings are not complete but are mere broken words. To make it ring true and perfect one must put his entire soul in the impression as well as in the word. And then the impression deepens and enriches itself, gathering round it the whole world and flowering spontaneously into Poetry; otherwise one feels imprisoned in the circle of a childish ephemiral pastime.

NAPLES, ITALY — BENEDETTO CROCE

DR. TAGORE AND CULTURAL PROGRESS

ONE of the many services rendered by Dr. Rabindranath Tagore to society is that of cultural progress. Culture is the sum total of the group experience of a people. The origin of culture lies in human nature itself. The object of life is to live and, in order to live, man must adapt himself to environment. Out of this adaptation of the inner self to the outer world arises the experience, which, becoming group habit, expresses itself in folk-ways, modes, laws and institutions. While a part of this experience is devoted to the technique of mere living, the other relates to ethical and æsthetic values, such as art, philosophy and religion.

Although culture is thus the product of group life, individual contribution to it is by no means negligible. In fact, the landmarks of cultural development are the contributions of great personalities. Like heredity, *i.e.*, the like producing the like, variation is also the law of nature and every individual differing from the rest is a potential centre of a new culture. The significance of a genius lies in the fact that a certain trait of human nature is developed in him in the highest degree. A genius is thus a great cultural focus, giving a social process a new direction of development or creating something of everlasting value to society. Dr. Tagore is a great creative genius. His contributions to religious, philosophical and political thought, poetry, music, painting, fiction, the drama, the histrionic art, and essays form a great treasure to the world's literature and art. He has given a new meaning to human life and created new ideals for human achievement.

The revival of the old cutural systems is another service of Dr. Tagore. Owing to the difference in racial traits and environmental conditions, cultures differ from one another both in time and place. This diversity is, however, a positive gain to society. It not only adds to its richness, but also paves the way to further development. Like the Hebrew, Greek and Roman cultures, Indian culture has also enriched the world and given rise to many new cultural ideals.

For sometime past, there has, however, been a distinct deterioration of Indian culture. There is a two-fold reason for this decline: First, India has been invaded and conquered by several peoples, who have directly and indirectly suppressed her cultural ideals. Second, in the presence of more vigorous, aggressive and dynamic cultures, Indian culture has lost some of its ideals and imitated others by the law of suggestion. From this condition, India is slowly but surely reviving her cultural ideals, especially since the beginning of the present century.

Dr. Tagore is a pioneer in this renaissance movement in India. Nationalism, *swadeshi*, and rural reconstruction all owe a good deal to him. His writings and his active participation in reconstruction processes have become a source of inspiration to his countrymen in their struggles for national emancipation and cultural regeneration. Even in reviving the old cultural systems, Dr. Tagore has added new values to them. Dr. Tagore is in fact a leader of mankind. His contribution to culture stands out as a great landmark in human progress.

GENEVA

RAJANI KANTA DAS

DR. TAGORE AS A UTILITARIAN IDEALIST

DR. Rabindranath Tagore has long been acclaimed as the world's greatest living poet. He has achieved immortality and, along with the names of such poets as Homer, Virgil and Dante, his name will undoubtedly pass to posterity.

That Dr. Tagore is a sage, seer and philosopher is also known to the world. He has personally brought the message of the East to the West and has preached the doctrine of peace and harmony among the nations. Recently his paintings have received recognition in various countries, especially in Russia. In fact, Dr. Tagore is a many-sided genius and one of the world's greatest artists.

As an artist, Dr. Tagore is naturally an idealist. He has sought after the perfection of human actions and human relations in "the good, the true, the beautiful," and has given mankind a conception of harmony in apparent conflict, a perception of the eternal in things ephemeral, and a vision of the beautiful in existing ugliness. He has thus created new values of human life and opened up new sources of human happiness.

While standing high among the world's greatest idealists, Dr. Tagore differs from most of them in being also a utilitarian. Idealism led Plato write his *Republic,* More his *Utopia* and Bacon his *New Atlantis,* but Dr. Tagore, as a utilitarian idealist, founded *Santiniketan,* the seat of Visva-Bharati or International University.

Nature herself has made Santiniketan a beautiful place. Azure sky, floating clouds, gorgeous sun-set, seasonal flowers and singing birds all add to the charm of the spot. But the significance of Santiniketan lies in the fact that here one of the world's greatest idealists has attempted to realise his dream of "the good, the true, the beautiful" in actual life. Gymnastics and dancing, drawing and painting, sculpture and architecture, music and drama, language and literature, and even arts and crafts are cultivated, and Hindu, Islamic and Western Cultures are studied under the direction of eminent Indian and foreign professors. The East and the West meet for the mutual understanding and appreciation of what is the best in art, philosophy and religion.

Dr. Tagore is a unique personality. He has combined in himself the vision of an artist and the benevolence of a utilitarian. On the occasion of his 70th Birthday, we all wish him many more years of his unique service to humanity.

GENEVA

SONYA RUTH DAS

INDIAN FREEDOM AND RABINDRANATH

It is generally asserted by many British Imperialists that the question of Indian Freedom will be determined by the will of the British people, expressed through the British Parliament. Some Indian nationalists think that India's destiny rests with them; and they do not need any outside help. Indian moderates and some British statesmen of liberal tendencies think that India's future will depend upon Indo-British co-operation. They advocate that India should remain as a part of the British Empire. But the truth is, the future of India concerns the whole world; and therefore many non-Indians have given their best efforts to serve the cause of Indian freedom. The problem of Indian freedom will be solved neither by the dictation of the British, nor even solely by the efforts of Indian nationalists. India will be free and independent through the combined efforts of the Indian people and the support of world forces—reflexes of world politics, international finance and commerce and international public opinion. In time there will be a Federated Republic of the United States of India, which will proclaim sovereignty of the people of India and contribute its share to human progress.

Intelligent and effective efforts for Indian freedom, on the part of the people of India, presupposes a thorough revolution of ideas. This cannot be achieved in a year or a decade. Fortunately for India, at least since the days of the late Raja Ram Mohun Roy (who may be regarded as the greatest modern-man of India), the needed revolution of ideas has been in progress. In recent years, through the accumulated efforts of unnumbered patriots, during the period of more than a century, many-sided activities in favour of Indian freedom have gained strength and power. As years pass by, it will be more clearly recognised that *Rishi* Rabindranath made a very substantial contribution to the cause of Indian freedom. His work and teachings have supplied the philosophical foundation of the ideal of assertion of India as a free and independent nation, which has taken root in the heart and soul of Young India. *Rishi* Rabindranath, through his writings and songs, has helped to revolutionise the political as well as social ideology of the Indian intelligentsia, who in their turn have awakened the masses. One may say that during the second half of the nineteenth century and early twentieth century, Swami Dayananda, Swami Vivekananda, *Rishi* Rabindranath, Lokamanya Tilak, Sri Aurobindo and others laid the spiritual foundation of the Indian Nationalist Movement. Swami Vivekananda and *Rishi* Rabindranath vitalised the struggle for Indian Independence with the doctrine of Fearlessness and Service. *Rishi* Rabindranath is not an Indian political leader nor is he a political revolutionist. He may be regarded as one of the preceptors of the Indian youth in the creed of Indian freedom. He may be compared with Fichte, who was one of the torch-bearers of the cause of German emancipation from foreign yoke.

The torch of freedom that has been held high by Rabindranath is not a dim one. He is sending forth messages for the political, social and religious emancipation of India. In his *Swadeshi Samaj* and other works and songs he has given us his ideas of political emancipation. In his poem *Brahmana*—the story of *Jabali-Satyakama*—and other works he has given us a clear insight into his social philosophy. In fact he has demanded that Hindu society should free itself from the degenerating influences of dead habits and superstitions. In his *Sadhana* and other works he has given expression to his religious convictions. At the 'Visva-Bharati' (Dr. Tagore's International University) he has tried to give practical demonstration of his ideal of 'creative unity' and a programme of cultural collaboration for world unity and promotion of peace with justice and freedom.

Rabindranath's unique contribution to the cause of Indian freedom has been in his cultural activities on an international scale. Not being engaged in leading the Indian nationalist movement, he did not make any attempt to lay the foundation for future foreign relations of Nationalist India ; yet he roused Japan and China with a feeling of sympathy and kinship for India. In the United States of America, in Germany, in France, in Italy, in the Scandanavian countries, and even in Great Britain, he has roused the consciousness of some people to the fact that dwarfing the people of India through political and economic slavery caused by an alien domination and the lack of education of the people of India, which was once the giver of civilization to the world, is a great and distinct loss to the world at large. Rabindranath's cultural activities, in some cases indirectly, helped those Indian statesmen and exiles, who are not narrow-minded isolationists and are trying to utilise world forces in favour of Indian freedom, by establishing international political contact with free and independent nations.

May he live long to promote the cause of Indian freedom ; because without Indian freedom, there cannot be any freedom for the East. Without freedom for the people of Asia, all efforts for better understanding between the East and the West will be futile.

BADEN-BADEN, GERMANY

TARAKNATH DAS

MYSTICISM OF RABINDRANATH

THERE is a good deal of divergence of views regarding the meaning of the term Mysticism. In the West it has been taken to be the feeling of ecstasy through which a mystic enters into communion with God. In my Harris Foundation Lectures on Hindu Mysticism I pointed out that such definitions are inadequate in the sphere of the various forms of Hindu Mysticism. I there defined mysticism as a view or belief that the ultimate reality, whatever may be its nature, though unattainable by merely logical or speculative means, can finally be realised through feeling or the development of the will-process, character or the like. The force of this definition lies in the fact that the mystic does not think that the ultimate reality can be attained merely through speculative philosophy or logic. He may believe in the fruitfulness of philosophy and he need not be anti-metaphysical. But though he may be willing to believe that philosophy is useful for the comprehension of the ultimate reality, he does not admit that philosophy alone can lead us to that goal. However great the philosophy may be, it must be supplemented by faith, emotion or the severe discipline of the functions of the will. As such one must distinguish between reason and higher conviction. We know that reason ordinarily leads to rational conviction. We believe what we find reasonable and such a belief is amenable to all the pragmatic tests. If I believe that the Chittagong Mail leaves Calcutta at 7 in the morning and if I am in need of catching that train, the belief would signify that under the circumstances I should start sufficiently early and take all due precautions that I may entrain myself before that time. Such a conviction naturally proceeds from a belief founded on reason. But there is a higher kind of conviction which proceeds not only from the satisfaction of reason but from the satisfaction of the person as a whole including his emotional and volitional selves. A person in this sense may be understood to mean the entity that is formed by the fusion as it were of the rational, emotional and volitional selves. The conviction that finds expression from this concrete person is naturally different from a merely intellectual decision or judgment, inasmuch as it involves the participation of the entire person in the conviction which is absent in the other case. When a man treads on the ground of traditional notions grounded on custom, popular religious beliefs, myths, wise sayings or the like, or when he merely argues in favour of a favourite proposition of his, it is his logical or historical faculty that he exercises and it may not in the least touch his concrete personality. Though in poetry as in every other work of art the artistic emotion may be regarded as an indispensable condition, yet there is an immense difference in the attitude of the artistic creation in accordance with the way in which the creator expresses himself in his creation. Thus when the poet is intoxicated with the joy of any particular piece of nature's beauty, say the evening landscape, a beautiful flower or the like, he may manifest his joy of this direct intuitive contact with nature or he may record his sympathy with the various aspects of the suffering humanity and present his distress in such universal forms that it at once touches the heart; we find therein the testimony of the poet's great humanity. But apart from this there may be occasions on which the poet not only reveals the particular tendency or temperament of his own but he seems also to record the deepest experiences of his own inner nature in which the various psychical, emotional or volitional functions of his self have melted away, as it were, into one whole. Such an experience is no longer temperamental and it cannot be said to be the expression of any particular part of the poet's nature, for here it is the integrated whole of the poet's personality that finds expression.

It is in this sense that we can speak of Tagore's mysticism in poetry as being the manifestation of his personality as expressed in his conviction of his place in the universe in relation to his fellow beings and to nature. It is no place here to illustrate it with copious quotations from his poems, songs and reflective prose compositions, but I may only indicate on very broad general lines the main characteristics of his mystic conviction. I call it mystic, because he has not formulated it as a result of logical speculation but it has come upon him in poetic enlightenment as it were through the insight of a seer. In his autobiographical sketch he refers to one fine morning when the sun shone before the tree tops and the houses before him and brought with it a new message which cleared away the darkness and delusion in which he was groping so long. He feels throughout all his mystic writings that man is but a part of the universe as a whole. He is related in an intimate connection with all other things in the world, be they however trifling; it is only because we take ourselves and our spheres of activities and ideals to be detached from other things, that we set up ourselves against them, and meet with a conflict. Our sense of misery and fear arises from the false individuality which centres itself in a delusive manner in our smaller interests and narrower ranges and thus feels the burden and crush of the mighty whole against it. If, on the other hand, we could broaden ourselves to see that we were like waves in a big ocean and that we had no separate existence apart from it, we should never feel ourselves to be lost and suffering will lose all its meaning. Suffering and privation, death and sorrow, can have place only so long as we raise our walls around ourselves and thereby obstruct the open air of the universe as a whole. The dynamic principle that runs through us is the same that runs through the universe and it unites us with it. What appears to be death is but a momentary disappearance which is to be revived again in another form. It is merely a game of hide and seek which can never mystify the wise man who knows how to look to himself and beyond. Egotism, pride and vanity can only appear when we move round our own orbits and refuse to believe that our real orbits are not around ourselves in our narrow circles but on the widest line which goes round us all. Our truth consists in the reality of that whole of which we are individual constituents. This does not mean the sacrifice of our individuality or personality but it merely means that our true personality or individuality, when properly interpreted, seems to extend further and further, wider and wider, until it permeates through all things in the world and loses itself in the infinite completeness of the whole. A true insight into our own personality reveals to us that it is infinite in its nature and cannot therefore be circumscribed to that form of it which is only apparent to us at the moment. Our true individuality is thus our cosmic personality through which alone our individual functions, interests, ideals and freedom of being should find their ultimate satisfaction. We realise the fact that the true logical, emotional and dynamic scope of such a personality gradually leads itself forward until it traverses the path of its self-development and completes the mystic circle that envelopes us all. Looked at from this point of view, all that may appear unaccomplished in this life, all that may appear as failures, is but only a sign that we have stopped in the mid-way and and have not taken into consideration our life's journey as a whole. For such a journey is not limited to this brief span of 60, 80 or 100 years, but it goes through eternity and in the eternal ideal completion of our life, all that has failed and all that has not yet come to pass, are already fully realised. He illustrates this idea in the dancing of the seasons in which the shivering, pale and languid winter changes its decrepit form into the rejuvenated, smiling and buoyant image of the spring. His religion of "no fear" goes for the conviction that, in spite of death and disease which constantly stare us in the face, from which the Buddha sought his relief in his wisdom of the doctrine of phenomenalism and momentarism and from which the Upanishads sought relief in their emphasis on the ultimate reality as pure consciousness, which was developed in the hands of their commentators as being a retirement from the domain of *Maya,* we have no reason to fear when we know things in their proper perspective, in which the being of every entity is commingled in its indefinite expansion with the being of every other entity, and the chasm of death is thus merely a plunge in the Ganges of rejuvenation. The chasm of death only obstructs our view for the moment and our sorrow is due to our foolish refusal to see and believe what comes next but what is not at the moment.

Side by side with this notion of a true individuality in which the being of every entity is commingled in its onward march of progress with the being of every other entity which thus smacks of pantheism in its conception of a whole, there is another vein of thought in which he seems to review the world-process in terms of the self-realising dance of the creative spirit.

Thus in his musical opera *Rituranga* he conceives that the spirit reveals itself in external nature in all its beautiful plumage of colour in the flying procession of the seasons which come and go and also in the mental forms which catch their flowing images.

Life and consciousness in man have an expansive existence which goes far beyond him and embraces life in all forms. In the inner region of man there is a continuous play of thoughts, ideas and emotions and in the outer world of nature there is a play or dance of heat and light, sun-shine and rain, leaves and flowers as manifested in the seasonal variations. In his mystic vision Rabindranath deeply feels that God is always approaching us in the various phenomena of nature, in the heat of summer, in the rains of the monsoon, in the corn-fields and sun-shine of autumn, through the shivering cold of winter and the rejuvenating touch of spring. Numerous songs of the poet testify to the feeling of communion with God through the various occurrences of nature. We also find that the poet feels himself to be like a toy or a musical instrument in the hand of God and all his poetical effusions are supposed to rush out from some perennial source of inspiration of a creative energy which is far beyond the control or touch of the man Rabindranath. It is this creative energy that uses the lips of the poet as its mouthpiece and reveals itself through him. In our appreciation and appraisement of art we come in touch with the surplus man which is entirely different from the economical or the practical man and it is this surplus man that constitutes the immortality and the infinitude of man, and it is this man that is the greatest *Brahman* in which all divisions, finitude and limitations are lost and in which we are all united. The mysticism of Rabindranath thus consists in the conviction of his personality, of his true relation with the higher man in himself, its place in the world of events and nature, and in the final fulfilment of the destiny of man, in the totality of the whole from which we can never be thrown away. Such a conviction must be distinguished from a mere intellectual notion which proceeds from logical judgment or from a mere emotional outburst of poetical fancy. It must proceed directly from out of the creative flow of the personality in which the diverse elements have all melted together into a concrete reality, the expressions of which must necessarily be something universal and infinite, far above the smallness of the economical or practical man.

S. N. DAS GUPTA

SANSKRIT COLLEGE,
CALCUTTA

TAGORE—THE PACIFIST

'Sprinkle the world with the water of Everlasting Life,
Thou who art the fountain of Peace, of Welfare, of Holiness, of Love.'

WITH this solemn hymn to Lord Buddha, sung in the Waisakha Celebration, Rabindranath Tagore sends all over the world the eternal message of India. Peace is the key-note of Hindu history and Peace and Fraternity are the greatest contributions of India to Humanity. Naturally the Poet Laureate of Asia, amidst the sunset-glow of his genius, is harping on that eternal theme to reclaim the benighted human beings from hatred and cruelty to sacrifice and love. The world has deservedly crowned him as the greatest living poet of the present age and one of the greatest of any age, but very few realize as yet that his silent and often unnoticed labour in the cause of World Peace, is one of his greatest titles to immortality. Poets will come and poets will go, but very few of the creative artists of the world would show this unique record of Tagore, as a spinner of the golden dream of *Maitri,* fellowship, making the whole world kin, silently removing the apparently irremovable barriers between nation and nation. Through his prophetic messages and passionate poems men and women all over the world have felt that they belong to one family ; and that is the greatest miracle which Rabindranath has worked in this age darkened by selfishness and savagery. May the blessings of all beings be on his noble life and may victory attend on his dreams, illumining the Future of Mankind!

THE MAHA BODHI SOCIETY — SRI DEVAMITRA DHARMAPALA

THE GREAT UTOPIAN

UNTIL we connect the spiritual life with the political and the political with the spiritual, both will remain paralysed. That is the riddle the sphinx sets to man, age after age; and civilization after civilization is devoured for inability to answer it. We are still waiting for our Oedipus; and we shall never find him by denying that the enigma exists. By nothing but by liberty can the problem be solved; and until it is solved, always, generation after generation, the prophets will rise like the Phoenix from the ashes of despair.

'Alas, alas!
   Thou hast smitten the world,
   Thou hast laid it low,
Shattered, o'erthrown,
   Into nothingness hurled
   Crushed by a demigod's blow!

We bear them away,
   The shards of the world,
We sing well-a-day
   Over the loveliness gone,
   Over the beauty slain.

Build it again,
   Great child of the Earth,
Build it again
   With a finer worth,
In thine own bosom build it on high!
   Take up thy life once more:
Run the race again!
   High and clear
Let a lovelier strain
   Ring out than ever before!'—(Faust).

CAMBRIDGE

G. LOWES DICKINSON

THE PROCESS

That which was crooked straightened
That which was defeated
Joined with that which was victorious
And that which was beautiful
Blended
With that which was ill planned
To be separated
And made crooked
Or straight again.

NEW YORK

THEODORE DREISER

INDIA AND AFRICA

THE great branches of the human family which have their chief dwelling place in Africa and India have much of common history in the past and common interest in the present.

The thing that India and Africa must learn to-day is that their interests have more in common than the interests of either have with the ideals of modern Europe. Granted that Europe is powerful and still dominant, yet she is to-day doomed. She has been weighed in the balance and found wanting. On the other hand, the dark millions of India and Africa and their descendants and kinsmen throughout the world, have upon their shoulders the vast responsibilities of re-making this world nearer to the ideals of true civilization and high culture.

Two things they forgot in the past and this forgetting gave Europe its chance. These things were:

The mastery of the technique of earning a living by subjugating the physical forces of the world. And the other thing was the faith in democracy; that is, the fact that out of the masses of people can be developed just as much power and genius, ability and culture as has in the past been shown by the aristocracy, by the favoured few. Africa and Asia did not know or did not realise these facts in the past and their contributions to civilization were marred by poverty and slavery, on the one hand; and tyranny on the other. Europe has given us the technique of industry. At terrible cost, to be sure, but nevertheless, the machine stands and is a marvellous tool but a horrible master. Europe and America have given us the beginnings of democracy, although with strange inconsistency they have tried to hem democracy in with a colour bar.

Here, then, is our chance for the future—our mighty opportunity. We borrow, as we have a right to borrow, and as Europe in other ages has borrowed from us,—the things that in modern days she has taught us. But we use these things for greater ends. Both Africans and Indians must seek to be rid of the spiritual and physical death of poverty. They must educate and develop the masses of their people. They must welcome genius and ability wherever it occurs,—among the lowest and most unlikely, as well as among those who have regarded themselves as the highest. It will be a revelation to see how wide-spread human ability is when it has a chance. And then, with the help and strength which decent income gives, and with the rise of the intelligent mass, the dark millions of Africa and India can go forward to set new standards of freedom, equality and brotherhood for a world which is in desperate need of these spiritual things.

It seems to me that no one has had a finer vision of such a future than Rabindranath Tagore. I greet him in his quest for common justice for all men.

W. E. BURGHARDT DU BOIS

Gurudeva, Revered Master,

If we may call you by this name so dear to your pupils, who express through it their consciousness that you are not only a poet and a teacher, but one of the voices of divinity itself, we thank you for coming to us, across so many dreary seas, to help to break down the barriers between the East and the West, so that, while India takes from us those inventions which would destroy all poverty if they were well controlled, we may learn from her something of her tolerant wisdom and her spiritual peace. We see in you not merely the poet who, many years ago, won the highest recognition of all nations, but the noblest symbol and representative of a people whose civilisation antedated the Pyramids, whose race was the mother of our races, and whose language was the mother of our languages ; whose village communities were the source of our democracy, whose religions preached Christianity before Christ, whose philosophers plumbed the depths of thought thousands of years ago, whose scientist has won this year the most famous of all rewards, whose architecture is rivalled in majesty only by that of Egypt, and in perfection only by that of Greece, whose arts and industries were once the marvel and magnet of the world. It is inconceivable to us that a nation capable of producing, even in the bitterest poverty and destitution, poets like yourself, scientists like Bose and Raman, and saints like Mahatma Gandhi, should not soon be welcomed into the fellowship of self-governing peoples.

We offer you, as you go from us, our admiration and our affection. We feel that we have been cleansed and ennobled by meeting you ; it gives us a new faith to see that a man may still live a life true to all the highest ideals of our youth. We were cynics before you came ; we thought that all ideals were false, and all hopes vain ; but one look at you and we know that we were wrong, that the battle between Right and Might is not yet lost, and that life may still have a meaning for us that will not be frustrated by our deaths. Something of the ancient idealism of the East has been poured into our blood by the wine and music of your verse, by the example and majesty of your life.

NEW YORK — WILL DURANT

A FRAGRANT MEMORY

IN September 1920, we had the joy of welcoming 'the Poet' to our home in Holland.

Our house was on the coast of the Zuider Sea and we had a wide and lovely view towards the setting sun. When I look back on the time the Poet spent with us, two vivid memories stand forth in pure relief against the background of many hours filled with joy. For that was for me the ground note of the whole symphony; joy, creative joy, life-giving joy,—his love for nature, the sky, the wind, the flowers. Often while he was with us I remembered the saying of One of the Great Teachers of Mankind: "Except ye become as little children, ye enter not the kingdom of Heaven." I have felt him as one who gets nearest to the heart of man, through the heart of Nature.

The first of the two vivid memories was when he entered our house. In the hall he stood still, raised his head, closed his eyes and was quite silent—then he bent his head as it were in greeting and moved on through the room; and as he passed a large bowl of red, living roses on the centre table, he let his fingers stray over the roses tenderly, full of understanding and love and recognition. That gesture revealed him to us as much as his poems.

The second memory is of an evening. A young girl sang some of his poems put to western music. At that time we did not know that each of his songs had music of its own, so we were ignorant of our very stupid attempt at entertaining the much-to-be-pitied poet. There were also some songs of Schumann, which were more appreciated. After the guests were gone, the poet sat in front of the fire, his hands folded on his knees, staring into the fire. I asked him: "Master, will you let us hear your own songs in your own words? May we take part in the life which is expressed when you sing your Indian music?" Great silence! Down in the hall the old Dutch clock ticked away time—the wood fell together in the fire and sent out a fountain of sparks into the silence—we waited—then he lifted his voice saying:

"This is the song we sing at sunset. We sit looking out over vast distances, we sing of the sadness of human existence, also of the longing in our hearts for union with God, we sing of the joy of our senses when we see the light, hear the songs, smell all the delicate odours from the Mother-Earth when the sun sets. We sing of the love in our hearts, not only the love of one man for one woman, but of the love in the heart of humanity, the longing, the sadness, the pain and the joy of all the world—that is our sunset song." The poet's voice rose and soared to the flame-lit rafters; it sank and became flute-like and again swelled out in waves or took over the shadows and pictures of the flames; hearing and seeing were merged into one great experience; joy and sorrow came from one source deep in the heart of the world, and from the heights above; time was not; the clock had lost its power of being a messenger to us—we heard it not. We were lifted up and merged into unity with Love and Compassion. That hour will live in our hearts as long as we live.

There are two sayings which I want to bring before you as so very typical of the poet's vision on life. One was uttered when we had been talking about the education of woman and of her place in life. The poet said: 'Teach girls to realise that their greatest influence is the personal contact with their surroundings in the making of a home or in educating youth. Therefore they should be trained to give out freely and pleasantly what they were taught. The atmosphere of culture and light which is so created, is the centre of beautiful home life. Great trouble should be taken to teach girls to express themselves in beautiful and simple language, to give out their knowledge and experience, and their wisdom, their thoughts, their dreams, their visions. The legends of the world are made eternal through woman's gift of story-telling. While man can express himself truly and well in work and deeds, woman does so best of all through personal contact with her surroundings. It is easier for children to learn through stories than through books. And so a cultured and beautiful home influence can be theirs through the gift of story-telling. The women who take care of the children of the world must be story-tellers, and so set free the children's own fantasy.'

The second saying was about a statue of Rodin's, called 'Protection.' The poet said: 'In India we would feel protection to be more of a static force, like a bird on the nest, or a Buddha sitting silent and full of inner peace; you in the West are too strenuous. Power is in stillness as much as in movement.'

I must stop writing about our well-beloved poet, but it is difficult. So many wonderful pictures pass before my inner vision.

NAARDEN, HOLLAND — MARY VAN EEGHEN-BOISREVAIN

'Free, henceforth, from doubts and desires which pass over it as water passes over the leaf of the lotus without wetting it; acting, henceforth, only as acts the potter's wheel when the potter has ceased to turn it: "If I know that my own body is not mine, and yet that the whole earth is mine, and again that it is both mine and thine—no harm can happen then".'

LONDON

HAVELOCK ELLIS

'IN THIS HALL OF THINE I HAVE A CORNER SEAT'

"Do you know Tagore?" People have a way of asking when the talk drifts, as it so often does, to India.

"Yes," I find myself answering, "I have known Rabindranath Tagore many years."

Yet do I? What do I mean when I say I know him? Somehow, on this autumn Sunday, with the sunlight that shifts between the tall buildings growing a little pale, and the tang of dead leaves beginning to drift across the memory—if not through the gray, treeless, city streets—it seems very presuming to imagine that one person can know another, much less a poet, who must surround himself with silence so that he can hear his own voice singing to himself his own songs. Something of the outer shell we may come to know, but the whole man never. These glimpses of Tagore, therefore, are set down here with the perfect realization of their incompleteness.

It was neither in America nor in India, but in Japan, that I saw Tagore first, nearly sixteen years ago. He had been invited to give a reading of his poems at the Imperial University of Tokyo, and in a hall packed to overflowing with hundreds of Japanese students I sat, eagerly awaiting the appearance of the winner of the Nobel Prize for literature; for it was as such that the western intellectual world, and Japan also, knew him at this time. In India, I have read, his songs were sung by peasants at work in the fields and by women drawing water at the well, long before the world honoured him.

When at last he stood before us, I felt that a prophet of the Old Testament had suddenly put on living flesh. The silver white of his long hair and beard melted into the white purity of his robe, and in the dark, aristocratic face the eyes burned with consciousness of power. Then I forgot how he looked; for in a high, delicate voice, the words following one another like a flight of wild birds across a sunset sky, he began to chant poems from *The Gardener* and *Gitanjali*.

My next contact with him came five years later, in India. Like so many visitors to India—one dreads to think how many—I, too, made a pilgrimage to Santiniketan. I remember that it was the 'hour of cowdust' when I arrived at the 'Abode of Peace,' the time when all over India the herds of humped white cattle and of blue-black water-buffaloes are returning to the thousands of villages. A room had been made ready for me, the room the poet himself formerly occupied, I was told, though now he was living in the upper storey of another of the small houses scattered about, part of the school he had founded here at his ancestral home. The room gave me odd pleasure. It was barely long enough for the cot which was its principal furnishing, and there was but a single window, yet its utter simplicity soothed—no clutter of possessions, no superfluous ornaments, not even, if my memory records accurately, a picture on the wall. But through the window the wide plain was visible, covered with some unknown magenta-colored bloom, and peace was there, outside and in.

A simple meal was served in the tradition of Indian hospitality; my hostess, Tagore's daughter-in-law, herself brought the dishes and set them before me. Then, when I had eaten, word came that the poet was ready to receive me. A teacher of science at the school, not then in session, led the way to Tagore's upper balcony. This time it was not the poet I found at first, but the educator.

It was of his university that he wished to talk. Here it was, the concrete expression of his vision of India's need and of his tireless energy. It embodies the spirit of the old forest universities of India—the students living in close association with nature, not cut off in the sterile atmosphere of modern city life; studying to grow wise, not learned; seeking no official reward for education: in short, following the old ideal of plain living and high thinking.

But in India toward the end of 1921 it would have been humanly impossible for any talk to stay long away from the burning topics of the hour. Amritsar was still painfully fresh in Tagore's mind. He had relinquished his knighthood in protest against what occurred there; yet he deplored the type of nationalism which was then sweeping across India. India was great in her own birthright; let her stand upon that birthright, confident and unafraid, but not blind herself to the truth that, though blood is thicker than water, without water there would be no blood. Always, humanity first, the nation second.

As Tagore talked, the full moon rose and silvered the dark earth. It shed its quiet radiance over the balcony and touched with new beauty the fine head of India's outstanding poet-philosopher etching it there vividly against the background of the

Indian night. It was true that the land was torn by much bitterness, but harmony was still worshipped in the heart of this faithful devotee.

It was my privilege, when Tagore came to New York last winter, to see something of him on a number of occasions. Two of these stand out above the others. Most precious, perhaps, was the evening spent in talk of Indian village life. As I entered the hotel room, he put down a copy of my *Voiceless India,* which he was just reading. My eyes had been opened by a year in an Indian village, not only to the pitiful economic struggle of the Indian peasants, but to their qualities of inner strength, and their fortitude. This book of mine, with its picture of village life, brought back to Tagore some of his own village experiences, which he recounted. It did more: it made him homesick, he said.

The last time I saw him was on the eve of his final home-going. He had moved to a friend's apartment, and here I found him, seated like a king, on a dais. The dais, as it turned out, was merely an artist's model-stand, and the kingliness of pose was to be interpreted as an expression of nothing but kindness. Deftly the sculptress smoothed her clay into a likeness. There was now the serenity of a northern winter in his face, something of the austere calm of snowy ranges, but the deep-set eyes were, as ever, compellingly alive. In India, they say, builders of temples always place some stone awry, leave some bit of the structure symbolically imperfect, since they know that whatever is finished in the realm of matter soon goes to death. Is it not the eternal quest for perfection that gives meaning to life and integrates all our varied activities? 'O my bird, listen to me,' Tagore's eyes seemed to say, in the words of one of his own poems, 'do not close your wings! The end of the quest is not yet.'

There was a stir, a sudden expectation, fitting the room. His secretary hurried to his side and whispered to him. Tagore arose and stepped down quickly from his platform. Instinctively everybody present stood up; for one had come to do him honor, one whom the world acclaims as perhaps the greatest mind the West has produced in three centuries—Albert Einstein.

What had the two men in common? As they sat together on a sofa, I felt the differences between them ringing like overtones, enriching a fundamental harmony. Tagore's gestures were restrained. Einstein's were abrupt. Einstein was squarer, stockier, more informal in his manner. His grey hair, brushed back from his forehead, stood out around his head as if charged with electricity. The fine mouth smiled frequently. The heavy-lidded eyes often held a quizzical look.

It came to me that, though they travel by different roads, surely the end they seek is one. The intangible bond linking these two great men from the East and from the West is the bond of personal surrender to the timeless and the eternal.

NEW YORK GERTRUDE EMERSON

NAISHKARMYAM

How real the mother to the child, the beloved to the lover, wealth to its owner, science to the scholar, beauty to the artist, one's own self to every man.

Still, no reality that is worldly, even the dearest one, can claim the privilege of becoming, sooner or later, a jot more than a dream.

To the thinker the thing that vanishes in ten or twenty or even one hundred years is as unsubstantial and deceitful as that which lasts a twinkling of the eye.

Indeed, we are all like black vesper's pageants: a cloud that is dragonish, a vapour sometimes like a bear or a lion, a towered citadel, a pendent rock, a forked mountain, or blue promontory with trees upon it, that nod unto the world and mock our eyes with air. Indeed, time makes us all indistinct as water is in water.

The realisation of the cosmic vanity brings as a result one only possible watchword: renunciation, naishkarmyam.

But, is it possible, on the other hand, to concentrate life in the one vision of transitoriness? Shall we say to the child: do not love thy mother for she is liable to perishing? On account of transitoriness shall we stop the hand of the tiller in the field, dissuade the genius from revealing new truths or forms of beauty?

Let not the great thought of impermanence, that leads the soul to God, resolve itself in destruction, in sheer impossibility.

There must be renunciation, there must be action. In the reconciling of the two terms the crown of life resides, and the seers of India, old and new, teach us how to reconcile them. It is not action that ought to be renounced but the fruit of action, and true naishkarmyam is attained to through complete unselfishness in our exertion. As long as the thought of transitoriness makes us pause and ask: 'What is the use of acting?' we may be sure that the ego has not been annihilated, that it is lurking under one form or other. Truly disinterested action gives a sense of eternity and of perpetual joy.

This is the doctrine, nay, the revelation of the Bhagavadgita, this is India's lofty message which triumphantly blends into a unity not only the incontrovertible truth of the dreamy nature of life and the no less incontrovertible necessity of action, but also the East sublimating itself in meditation and the West raising work to wonder.

Renunciation is good, action is good. The East is right, the West is right too.

That the world should know and love renunciation and action, East and West, a poet, made of light and of music, sang and is still singing luminous and melodious songs:

Rabindranath Tagore.
Let humanity bless him.

ROYAL ACADEMY, ROME

CARLO FORMICHI

DANK AN RABINDRANATH TAGORE

Dein Wort bricht dem meinen Bahn,
Schlafendes beginnt zu wandern.
Wundersamer Drang hebt an,
Zieht mich mächtig zu den andern.

Zieht mich hin zu allen Dingen,
Weil ein Strahl aus ihnen bricht,
Der wie innig-leises Singen
Trifft erschütternd mein Gesicht.

Zieht mich zu den Menschen allen,
Denen ich bisher so fern,
Weil ein Durchblick wie kristallen
Dringt zu unsers Wesens Kern.

Zieht durch Zeiten und durch Räume
Mich zur letzten Klarheit hin,
Öffnet jenseits aller Traüme
Pforten zu dem tiefsten Sinn.

Innre Schönheit strahlt zur Stund
Aus der Schimmerglanz der Zähren.
Innre Einheit tut sich kund:
Sein ist bitter-süss Gebären.

Innrer Friede senkt sich ein
Ganz erwachendem Gemute.
Pochend Herz in allen Sein!
Lauter Freude! Lauter Güte!

MARBURG — HEINRICH FRICK

In the name of American Womanhood I send you love and heartfelt wishes for great many more joyful and creative years.

PHILADELPHIA — ERNESTINE FITZMAURICE

AN OPEN LETTER TO TAGORE

DEAR Poet and Honoured Teacher—whom I am also happy and proud to call Old Friend—I welcome this opportunity of expressing, in company with so many others, my heart-felt appreciation of your personality and of your life-work, and of warmly participating in the good wishes you are now receiving from all sides. All these not only from your fellow-countrymen in Bengal, and over India, but also from so many of us in other lands, who recognise in you their Laureate also, and even the wide World's ; as this occasion will more fully help to make known.

Among these good wishes, we hope above all that despite all your difficulties, from shaken health to manifold cares, you may be able to surmount these, throughout active and productive years to come. It is encouraging and hopeful to us all, as I trust to you, to recall how your brothers, whom we remember as also men of Wisdom, reached its normal reward, of longevity, and up to its ever-ripening best. That association and assurance—of wisdom towards its persistence for many days—is often and admirably stated in the Wisdom Books of Israel of old. It is verifiable throughout observation and in biographies up to this day ; and it is also demonstrably justified by biology and psychology, by medicine and hygiene in their current advance.

So thus while we wish long life to you, be encouraged to live it : thus with your very best work before you, still to be accomplished, even perfected.

I pass however from your vast and varied contributions to literature, from its natural base in folk-song to its highest levels, to that interest and activity in Education, again at all levels, of which let me more fully speak. Your combination of "plain living and high thinking," in which India has throughout the ages given the very foremost example to the world, has been with you most fully associated with active participation in the highest cultural interests of other lands, and these in the West as well as further East. Thus you have been helping forward the wide world, and even more widely than you can know ; though often before now you have had many and cordial assurances of it. Yet though I know of your wide helpfulness, and not only from my own son and his fellows, but widely over Europe, and indeed from Japan to North and South America as well, I have realised the actual and the coming values of your example and influence most clearly of all at Santiniketan itself ; with its boys and students, its teachers and professors and yourself, all starting their days from sunrise appreciation of Nature in its beauty, to meditation upon Life, towards its highest and best. Hence the fundamental preparation—as some of us Westerners can confirm—for thoughtful and serious studies, and for better aiding of them : so next for due professional preparation ; and this not only towards individual proficiency, and even originality, but beyond all to social service. Thus in method, in principle, so in very essence, you have long been giving example of encouragement towards that revitalisation of the school and university curriculum of Western type, now too dominant, even in India. I have indeed high hope of our Indian College here—which you have honoured at its outset by your acceptance of its presidency, and which I trust you may be able some day to visit and thus re-inspire—that it may pass on your educational example and its impulse to the incipient sister-colleges of our nascent "Cité Universitaire," Scottish, British and American, Swiss, German and Austrian, etc., and of course French as well: so hence again throughout the Western universities from which we mostly come. There, too, we are studying and striving to aid beyond their too dispersive specialisms, and towards synthesis; and this through studies of Life, in Evolution;—Life both on its organic and its social levels; so in terms of Nature and Civilization; and thus beyond the too simply mechanistic presentments still so largely in power.

Primary education in Europe has had many pioneers, as from Rousseau, Pestalozzi and Froebel to Montessori and now many more; and in secondary education, too, notable advances are in later progress. But alas, our University Entrance Examinations inhibit rather than aid the best work of teachers in their schools; while even in the Universities themselves, "exam and cram" too readily go on together. Hence that "Parrot's Training," which you have so justly satirised, and reinforced by your admirable illustrators. Let me beg you will re-publish this; and let your publishers in all countries give it that widening circulation for which the public are more ready than when you wrote it. Thus both universities and schools will profit by it, even towards the increasing replacement of examinations, too much of memory and routine, by estimation, or real attainments and powers, and of character combining all these.

How such collaboration of East and West is needed towards vital studies, has been sadly illustrated for me in this past month: in which two patriotic and well-meaning Indian graduates in this country have sent me their manuscripts in hopes of encouragement before publication, the subject of each being "Education for India." But, alas, in each case, they consider its needs in terms of our relatively greater European literacy, that is of "the three R's" (Reading, 'Riting and 'Rithmetic). And they alike insist that this be made compulsory, and that without delay! You can imagine how uncongenial had to be my replies! What we in English call "the Ministry of Education" is for the clearer-headed French, but "the Department of Public Instruction"—though still too much akin. In both countries happily however, by the better members of the bureaucracy, by rural teachers and awakening urban ones, it is at length becoming realised how such centralized drilling into the print-habit, and the scribble-habit and the money-habit, now so predominant in the urban mass-mind, and in that of its leaders, with their verbalistic empaperment and their pecuniary obsession accordingly, are deleterious, indeed often destructive, to the rural mind, and thus to village life; even leading to its growing depopulation, with deterioration of what remains. What you can see of this too much beginning in India, is now far surpassed in France, throughout its 40,000 villages ; while as you know our Scottish and English rural life has been depressed, sucked well-nigh dry, when not even devoured by our great towns. Yet the remedy is also plainly within our reach, and even its application ; that of "the New Education" (real and ancient)—of "the three H's"—Heart, Hand and Head. From these all that any can require and use of reading, writing and arithmetic, speedily "explode" into clearness and power, as Madame Montessori has so well proved, and as many others as well as myself have clearly verified in practice ; hence without those wasted years of weary drudgery, which the dominant mis-instruction system compels, and leaving the mind ready and keen for all that Song, Literature and Drama, and Science too, have to offer. And this plainly, from your remotest Bengal villages to those of our Scottish Highlands and Hebrides, hence alike vitally and spiritually rich ; despite that material poverty which such villages too similarly share.

I have learned much too from your professional courses, as notably from Agriculture to Painting ; so again I have to congratulate and thank you. For though our Western schools of these, here and elsewhere, are more largely equipped and attended, more developed and specialised than are yours, you have not only potently aroused the noble idealism of the Bengal School of Painting (even before discovering the original painter in yourself!) as well as by setting a true artist to inspire his pupils in your College. In Agriculture you have shown example to all our Western colleges, in turning your students to advancing village practice in ever-widening circles, year by year.

Even beyond Literature, and Education too, we rejoice in your widening moral influence ; this again, not only in India, but literally from "China to Peru." Yet the world needs your further impulse,—and so is ready for it ; since now in all lands becoming awakened, through recent and impending crises, of late years extending to all countries, until now so gravely threatening each of our own. These crises are not "simply financial," nor even of unemployment, as London mostly too simply thinks ; nor even political, as many also do. For all these stresses and strains are but so many conspicuous symptoms, though each dangerous enough, of far deeper change ; nothing short of the decadence, even towards breakdown, of our Industrial Age ; with its too prolonged subordination of Men to the Machine ; and of both to Money, now also failing him. Yet much as in our European fifteenth century, while the Medieval World was breaking down, the Renaissance was arising. In turn, it declined, giving place to this Industrial, Commercial and Mechanical Age : with its rival political economies as its contending faith, Individualist and Socialist, Bolshevist and Fascist ; and with the "Struggle for Existence" as its general doctrine for all concerned, from individuals to parties, and to States, as in fact its prevalent philosophy. No wonder then that all this should be in decadence! Hence you and I, and others, increasingly remain outside the political struggles of the present ; not from apathy, but for our best work, that of aiding the better social order now also at many points in germination and growth, and towards its future foliage and flower, its fruit, and seed beyond. Yet how shall we make this nascent age, of Revivance, clearer to ourselves and others? "Where no vision is, the people perish." Your vision has been clear as was Ruskin's, and happily more gently stated and practically applied, that "there is no wealth but Life!" If so, in the subordination of mechanism to Life lies the secret; as Denmark and other small countries have been seeing and practising, so much better than "the Great Powers." You doubtless know your nearest analogue, alike as ruralist and poet, A.E. (George Russell of Dublin), one of the very foremost of Western re-educators, though still in the day of small things. Though none can wholly escape the pressure of the struggle for existence, its present pains are also birth-struggles, those of the new and better order. This Social Revivance is destined increasingly to supersede the prevalent mechanistic and mammonistic age, with its everthreatening international and civil wars by turns, each worse than before. How so? By the discernment of Life, in Evolution; so long perverted, and misunderstood, as mere Struggle for Existence—but now increasingly discernible, as in past ages at their best, as to and through the Culture of Existence. Those immersed in prevalent illusions, as of conflict on all levels, find it hard to see this; for one these mechanistic and mammonistic thought-levels, the practice and even the scientific theory of Struggle have seemed alike clear and convincing. But as we are now passing from the long domination of physical science during the Industrial Age towards the discernment of the processes of life and mind, and even of society and morals, so "we speak what we do know, and testify what we have seen"—the beginning of a new period and phase of civilization, a veritable Revivance.

How can we verify this in direct observation? and next in terms of these later sciences and their application? For observation I have seen your own vital sowing and then growings at Santiniketan; and I can show at least something of the like when you or your students come to Montpellier, or to our Outlook Tower at Edinburgh, or to our kindred and other centres in London itself. Yet even great scale illustrations are not lacking, as conspicuously that of Krupp, who, until November 1918, was the most terrible of efficient munition-makers; yet since Peace was dictated by the victors, has not been allowed to make a single weapon. So now he has literally turned sword to plough-share. He has been redeeming the equivalent of a new and fertile little Denmark from the heaths and wastes of Germany; and with such prosperity that he is building more garden villages for his own many workers than before. So, in common sanity, apart from pacifist sentiment, other countries can learn thus to realise, beyond our present "peace" (too little better than War-Truce, from mere fears) the possibilities of the needed Peace-war, of constructive Help-will, inspired by renewing Hope. At this critical time too, the old conceptions of Nationalism and Imperialism are giving way with us as in other lands; and towards better ones Regional, from small scale to great, International, and even Mondial.

Here again you have been at once an example at home in Bengal, thence increasingly to India, and throughout the World. With the change of the Industrial Age on the one side towards breakdown, yet on the other towards an age of Revivance, the like is becoming even plainer in Politics, on one side intensifying to crises, yet on the other hand to beginning of further and more advanced changes, beyond all schools of politics. Imperialistic and Nationalistic alike and even beyond the often useful endeavours of the League of Nations itself.

Yet as we all begun with appreciation of you as our foremost Poet, so let me close. With your keen and sympathetic ear, you have appreciated the best of English poetry, and enriched it with your own voice. As our old friend, Jagadis Bose, with his subtle brain and skilful hand, has been a "cutting edge" in European science-progress, yet all the more because fundamentally Indian too, so we of the West have all the more welcomed you among our poets, because your mastery of our tongue has been enriched from the spirit and the rhythming of your own home-singing. So now my final word.

Among our poets, let me recall our last Laureate, Robert Bridges ; and above all for his well-named "Testament of Beauty" ; his bequest ere he passed away at the ripe and happy old age we hope for you. Your works so far have surpassed his before that one ; yet let us plead that you consider his final example, and prepare for the world your "Testament" in turn. You also have long been seeking and finding, discerning and expressing, the Beautiful, the True, the Good ; and so what man now living can so fitly and so fully concentrate his powers towards such final and consummate poem as that of their presentment anew? Does not your greatest work thus lie before you? Its full design, its high purpose and resolve, will give you new strength, and length of days for its achievement.

Yours ever,
PATRICK GEDDES

THE INDIAN COLLEGE
AT THE UNIVERSITY OF MONTPELLIER,
FRANCE

Very hearty Good Wishes to Rabindranath Tagore on his Seventieth Birthday.

LONDON JOHN GALSWORTHY

RABINDRANATH Tagore ne comptait encore, en Angleterre même, que de très rares lecteurs, lorsque en 1912, je traduisis son *Gitanjali*. L'incomparable pureté poetique de ce petit livre rayonnait à mes yeux d'un tel éclat que je tien a honneur d'en apportor un reflet à la France. A travers la guerre, au dessus de toutes nos dissensions politiques ou confessionnelles cette étoile fixe a continué de luire et de verser sur le monde une tranquille lumière d'amour, de confiance et de paix. Je suis heureux d'apporter aujourd'hui mon tribut d'hommage et de reconnaissance à la grande figure que vous vous proposez d'honorer.

PARIS ANDRÉ GIDE

ON TAGORE

I.

"DUHKHABHISAR" by Rabindranath Tagore is one of those poems in which the peculiar inimitable quality of our greatest lyric poet comes out with supreme force, beauty and sweetness. Rabindranath has a legion of imitators and many have been very successful in catching up his less valuable mannerisms of style and verse, as is the manner of imitators all the world over. But the poignant sweetness, passion and spiritual depth and mystery of a poem like this, the haunting cadences subtle with a subtlety which is not of technique but of the soul, and the honey-laden felicity of expression, these are the essential Rabindranath and cannot be imitated, because they are things of the spirit and one must have the same sweetness and depth of soul before one can hope to catch any of these desirable qualities. We emphasise this inimitableness because the legion of imitators we mention are doing harm to the progress of our poetry as well as to the reputation of their model and would suggest to them to study this poem and realise the folly of their persistent attempt. One of the most remarkable peculiarities of Rabindranath's genius is the happiness and originality with which he has absorbed the whole spirit of Vaishnava poetry and turned it into something essentially the same and yet new and modern. He has given the old sweet spirit of emotional and passionate religion an expression of more delicate and complex richness voiceful of subtler and more penetratingly spiritual shades of feeling than the deep-hearted but simple early age of Bengal could know. The old Vaishnav *bhava*—there is no English word for it,—was easily seizable, broad and strong. The *bhava* of these poems is not translatable in any other language than that the poet has used,—a striking proof is the unsatisfactory attempt of the poet himself, to explain in prose his own poem, *Sonar Tari*. But while the intellect tries in vain to find other intellectual symbols for the poet's meaning, the poetry seizes on the heart and convinces the imagination. These poems are of the essence of poetry and refuse to be rendered in any prose ; equivalent poetry is not created from the intellect or the outer imagination, but comes from a deeper source within to which men have no means of access except when the divine part within seizes on the brain and makes it a passive instrument for utterance the full meaning of which the brain is unable at the moment to grasp. This is the divine mania and enthusiasm which the subtle spiritual discernment of Plato discovered to be the real meaning of what we call inspiration. And of this unattainable force the best lyrics of Rabindranath are full to overflowing.

II.

The first condition of the complete emergence of this new poetic inspiration and this vaster and deeper significance of poetic speech must be the completion of an as yet only initial spiritualised turn of our general human feeling and intelligence. At present the human mind is occupied in passing the borders of two kingdoms. It is emerging out of a period of active and mostly materialistic intellectualism towards a primary intuitive seeking to which the straining of the intellect after truth has been brought in the very drive of its own impulse by a sort of slipping over unexpected borders. There is therefore an uncertain groping in many directions, some of which are only valuable as transitional effort and, if they could be the end and final movement, might lead only to a brilliant corruption and decadence. There is vitalistic intuitivism, sometimes taking a more subjective, sometimes a more objective form, that lingers amid dubious lights on the border and cannot get through its own rather thick and often violent lustres and colours to finer and truer spiritual vision. There is an emotional and sensational psychical intuitivism half emerging from and half entangled in the vitalistic motive, that has often a strange beauty and brilliance, sometimes stained with morbid hues, sometimes floating in a vague mist, sometimes (and this is a common tendency) strained to an exaggeration of half vital, half psychic motive. There is a purer and more delicate psychic intuition with a spiritual issue, that which has been brought by the Irish poets into English literature. The poetry of Whitman and his successors has been that of life, but of life broadened, raised and illumined by a strong intellectual intuition of the self of man and the large soul of humanity. And, at the subtlest elevation of all that has yet been reached, stands or rather wings and floats in a high intermediate region the poetry of Tagore, not in the complete spiritual light, but amid an air shot with its seekings and glimpses, a sight and cadence found in a psycho-spiritual heaven of subtle and delicate soul-experience transmuting the earth tones by the touch of its radiance. The wide success and appeal of his poetry is indeed one of the most significant signs of the tendency of the mind of the age. At the same time one feels that none of these things are at all the whole of what we are seeking or the definite outcome and issue. That can only be assured when a supreme light of the spirit, a perfect joy and satisfaction of the subtlety and complexity of a finer psychic experience and a wide strength and amplitude of the life-soul sure of the earth and open to the heavens have met, found each other and fused together in the sovereign unity of some great poetic discovery and utterance.

III.

The most considerable representatives of this new and free form of poetic rhythm are English and American, Carpenter and Whitman. Tagore's translation of his lyrics have come in as a powerful adventitious aid, but are not really to the point in the question at issue ; for these translations are nothing but a rhythmically poetic prose and that kind of writing, cadenced prose poetry, a well recognised form, cannot and does not try to compete with the established principle of measure : it is an indulgence, a minor variation which has yet its definite place and serves certain purposes which could not otherwise be fulfilled with any adequacy. It is perhaps the only method for the work Tagore intends, a poetic translation of poetry reproductive of the exact thought and spiritual intention of the original; for a version in the fixed measures of another language not only substitutes another mould for the original movement, but by the substitution gives it almost another soul, so powerful, distinct and creative a thing is poetic rhythm; but the more flexible, less insistent cadence of poetic prose does not so seize on and recast the spirit of the original movement; it may even give a far-off minimised shadow, echo, illusion of it, if the same or a similar spirit is at work; it can never have the same power, but it may have some echo of a similar suggestion. When for instance Tagore writes in English:

> "Thou settest a barrier in thine own being and Thou callest thy severed self in myriad notes. This thy self-separation has taken body in me. The great pageant of thee and me has overspread the sky. With the tune of thee and me all the air is vibrant, and all ages pass with the hiding and seeking of thee and me."

we have a very beautiful delicately cadenced poetic prose and nothing more. Tagore is what some of the French writers of *vers libre* and Whitman and Carpenter are not, a delicate and subtle craftsman, and he has done his work with a perfect grace and spiritual fineness; but there is no attempt to do anything more than the work just in hand, no intention of displacing the old way of poetry, in which he has done in his own language such wonderful things, by a new principle of poetic movement. If there were any such intention, it would have to be pronounced a failure. One has only to compare this English prose, beautiful as it is, with the original poetry to see how much has gone out with the change; something is successfully substituted which may satisfy the English reader, but can never satisfy the ear or the mind that has once listened to the singer's own native and magical melodies. And this is so, even though the intellectual substance, the intellectual precision and distinctness of the thought are often more effective, carry home more quickly in the translation, because in the original the intellectual element, the thought limits are being constantly overborne and are sometimes almost swallowed up by the waves of suggestion that come stealing in with the music; so much more is heard than is said that the soul listening goes floating into that infinity and counts the definite contribution of the intelligence as of a lesser value. Precisely there lies the greatest power of poetic rhythm for the very highest work that the new age has to do, and that it can be done by a new use of the poetic method without breaking the whole form of poetry, Tagore's own lyrical work in his mother tongue is the best evidence.

IV.

The spirit gives us not only a greater light of truth and vision, but the breath of a greater living; for the spirit is not only the self of our consciousness and knowledge, but the larger self of life. To find our self and the self of things is not to go through a rarefied ether of thought into Nirvana, but to discover the whole greatest integral power of our complete existence.

This need is the sufficient reason for attaching the greatest importance to those poets in whom there is the double seeking of this twofold power, the truth of things and the insistence of life. All the most significant and vital work in recent poetry has borne this stamp ; the rest is of the hour but this is of the future. It is the highest note of Whitman, in him, as in one who seeks and sees much but has not fully found, it widens the sweep of a great pioneer poetry but is an opening of a new view rather than a living in its accomplished fullness. It is constantly repeated from the spiritual side in all A. E's work, moves between earth and the life of the worlds behind in Yeats' subtle rhythmic voices of vision and beauty, echoes with a large fullness in Carpenter. The poetry of Tagore owes its sudden and universal success to this advantage that he gives us more of this discovery and fusion for which the mind of our age is in quest than any other creative writer of the time. His work is a constant music of the overpassing of the borders, a chant-filled realm in which the subtle sounds and lights of the truth of the spirit give new meanings to the finer subtleties of life. The objection has been made that this poetry is too subtle and remote and goes away from the broad near, present and vital actualities of existence. Yeats is considered by some a poet of Celtic romance and nothing more, Tagore accused in his own country of an unsubstantial poetic philosophising, a lack of actuality, of reality of touch and force of vital insistence. But this is to mistake the work of this poetry and to mistake too in a great measure the sense of life as it must reveal itself to the greatening mind of humanity now that mind is growing in world-knowledge and towards self-knowledge. These poets have not indeed done all that has to be done or given the complete poetic synthesis and fusion. Their work has been to create a new and deeper manner of seeing life, to build bridges of visioned light and rhythm between the infinite and eternal and the mind and soul and life of man. The future poetry has not to stay in their achievement ; it has yet to step from these first fields into new and yet greater ranges, to fathom all the depths yet unplumbed, to complete what has been left half done or not yet done, to bring all it can of the power of man's greater self and the universal spirit into a broadened and even the broadest possible all of life. That cannot and will not be achieved in its fullness all at once ; but to make a foundation of this new infinite range of poetic vision and creation is work enough to give greatness to a whole age.

PONDICHERRY

AUROBINDO GHOSH

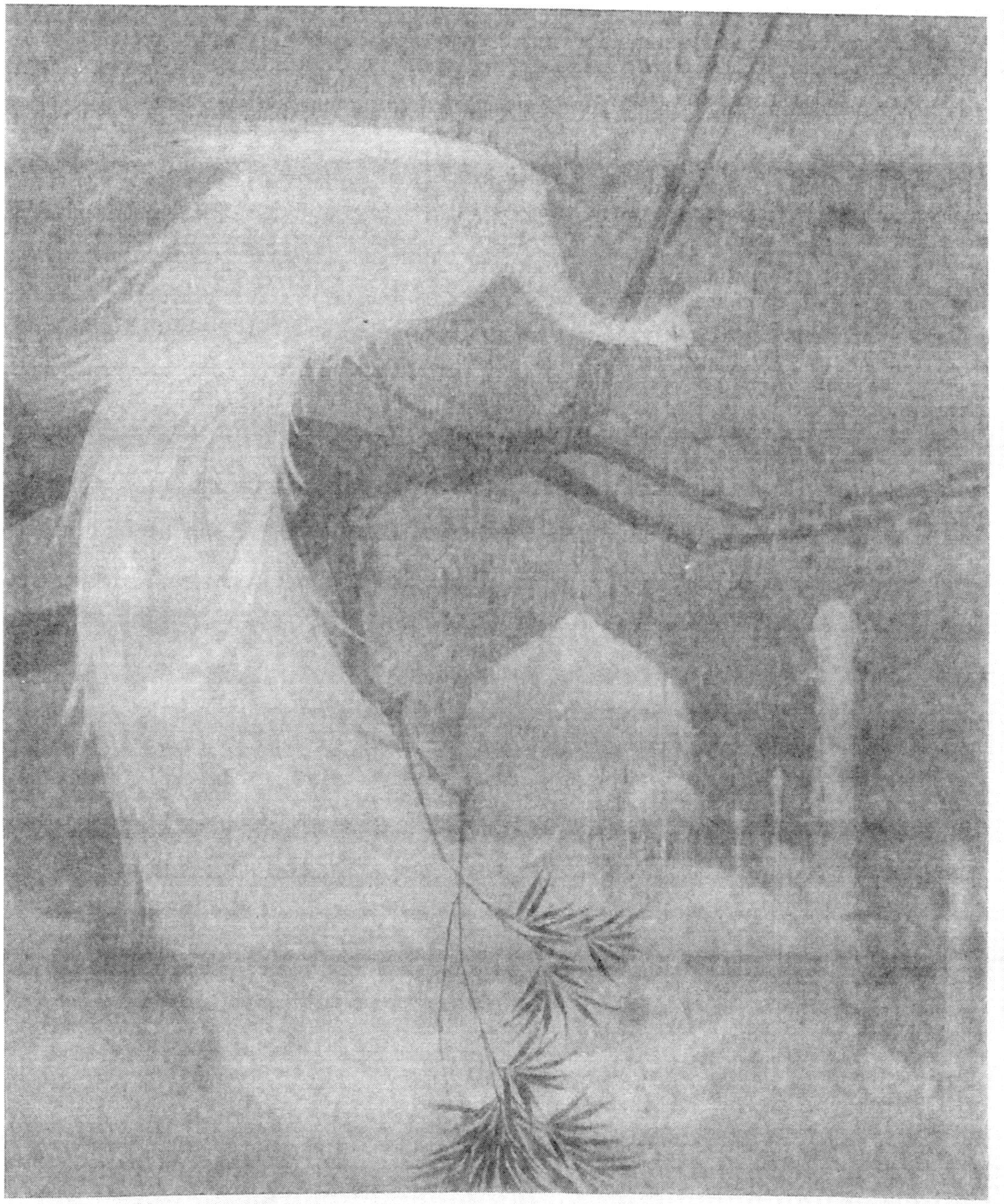

A RABINDRANATH TAGORE

(En hommage, avec toute l'humilité et la joie de mon cœur!)

Aux lèvres du maître
la bonté souriante
fleurit ;
et chante,
en paroles aimantes,
sa claire sagesse humaine.

La plaine, au soir lunaire,
est fluide ;
et languide, la rivière
frâle le silence nocturne.

Urne mystérieuse,
l'âme du maître
brûle
les parfums secrets
et précieux des idées.

Tel un vol de colombes blanches
que balance les nuées ;
la pensée
monte et s'exalte
au rythme délicat des periodes dorées.

BRUXELLES — O. P. GILBERT

AN RABINDRANATH TAGORE

DICHTER und Philosoph der durch sein Lebenswerk die tiefsinnige und erhabene indische Philosophie und Dichtkunst weiten Kreisen der übrigen Welt erschlossen hat, entbietet der Unterzeichnete, im Bewusstsein der innerlichen engen Verbundenheit deutschen und indischen Geisteslebens, die ehrerbietigsten Glueckwünsche zum ciebzigsten Geburtstage. Möge es dem hochverehrten Jubilar vergönnt sein, noch viele Jahre hindurch in ungebrochener Schaffenskraft seine segensreiche Tätigkeit im Dienste der Mitwelt fortzusetzen nach den hehren Worten der Bhagavad Gita "im Mittelpunkt des Herzens einsam wohnend, von wo in Liebe er das All betrachtet."

HEIDELBURG — EMIL GOTSCHLICH

INDIA'S CONTRIBUTION TO WORLD THOUGHT

I welcome this opportunity, furnished to me by the editor of the *Golden Book of Tagore,* to make my contribution to that Memorial Volume on the completion of the seventieth year by the Poet-Philosopher of India. I wish I could write something about the Poet himself, but my knowledge of him is limited and derived from his works ; for I have never had the good fortune of meeting him. But all the same, it does not preclude me from realizing his greatness and the value of his contribution to world thought.

The Indian mind has for generations been essentially a religious mind. Its thoughts are enveloped in the mysticism of its faith, its ideas circumscribed by the confines of its dogmas. History records several notable examples of break-aways from this system. The first, the greatest and the noblest example of them all is that of Gautama Buddha, the World Master of Thought and Philosophy. He was the first notable Indian to depart from the surrounding creed and social order and create for the people of his land the re-invigorating atmosphere of free thought and rational living. The history of that great world movement is forgotten in the clamorous claims of the lesser Lares and Penates for popular tribute. But in the academy, though not in the market-place, the sublime contribution of this greatest of thinkers is well recognized. For it is he who was the first to break down the galling barriers of caste, it was he who established the unity of all life, the equality of all men including women, and the redemption of man from the thraldom of priestcraft.

The poet, Rabindranath Tagore, belongs to the same family of political, religious, social and literary free-lances. His writings breathe, not the musty fumes of the lamp, but the green aroma of the corn fields. Unlike many a Hindu poet, he has not confined his poetry to describing the imaginary exploits of the great heroes of Hindu legend like Sri Ramachandra and Sri Krishna ; but he has followed the lead, if I may be permitted to say so, of the great humanist poets of the West for whom humanity counts and of which they are the heralds and the symbols.

Except in Bengal, where he was fully appreciated by those whose appreciation is worth having, Rabindranath Tagore had worked unhonoured and unsung for many a year till he attracted the admiring gaze of a distant band of literary critics who placed round his head the laurel wreath of the Nobel prize. The Government, ever tardy to recognize merit, woke up to its obligations and conferred upon him its own tribute of knighthood. Poets and philosophers do not work for the applause of men ; they work because they must. The inner fire within them burns too strong and must find an escape, even though its light perish unseen by the *habitués* of the Court or of the ball room. True poetry and true art can only be developed in such free and unfettered atmosphere, which Rabindranath has created for himself. His school at Santiniketan is truly an Abode of Peace. It conforms to the ancient ideal of a University of which Nalanda and Taxila are shining examples. The preceptor and the pupil become spiritually one and their lives during their period of preparation and probation are the lives, not of the master and servant, the preceptor and the scholar, but of the father and son, or rather of the elder and younger brother. This intellectual brotherhood creates a new bond which no time can sever. It instils into the young impressionable youth the love of knowledge, just as the young offspring receives with mute silent devotion the teachings of its mother. Santiniketan fulfils an ideal, a glorious and noble one, of a seat of learning and good conduct.

A great poet and a great thinker cannot be impervious to the throbbings of a new nation. For India of the old has ceased to be, and an India of the new is emerging out of the toils of men like Mahatma Gandhi and Rabindranath Tagore, who have by their self-sacrifice and incessant prayers made the Indian feel a craving for a fuller life. The voice of Tagore has been the voice of a Messiah preaching in the wilderness from which there has emerged an abundant crop of patriotic endeavour and a craving for liberty. India of yesterday is the India hide-bound in superstition, enslaved by self-seeking spiritual marauders, atrophied by their gloomy philosophy. The India of to-day is the India crying for more light, struggling for greater liberty—liberty not merely political, but in all domains. The India of to-morrow will be the fulfilment of the promise of to-day.

NAGPUR — HARI SINGH GOUR

More than any other man, Rabindranath Tagore has, through his own works, taught the world the marvellous beauties of Indian literature and song.

BOSTON, MASS., U.S.A. — RICHARD B. GREGG

AN RABINDRANTH TAGORE

Hochverehrter Freund!

AUS Ihren Büchern kannte ich Sie als den grossen Dichter, den universellen, tiefgründigen und erfolgreichen Mittler zwischen morgen und abendländischen Kultur, den tapferen Kämpfer für die Befreiung der Erziehung von der Pädagogik, den genialen Künder der Kindesseele, dem in Santiniketan das einzigartige Glück gelang, denen, die dort heranwachsen, eine ganz glückliche Kindheit und Jugend zu sichern, religiöse Menschen sich in völliger Natürlichkeit und Unbefangenheit, durch keinerlei Dogmatismus gestört, zu Gotteskindern entwickeln zu lassen, geschützt von jeder äusseren oder geistigen Vergewaltigung durch Erwachsene.

Seitdem ich am Sommer vorigen Jahres das beseligende Glück gehabt, Ihnen persönlich zu begegnen, weiss ich, dass Sie, den Titel eines Philosophen ablehnend, einer der grössten Weisen aller Zeiten und Völker sind, die einzige Persönlichkeit der neueren Zeit, die an menschlicher Grösse neben Goethe, den grössten Deutschen, zu stellen ist. In den hundert Jahren aber seit Goethe hat die Welt sich insofern verändert, als den Nationen und Rassen der Erde ihre Zusammengehörigkeit in der Menschheit zum Bewusstsein gekommen ist. Möge die Vorsehung es fügen, dass in den nächsten hundert Jahren Sie für die kulturelle Entwicklung Indiens die segensreiche Bedeutung erlangen, die Goethe für die deutsche Kultur erlangt hat, und über die ganze Erde hin als der Prophet der Menschheitskultur erkannt und gefeiert werden.

In herzlicher Liebe und Verehrung bin Ihr dankbarer Schüler.

ODENWALDSCHULE PAUL GEHEEB

"DEATH, O MY DEATH, COME AND WHISPER TO ME"
—*Gitanjali*

By Mr. Gogonendranath Tagore.

A TRIBUTE FROM TRINIDAD

Love is the great Amulet that makes this world a garden ; and 'Hope that comes to all' outwears the accidents of life ; and reaches with tremulous hands beyond the grave and death.

R. L. S.

Many thousands of miles of sea flow between the vast continent of India, and the little Island of Trinidad in the West Indies, more picturesquely called by the Arawaks, the original inhabitants, Iere, the Land of the Humming Bird.

Trinidad lies off the delta of the Orinoco river, about 16 miles to the east of Venezuela in the north of the Continent of South America. The area of Trinidad is small, being only 1,754 square miles. It is a beautiful and fertile land, being verdure-clad from the tip of the highest peak El Tuchuche, 3,000 feet, down to the sea. The products are sugar, cocoa, coffee, coconuts, rice, Jonca beans and petroleum.

The inhabitants made up of many nationalities, number between three and four hundred thousand, of which a third are of Indian birth, being the descendants of agricultural emigrants brought from Mother India to help to build the prosperity of the island, and for the greater part to find health, happiness and a fair measure of prosperity for themselves.

And so from the capital town of Port of Spain, throughout the length and breadth of the island, the sons and daughters of India may be found, Panjabees. Bengalis, Madrasis, and others. And whilst each section may speak in English, its own vernacular, or in the dialect that has gradually evolved between them all, with an admixture of English, each and all revere and love the name of Rabindranath Tagore. His books of poems and essays are in constant demand from the public library. Particularly is this true of "Letters To A Friend."

And his portrait adorns the walls of many a humble as well as wealthy home. And equally are his writings loved, appreciated and quoted by the educated men and women of African descent. Indeed one could fittingly adapt the lines written by the poet Alfred Tennyson, to welcome the beautiful young Princess Alexandra when she came to England from Denmark to be the wife of the Prince of Wales, afterwards Edward VII, and say :—

"Indian, African, European,
Whatever we be,
We are all one
In our homage to thee,
Rabindranath."

And happily there is a cord, a golden, though invisible cord of love that binds them to Santiniketan, for in a quiet garden where widespreading fruit and shady trees invite repose there is a little cottage called Santiniketan and in which a greeting from the Poet hangs. And to this little abode of peace come tired school-teachers to gather strength and refreshment of mind and body to carry on their arduous task of educating the children of the island, a large number of whom are of Indian descent.

Very deeply do I realize the great honour that has been conferred on me to be privileged to represent as it were, the sons and daughters of Trinidad, of Indian, European and African descent, and to write for *The Golden Book of Tagore* the expression of the homage, love and devotion that they would lay at the feet of the revered Poet on the occasion of the celebration of his seventieth birthday.

Oh Poet! who in tender youth
Beneath a tree sat singing,
Your voice upraised in prayer and praise,
Your father solace bringing,
No thought had you that round the world
Your songs would go a-winging.

And as in Trinidad's fair isle,
Where temple bells are ringing,
Your songs and portrait are the means
Of peace and solace bringing,
Then back to you our eager hearts
With love and praise are winging.

HEARTSEASE,
TRINIDAD

BEATRICE GREIG

A GOLDEN SINGER

If length of years were the only claim to remembrance few men would live in the memories of men, for life at its longest is only a brief span and is obliterated by death. What we call a man's personality, his striking presence, the nobility and beauty of his features, his aplomb are evanescent, for the body is built up of perishable material. There is something, however, apart from a man's physique which occasionally helps him to conquer death and enables him to leave behind a record of achievement which does not pass away. Rabindranath Tagore has attained the biblical age of three score and ten years and the tributes that will be paid to him will be an acknowledgment of the work he has been able to accomplish in these years, an expression of gratitude for the great gifts he has made to humanity.

Even now while he is still amongst us the world hails him as a world-poet, a singer whose melodies contain a world appeal, who has voiced the yearnings and aspirations of all humanity in verses of singular sweetness and penetration. His poetry radiates light, it is illuminating, resplendent with the glorious rays of the morning sun, lighting up the hill-tops and flooding the dark recesses of grottoes. The scorching and blinding glare of the noonday sun is not reflected by his muse. His exaltation comes of invincible and abiding faith, not from fitful gusts of passion. This is the secret of his rapid and universal popularity. The world has reacted promptly and eagerly to the magic of his songs, because the world longs for words of faith and the harmony of peace and beauty.

There is an inscrutable purpose behind the unprecedented and world-wide success of Rabindranath Tagore. He belongs to a subject race which has no recognised place among the free nations of the world. Many centuries of alien rule have reduced his people to the position of helots in their own land. They have been traduced and calumniated by foreign writers and visitors from other lands. Abroad they are either despised or barely tolerated by western people with an undisguised consciousness of superiority. The language in which he writes is written and spoken in only one province of India. Although derived from one of the greatest classical languages of the world, it is obscure and practically unknown out of Bengal. It does not yet possess a great literature, nor has it acquired an assured position among the literary languages of the world. Yet these handicaps, heavy as they undoubtedly are, have not stood in the way of the personal and literary success of Rabindranath Tagore. The man as well as his work have had universal acceptance ; Rabindranath himself has been welcomed with open arms and warm hearts wherever he has gone, east, west, north and south, and his writings have found a permanent place in the literature of almost every country in the world. The greatest name in the literature of to-day is not to be found in the west, among great and powerful nations, but in the ancient east among a humble people held in bondage by a western race. So do the mysterious ways of Providence fulfil themselves and East and West stand side by side rendering homage to the poet and prophet.

Genius would not be great, if it were not unconditioned. The limitations of language and country, the restrictions of personal liberty are burst asunder by the unshackled spirit soaring fancy-free in the empyrean and pouring forth its treasure of song. In the original, the poems and songs of this eastern poet are read and understood by only a small section of the human race. It is only through the medium of translations in many languages that his fame has spread in many lands, and many readers of many nationalities have found his message good for the soul. The essence has been retained in the translations, the beauty of thought and the subtlety of suggestion cannot be conveyed in another language. That the gist of the writings has been understood and appreciated is evident from the large sale of the translated works and the enthusiasm with which Rabindranath has been greeted wherever he has gone. Still the regret remains that the garb in which his muse is originally clothed has to be stripped in order that others may recognise her in other garments familiar to them. The glowing light of the jewel remains, but the setting has to be replaced. Else the world would have known the marvellously musical capacity of the language in which the poet writes: the mellifluous cadence of the words, the twinkling lilt of the verse. Bengali is a language that lends itself charmingly to the composition of poetry and all its resources have been wielded with consummate art by this poet.

What is the secret of this poet's appeal to all lovers of literature, without distinction of country and race? Why is it that his writings are so much sought after in the Far East and the Far West, among nations divided from one another not only by great distances but by tradition and custom and different habits of thought? Rabindranath's writings have proved, if any proof were needed, that there are certain characteristics, certain fundamental ways of thinking common to all humanity, and the heart of the East and the West is stirred alike if it can be touched the right way. Our poet does not employ exotic methods, the colouring is local and the aroma is racy of the soil. But the deeper truths that he explores and expounds are the truths of all time and all humanity, and hence the universality of his appeal. Deep down in the hearts of all thinking men, no matter what their race and what their colour, is the desire to understand and to hold to the truth, to attempt to attain to the higher destiny of the human race. It has been given to this eastern poet to reveal the deep and steadfast truths of life and to illuminate the depths of human thought.

It is yet too early to say that the world has arrived at a final and accurate estimate of the genius of this poet. There is no difficulty at all in appreciating the universal welcome extended to him, or in realising the profound admiration with which his works have been read all over the world. It is not yet possible, however, to assign finally his place in the world's literature. That must necessarily be a matter of time. Criticisms and high praise of his work, based mainly on translations, have appeared in many countries. In his own country and among his own people there is considerable enthusiasm but not much by way of an elaborate examination of the predominant features of his genius. The one outstanding fact beyond all dispute is the unparalleled recognition that has come to him in his own lifetime. With changing conditions in the world, the rapid spread of publicity, the growth of internationalism, the broadening of human interests, fame spreads more quickly than it used to do in the past; but even these favourable conditions do not wholly account for the phenomenal success of Rabindranath Tagore as an international, nay, a universal poet. There have been and there are other famous writers for whom the same facilities for world-wide celebrity were available, the Nobel prize for literature is conferred every year, but the works of no other modern writer have been, in such a short space of time, translated into so many languages as those of this Indian poet. It is obvious that there must be some special fascination, some irresistible appeal in his writings.

The present occasion, the completion of the seventieth year of the poet's life, has been marked by a spontaneous offering of tributes by the poet's friends and admirers all over the world. It is a grateful acknowledgment of what the world owes to him. It is a personal tribute inseparable from the great work done by him and which has brought his personality into such prominence. This may be considered a fitting occasion to strike a personal note. There may be a few friends still left who have known him young and have known him old, and who may recall personal memories of the years gone by. As a matter of fact, however, the life of the poet is an open book of which all the chapters are known to the world. There are no obscure pages, no elements of romance. His has been a life of high purpose, clean and pure, and of steady and ceaseless work. His literary activities cover a wide field. Although his chief distinction is that of a poet, he is no less distinguished as a dramatist and a writer of fiction, while his work as a critic and essayist is by no means inconsiderable. His intense patriotism has found expression in his patriotic songs; the different phases of the political evolution in his own country have found him alert and watchful, and, whenever necessary, he has fearlessly expressed disapproval of some particular form of political creed or activity. There has never been any question of the sincerity of his convictions and the selflessness of his motives.

These are matters which do not call for more than a passing mention. The world knows and will remember Rabindranath as a maker of exquisite melodies, a seer who has seen the truth and celebrated it in matchless song, a poet who has devoted his art to the exposition of the pure and the beautiful, a man of a living faith which has been a source of unfailing inspiration to him. This is why hands and hearts have been stretched out to him from every point of the compass and his message has found willing listeners in every part of the world. His verse has caught and sounded the harmony of the spheres; it has the abiding peace of a deep faith and also the strange pain that accompanies it. Apart from the profound truth that 'our sweetest songs are those that tell of saddest thought', there is an indefinable heart-ache in the realisation of the truth, throbbings of pain that finally cease in peace. It is only rarely when a man is far more subtly gifted than his fellows that he realises in himself the travail of creation, the paroxysm of pain which is the inevitable prelude to peace. This is an experience that cannot be communicated to others. It is an individual realisation and the result alone can be shared by others.

The impersonal aspect of a man's genius must transcend his personality. When we say of any man that he is greater than some achievement that has brought him fame, we are perfectly aware that the man's fame will outlive him. Aware of our own transitory existence we endeavour to hold fast to the passing image of a man. It is the light that illumines the lamp ; quench the light and the lamp serves no purpose. We attach so much importance to personality, because we are utterly ignorant of the personalities of the greatest men of ancient times, men whose claim to greatness is still beyond dispute. They were wise with a great wisdom and they did not concern themselves with the trivialities of personality. They have left no record of themselves and others have said nothing about them. How a man lived his life, how he looked, how he comported himself were apparently matters of no moment. Great poets found great commentators but no biographers. There were numerous and varied glosses upon theological and philosophical works, but no word was written about the authors. The ancients easily and instinctively distinguished between the permanent and the impermanent.

The ancient lack of curiosity about the personal history of famous men has now given way to a spirit of keen inquiry and a strong desire to know all that may be possible about the life of a man distinguished above his fellows. It so happens that the personality of Rabindranath Tagore apart from his remarkable genius is eminently attractive. He would attract attention anywhere in any gathering of men by his physical and intellectual distinction, the beauty and nobility of his features. Added to his personal appearance is the singular dignity and purity of his life. The great strength of his character has been manifest throughout his life, in the hours of trial and grief. The more one knows the story of his life the greater will be his respect for the man. One looks in vain for another personality so great as his, so fascinating in its beauty, so impressive in its strength.

It is a great privilege to have an opportunity of paying our homage to the genius and character of such a man. For him there are no bounds of nationality or country. His gift is the heritage of humanity, his voice is the clear expression of human thoughts struggling for utterance. The world is grateful because he has given the truth to the world set to beautiful music. It is not for us to worry about the future, for it does not concern us, though the poet's own place in the future may be assured. We make our bow and pass on, but we feel our lives have been fuller and richer for what we have learned from this latest of the world-poets. If our hands cannot lift the veil of the future, nor our eyes penetrate its folds, we can still hear faintly the music of the future and distinguish the poet's songs ringing down the golden steps of time.

BOMBAY NAGENDRANATH GUPTA

My respectful salute to the teacher, poet and prophet.

NORHOLM, NORWAY

KNUT HAMSUN

PORTRAIT-SKETCH

Firm lips and shaggy brows,
Hands that a little tremble;
Deep eye that knows
Work; and white hairs which resemble
Pure and perennial snows
On a mountain that once grew green,
But now by a glacial age of its own invaded,
To snowy repose by that cold hand persuaded,
Grows to an end more stern but most serene,
Remembering days that have been.

LONDON

JULIAN S. HUXLEY

TAGORE.

IT has been suggested to me that I should make a slight contribution to the Birthday Volume in which the admirers of Rabindranath Tagore are expressing their loyalty to their teacher, and their appreciation of his work. For me, however, it is not easy to comply with the request. I am more than an admirer of his genius; lover would be nearer the mark; but when one expresses himself in such terms one remembers that restraint in expression increases with the affection that would be expressed. One does not send one's love-letters to be published in the London *Daily Mail*, or in what answers to the *Daily Mail* in Calcutta or Delhi. Such things are kept, as one preserves a rose-leaf in a book, so that the leaf, even if faded, may recall the open flower that one would preserve from fading. Lie there, Fair Memory, we say; we shall know how to turn the pages and find you. Let me see what it is that I shall find, always keeping in mind that we have still the full-blown rose with us, as well as any leaf-memories.

We found our fellowship, which is our friendship and our deepening affection, on the day when Tagore first came to our little group of Truth-seekers at the Woodbrooke Settlement; he did not come in person, but the door was wide enough open between East and West to allow of a book being pushed in for our notice; if ever a book is the same thing as a person, it was so when we read *Gitanjali* for the first time, either alone or in company with those who could value it as such a guest ought to be valued. That was the Poet's first visit to Woodbrooke; he will come in person later, and Woodbrooke must always be his home.

After reading, or rather revelling, in the pages of *Gitanjali*, it was natural to ask questions about the new friend who was behind the new book. What one said to oneself was as follows:

"The things that are said here sparkle like diamonds with many facets; one moment you seem to be reading a handbook of Christian devotion; the next moment, after the manner of the Sufis, all creeds, all buildings that house creeds, mosques as well as churches, are left far behind, and the Soul is heard singing like a lark,

'Sucked up out of sight,
In vortices of glory and blue air.'

Is he, then, a Sufi, or just one of the lovely company that are almost Christians, because in so many ways they are beyond what is called Christianity? Where did the man find this secret hunger after God which burns his heart away in great flames of desire, and will not be satisfied till the whole world is aglow with the heat from the same central fire and radiant with the light from the same central flame?"

Such were some of the questions that I asked myself when meditating on 'God and the Soul in the Songs of Tagore.' We had found, indeed, a Poet, and more than a Poet. I am ten years his senior, but am glad to sit down at his feet, with the rest of his disciples.

WOODBROOKE, ENGLAND

RENDEL HARRIS

TO TAGORE

IT has been my great privilege to enjoy the friendship of Rabindranath Tagore and of his distinguished relatives, Gaganendranath and Abanindranath, almost from the date of my arrival in Calcutta thirty-five years ago, when the poet's father, the Maharshi Debendranath, was the illustrious family's venerated head. It is, therefore, a peculiar gratification to me to be permitted to join in the world-wide tribute of respect and admiration which will be offered to the poet in celebration of his seventieth birthday this year.

Rabindranath Tagore's creative energy, incessant and wide-spreading, inspired by the highest ideals of Indian culture—yet universal in its appeal like all great art—has been a pure life-giving stream flowing through the arid sands of political strife, bringing spiritual joy and clear-sightedness to those who have drunk of its unsullied waters. May the happiness and strength he has given to so many lives replenish his own for many years to come.

Happily his freshness of spirit seems to defy the oncome of years. Only last year he demonstrated this in several public exhibitions of his pen-drawings which revealed remarkable originality in design and technique. In spite of his preoccupations in poetry, drama and music, and the work which a great educational undertaking imposes upon him, he yet finds time for and the keenest delight in exploring new avenues of art. All will rejoice in thinking that this augurs well for many more happy and fruitful years being added to his life.

OXFORD

E. B. HAVELL

AUSTRALIA, newest of the new civilizations, might not seem likely to have admirers of Tagore. Yet they are many and would not wish to miss this opportunity of adding their contribution to the world's tribute of admiration and gratitude. It is not merely that the Poet and Philosopher in him are universal and appeal to hundred spirits whatever the outward circumstances of their lives. No Australian who passes through the sunburnt plains of India and sees its people living close to the earth and the elemental things of life, can fail to realize that despite all the differences, there are common elements in the lives of the two peoples. He too comes from a people who live with the earth and not merely upon it, who know the night and the dawn and water, air and fire. To some of them at least Tagore has given a fuller vision of the inner beauty of that fusion of nature and the human spirit which is part of their daily lives.

SYDNEY, AUSTRALIA

H. DUNCAN HALL

TO MY DEAR FRIEND RABINDRANATH TAGORE,

IS it really true that you are only 70 years old! Judging from your work, your wise thoughts and the influence you have had upon our time, one would believe you were much older.

I remember so well when our great poet, Dr. Verner von Heidenstam, first told me you had got our Nobel prize for the year 1913, and how happy I was that the greatest thinker and philosopher of my beloved Asia had been honoured. Later, the same year, I myself became a member of our Swedish Academy that has to distribute the literary Nobel prize to the greatest author of the running year.

Several years later you came to Stockholm to deliver the public lecture that every receiver of a Nobel prize has to give. Our Academy at that occasion gave a dinner in your honour. Several Swedes of fame were present. The Secretary of the Academy, Dr. Erik Axel Karlfeldt, held the great speech to you. Our Archbishop Dr. Nathan Söderblom of Upsala also made a beautiful speech. Amongst those present were also the great historian Professor Harald Hjärne of Upsala and the famous archæologist Dr. Oscar Montelius. All those four members of the Academy are dead now.

I remember your speech at that informal dinner where nine of the eighteen members of the Academy were the hosts and where you and your two secretaries were the only guests. I have a special reason to remember your speech as you mentioned my expeditions in Asia in the kindest and most encouraging words.

Later on, in 1926, you again came to Stockholm for a day, and that day you passed in my home, and we made a trip together round Stockholm seeing something of its beautiful surroundings.

In 1929 I again had the honour and pleasure of meeting you in Tokio, and again we had a long talk about the extraordinary and deplorable situation in the world. We found it a great pity to the whole humanity that our time did not possess one single really capable and wise statesman, a man whose actions were dictated entirely by righteousness, justice and love. If all those in power now were sent to an uninhabited island where they could continue their fights in words, words, words, and you were made the dictator of the world, there would be peace, confidence and mutual respect, there would be love and sympathy for the sufferings and depressions of the whole humanity in all countries of the earth.

I know that nothing could give you a greater happiness on your 70th birthday than the appearance of a Saviour who was strong enough to lead men and nations according to your noble and human principles.

May God bless you and let the evening of your wonderful life be long and happy!

SVEN HEDIN

STOCKHOLM

THE SONG OF ABEL'S DEATH

Dead in the grasses lies Abel,
Brother Cain in fright has fled;
A bird dips his beak in the blood—
Shudders—flies swiftly away.

The bird flees restlessly over the world,
His flight is shy, and his voice is shrill,
Unceasingly wailing his sorrow:
For the lovely Abel, who far away lies slain,
For the gloomy Cain with grief tormenting his soul,
For his own days of youth, gone for ever!

Soon will Cain's arrow wound his frightened heart,
Soon will he bring dispute and war and death
To startled homes, to peaceful cities,—
Ever making foes for himself and slaying them,
Despairingly hating them and himself,
Pursuing them and himself into all the byways,
Torturing them till another darkness takes the world,
When Cain, at last, himself was slain.

The bird flies on and from his bloody beak
Laments of death re-sound over the world,
Cain hears him, the mother of Abel hears him,
Thousands under the heavenly tent hear his voice.

But many more thousands are deaf to his woes,
They will not know of Abel's death,
Nor of Cain and his anguish of soul,
Nor of the blood flowing from so many wounds,
Nor of the war which was of yesterday only—
Now told in novels for bored women to read!
For all those, for the satiated, the flippant,
The strong and the brutal,
There is no Cain, no Abel, no death, no sorrow,
No hatred, no war—at the most "a jolly good time!"

They do not heed his warnings whenever the sorrowful bird flies by ;
They call him Pessimist, (which, perhaps, he really is)
They feel themselves strong and unconquered
And throw stones at the bird, to drive him away from their homes,
They laugh, they make music so that he cannot be heard,
For his doleful voice disturbs their life's play.

The bird, with the small drop of blood
On his beak, flies from place to place,
And his wailing for Abel thrills the vast void.

HERMANN HESSE

MONTAGNOLA,
SWITZERLAND

[In the spring of 1924, Tagore came to Peking, China. A reception wa accorded to the poet at the Fe-yen temple, the abbot of which was His Highnes Rev. Tao Kai, the famous Buddhist scholar and monk of China. The poem wa composed on the occasion.]

He comes from the glorious India, queen of peacocks, which gave him th splendour of spirit. He comes from our holy place, the motherland of Buddha, an the Bodhi trees provided him with supreme intelligence.

He breathed the cloud-kissed air of the Himalayas, and washed his body in th sacred river Ganges. His touch revived the ancient soul of India. The Vedas Upanishads, and Brahmanas stood by him.

Our dream in a dark night ends thus on a sudden. Truth shines forth and mai says, "It is I." Thus do scented flowers open up in the air, and freely do the swim ming fishes run to and fro ; a thousand rivers flow gently to the ocean, and tides ebl and flow between the East and the West.

The East has its rebirth through our Poet-seer. May he live for ever!

LIU YEN HON

PEIPING (PEKING)

THE POET & THE DANCE

After an woodcut by Mr. R. Chakravarty, Govt. School of Art, Calcutta

TAGORE

THE seventieth birthday of Rabindranath Tagore may wisely be acclaimed in a world-wide celebration. For Tagore holds great place to-day in the life not merely of his nation but of all mankind.

We think of Rabindranath here in the West, first of all, as one of the supreme poets of all time. As native to the genius of his own culture as Homer to that of ancient Greece or Dante to that of medieval Italy, Tagore has yet made his voice, as Homer and Dante made theirs, a part of the lifted chorus of humanity. The *Gitanjali* and kindred volumes are the pure distillation of Indian thought and life and vision. Yet they have already become an immortal part of the literature of mankind. It is not only natural but inevitable to include in the company of the world's great poets the exalted figure of this eastern bard.

But Tagore is philosopher as well as poet. In his earlier *Sadhana,* and in his latest work, *The Religion of Life,* he has expounded in prose as noble as his poetry, and in thought as clear as it is beautiful, the sheer idealism of the East. In an age when this type of speculation and belief has all but disappeared here in the West, Tagore's philosophical and religious writings have come like the pouring of a pure spring of living water into the parched areas of a desert land. Machinery, manufacture, wealth, war have possessed our world, and have reflected their mastery in the production of materialistic or mechanistic forms of thought. But all the while, from the far horizons of another world, has come the calm but magically clear voice of this Indian sage, reminding us that the inner spirit is the sole reality, and that the fulfilment of this spirit is the secret of all life. Will it not be recorded in days to come that Tagore was one of the influences which served to keep alive, in this disastrous period of history, the essential soul of man?

As poet and philosopher alike, Rabindranath Tagore has been the supreme reconciler of East and West. To each, as a sort of inspired mind, he has been the interpreter of the other. More than any other oriental of whom I know, he has understood the West, seen the good in the midst of its evil, discerned in its mastery of the material world an indispensable and permanent contribution to the life of man, and commended to the East this vast achievement. But just because he has known the West so well, he has seen its need of what the East could bring—namely, a mastery of the inner life to match the West's great mastery of the outer realm of things. If the West has developed the means of living, the East has found the end of living. Her people have laid hold upon the spirit, without which no people, whatever their mechanistic miracles, can hope in the long run to survive. So here was a severed world, each part of which needed the other, as the two halves of Plato's mythical man hungered and searched for one another. To bring these two divisions of mankind together has been Tagore's great mission. He has journeyed ceaselessly in his own country, and far afield in China, Japan, Europe, America, even Soviet Russia, to speak his message of reconciliation and mutual co-operation. That he should have come at just the time when all the East is awakening to individual and national self-consciousness, and is in imminent danger of building its new life in hatred of and hostility to the West, is one of those accidents of circumstance which would seem to indicate not accident but purpose in the world.

What Tagore has thus done extensively abroad, he has undertaken to do intensively in his own country. To many of his fellow-countrymen, Tagore's work as a teacher must mark his greatest contribution at least to the life of his own people. He has seen precisely what Gandhi has seen in the threatened extinction of Indian culture before the ruthless invasion of western materialism and militarism. Gandhi has met the issue by leading his people in a national revolution which has compassed in one vast movement the economic, political and social forces of his age, and therewith has proved himself the greatest statesman of his time, as well as the purest saint and most potent popular leader of all time. With the spirit and purpose of Gandhi's nationalist cause, if not with every detail of method, Rabindranath Tagore has always been in basic sympathy. But the poet and philosopher, like the Mahatma himself, has had his own approach to the one problem—his own way of contributing to the salvation of his people's life. This has been, as a specific work apart from the general work of writing and speaking, his task of education as embodied in his school which has become one of the most important educational institutions not only of India but of the world. Here he has awakened the soul of India to itself, and laid down methods by which the awakening may continue, and spread to the remotest corners of the land, long after his own inspired presence has been withdrawn. Tagore the teacher takes rank with Tagore the poet and philosopher. Side by side with Gandhi, he serves the age's cause. As different as Erasmus and Luther, these two men, each in his own distinctive way, labor to bring in that new period of world history which must mark an epoch in the annals of mankind.

Rabindranath Tagore is one of those happy men who look the part they play. Who that has ever seen him can forget that serenely beautiful countenance, that tall and noble form, that mien of ineffable dignity and exaltation! I remember, when first I saw his figure clad in its softly flowing robes, that I thought myself in the presence more of a god than of a man. Later I came to feel that this presence was the veritable incarnation of the poetic soul—the outward and visible form of the inward and spiritual grace. Surely it is this which makes a meeting with Tagore to partake of the nature of a sacrament. More than by any ceremony before an altar, I was made to feel by the man himself the sense of mystic reverence and awe.

COMMUNITY CHURCH
NEW YORK

JOHN HAYNES HOLMES

THE DREAM OF LIFE

Our days of love are over;
    But other loves abound,
And sweetly springs the clover,
    And in new woods around
    Are birds of happy sound.

In the grass-covered meadows,
    Where the low swallow gleams,
Beneath the sky-laid shadows—
    Beside light-stepping streams,
    The bending willow dreams.

There, under grey leaves leaning,
    The brook goes waving by.
O man, read here the meaning
    Of life, and feast your eye:
    Things pass, and we must die.

On streams that have no finish
    Our little lives are writ.
Time's flow shall not diminish,
    While down the course of it
    Like withered leaves we flit.

Below the leaning willow
    The grey leaves fall, and fall:
Down on a watery pillow
    They drift beyond recall;
    And the stream takes them all.

Stone, stream, and time are deathless;
    And in them dwells no sense:
Dumb in their bonds, and breathless,
    Blind in their providence,
    They roll, and bear us hence.

But we—O eyes that waken!
O feet that walk on light!
For all the breaths we've taken,
And the long day's delight,
Now thank advancing night!

Had night not lain around us
How little should we know!
Light through the darkness found us;
And, wakened by its glow,
We kissed, and now must go.

Our day of love is over;
But other loves abound;
And life is still in clover;
And in new woods around
Are birds of happy sound.

In the grass-covered meadows
Where the low swallow gleams,
Beneath the sky-laid shadows—
Beside light-stepping streams,
Old willows dream their dreams.

SOMERSET, ENGLAND LAURENCE HOUSMAN

EL MISSATGE DE CATALUNYA

ELS grants poetes suren en mitg de les ones de la civilizatció quant un' era grant s' acosta. Son els portaveus de la generació futura. Aixis el grant Kalidasa aparagué en el nord de l' India quand Chandra Gupta Vikramaditya preparava els seus exercits per la victoria, quand la grand era de Nalanda se dibuixava en l'horitzó, quand els peregrins de la China pensavan en visitar l' India com l' empori de l' educació de l'Orient.

Aixó is Tagore per l'India moderna. Ell li ha ensenyat lo qu' es i lo que será. Vullga Deu que' ella, i el seu poeta amb ella, tornin llurs mirades envers la font de tota grandesa. Llavors la civilizatció de l'India sera grand. Llavors Tagore será el verdader missatger de la grand India.

BOMBAY H. HERAS, S.J.

THE POET AT WOODBROOKE

THE month of May, 1930, has become memorable in the annals of our community, because it was the occasion of the visit of the famous Indian poet and internationalist, Rabindranath Tagore. His visit had been most eagerly looked forward to, but all our expectations were exceeded. The Poet was with us for a number of days on three several occasions. He shared in the common life of our colleges at Selly Oak (for Woodbrooke is one of a family of eight colleges); and wherever he went he left the impression of spiritual beauty, calm and strength. He was present on several occasions at the devotional meetings with which we begin our day—silent meetings for the worship of God. At three of these he spoke briefly, and the words which he said and even more the spirit in which he said them made a very deep impression upon all his hearers.

One afternoon the Poet went with some of us to see the spring flowers in the beautiful Forest of Arden, which lies some distance to the south-east of Birmingham, on the outskirts of which great city our community is situated. Those of us who went with him on this occasion will not soon forget the happiness which the sight of those flowers gave to him.

On one occasion, when the Woodbrooke family was gathered to hear a reading by our guest from some of his own works, the proceedings began with the presentation of a boquet of wild flowers to the Poet by the youngest child of our community, a little girl of three. It was a pleasant sight to see the grave kindliness with which the famous writer received the simple gift.

What remains in my mind, above all, as a memory of Rabindranath Tagore's visit, is the picture of him sitting amongst us in our Common Room, and reading to us from *Gitanjali* those great words:

"Our Master himself hath joyfully taken upon him the bonds of creation.
He is bound in our midst for ever.'

WOODBROOKE, BIRMINGHAM — JOHN S. HOYLAND

Minél többet ismerek meg India lelkébo˝l, annál ero˝sebb lett bennem a gyanu, hogy az igazi kereszténység elhagyta Európát és Azsiába költözött.

BUDA-PEST — HERCZEG FERENC

[TRANSLATION]

The more I know the soul of India the stronger does the suspicion grow in me that the spirit of Christianity has migrated from Europe, and has again appeared in Asia.

'THE GODS' OWN WAY' AND WORLD PEACE

IN this our Land of the Rising Sun there has been in force from time immemorial a moral code called 'The Gods' Own Way.' This code has formed throughout the ages and will continue to form for all times the corner-stone of our civilization.

True it is that stimuli and impulses from without have often contributed to our peculiar form of culture, but the 'Gods' Own Way' has for ever proved a happy check on undue exotic influences, and has thus enabled us to maintain our assimilative capacity and the desire of adopting only that which is good.

In its earliest form the 'Gods' Own Way' set great store by innocence and purity of heart, and this becoming the traditional characteristic of the nation, we Japanese have come to judge our every word and deed by the degree of our conformity to this standard.

In ancient China three, and sometimes five cardinal virtues were spoken of, while classical Greece recognized her four supreme moral excellences. What is cherished by a nation as its guiding principle is often found to change with time. We have, however, throughout all ages been true to that one and only teaching of pure-heartedness, peculiar to our people.

In the reign of Emperor Temmu (673-686 A.D.), we find that the four supreme virtues of guilelessness, purity, uprightness and honesty were held in high esteem. Yet all these may with propriety be considered as but synonyms of pure-heartedness, our national virtue *par excellence*, which has gradually developed into what is known as *nori* (law) and *michi* (way), until it is now known as *Kan-nagara-no-michi, i.e.*, 'The Gods' Own Way.'

The wholesale adoption of Western civilization by this country after the Meiji Restoration of 1868 has for a few obscured the real direction and significance of the 'Gods' Own Way,' and has caused no little confusion in our manner of thinking, more especially noticeable among our young students. Yet it is indisputable that the unshakable 'Gods' Own Way' still reigns over the great majority of the Japanese people.

What is then the 'Gods' Own Way'?

It may literally be rendered as the 'Way the Gods Themselves Follow'. Yet such a description does not bring us to a clearer understanding.

Old archives show that our forefathers did not call their guiding moral principle *michi* but *nori*. Now *nori* means the 'law', *i.e.*, the way all people should follow. To this day every Imperial Rescript is known as *mikotonori* or 'what the Emperor has spoken to His people.' This, of course, because His august edict is proclaimed as a law for His subjects to obey. If the word *michi* were used in early times, it would appear to have been in its literal sense of 'a road' along which to walk or ride. Not until after the introduction of Confucianism in A.D. 285 did the figurative use of the word as 'way' come into use. Then did *michi* in most cases come to replace *nori* as meaning 'law', and to stand for the Chinese character *tao* in its abstract sense. Yet must it not be forgotten that *michi* was not understood in its Confucian application, but that it came to represent that peculiar moral principle which had already been developed among us Japanese.

Michi or the way is something unchangeable and everlasting; it is universal in its application, belonging to the world at large, and no one country may call it her own. In other words, it is an absolute existence, knowing no distinction of race, time or space. Hence its designation as the 'Just Way of Heaven and Earth.' It corresponds to what some understand by the term *logos*. This principle, abstract and unique as it is in its very essence, assumes, however, different forms as it reveals itself through an endless variety of environments, giving to us that *michi*, the 'Gods' Own Way', peculiar to us Japanese people, Confucianism and Taoism to China, and Buddhism to India, while it inspired the idea of the *logos* in the mind of the ancient Greek philosophers.

Michi may well be unique and absolute in its origin, but in its relation to human affairs it is liable to a certain modification depending upon circumstances. In Japan too, the original *michi* has undergone inevitable changes in the course of its adjustment to the soil where it was ultimately to take root.

In this 'Land of the Rising Sun' all without distinction of social rank are expected to conduct themselves consciously or unconsciously according to the teaching of the 'Gods' Own Way.' As practised by the Emperor himself, this way is called the *Kodo*, or the Imperial Way, in contradistinction to the *Shindo*, which means the *michi* as observed by his faithful subjects. The practice, because of its ancient origin, is sometimes spoken of as *Kodo* or the 'Old Way'; but as it is not limited by considerations of time only, the word is but rarely used.

The practice of deifying some of Japan's great men of recent times may be explained as the process of converting them into so many objects of Shinto worship and personifications of the 'Gods' Own Way.'

Bushido, a word now widely understood in the West, is the *michi* or 'Way' as practised by the *Samurai*. These members of the warrior class in the feudal days of Japan considered it a point of honour to conduct themselves in time of peace, but more especially on the battle-field, in strict accordance with their *michi*. They, moreover, firmly believed that any show of prowess unworthy of this moral code was nothing but a mere savage display of animal courage, entirely alien to *Bushido*.

Judo, the 'way of suppleness,' *Kendo*, the 'way of fencing,' *Kyudo*, the 'way of archery,' *Sumodo*, the 'way of wrestling,' and all the other *'dos,'* as applied to the arts of physical training, derive their true meaning as they seek to remain true to the spirit of *michi*, the 'Gods' Own Way.' The same came to be said of indoor occupations such as *Chado* or the 'Way of the Tea-ceremony,' the *Kwa-do*, the 'Way of Flower-arrangement,' *Kodo*, the 'Way of Incense-burning,' etc.

Generally speaking, all the forms of art base themselves on the divine *michi*, the 'Gods' Own Way.' We sometimes refer to this as *Shido i.e.* 'the way *par excellence*,' which in China is used to designate the exclusive doctrine of their own, which is Confucianism. To us Japanese it is *Sotten*, that is our 'imperative duty.' To lose it would mean the loss of our very essence. It is therefore with a sense of deep regret and shame that we see how the radiance of this 'God's Own Way,' so dear and sacred to us, has become somewhat dimmed, by the importation from the West of foreign doctrines like imperialism, utilitarianism and materialism. Yet do we stand in no danger whatsoever that complete darkness may overcloud the moral principle of this land of ours.

When our nation is threatened by evil and crafty dealings, we are not backward in rousing our whole people to that strong sense of righteous indignation which impels us to strive unceasingly until the cause of the threatened corruption is removed. This does not mean that our *michi* does not embrace the doctrine of non-resistance, but that it considers the realization of abiding international peace and goodwill as more worthy of its dignity. Indeed, it may rightly be said that its aim and ultimate end is the bringing about of world peace. In this connection, we might quote the song of the great Emperor Meiji:

Yomo no umi
Mina harakara to
Omou yo ni,
Nado namikaze no
Tachisawagu ran?

(When I am firmly convinced of the universal brotherhood of the peoples across the seven seas, why is it that some prove so very violent and insurgent?'

The spirit of world-wide fraternity is here breathed nobly in every syllable of the poem, and it is well worthy of the One Who identified Himself with the 'Gods' Own Way.' It is the ideal of our *michi* that it should not only affect peaceful rule within the boundaries of this Empire, but also that it should eliminate all those refractory elements in the world at large which are an impediment to the establishing of international calm and happiness, and which would tend to destroy the purity and innocence of our world. When this spirit of peace and humanity holds sway over us, then may we say that the whole nation is permeated by that true spirit of Yamoto of old. To speak of it as something anti-foreign is but to betray one's lack of understanding and narrow-mindedness. No nation is free from lowering clouds that would sometimes threaten to burst upon even its purest members. Yet no people, even at the darkest hour of its danger, is ever without its men endowed with the righteous spirit needed. It should be our aim that those great souls be inspired to work together so that a real and lasting peace may be established in the world.

TOKYO — TETSUJIRÔ INOUE

THE EAST AND THE WEST

TIME after time, the wisdom of the East has been offered to the world, and its civilization has been given a turn for the better; and the interpreters of this wisdom have ever been the sons of the Aryan race.

In a dim and distant past, Zarathushtra, the Prophet of the Aryan race, gave to the world the Message of Truth. Mankind had hardly learnt the art of living in peaceful and ordered agricultural settlements when Zarathushtra raised his protest against a nomadic and savage existence, and showed to his followers and the world the advantages of a peaceful existence of a well-ordered society. On the spiritual side, he showed them how to attain to perfection and happiness in this world and to salvation and immortality in the presence of the Divine Beloved in the life hereafter by choosing the Path of Truth (*Asha*) and following the triple principles of Good Mind (*Vohumana*), Holy Power (*Khashthra*), Love and Devotion (*Armaiti*), the fruitful ways of Wisdom, selfless Action, and devoted labour of Love. Through these Paths, Zarathushtra assured mankind that everyone would meet and see the Divine Beloved as he himself had met and seen.

That sister portion of the Aryan race that were leaving their Iranian brethren in the North-west, and were crossing over the Hindu Kush and were entering the land of the seven rivers, had their own great sages, propounding the same great wisdom that we see culminating in the Upanishads and the Bhagavad-Gita. The Path is again indicated as lit by the beacon light of Truth (*Sat*), and the Divine Essence is again described approachable through the *Jnana Marga*, the *Karma Marga* and the *Bhakti Marga*, the triple ways of Wisdom, Action and Devotion.

This wisdom of the Aryan race, of the ancient Iranians and the ancient Indians, has remained unassailed and unassailable through the passage of time. Fearful cataclysms both the component parts of the Aryan race have gone through, but the intense heat of all calamities, has only made the Wisdom come out of the ordeal, purer and brighter like the purest gold. Princes of poets like Hafiz in Persia and Kabir in India have given expression to the same wisdom, although then the world about them was in the throes of turmoil and strife.

During all these times, the West and the rest of the world gleaned the corn from the harvest of the East through its travelling philosophers. The very first of them, Pythagoras, came to Persia and learned the wisdom of the Magians; and he must have learnt it well too; for, in a fragment that is left to us, he describes the Persians as contemplating the Supreme Creator exactly as the sacred Avesta describes Him, *viz.*, that His body is Light and His Soul is Truth and that the way to meet Him was the Way of Truth. The last statement is an exact translation of the Avestan fragment which says: "There is only One Path, and that is the Path of Truth."

But now in the twentieth century, almost a miracle has happened. Both the wisdom of the East and its deep philosophy, which have hitherto been offered in weak or inadequate translations, have been offered to two continents of the West,—Europe and America, in original English itself,—the current language of the cultured of the present age; and this has been done through the superb and soul-elevating productions of Tagore and Gandhi. In Rome, in Vienna, in Paris, in London,—in these big cities, the political and intellectual centres of the great nations of the West, one feels and realises how these two great Indians, have not only raised the name of India and the Indians in the estimation and esteem of the West; but that by their writings which directly approach them and appeal to them, a veritable thirst has been created in the West for the wisdom of the East.

Unless there is a better and a more intimate cultural and spiritual understanding between the East and the West, a great calamity stares the world in the face. But should such an understanding be an accomplished fact, it might be the precursor of universal peace and brotherhood in this world. If this vision ever comes true, the future history of the world, will attribute it most to the two great men of the present age, Gandhi and Tagore, both coming from the ancient land of India, both sons of the great Aryan Race.

D. J. IRANI

BOMBAY

HOMAGE TO RABINDRANATH TAGORE

The Truth shall make you free.

What is Truth?

Truth is the reality of *knowledge*, as good is the reality of *being*. It is the essence of life, and must be the principal object of realization of man.

What is Reality?

Reality, the first principle of Reason, is the form of the Divinity, the form of the Absolute, the full Identity of being and knowledge of Ego and non-Ego in man,—the Identity, seized by the same knowledge.

What is Knowledge?

Knowledge, the creative faculty of reason, is one of the two poles of Reality, which tends ever to the union with the second one, the Being, in order to become the fullness of Reality, a form of Divinity, absolute.

What is human truth on the earth?

The human truth on earth is a relative truth, that is not entirely fulfilled as the imperfect union of being and knowledge, the incomplete reality of knowledge in man, yet ever on the way to the full one. The Absolute Truth is the Perfect Union of Being and Knowledge, the Perfect Reality of Knowledge in man.

What is the criterion of Absolute Truth in man?

It is the quantity, the extent of the Absolute Reality, of the Divinity's form in man, conquered by his sacrificing merit (the creative word in man).

What is this criterion called in the current human language?

It is called the creative inspiration in Art and revelation in religion.

What is Art, then?

Art is the self-creation of Absolute Reality, of divine Harmony between Being and Knowledge in man. It is verily a God's gate in man, God's Word leading to God, to Truth, to Reality.

Is man able to open this gate entirely?

More or less. Human values and merits decide his tendencies and efforts.

Rabindranath Tagore is one among those few who are gifted with the highest inspiration of God, of Truth, of the Absolute Reality. He is on the way to God. He is nearest to His Reality.

Therefore, let Immortal Glory be to Him!

WARSAW — JOSEPH JANKOWSKI

TAGORE IN GUJARAT

THE Tagore family has been known to Gujarat for more than a generation. The late Narayan Hemchandra was the first writer who made Gujaratis familiar with the beauties of Bengali Literature and in a way introduced the Tagore family to them. But this introduction was not to remain impersonal or merely academic. Maharshi Debendra Nath Tagore visited Ahmedabad, very early in the life of its Prarthana Samaj and delivered a sermon in the Samaj Mandir. Satyendra Nath Tagore was stationed in Ahmedabad for a long time as a District and Sessions Judge, and he had picked up sufficient Gujarati, not only to be able to converse in that language and thus mix with Gujaratis, but his knowledge went further and he very often delivered sermons in Gujarati from the pulpit of the same Mandir. Dr. Tagore visited his elder brother (Satyendra Nath) in those days and was thus not an utter stranger to Gujarat. The ball set rolling by Narayan did not stop in its motion and the interest in Bengali Literature aroused by his writings (mainly translations) in the minds of Gujaratis was kept alive by others who followed in his wake. So that when Dr. Tagore brought out his *Gitanjali*—the great work which at a bound made him famous in both hemispheres—it was hailed in Gujarat, and received with open arms, because the soil was prepared for it: Gujaratis had already become familiar with the spirit of Bengali literature, prose and verse. Translations were made of its most beautiful songs, and articles dealing with the work and its author became a feature of Gujarati journals and monthlies at that time. On the top of this popularity came his visit to Ahmedabad in April, 1920, when the Sixth Gujarati Sahitya Parishad was in Session. Mahatma Gandhi was instrumental in getting the Poet to consent to come to Ahmedabad, at a time when the weather there is none of the pleasantest, there being unbearable heat, unrelieved by any breezes. He attended the Session of the Parishad as an honored guest, an address was presented to him and he replied to it in a memorable speech. A meeting in a large open maidan was held later in his honor, speeches were made by him and others. Sarala Devi Chaudhurani, who happened to be present there, sang *Ayi Bhuvana-mano-mohini,* in her beautiful voice, and a most successful gathering of thousands, men, women and children, dispersed after doing him homage, singing *Bande Mataram.* He was cheered, he was fêted, he was apotheosised. A large evening party was given by Sheth Ambalal, a millionaire of Ahmedabad, with whom he had put up, and the Poet relaxed so far as to sing some of his own songs in response to the repeated requests made to him by the guests, and those who were privileged to hear the music of his voice, amidst the charming surroundings of Sheth Ambalal's Bungalow at Shahibag that night, will for ever cherish in their minds the memory of that unique occasion. At a public garden party, Dr. Tagore was made to witness a scene, familiar enough in Gujarat, but not met with elsewhere, which he had never witnessed before, and he was charmed with it. I mean the *Garba,* in which girls, small and big, sing songs, while moving round and round a circle, with movements of hands which entrance by their rhythm, and movements of the body that magnetise by their mechanical regularity. Dr. Tagore was so impressed by the music and rhythm of this indigenous feminine sport and mode of enjoyment, no less than that of worship, that he expressed a desire to take the girls away to Santiniketan with a view to transport the *Garba* to Bengal. This welcome, sincere and heartfelt, as it was, no doubt greatly moved the Poet, and it seems to have convinced him of the influence he wielded and the impression he had made on the people of Gujarat, especially its youth. After that Dr. Tagore's writings and books followed in rapid succession, and Gujaratis did not fall behind others, both in and and outside India, in profiting by them. Such costly institutions as the educational and other classes conducted at Santiniketan are always in want of funds, and the generosity of Gujarat and Kathiawar has responded nobly to the call of the Poet. Whenever he chose to tour our province for the purpose, Ahmedabad, Baroda (whose generous-hearted and cultured Maharaja never failed him), and even a comparatively small State like Limbdi, have helped him to the best of their ability. The Poet has thus been able to make many friends in Gujarat. His admirers are, however, far greater in number, and his influence is sure to abide for ever. Many young men and to some extent women, have taken to the study of Bengali, so as to be able to follow his writings the better in the original. It is thus that the Poet has helped, unconsciously, the cause of interprovincial amity, for surely nothing promotes the cause so well and cements it so firmly as the knowledge on the part of one province of the language and literature of another. Gujarat will ever remain proud of the fact of its having entertained the Poet right royally and helped him, however inadequately and slightly, to go forward with a scheme, which is his pet and which for ever lies next to his heart.

BOMBAY — K. M. JHAVERI

Please accept Humanistic Club's and mine hearty congratulations on your seventieth birthday. May you live long to see humanity appreciate and practise your cherished ideal of the world as one big happy family.

BANGALORE — RAJA JAIPRITHVI

BELOVED FRIEND,

I like to think of the contributors to *The Golden Book of Tagore* as a large family of children who, on your birthday, bring you a token of their affection and gratitude. Each one of them will make a different offering and most probably in a different manner; some will make their offering in themes of verse and prose, with some little devices as their hearts dictate, or according to what they think will please; and I, who cannot do any of these things greatly, ramble into the garden of my mind and the fields of my spirit, and gather the fairest flowers I can find. Though they be but simple wild-roses, I know you will be more gratified by such a variety than if all your friends brought you stately wreaths of eulogy.

As our thoughts dwell lovingly on your noble and wise work, we are lifted to a higher level of effort and devotion. To realize the meaning of your message of friendship and co-operation is to deepen the furrows from which shall spring richer harvests of inspiration.

In the sweet solitude of a Poet's life you heard a Voice bidding you look into the hearts of your fellowmen and seek the way to deliver them from the grotesque gods of their own creation. You stepped forth into the crowded abodes of men where strife is bitter, and ignorance is deep. Taking little children by the hand, you led them into gardens of delight and taught them to live in sympathy with all that is beautiful, and to live all that is love-worthy.

Again the Voice bade you go from land to land in search of knowledge. With observing eye and listening ear you journeyed, and saw the curse of division, the darkness of prejudice, the deafness of hate in which men live as strangers and enemies. But, looking long and patiently, you found the dynamic force of love hidden in humanity . . . . the force which, understood, shall transform their life of self-destruction into a life of creative work and peace. To a world living under the law of fear you are a Prophet of the Law of Love.

Your school at Visva-Bharati is a bright pledge of a nobler civilization; for it is a meeting-ground of the East and the West. There you teach in object-lessons of sympathy and good-will that the true happiness of individuals and nations is identified with the highest good of mankind. When this supreme truth is grasped, the dream of all the greatest teachers spoken through the ages shall be fulfilled; "Wars will be dead; hatred will be dead, boundaries will be dead; dogmas will be dead; man will live, he will possess something greater than all these . . . . the whole of earth for his country and the whole of Heaven for his hope."

Long may you be spared, dear Master, to foster the unitive love from which shall spring constructive thinking and the upbuilding of a new social order!

With affectionate memories of our fleeting but precious few minutes together and the warmth of your hand in mind, I am,

Faithfully and gratefully yours,

NEW YORK

HELLEN KELLER

TAGORE

TAGORE represents in the very finest way the spiritual history of India flowing forth into the future, leaving behind its outworn parts and blending itself with the best in the cultures of all the worlds. He and his University represent India in the dignity of her past taking the next step forward.

His appreciation of the West goes much deeper than that of most other leaders of India. He has often been criticized in India by extremists because he will not speak against the West as they would have him do. Instead he defends the West for its practical idealism and its broad vision. He senses with the clarity of a Prophet that the East and the West are great and how much greater they could become if they could be brought into closer co-operation with each other. His social and international programme is highly practical and far-sighted and is well expressed in the policy of his University.

COLUMBIA UNIVERSITY, NEW YORK — WILLIAM H. KILPATRICK

I revere and love you, the painter and the poet, in equal measure.
May long years be yet granted to you.

BAD TOLZ, BAVARIA — KÄTHE KOLLWITZ

I have suffered very much in our Western materialism and barbarism ; and I have prayed to God, he might send me a spirit from the Orient to give me a true perspective of life, and Tagore came like the fulfilment of my prayer.

UNIVERSITY OF ILLINOIS, U.S.A. — J. KUNZ

THE BEAUTY AND VALUE OF TAGORE'S THOUGHTS

FOR countless ages from the beginning of society mankind has depended upon the seers, poets, and heroes for all the knowledge which has enabled the human family to emerge from the obscurity of savagery to the dawn of civilization. Some races have contributed more than others in producing the prophets who have the intuition to comprehend subtlety of truth, and to foretell what destiny has in store for the race. Others again produce men of genius with diverse gifts, who become leaders, teachers or poets, and excel in their exposition of the mysteries of existence, in their description of phenomena or abstract concepts, or in the discovery of contrivances for the needs of the race, struggling for existence in a world of endless conflicts.

From the start surely human life has been made possible by the emergence of Reason, which has slowly but steadily provided the arguments which justify the belief in a possible world of peace and happiness for mankind despite the fearful carnage and cruel destruction all around. These problems received the attention of Indian seers in very ancient times. They left the heritage of their speculations in their literature which has reflected throughout the ages the light of Truth and Wisdom, that have made India the home of poetry, mysticism, religion and philosophy.

The outstanding feature of the genius of Tagore is the wonderful capacity for minute observation of all aspects of Nature, and of perceiving, true to the instincts of an Indian sage, the mute language of creation with its infinite variations of melody and harmony. His mind is a perfect mirror to reflect the infinite apparitions of Beauty. The weird phantasmagoria of Life appears to him as quite an unmistakable manifestation of the Eternal. But stern reality is not lost sight of. None lives for ever. Whence come our miseries? Can the ordinary man see in the bud, or in the drop of dew on the lotus leaf emblems of life? But to the philosopher, when life ends, the mystery of Death begins.

On this subject of Death, which is so commonly distorted by fear, misconception and superstition, Tagore expresses his innermost feelings in simple but profound language. He experienced its awful advent quite early in life. Yet in mature years he says:

> 'Death had given me the correct perspective from which to perceive the world in the fulness of its beauty, and as I saw the picture of the universe against the background of Death, I found it entrancing.'

Tagore sees in death an inevitable phase of life, and his philosophy finds a ready solution, which enables him to see in the inexorable rôle of Death visions of Joy! Is it not the portal through which to meet the Eternal?

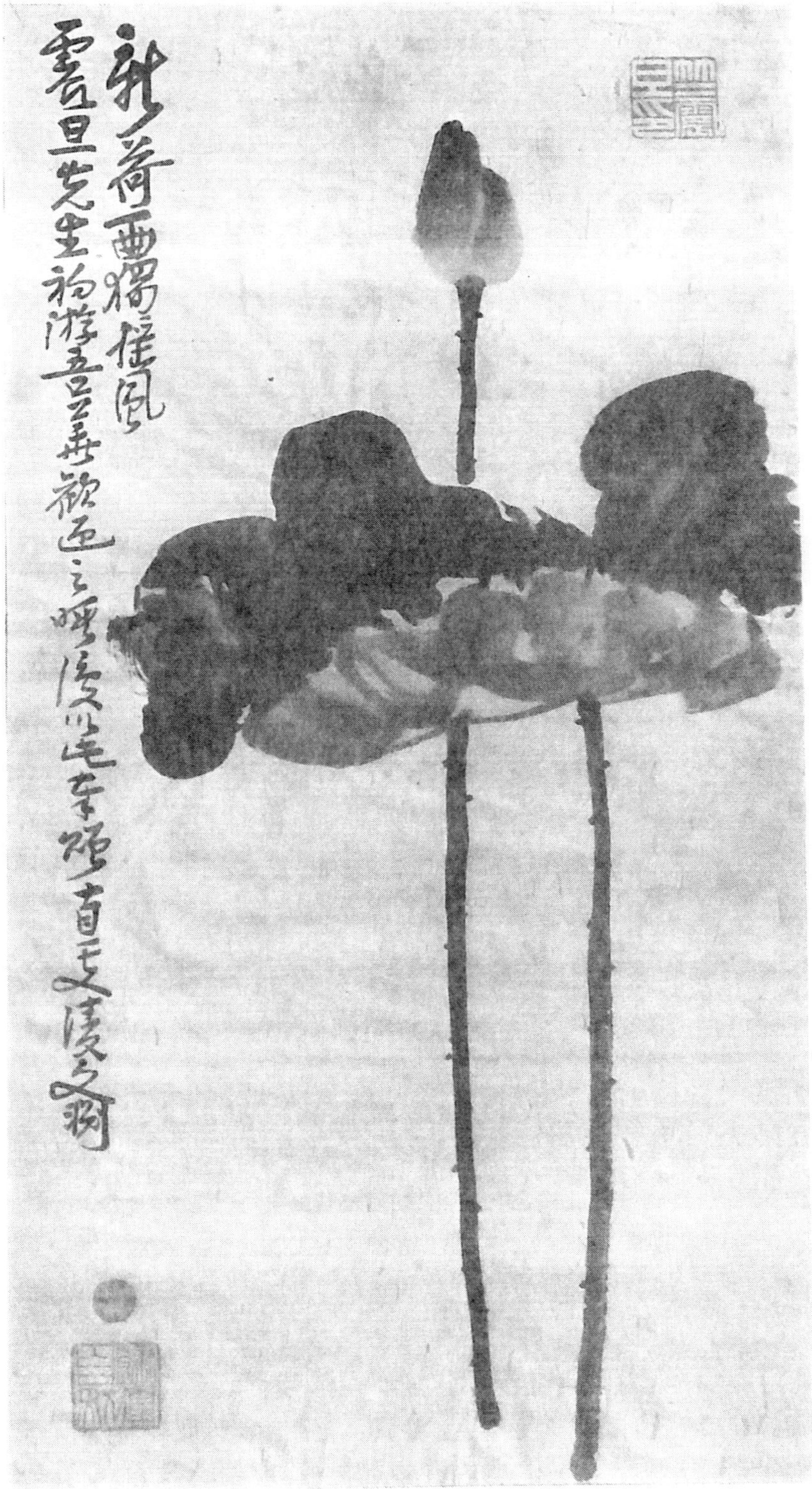

It is only natural, however, that Love should be an entrancing theme to the gentle and amiable poet, who sees everywhere, in each blade of grass, in every flower, in the song of birds, and in everything, the evidences of the Beautiful. The origin of the instinct, which impels man to seek love at its fountain may be lost in the remotest antiquity. The poet, however, needs no Freudian analysis to discover in woman the source of so much happiness and of so much tears.

'O woman! You are one half woman and one half dream.'

In a brief survey like this, it is impossible to do justice to the philosophy of Tagore, but perhaps it may be summarized by calling it the Gospel of Nature, since it draws its parables from the grass, the rocks, the streams, the song of birds, and the light of the heavens.

Not only does it reveal to us the arcana behind these appearances but also, what is more important, it points in emphatic and unmistakable language to the avenue through which the willing one seeking the Truth may behold the Good in all its Majesty and Glory.

It is indeed difficult to appreciate fully the profundity of the apparently simple thoughts which Tagore gives expression to in response to the appeals of his delicate senses when they come in contact with Nature. His soul seems at once to vibrate in full harmony with the orchestra of melodies and echoes reflected from the sound of rushing waters, from the songs of birds, from the gushing of winds, from the rustling of leaves, from the babbling of babes, from the laughter of lovers, from the roar of thunder or from the noise of the crowd.

In the depths of nature, the eye of faith sees the illumination of Love. The music of a seer makes the echoes of its mysterious movements resound in our ears as captivating song and melody. Thus from the infinity of space, love finds its abode in all things. In the discovery of Love, Tagore finds the matrix, which binds humanity into the solid frame of a conglomerate, which must find its fitting place in the harmony of the cosmos. Mankind must get knowledge and wisdom to behold the light of Truth, which will show the path of Freedom and Happiness,—mere shadows and vain illusions, unless in the presence of the All-good.

The unity of the entire universe is best seen through rhythmic vibration. The oscillations in each human soul must move in harmony with its entire environment. Then surely beauty will find its due place, and every movement and every sound will pass on to finite space in full accord with the eternal law. There is no break possible. The wildest chaos—the cataclysms of the stars—reveals in fact a perfect sample of the invariability of the order of Nature. The mind of man must learn how to discover the harmony of colour and sound. It must also learn to attune the soul to the music of the spheres and to find peace and happiness in the world.

Then a revelation comes as the light with the dawn. The pains and miseries of life disappear, as the darkness and the mist when the sun rises. Death itself, in this ecstasy of living in full accord with the spirit of the Eternal, approaches as the harbinger of Peace, bringing the consolation that the wheel of existence thus turns on, making way for new births in the march of time and change. Like all mortals, Tagore had suffered at first from the pangs and sorrows which Death's visit brought to his family. But his philosophy surmounted all the obstacles which obscured the truth at first, until he had ascended the top of the mountain of experience and could perceive over all the hills and the woods, the purifying work performed by merciful Death. Death has for ages been a source of fear, misery and pain, because people have not pondered over the Truth.

O! ye who suffer and fear the approach of Death, hear the music of Tagore. Learn from him to lose yourselves in the Infinite and the Eternal!

Just tune the chords of your being and make them move in harmony with the music of the cosmos, then Death just becomes the prelude to a change of melody on another key!

So throughout Tagore's philosophy everything is worthwhile. Every man and woman should strive to secure the light of Truth, and live simply and wisely for the common good.

Thus the philosophy of Rabindranath Tagore, in essence, is identical with the profound Monism of the ancient Chinese cult, preserved for the world by Confucius. All existences constitute the one organism of the entire cosmos, emitting love as the highest manifestation of its vital energy, and having as its rational soul the centre of the spiritual galaxy.

In presenting this humble tribute to the Indian sage, whom the world honours, the author takes this opportunity to express this earnest prayer on behalf of the Chinese people, that he may live long to give the world more of his noble teachings out of his inexhaustible mind.

UNIVERSITY OF AMOY,
CHINA

LIM BOON KENG

RABINDRANATH Tagore is the greatest man I have had the privilege to know. He is very much greater than his world reputation and above all, his position in India imply. There has been no one like him anywhere on our globe for many and many centuries. That is, Rabindranath is the creator of a nation. Everywhere, the Logos has been the first creator of things; it is only in decadent ages that he becomes a mere interpreter. And, in most cases, he becomes incarnate in a poet because the latter's love of metre and rhyme makes him, more than the pure philosopher, one with the rhythmical nature of the phenomenal Universe. Thus most nations have been created by some blessed poet who gave voice to their stammering longing.

The last historical figure of this kind in Europe has been Homer, though Orpheus probably was the true creator of Greece. In a few centuries mankind will realize that Rabindranath Tagore means very much the same to India. His were the greatest songs of her aspiring Liberty; his was the creation of the first all-human prestige of modern Indian man. That other figures seemed to mean more than Rabindranath to present-day struggling India is due to the fact that modern India is in her birth-pangs. Rabindranath, however, is the great model of the full-grown œcumenic Indian of centuries to come. In this he should mean much the same to India as Goethe has meant and means to Germany.

I will say no more. I admire my great friend Rabindranath Tagore as I admire no other living man, because he is the most Universal, the most encompassing, the most complete human being I have known. A while ago, the inventor of the science of Graphology, the old Frenchman Crépieux-Zamin, came to see me in search of handwritings of what he called "noble souls." He found very few in my collection that could satisfy him. But when I showed him Rabindranath's handwriting, the old man—much older than the Hindu poet, burst into tears: "How beautiful and how noble! I know of no handwriting of this level since the great days of the European Renaissance."

May my great friend continue to live and work for the benefit of all of us for many many years.

DARMSTADT, GERMANY — HERMANN KEYSERLING

OUR enemies very often accuse us of having "destroyed culture." Meanwhile, perhaps no nation shows such a strained attention to the world's culture and its greatest representatives as the delivered nations of the Soviet Union. In 1930, Rabindranath Tagore paid us a visit and could convince himself how our workers respect and honour the great writer. In every place, where he showed himself, he became the object of enthusiastic triumphs ; the auditoria where he spoke were overcrowded with the public, thousands visited the exhibition of his pictures, which was organised in Moscow, and we all remember how the enormous auditorium of the Union House listened breathlessly to the great poet, reading his own poems ; they listened with respect and admiration, feeling the beautiful music of the language of Bengal, though not understanding the words, but feeling themselves in the presence of a great soul.

It must have seemed that Tagore, avoiding all political struggle, absorbed in his deep meditation, must be foreign to us and far away from our life, which is spent in an atmosphere of stormy political discussions and feverish reconstructions. But it is an error. A thinker, reflecting on the Eternal, and a Revolution full of to-day's interest and immediate problems, are not enemies. There is no rupture between them, and somewhere high up on the last summit they will hold a friendly meeting. Our revolution does not reject the hope of a "golden age," of a future brotherhood of humanity, the idea which during many thousand years animated all religions and also the best representatives of humanity. The communist revolution has traced on its banner the practical realisation of these ideals. The revolution is not a destroyer, an enemy of noble thinkers. On the contrary, the proletariat looks upon itself as the lawful heir who is called to translate these ideals into life. That is why the songs of Tagore are resounding in our hearts as a beautiful call for liberation. He is longing for God. "Thou hast made me endless, such is thy pleasure," these are the opening words of his *Gitanjali*. We have no mystics, our cravings are limited by the boundaries of our planet, by organisations of a wise life of labour here on earth. But when the great Hindu poet shows us the treasures of his soul, when the old rags that cover the every-day man fall to pieces, when he describes, as nobody else can, the rapture of longing for the Ideal, I am sure that it is the expression in idealistic form of the joy of Creation which burns in the soul of each warrior of our revolution, and each of our fighters feels the charm of these songs ; he does not feel them less deeply, because the longing of the poet for higher spheres goes over the boundaries of our planet and we think its limits give us space enough. The nature of the sublime is always the same ; and all those who can rouse the sentiment of elevation in man's soul as Tagore does (and there are also our poets), they are the singers of our sentiments and moods, because in the old world—in the world where all idealistic impulses were stifled by the craving for gain and by cruel competition—there is no more place for such sentiments.

Tagore is also very near and dear to us in another way. He is seeking his God there where we seek ours. How often do I read over his splendid hymns (10th and 11th) out of his *Gitanjali*; his allocution to God: "Pride can never approach to where thou walkest in the clothes of the humble among the poorest and lowliest and lost."

"Leave this chanting and singing and telling of beads: Whom dost thou worship in this lonely dark corner of a temple with doors all shut? Open thine eyes and see thy God is not before thee!

"He is there, where the tiller is tilling the hard ground and where the path-maker is breaking stones. He is with them in sun and in shower and his garment is covered with dust. . . . .

"Come out of thy meditations and leave aside thy flowers and incense! What harm is there if thy clothes become tattered and stained? Meet him and stand by him in toil and in the sweat of thy brow."

We have in our country an army of many millions of men and women formed out of those tillers and pathmakers. This army is fighting for the deliverance of humanity.

The new labour country puts into practice those ideals that were the dream of the best thinkers and poets, and the country looks at them as her own.

That is the reason of our enthusiastic welcome to Tagore.

I am very sorry not to know the language in which he wrote his songs, the beauty of which I felt when listening to his inspired reading in the Column Hall of the House of Union in Moscow. But even the pale reflection of his poetry in translation into European languages shows the high flights of his soul, the greatness of his thoughts, the sincerity and depth of his sentiments. In this *Golden Book*, where his friends' greetings are gathered, I should wish to tell that in our country we know and honour Tagore's name, we have very good translations of his works, and our toiling masses, only recently so oppressed through injustice and ignorance, are now delivered and already united to culture. They are now occupied with the great work of economical and cultural renewal of their country, and the quicker this work will be accomplished, the nearer and dearer to us would be the names of the great teachers of humanity, in whose constellation the name of Tagore burns with such a fascinating bright light.

MOSCOW P. S. KOGAN

RABINDRANATH TAGORE

TO millions in Asia India's wealth of thought and spiritual ideal has, from early times, exercised an influence which is hardly less than that of Greece in the West. But for centuries Europe did not know anything about this fact.

India was considered to be a country where wealth could be accumulated and where wondrous things were to be found. And it was the tales about such marvels which chiefly interested the mind.

It was an Indian poet who at last opened the eyes of the West. Through William Jones' translation of Kalidasa's *Sakuntala* Europe came to know something about India's soul, about the ideals, the aims, and the aspirations of the people of India. And this led to a keen interest in India, her history and civilization.

It was, however, chiefly ancient India which attracted the interest of the West. Kalidasa was the poet, and the ancient seers and thinkers were the last and noblest product of India's genius.

Even when modern Indians came to play a role in the spiritual development of the West, it was chiefly as interpreters of the wisdom of the past that they were greeted and admired.

Then came the day when another Indian poet conquered the West. This time it was not one of bygone times, but one who lived and sang in modern India, whose tune was that of the Indian landscape, the Indian river, the Indian forest and the Indian village of to-day.

Again the West listened, and marvelled. It found the same authentic beauty, the same sublime flight of thought as in Kalidasa's immortal works: the old spirit was still alive.

Europe's interest in India was renewed and strengthened. And now it was not only directed towards the bygone poet, but often chiefly towards the living forces that shape the modern India, towards the world of beauty and harmony which his poems revealed, and towards the people to whose feelings and aspirations they gave expression.

The consequence was an ever-growing interest and sincere sympathy. To-day India has countless friends and well-wishers all over the world: he who bears the Sun-god's name has warmed the hearts towards his country and been her best ambassador.

He has taught the world to look on India not only as the source of an ancient civilization and spiritual culture, but just as much as the home of living men and women, whom we must love, and who belong to the same great human community as we. India has come nearer to us. Our attitude has changed,

As long as we were under the spell of India's past, we could admire her old achievements, sometimes in blind admiration, without understanding. We were thankful for them, and we sometimes showed our gratitude in an attempt at giving India a share in our own achievements. But few people believed that the India of to-day could give us as much as we could give her.

Now we know that the Indian genius which gave the world the Vedas, the Upanishads, the Bhagavad-gita, the inspired poets, is still alive, and that its voice must be heard in the great concert where every nation has her own tune. Indians and Europeans are brothers, living in the same world and the same time, and their highest interests are inseparable.

We do not want to become Indians, and we do not want the Indians to become Europeans in their mind and in other ways. But we want the East to join hands with the West, in a noble contest for the promotion of the highest ideals, which are common to the whole world.

We feel that Rabindranath Tagore has been our best guide towards this deeper understanding. And we also feel that he, with his deep sympathy, will be able to show the East, and above all India, that we are her brethren, and not her enemies.

We called him *Guru Dev* in Santiniketan. And he has become our *Guru*. He has shown that oceans and continents cannot separate what is one: the human mind in its longing for peace and harmony, for beauty and lofty ideals. Our hearts go out to him, in gratitude, and in hope, the hope that he will long be able to continue his noble work for mutual understanding and love. The world is in need of it.

OSLO, NORWAY

STEN KONOW

GURUDEV

In the mould of his limitless genius all different Arts become one:
He paints with words and plays with colours;
He draws with rythm and dances with thought;
His lines are philosophy, his ideas sculptures;
He builds with dreams and teaches with silence.
Unveiled by him, Death's mysterious image
reveals her misunderstood Beauty.

PARIS

ANDRÉE KARPELES

CONTRIBUTION OF NATIONALISM TO INTERNATIONALISM

MAN is only one of several species of gregarious animals which get together for various reasons, some for defence, some for aggression, some from a social instinct. Seldom does man prefer isolation to group life. Association of persons may form small groups or nations. The most simple and common unit is a family, the adhesive force being love. From this, wider circles of tribes, communities, castes and nations are formed. Being a good father does not preclude one from being a good patriarch of a tribe or head of a community, or a leader of a nation ; on the other hand, it is the same attribute that makes a good father that goes to make a good leader. The adhesive force that results in a nation is termed nationalism. It is a form of social mind that pervades a whole group of people.

When animals get together for hunting, like a pack of wolves, their purpose is aggression, and their motive selfish. The damage done by such a pack may be wanton and the behaviour of the pack will be far more ferocious than the total ferocity of the units composing the pack. In the same way, amongst human beings nationalism may form the dynamic force for aggression and exploitation to satisfy their own selfish greed. In this we find the worst manifestation of human nature, and the ethical standard of a nation urged to action by the type of what may be called Functional Nationalism is, as a rule, much lower than the standards of the individuals forming the nation. The western nations of the present day are labouring under the grip of such a degrading nationalism as this. Europe has always peopled hunters and fishers, and their present nationalism discloses the origin of the purpose for which they have clung together. The contribution of such a nationalism to International affairs is strife, dissension and discord. It is this type of Nationalism that Poet Rabindranath has in mind when he observes: "The political civilisation of the west is always watchful to keep the aliens at bay or to exterminate them. It is carnivorous and cannibalistic in its tendencies, it feeds upon the resources of other people and tries to swallow their whole future," and feels that "the spirit of conflict and conquest is at the origin and in the centre of western nationalism." This insular and virulent type of Nationalism has set nation against nation and has lowered man below the level of brute beasts. It has directed Science into producing poison gas and inventing methods of wholesale murder, and has degraded God-given talents to gratify its insatiable rapacity. As the poet puts it: "The vital ambition of the present civilization of Europe is to have the exclusive possession of the devil." The individuals composing the nation as a rule stand aghast at the achievements of their own nation when they stop to reflect on the results. Such a functional nationalism which is motivated by greed and selfishness is indeed a curse to humanity.

We find some animals get together, not because they are engaged in the same venture on formation function, but because they belong to the same family, as in the case of a herd of elephants, or a flock of sheep. We have a similar brotherly spirit manifested in a form of nationalism, which we may call Ethnic Nationalism. This is also somewhat exclusive, but it is not based on selfishness and usually the binding factor is a common culture, religion, or birth. The best example of this type of social mind is seen amongst the followers of the Prophet of Mecca. Their fellow-feelings are not circumscribed by caste or colour and transcends geographic and economic barriers. Prince and peasant, black and white, Turk or Negro, all form an universal brotherhood within the pale of one religion. Their love is all comprehensive within its boundaries; outside the religion the brotherhood refuses to function and forms the limitation to its approaching an internationalism which is so eagerly sought for.

Then we come to the third type of Nationalism, which does not seek to gain by another's loss, has no predatory designs and is not limited in its operation. It seeks to protect itself not by violence but by binding its constituents by regulations. This type we may call Constitutional Nationalism. It is to be mostly found in Asiatic countries. In our own land, the binding factor has expressed itself in the caste system and in the rules and regulations attached to everyday conduct. Japan has abandoned this constitutional nationalism and has adopted the functional nationalism and so has been recognised as one of the Powers of Destruction to-day. Baron Hayashi, formerly Japanese ambassador at Paris, says: "As long as we were engaged in peaceful pursuit of arts and literature, we were despised as barbarians, but as soon as we learnt the use of arms and the art of killing, we were hailed as civilised and as equal of the Europeans."

Constitutional nationalism, like the banks of a river keeps and conserves the life-giving streams. Indian Nationalism to-day distributes the *charkha,* while western nationalism is carrying out experiments in the manufacture of Poison Gas. In ancient India, it was this type of nationalism that discouraged competition and formed joint families and trade gilds to provide for all.

A nation that is consolidated by constitutional nationalism need fear no disintegrating forces. It is due to this power that our society has withstood the storms and ravages of centuries, while Babylonian and Egyptian civilizations have succumbed. Having composed itself, the nation expands and is prepared to receive anybody. India received all foreigners with open arms. Such nationalism is not exclusive, but, if fully developed, will result in an international life which will usher in peace and brotherhood. As C. R. Das said: "If Indian Nationalism is to live, it cannot afford to isolate itself from other nations. We must have a home before we can receive a guest. She (India) must vibrate with national life, and then we can talk of the union of the two civilizations." Gandhiji says: "Indian Nationalism is not exclusive, nor aggressive, nor destructive. It is health-giving, religious, and therefore humanitarian. India must learn to live before she can aspire to die for humanity." We find it is this type of nationalism that impels Gandhiji, who said before embarking for England, in his parting message: "To me service of India is identical with the service of humanity." Nationalism like charity begins at home, but if it stops there, it is not worth much. It has to reach out to all sorts and kinds of men all over the globe. We cannot seek to develop an international mind without a foundation of a strong national mind, "for he that loveth not his brother whom he hath seen, how can he love God, whom he hath not seen?" Development of such a nationalism, not based on selfish greed or avarice, nor limited to any particular belief or creed, but one that is sure of its own grounds, and reaches out to the rest of humanity, can only hasten the day when all peoples will beat their swords into ploughshares and their spears into pruning hooks: "Nations shall not lift up sword against nations, neither shall they learn war any more. But they shall sit every man under his vine and under his fig tree ; and none shall make them afraid," and there will be "Glory to God in the highest, and on earth Peace, Goodwill towards men."

SABARMATI, AHMEDABAD

JAGADISAN C. KUMARAPPA

RABINDANATH Tagore, grand Cygne de l'Orient et de l'Humanité, Prophéte visionnaire et Chanteur passionné de l' Unité et de la Réalisation, Etoile douce qui veille sur le monde tumultueux et sombre, Grand Ame qui s'accorde avec la musique grandiose, Mystique de l'Univers sans fond, ainsi qu'avec celle des appels tatonnants des lârmes cachées dans les êtres les plus humbles, sage Annonciateur de l'harmonie naissante d'un avenir plus vaste, Sculpteur patient et pieux des âmes enfantines qui doivent être les concitoyens des temps nouveaux. O Poète de l'eternel printemps de l'âme, par qui la raison rêve et le rêve se cristallise intellectuellement en poesie et en action, en qui se reconcilent fraternellement les ideaux vivants de l'Orient et de l'Occident, O Poète-Homme, Rabindranath Tagore, votre voix est parvenue, et parvient, au-dessus des mûrs aveugles de haines, de prejuges, toujours melodieuse, puissante, parfois tremblante par suite de la tristesse paternelle, jusqu'à nos cœurs ; en vous remerciant, ils vous félicitent, du cœur de notre pays de l'Extrême-Orient, qui gardent heureusement en souvenir votre figure lumineuse et meditative.

TOSHIHIKO KATAYAMA

RABINDRANATH TAGORE

Många år ha förgått sedan den dagen,
då jag hörde Rabindranath Tagore säga tack för Nobelpriset,
men jag bevarar ännu minnet av en högrest gestalt,
draperad i några löst fallande våder av grått siden
och av ett ansikte av en underbar höghet.
När man såg det bredvid andra ansikten
tycktes det utmejslat med vida större omsorg och skicklighet.
En ande gegåvad med en mera vaken skönhetstörst
eller kanske med en tydligare hågkomst av det himmelska urhemmet,
än som vanligen beskäres oss,
hade format denna kropp och detta huvud till sin jordiska boning.

Jag såg honom stå i en kateder i en vanlig föreläsningssal.
Högtidsklädda herrar och damer fyllde den till sista plats,
överallt mötte man bekanta ansikten,
inte ett ögonblick kunde man glömma,
att man befann sig i Stockholm, i gamla Sverige.
Föreläsaren själv talade engelska, en tydlig lättbegriplig engelska,
inte ett ögonblick kunde man glömma,
att man befann sig i Europa, i Västerlandet.
Men den främmande skalden började tala till oss,
och med några få enkla ord
flyttade han oss bort till ett fjärran underland.
Jag vågar inte säga om det just var Indien.
Men det var ett land, som han bar i sitt hjärta.
Ett land av frid,
ett land utan oro, utan ärelysten strävan,
utan jäktande maktbegär.
En himmelsk ro omgav oss,

vi vandrade utmed stränderna av längsamt glidande floder,
i ljumma stjärnenätter lyssnade vi till milda visdomsord,
och av sköna, lyckliga människor omskapades tillvaron
till välvilja och poesi.

När den dag kommer, den avlägsna, den efterlängtade,
d*a* livet har n*a*tt sitt m*a*l, d*a* den stora harmonien är uppn*a*dd,
och den gamla paradisdrömmen har blivit till verklighet,
d*a* skola den tidens människor p*a*minna sig den indiske siaren
s*a*som en bland dem, som förberedde den goda framtiden,
s*a*som en bland dem som i osvikligt hopp
utrotade hatets giftblomster
för att i deras ställe uts*a* kärleksäpplen och fredsrosor.

STOCKHOLM SELMA LAGERLOF

TO TAGORE

I find it difficult to express through a foreign medium all I want to say about his great personality. India through him has given proof to the world, of the greatness of her religion, her philosophy and of her spiritual heritage.

Tagore was not educated in any of the modern Universities, in fact, he had a dislike, when a youth, to modern schools and we may say that he educated himself in the Nature's school. True to the spirit and teachings of Hinduism, he has been advocating absolute equality, equal rights and equal opportunities between the sexes and his speeches and writings breathe a deep veneration and love for womankind. He believes that India's redemption, nay, the redemption of the whole world from greed and quarrels and the establishment of international Peace and Goodwill is possible only with the help of a refined, pure and devoted womanhood. Women of the East and the West look upon him as their friend, champion and *Guru*. Humanity is indebted to him for bringing nations and creeds together through his school of international culture and through his song of love.

May he be blessed with a sound health so that he may see India free and happy.

MADRAS MUTHULAKSHMI

GITANJALI

WHEN I turn the pages of my *Gitanjali,* fragrant memories awake.

One of them brings to my mind a centre of fashion on the Riviera some years before the War. The quality of its beauty was elusive, only to be discovered in serenity by the spirit of discernment, rare in the cosmopolitan, over-stimulated crowd of idle-rich. So I took as my companion when I walked, the Poet's volume. And now for me these two are inextricably mingled, the golden sunlight of the South and his verse.

Another takes me back to a Bengali garden after sunset. I had been sitting indoors alone with the *Gitanjali,* but the garden called me and I roamed out into the scented night, and found the darkness illumined by fireflies, the first I had seen during my brief stay in India. Thenceforward the Poet's lines have never been far from my mind: 'Thou hast pressed the signet on every fleeting moment.'

By contrast, the scene is a ramshackle old hall in a back street in East London on a Sunday night. People from adjoining courts and alleys have gathered together, men and girls from adjacent factories, mothers from over-crowded one-roomed homes, teachers, a musician or two and some intellectuals. They are in dead earnest, these pale, eager-eyed men and women met together for worship. They are realists. They know the desperate need the world is in. They know the snares of poverty and of power. They have learnt how soon the most trusted leader may desert his people, betray his trust, forsake the way of the Cross; the handful of silver may be disguised now-a-days, exchanged for commodities not so easily recognised as a bribe. They read together from the Gospels, they pray together in silence, and they study the Sermon on the Mount. Then they hear about the beggar who expected much from the visit of a king: 'I thought the luck of my life had come at last.' The king asks the beggar for alms, whereon the man, hiding his bitter disappointment as best he can, hands him a single grain of rice. But that night among the crusts in his begging bowl he finds a single grain of gold. 'I bitterly wept and wished that I had had the heart to give thee my all.' The Poet's story reinforces the truth the lowly worshippers have already learnt in the hard school of experience.

Together they repeat as a final prayer one of the Poet's 'Song Offerings': 'Life of my life, I would ever keep my body pure.' Line by line they pray, each lovely word making their aspiration more clear to their own minds. And as they return to their sunless homes, their lives are gladdened and enriched by the wisdom of the East.

KINGSLEY HALL, EAST END, LONDON — MURIEL LESTER

A great soul of an incomparably great nation.

NEW YORK — SINCLAIR LEWIS

Rabindranath Tagore's life has been a noble example of disinterested service to high ideals. I hope he will long be spared to see the new India he has so largely helped to make self-conscious both free and happy.

LONDON — HAROLD J. LASKI

TAGORE—WHAT HE MEANS TO ME

A touch of the Infinite—an echo from the deeps of Being, an illumined presence, draped in flowing lines. As he walks, one feels the rhythm of his cosmic union with the Unseen Mysteries of the Silent Things.

He is the human Stradivarius for Gods to play upon. Tones of the master chords sing—we listen wrapt in wonder—we become singers too.

His poems make one feel as though one were To-morrow, with a better, holier growth.

His prose heals the wounds that ache and makes them whole again.

Once upon a time the writer, a strange child of tender years, found fear within the walls of the school-room in the West. Later, as she read of Santiniketan, far away in the Eastern clime, she felt comforted to know someone—somewhere—had suffered as she, and in suffering, had builded a School where little men and women could find a Master-Comrade, bending the delicate twigs towards the Sun. These little green shoots are the men and women of to-day—they are the torch-bearers out of the Greater India of the past to a Still Greater India, loosening her bleeding chains. These are the Sons and Daughters, walking the Way with the Master. He with his song helps—when pain and grief and questioning come—to find the way back—over There—beyond the Here.

Master, Thou art the Perfect Instrument,—sounding the plaintive notes . . . it is the call to Brotherhood—the hymn of "Mother India and the World", together, walking together.

Sometimes I cry out, are Gods like this—this Presence all in white?

NEW YORK ALMA L. LISSBERGER

FRIEND OF US ALL:

THIS is your seventieth year. It is also the hundredth year of electric power, which we chiefly owe to Faraday. To speak of his discovery of electro-magnetic induction is to speak plain prose, but we who have faith in the ultimate unity of poetry and science will celebrate Tagore in May and Faraday in September. He is a great gift to the East, you are a great gift to the West, and both are a great gift to the World.

He revealed depths of unused force, and you have revealed depths of unused love. He cut lines of physical power and let it flow into our hands; you have cut lines that divided men and let love flow into our hearts. By dynamo and cable he has brought men nearer together, but you have reminded us that men who hate each other are better sundered. He began the net-work of obedient fire that now flashes round the earth ; you have given us the sanest words to send with utmost speed. He could not give us a smaller world without increasing the dangers of haste, but you have given us hope of world-wide sobriety. He increased material wealth incredibly, but would take no penny of it for himself, and sadly summed up the faults of men in three weighty words: *deficiency of judgment*. You have shown us that respect for persons goes far to remove that deficiency, and convinced us that reverence for persons renders judgment sound.

It was Faraday who first divined that there is a unit charge of electricity. Though this was not discovered and measured till you were nearly fifty years of age, we are now beginning to think in terms of this minutest charge, and to find beauty where once we found but means to satisfy our greed. We lust far less for gold when we find the tissue of earth all golden. To put it with the utmost literalness, the actual tissue of earth is not unlike the tissue of the midnight sky, thick sown with stars.

It was Faraday too who framed the first equation of organic chemistry, which gives us at least the means of making life happier for all men, and now we are beginning to read organisms in terms of electric units, till the human body itself seems but a starry pattern within the starry whole. Here again poetry and science unite in rendering it difficult to separate men from nature or from each other.

But never did Faraday pretend to solve by chemistry or by electricity the inviolable secret of personality, and never did he question the love of the Person in whom all persons may find their peace. No man would have been gladder than Faraday to echo these words of yours: "It costs me nothing to feel that I am ; it is no burden to me. And yet if the mental, physical, chemical, and other innumerable facts concerning all branches of knowledge which have united in myself could be broken up, they would prove endless. It is some untold mystery of unity in me, that has the simplicity of the infinite and reduces the immense mass of multitude to a single point."

If such words can thrill and comfort those who recognize the limits of scientific method—words written in a language not your own and in the lowly harmony of prose—how piercing sweet to native ears must be your native songs! If thus you lift a burden in the West, who shall measure the burdens that you lift in the East! And if in the West we dimly discern the beauty of the vision you unfold, how brightly in the East must you reveal the vision of sunrise! May you live long! We wish ourselves many happy returns of your day and yourself, for wherever you go on earth you make life easier to live, and sweeter.

Ever yours,

EDWIN HERBERT LEWIS

LEWIS INSTITUTE, CHICAGO

AS A BOY

A TAGORE

JE considère certains pages du *Gitâñjali* comme les plus hautes, les plus profondes, les plus divinement humaines qu'on ait écrites jusqu'à ce jour.

BRUXELLES MAURICE MAETERLINCK

RABINDRANATH TAGORE

NIE werde ich den Tag vergessen, wo mein Mann mir *Gitanjali* brachte und wir die ersten Lieder zusammen lasen. Es war wie ein Nachhausekommen—ich weiss kein besseres Wort für das beglückende seelische Heimatsgefühl,—das mich beim Lesen dieser herrlichen Psalmen durchströmte. Ein köstliches Geschenk nach dem andern kam von ihm zu uns herüber: die glutvollen und doch lilienreinen Liebeslieder des Gärtners, die zarten und tiefen Gedichte vom Kinde, und dann die weisheitsvollen Sammlungen der im Auslande gehaltenen Reden aus der Zeit des grossen Krieges. Da war es, dass Rabindranath Tagore ganz zum Zentrum meines Lebens wurde, dass ich meine Lehrarbeit niederlegte und mir die Übertragung und Verbreitung seiner Werke in Deutschland zur Lebensaufgabe machte. Denn diese Werke bergen in sich die Erfüllung der tiefsten Sehnsucht der deutschem Volksseele,—der Menschenseele überhaupt.

Rabindranath Tagore, Du begnadetes Gefäss Gottes, Du goldenes Buch der Weisheit und Schönheit, das Gott den Menschen schenkte, Du tausendfach Gesegneter, sei gegrüsst.

WANDSBEK, GERMANY HELENE MEYER-FRANCK

RABINDRANATH AND THE PHILOSOPHY OF PERSONALITY

THE present age is witnessing a gigantic struggle between personality and machine. The growth of Science and the industrial civilization resting upon it have led to an apotheosis of the purely mechanical aspect of life. This struggle has been described by Rabindranath as the struggle between Jack and the Giant. Only the Giant here is not a "gigantic person but a multitude of men turned into a gigantic system". The tragedy that we are daily witnessing to-day is the tragedy of a vast soulless organization slowly eating up all humanity within us.

The present Western civilization appears to us to be an embodiment of this soulless organization. Its very bigness is its most dangerous feature. Its impersonal character is precisely what makes it so awful. Its abstract nature and its aloofness smother all our humanity. The view that we obtain of its is "that of a Titanic power with an endless curiosity to analyze and know, but without sympathy to understand; with numberless aims to cover and acquire, but no serenity of soul to realize and enjoy."

It is sad to reflect that this soulless civilization is the creation of Science. For Science in its inception is not soulless. It is, on the contrary, distinctly spiritual in its aim. For it is animated by nothing else than a pure love of truth, the most spiritual of all the possessions of man. The motive force which drove a Galileo or Newton is essentially the same as that which moved a Buddha or a Shankara.

Science as Science, therefore, is not to be condemned. If Science is to be suppressed, then the noblest activity of man, the disinterested service of truth, will disappear. No poet or philosopher worth the name has ever proposed any such thing. Rabindranath will be the last person on earth to be a party to it. Yet nobody can be blind to the evils which the progress of Science has brought in its train. They are so palpable that nobody can ignore them. Everyday we feel them, every hour we realize their presence.

The fault of Science, then, does not lie in its aim but in its method. Its method is the impersonal method of abstraction. It has carried the principle of disinterestedness to such an extent that it has banished all human interest out of its sphere. Its method has coloured (or rather discoloured) its conception of truth. For truth comes out of its hands a mere skeleton, a spectral form which has carefully left all its substance behind.

If modern civilization, therefore, is to be saved, the impersonal method of Science must give way to one in which Personality plays the dominant part. If human culture is not to come to an end, then the force of personality must be allowed to break through the barriers of abstraction.

This is the message of Rabindranath. This is also the substance of Bergson's teaching. This is, moreover, the central theme of the philosophy of values, as well as of that movement led by Alfred Fouillée and Emile Boutroux and known as the

French philosophy of freedom. Rabindranath has joined here all the great constructive forces that are ranged against the impersonal worship of abstract symbols. If the world is to be made safe for humanity, it is essential that Personality and not abstract mechanism should be made the dominant note of civilization.

This is the substance of Tagore's protest against the soulless mechanical civilization of the present age, as well as of his vindication of the philosophy of Life, as we find it in the *Cycle of Spring* and the *Crane*. In the *Cycle of Spring* the principle of Life appears as the Spirit of Youth which makes short work of disease and decrepitude. It appears as the maddening south wind, the herald of youth and joy:

> O South Wind, the Wanderer, come and rock me,
> Rouse me into the rapture of new leaves.
> I am the wayside bamboo tree, waiting for your breath
> To tingle life into my branches.

It is the fire of April which

> . . . . . . leaps from forest to forest,
> Flashing up in leaves and flowers,
> from all nooks and corners.

It is the "rushing river as it runs splashing from its mountain cave".

"Haven't you noticed the detachment of the rushing river, as it runs splashing from its mountain cave? It gives itself away so swiftly, and only thus it finds itself. What is never-changing, for the river, is the desert sand, where it loses its course."

The play ends with the triumph of life, with the victory of youth over old age:

> The Song of Burdens dropped.
> Do you own defeat at the hand of Youth?
> Yes.
> Have you met at last the ageless Old,
> Who ever grows new?
> Yes.
> Have you come out of the walls that crumble
> and bury those whom they shelter?
> Yes.

(*Another group sings*):

> Do you own defeat at the hands of life?
> Yes.
> Have you passed through death to stand
> at last face to face with the Deathless?
> Yes.
> Have you dealt the blow to the demon dust
> that swallows your City Immortal?
> Yes.

And the closing words of the last scene of the play are perhaps the most glorious vindication of Youth and Life that exists in any literature.

April is awake,
Life's shoreless sea
  is heaving in the sun before you.
All the losses are lost,
  and death is drowned in its waves,
Plunge into the deep without fear,
  with the gladness of April in your heart.

In the *Crane* the Spirit of Life becomes definitely the Vital Urge which is the underlying reality not only of human nature but of the whole universe. Its nature is best represented by a ceaselessly flowing river:—

O river, vast and free,
  Thy viewless waters rush and sweep,
  Resistless, deep,
  In silence ceaselessly.
The great void shivers at thy fierce and formless speed.
  The dash terrific of thy currents breed
  Glittering foam in heaps and clustered rings
    That live as Things;
  Life bursts in dazzling gleams, in coloured streak and spark,
    Through the hurrying dark.
  On whirling eddies' edge are spun,
  Like bubbles, moon and star and sun.
  O mighty Amazon, O Titan dame,
  The wordless cadence of thy being
  Is thine own journeying
  Without an end, without an aim

And just as Bergson says that Matter arises as soon as the movement of life is checked, so the poet says that as soon as the flow of the river is checked, there arises a "mountain-heap of things":

If in a moment's mood
    Of lassitude
Thou stoppest on thy path,
The Universe, in sudden wrath,
Would bulk gigantic with its mountain heap of things.

In the *Waterfall* the conflict of the Universe becomes more definitely the struggle between life and mechanism. The engineer Vibhuti wants to curb the free flow of the river by erecting embankments, and the people destroy the embankments and allow the river to reassert itself. Vibhuti had to bow before the Spirit of Life: mechanism had to retreat before the triumphant march of the vital spirit.

It is, however, in the *Red Oleanders* that the Vital Urge takes the distinct form of Personality. The struggle depicted here is the struggle between personality and machine. Nandini, the heroine, represents concrete personality, and there is ranged against her the abstraction called industrial civilization, represented by the King. It is significant that the King is described as a Voice, for he is nothing but a bare abstraction. The theme of the drama, as the poet himself has described it, is as follows: "Nandini, the heroine, represents a concrete personality. She is pursued by the abstraction, known as the King." "Nandini is a real woman who knows that wealth and power are *maya,* and that the highest expression of it is in love, which she manifests in this play in her love for Ranjan. But love-ties are ruthlessly molested by megalomaniac ambition, while an acquisitive intellect plies its psychological curiosity, probing into the elusive mystery of love through vivisection."

But Personality in its most concrete form is here conceived as feminine. As the poet says: "This personality—the divine essence of the infinite in the vessel of the finite—has its last treasure-house in woman's heart." Here the poet comes very close to the conception of Goethe, who similarly speaks of the guiding principle of the universe as feminine: "Das Ewig-Weibliche zieht uns hienan." The poet believes that the pervading influence of woman will some day restore the human to the desolated world of man. "The joy of this faith," he says, "has inspired me to pour all my heart into painting against the background of black shadows—the nightmere of a devil's temptation—the portrait of Nandini as the bearer of the message of reality, the saviour through death."

It is significant that the poet believes that in the heart of mechanism there is installed a power that can emancipate us from mechanism. He has compared mechanism to a tired mountain. There is a trepidation within, a slowly moving process of disintegration, as a result of which the gigantic mountain will gradually crumble down and slip into the valley. This is how Personality will re-assert itself. Mechanism, therefore, is a temporary eclipse of Personality and will disappear before the incoming tide of Personality.

The parallelism here between the poet's thought and that of Bergson is remarkable. Bergson believes that it is when the Life-force suffers a check that mechanism makes its appearance. Mechanism, however, disappears again with the restoration of the Life-force. It, therefore, represents only a temporary slowing down or retardation of the Vital Urge.—Why the Vital Urge should suffer a retardation, even of a temporary nature, has not, however, been sufficiently well explained by Bergson. In place of explanations he has only given us illustrations. One illustration which he has given is that of a vase from which jets of vapour come out, which, however, gradually condense and come down in the form of minute water-particles. In a similar manner, he says, the movement of life, after proceeding for some time, slows down and ultimately is reversed.

It is in this faith in the ultimate triumph of Personality that the mysticism of Rabindranath lies. The central idea of this mysticism which runs through the plays, *Post Office, King of the Dark Chamber, Cycle of Spring, Waterfall* and *Red Oleanders* is that there is an irresistible force shaping the course of the world, fighting and conquering mechanism. To the rule of law, which apparently seems to be the last word of Science, there is opposed a force which, though invisible, is gigantic. This force is the force of Personality. Science tries to crush it, but it refuses to be crushed.

Nandini. What is it you see in me?

Voice. The dance rhythm of the All.

Nandini. I do not understand.

Voice. The rhythm that lightens the enormous weight of matter. To that rhythm the bands of stars and planets go about dancing from sky to sky, like so many minstrel boys. It is that rhythm, Nandini, that makes you so simple, so perfect.

This force of Personality strikes at the very root of soulless mechanism. Hence the desperate efforts of the latter to smother Personality.

Voice. The hidden mystery of life, wrenched away by me, bewails its torn ties. To get fire from a tree you have to burn it. Nandini, there is fire within you, too, red fire. One day I shall burn you and extract that also.

Nandini. Oh, you are cruel!

Voice. I must either gather or scatter. I can feel no pity for what I do not get. Breaking is a fierce kind of getting."

"Breaking is a fierce kind of getting." It is the desperation of autocratic power when it is haunted by a sense of its weakness.

In this struggle of mechanised autocracy with Personality, the latter triumphs. Autocracy is from the beginning conscious of its emptiness. Thus the Voice says to Nandini: "I, who am a desert, stretch out my hand to you, a tiny blade of grass, and cry: 'I am parched, I am bare, I am weary.'" The very wealth of natural resources reveals their essential hollowness. The King is fully conscious that in spite of his absolute power, or rather on account of it, there is lurking within him an essential weakness.

Voice. All I possess is so much dead weight. No increase of gold can create a particle of a touchstone, no increase of power can ever come up to youth.

Again—

Voice. Shall I explain? Underground there are blocks of stone, iron, gold—there you have the image of strength. On the surface grows the grass, the flower blossoms—there you have the play of magic. I can extract gold from the fearsome depths of secrecy, but to wrest that magic from the near at hand I fail.

On the other hand, Nandini is fully conscious of her strength. When asked by the King whether she is not afraid of him, she replies with an emphatic "No."

The iron fortress of autocracy falls like a house of cards at the very touch of Personality. The King himself goes out in quest of the "Secret of Life" and hears the call of Nandini. The body of Ranjan is found lying on the road. And there is found the red streak which is the marriage tie of Nandini and Ranjan. And in the dust lies Nandini's wristlet of red oleanders. What a union and what a death is this! It is in this tragic manner that the life-stream bursts through the network of rules.

This tragedy is the tragedy of Life. The keynote of Life is not sacrifice but conquest. This is why Fichte said that the world is not given but surrendered ("Die Welt ist nicht gegeben, sondern auf-gegeben"). There can be no truce with the reign of law. What is necessary is a root-and-branch work that will destroy the whole machinery of soulless rules. This eternal conflict between Life and dead rules is the source of all movement. You may call it original evil if you like, but it is the fundamental motive force of the universe.

In his Hibbert lectures on *The Religion of Man,* the poet has shown the same principle of Personality in its creative aspect, as the guiding thread of human evolution. The evolution of Man is the evolution of creative Personality. Man alone has the courage of standing against the biological laws. His erect posture itself is an adventure. When every possible biological advantage was on the side of his following the orthodox method of walking on all fours, he chose a new method of progression for himself. This is his first great experiment and the whole of his subsequent evolution is a continuous series of experiments in breaking established rules. It is here that his Personality reveals itself. As human evolution, however, hardens into civilization, the elastic force of Personality is more or less obscured by the artificial standards that civilization sets up. It is then that human tragedy begins. Our real tragedy, therefore, lies not "in the risk of our material security but in the obscuration of Man himself in the human world."

Oswald Spengler also in his celebrated book, *The Decline of the West,* speaks of the hardening of culture into civilization. When culture loses its vitality, when it stiffens into rigid forms, it passes into civilization. Civilization, therefore, is a diseased or degenerate form of culture. Rabindranath's protest against the tendencies of modern civilization is quite as strong as that of Spengler. He has, however, faith in the ultimate triumph of Personality over Science. Science will lead slowly but steadily to its own self-redemption. This is what he means when in the *Red Oleanders* he compares the present mechanical civilization to a tired mountain. The present civilization is a necessary preparation for a higher civilization, resting upon Creative Personality. Moreover, with all its faults, the poet believes that the present age is better than the ages that have preceded it. He would, therefore, be the last person to raise the cry: "Back to the mediæval ages."

THE UNIVERSITY, BENARES SISIR KUMAR MAITRA

DAS BUNTE KLEID

NICHT, wie vorgesehen, zu den Erntearbeiten, sondern schom zur Nacht des Frühjahrsvollmonds kehrten die Lea-Söhne Hals über Kopf von den Weiden Schekems nach Hebron zurück. Sie kamen angeblich, um das Pesach-Schaf mit dem Vater zu essen und mit ihm den Mond zu beobachten, in Wirklichkeit aber, weil sie eine aufregende, alle Brüder nahe angehende Nachricht empfangen hatten, von deren Wahrheit sie sich unbedingt sofort an Ort und Stelle mit eigenen Augen überzeugen mussten, ob nun etwas daran zu ändern war order nicht. Die Sache war dermassen wichtig und erschreckend, dass die Söhne der Mägde nichts Eiligeres zu tun gehabt hatten, als einen der Ihren abzuordnen und ihm die viertägige Reise von Hebron nach Schekem zuzumuten, nur damit er den Fernen die Kunde bringe. Selbstverständlich hatte man Naphtali, den Geläufigen, mit der Botschaft betraut. Im Grunde war es, die Schnelligkeit angehend, ganz gleichgültig, wer reiste. Auch Naphtali ritt zu Esel, und ob ein Paar langer oder kurzer Beine an den Seiten des Esels herunterhingen, machte genau genommen nichts aus: der Weg nahm jedenfalls ungefähr vier Tage in Anspruch. Aber Naphtali, Bilhas Sohn, war es nun einmal, mit dessen Person die Vorstellung der Geläufigkeit verbunden war; die Rolle des Boten war nach feststehender Übereinkunft die seine; und da auch seine Zunge geläufig war, so traf schon zu, dass wenigstens im letzten Augenblick die Brüder durch ihn den Sachverhalt etwas schneller erfahren würden, als durch einen anderen.

Was war geschehen? Jaakob hatte dem Joseph ein Geschenk gemacht.

Das war nichts Neues. Dem "Lamm", dem "Reis", dem "Himmelsknaben", dem "Sohn der Jungfrau", oder wie die eigensinnig gefühlvollen väterlichen Bezeichnungen für den Steineleser nun lauteten, war von jeher unter der Hand an Sondergaben und zärtlichen Aufmerksamkeiten, an hübschen Töpferstücken, Huldsteinen, Purpurschnüren, Skarabäen dies und jenes zugekommen, was dann die Brüder mit finsteren Brauen in seinem lässigen Besitz sahen, und um was sie sich verkürzt fanden; an Ungerechtigkeit, eine grundsätzliche und fast lehrhaft betonte Ungerechtigkeit, hatten sie Musse gehabt, sich zu gewöhnen. Dies aber war ein Geschenk von erschreckender Art und eines, wie zu befürchten stand, entscheidenden Sinnes; es bedeutete einen Stoss vor den Kopf für sie alle.

Hier ist der Hergang. Es war Zeltwetter, die Spätregen waren in Gang gekommen. Jaakob hatte sich nachmittags in sein "härenes Haus" zurückgezogen, dessen verfilztes Gewebe, schwarz, aus Ziegenhaar, über feste Stangen gespannt und mit starken Seilen an den gerammten Pflöcken befestigt, vollkommenen und sicheren Schutz vor der Segensnässe bot. Es war das grösste der ziemlich weit verteilten Siedlung, und als reicher Mann, der darauf hielt, den Frauen ein eigenes Obdach zu bieten, bewohnte der Herr es allein, obgleich es durch ein an den mittleren Pfählen

AS A STUDENT IN LONDON

von vorn nach hinten hindurchgezogenes Gehänge in zwei Räume geteilt war. Der eine diente als Privat-Magazin und Vorratskammer: Kamel-Sättel und Taschen, unbenutzte Teppiche in gerolltem und zusammengelegten Zustande, Handmühlen und anderes Gerät lagen umher, und Schläuche mit Getreide, Butter, Trinkwasser und aus eingeweichten Datteln gekeltertem Palmwein waren aufgehängt.

Die andere Abteilung war der Wohnraum des Gesegneten und zeigte im Verhältnis zu der halbbeduinisch lockeren Lebensform, an der er festhielt, viel Wohnlichkeit. Jaakob brauchte diese. Seine Ablehnung dauernder Bindung durchs Städtische hinderte nicht, dass er einigen Behagens bedurfte, wenn er sich zu Betrachtung und denkerischer Gottesarbeit vor der Welt in sein Eigenstes zurückzog. Auf der Vorderseite in Manneshöhe offen, war der Boden des Gemachs mit Filz und darüber noch mit Teppichen in Buntwirkarbeit warm bedeckt, von denen andere sogar die Wandgehänge überkleideten. Ein Bettlager, mit Decken und Kissen belegt, aus Zedernholz, stand auf erzenen Füssen, im Hintergrunde. Mehrere Tonlampen auf verzierten Untersätzen, flache schalen mit Schnauzen für die Dochte, brannten hier immer, denn armselig und einem Gesegneten nicht anständig wäre es gewesen, im Dunklen zu schlafen, und auch bei Tage unterhielt die Bedienung immer das Öl, damit nicht eine Redensart, die schlimmen Untersinn führte, auch nur im eigentlichen Sinn anwendbar würde und man nicht sagen könne, Jaakobs Lampe sei erloschen. Bemalte Henkelkrüge aus Kalkstein standen auf dem flachen Deckel einer Truhe aus Sykomoren-Holz, deren Wände mit blau glasierten Toneinlagen geschmückt waren. Der Deckel einer anderen geschnitzten und beschriebenen Truhe auf hohen Beinen dagegen war gewölbt. Es fehlte nicht an einem glühenden Kohlenbecken im Winkel, da Jaakob zum Frösteln neigte. Stuhlhocker waren vorhanden, dienten aber selten zum Sitzen, sondern vielmehr zum Abstellen von Gebrauchsdingen. Ein kleiner Räucherturm stand auf einem, aus dessen fensterartigen Öffnungen feine, nach Zimmet, Styrax-Gummi und Galbanum duftende Rauchwolken hervorkräuselten; ein anderer trug einen Gegenstand, der von der Wohlhabenheit des Besitzers zeugte: ein wertvolles kunstgewerbliches Stück phönizischer Herkunft, golden, eine flache Schale auf zierlichem Untergestell, das dort, wo man es mit der Hand anfasste, eine musizierende Frauenfigur zeigte.

Jaakob selbst sass mit Joseph in der Nähe des Eingangs auf Polstern an einem niedrigen Taburett, auf dessen gravierter Bronzeplatte das Brettspiel aufgeschlagen war. Er hatte den Sohn zu diesem Zeitvertreib, bei dem früher Rahel seine Gegenspielerin gewesen war, zu sich gerufen. Draussen rauschte auf Ölbäume, Busch und Stein der Regen nieder, der nach Gottes Gnade dem Korn des Tales die Feuchtigkeit verlieh, die es brauchte, um die Sonne des Frühsommers bis zum Schnitt zu ertragen. Der Wind klapperte leicht mit den Holzringen am Zelttuch, an denen die Spannseile befestigt waren.

Joseph liess den Vater im Spiele gewinnen. Er war absichtlich ins Feld "Böser Blick" geraten und dadurch so in Rückstand und Nachteil gekommen, dass Jaakob zu seiner angenehmen Überraschung—denn er hatte mit grosser Unaufmerksamkeit gespielt—, ihn schliesslich schlug. Er gestand seine Zerstreutheit ein, und dass das Glück mehr Anteil an diesem Ende gehabt habe, als sein Scharfsinn.

"Wärest du nicht so zeitig zu Fall gekommen, Kind," sagte er, "so hätte ich notwendig unterliegen müssen, denn meine Gedanken schweiften ab, und ich habe zweifellos schwere Fehler begangen, du aber hast sinnreich gezogen und nichts versäumt, dein Missgeschick wieder gut zu machen. Deine Art zu spielen erinnert sehr an Mamis, die mich so oft in die Enge trieb. Sowohl ihre Art, beim Nachdenken den kleinen Finger zu beissen wie auch gewisse Listen und Kunstgriffe, die sie liebte, erkenne ich zu meiner Rührung bei dir weider."

"Was hilft's?" antwortete Joseph und reckte sich, indem er den Kopf zurücklegte, einen Arm zur Seite streckte und den anderen zur Schulter bog. "Der Ausgang spricht gegen mich. Da das Väterchen obsiegte bei zerstreuten Gedanken, wie wäre es dem Kind wohl ergangen, hätte es deine volle Aufmerksamkeit gegen sich gehabt? Der Gang wäre rasch zu Ende gewesen."

Jaakob lächelte. "Meine Erfahrung," sagte er, "ist die ältere und meine Schule die beste, denn schon als Knabe habe ich mit Jizchak gespielt, deinem Grossvater meinerseits, und später gar oft mit Laban, deinem Grossvater vonseiten der Lieblichen, im Lande Naharin, jenseits der Wasser, der ebenfalls ein Spieler von zäher Überlegung war."

Auch er hatte Jizchak und Laban mehr als einmal absichtlich gewinnen lassen, wenn es ihm um ihre gute Laune zu tun gewesen war, kam aber nicht darauf, dass nun Joseph es so gemacht haben könnte.

"Es ist wahr," fuhr er fort, "dass ich es heut habe fehlen lassen. Wiederholt überkam mich ein Sinnen, das mich den Stand der Steine vergessen liess, und siehe, es galt dem Fest, das sich nähert, und der Opfernacht, die herankommt, da wir das Schaf schlachten nach Sonnenuntergang und tauchen den Ysopbüschel ins Blut, um die Pfosten damit zu bestreichen, damit der Würger vorübergehe. Denn es ist die Nacht des Vorübergehens und der Verschonung um des Opfers willen, und ist das Blut an den Pfosten dem Umhergehenden eine Beschwichtigung und ein Zeichen, dass der Erstling geopfert ist zur Versöhnung und zum Ersatz für Menschen und Vieh, die es ihn zu würgen gelüstet. Darüber fiel ich mehrfach in Sinnen, denn der Mensch tut manches, und siehe, er weiss nicht, was er tut. Wüsste und bedächte er's aber, so möchte es sein, dass sich das Eingeweide ihm unwendete und ihm das Unterste zuoberst käme in Übelkeit, wie mir's mehrmals im Leben erging, nämlich zum zweitenmal, da ich erfuhr, dass Laban zu Sinear überm Prath einstmals sein erstgebornes Söhnchen geschlachtet habe als Darbringung und es in einer Kruke beigesetzt habe im Fundament zum Schutze seines Hauses. Meinst du aber, es hätte ihm Segen gebracht? Nein, sondern Unsegen, Fluch und Lähmung und wäre nicht ich gekommen und hätte ein wenig Leben verbreitet in Haus und Wirtschaft, so hätte alles in Trübsal gestockt, und nie wieder wäre er fruchtbar geworden in seinem Weibe Adina. Und doch hätte Laban das Söhnchen nicht eingemauert, wenn es nicht Altvorderen vor ihm Segen gebracht hätte in anderen Zeiten."

"Da sagst du es," antwortete Joseph, der die Hände im Nacken gefaltet hatte, "und machst mir klar, wie sich das begab. Laban handelte nach überständigem Brauch und beging schweren Fehler damit. Denn es ekelt den Herrn das Überständige, worüber er mit uns hinaus will und schon hinaus ist, und er verwirft's und verflucht's. Darum, hätte Laban sich auf den Herrn und auf die Zeiten verstanden, so hätte er an Stelle des Knäbleins ein Zicklein geschlachtet und mit dem Blute Schwelle und Pfosten bestrichen, so wäre er angenehm gewesen, und sein Rauch wäre gerade aufgestiegen gen Himmel."

"Da sagst nun du es wieder," erwiderte Jaakob, "und nimmst mir den Gedanken vorweg und das Wort vom Munde. Denn den Würger gelüstet's nicht nur nach dem Vieh, sondern auch nach des Menschen Blut, und nicht nur in Ansehung der Herde beschwichtigen wir seine Gier durch das Blut des Tiers an den Pfosten, sowie durch das Opfermahl, das wir abhalten gründlich und eilig bei der Nacht, damit bis zum Morgen nichts übrig bleibe vom Braten. Was für ein Braten ist das, wenn man's besinnt, und büsst wohl das Lamm nur für die Herde, da wir es schlachten? Was würden wir schlachten und essen, wenn wir töricht wären, wie Laban, und was ist geschlachtet worden und gegessen in unflätigen Zeiten? Wissen wir also, was wir festlich tun, wenn wir essen, und müsste uns nicht, wenn wir's bedächten, das Unterste zuoberst kommen, so dass wir erbrächen?"

"Lass uns tun und essen," sagte Joseph mit leichtsinnig hoher Stimme und schaukelte sich in seinen gefalteten Händen. "Brauch und Braten sind wohlschmeckend, und sind sie eine Lösung, so lösen auch wir uns fröhlich damit vom Unflat, indem wir uns auf den Herrn verstehen und auf die Zeiten! Siehe, da ist ein Baum," rief er und wies mit ausgestreckter Hand ins Innere des Zeltes, als wäre dort zu sehen, wovon er sprach, "prächtig in Stamm und Krone, von den Vätern gepflanzt zur Lust der Späten. Seine Wipfel regen sich funkelnd im Winde, da seine Wurzeln im Stein und Staube haften des Erdreichs, tief im Dunkeln. Weiss wohl auch der heitere Wipfel viel von der kotigen Wurzel? Nein, sondern ist mit dem Herrn hinausgekommen über sie, wiegt sich und denkt nicht ihrer. Also ist's meines Bedünkens mit Brauch und Unflat, und dass die fromme Sitte uns schmecke, bleibe das Unterste nur hübsch zuunterst."

"Lieblich, lieblich, dein Gleichnis," sprach Jaakob mit Kopfnicken und strich sich den Bart, indem er ihn von den Seiten zusammenfasste und ihn durch die hohle Hand streichen liess, "witzig und wohl erfunden! Das hindert nicht, dass notwendig bleibt das Sinnen, sowie das Sorgen und die Beunruhigung, die Abrams Teil waren und unser Teil sind je und je, damit wir uns lösen von dem, worüber der Herr hinaus will mit uns und vielleicht schon hinaus ist, das ist die Sorge. Sage doch an: Wer ist der Würger, und was ist sein Vorübergehen? Geht nicht der Mond in der Nacht des Festes voll und schön durch den Pass, der da ist der Nord-und Scheitelpunkt seines Weges, woselbst er sich wendet in seiner Fülle? Aber der Nordpunkt ist Nergals, des Mörders; sein ist die Nacht, Sin regiert sie für ihn, Sin ist Nergal bei diesem Fest, und der Würger, der vorübergeht, und den wir versöhnen, das ist der Rote."

"Offenbar," sagte Joseph. "Wir bedenken's kaum, doch er ist's."

"Dies ist die Beunruhigung," fuhr Jaakob fort, "die mich zerstreute beim Spiel. Denn es sind die Gestirne, die uns das Fest bestimmen, Mond und Roter, die die Vertauschung eingehen in dieser Nacht, und tritt dieser an jenes Stelle. Sollen wir aber den Gestirnen Kusshände werfen und ihre Geschichten feiern? Müssen wir uns nicht grämen um den Herrn und die Zeit, ob wir uns denn auch noch auf sie verstehen und uns nicht versündigen an beiden, da wir sie festhalten durch träge Gewohnheit beim Unflat, über den sie hinauswollen? Ich frage mich ernstlich, ob es nicht meine Sache wäre, unter den Unterweisungsbaum zu treten und die Leute zusammenzurufen, dass sie meine Sorgen vernähmen und anhörten meine Bedenken in Sachen des Festes Pesach."

"Mein Väterchen," sagte Joseph, indem er sich verbeugte und seine Hand neben dem Brett, das seine Niederlage zeigte, auf die Hand des Alten legte, "ist von allzu genauer Seele, man muss ihn bitten, sich davon nicht zur Übertreibung bewegen zu lassen und zur Zerstörung. Darf sich das Kind als befragt ansehen, so rät es, das Fest zu schonen und es nicht eifernd anzutasten um seiner Geschichten willen, für welche vielleicht mit der Zeit eine andere eintreten könnte, die du alsdann erzählst beim Bratenmahl: beispielsweise die Bewahrung Isaaks, die sehr passend wäre, oder aber wir warten ab in der Zeit, ob nicht Gott sich einmal durch eine grosse Errettung und Verschonung verherrliche an uns, — die legen wir dann dem Fest zugrunde als seine Geschichte und singen Jubellieder. Sprach der Törichte wohltuend?"

"Balsamisch," erwiderte Jaakob. "Sehr klug und tröstlich, was ich eben in dem Worte 'balsamisch' zusammenfasse. Denn du sprachst für den Brauch und zugleich für die Zukunft, das sei dir angerechnet zu Ehren. Und sprachst für ein Verharren, das dennoch ein Unterwegssein ist, darob lacht dir meine Seele zu, Joseph-el, du Reis aus zartestem Stamm, — lass dich küssen!"

Und er nahm Josephs schönen Kopf über dem Spielbrett zwischen seine Hände und küsste ihn, grundglücklich in seinem Besitz.

"Wenn ich nur wüsste," sagte Joseph, "woher mir Klugheit kommt zu dieser Stunde und der geringste Scharfsinn, der Weisheit meines Herrn damit zu begegnen im Gespräch! Sagtest du, deine Gedanken seien abgeschweift beim Spiel, so taten's, offen gestanden, meine nicht minder: Immer nach einer Seite schweiften sie von den Steinen weg, und die Elohim wissen, wie mir's gelang, mich auch nur so lange zu halten."

"Wohin denn, Kindchen, gingen deine Gedanken?"

"Ach", erwiderte der Junge, "du errätst es leicht. Ein Wort jückt mich im Ohre Tag und Nacht, das das Väterchen kürzlich zu mir sprach am Brunnen; das hat mir die Ruhe geraubt, so dass die Neugier mich plagt, wo ich gehe und stehe, denn es war ein Wort der Verheissung."

Jaakob errötete, und Joseph sah es. Es war eine leichte, rosige Röte, die in die feine Greisenhagerkeit seiner Wangen emporstieg, und seine Augen trübten sich in sanfter Verwirrung.

"Wie denn, es war nichts", sagte er abwehrend. "Umsonst macht das Kind sich Gedanken. Es war unbedeutend dahingesagt, ohne feste Meinung und Absicht. Schenke ich dir nicht dies und das, wann's das Herz mich heisst? Nun denn, einzig so war's gemeint, dass ich dir irgendein schmuckes Ding zu gelegener Stunde . . ."

"Nichtsda, nichtsda!" rief Joseph, sprang auf und umschlang den Vater. "Dieser Weise und Gute sagt nichts unbedeutend dahin, das wäre das Neueste! Als ob ich's ihm nicht angesehen hätte beim Sprechen klar und deutlich, dass er mitnichten ins Leere sprach, sondern ein Ding im Auge hatte, bestimmt und schön, nicht irgendeines, — ein Besonderes und Herrliches, und dachte mir's zu. Aber nicht zugedacht nur hast du mir's, sondern zugesagt und verheissen. Soll ich nicht wissen, was mein ist und was mich erwartet? Scheint es dir glaubhaft, ich könnte Ruhe finden und könnte dir Frieden geben, eh' ich's weiss?"

"Wie du mich drängst und bedrängst!" sagte der Alte in seiner Not. "Schüttle mich nicht und nimm die Hände doch von den läppchen meiner Ohren, dass es nicht aussieht, als sprängest du mit mir um! Wissen — du magst es wissen, warum nicht, ich sage dir's und gebe zu, dass ich Eines im Sinne hatte, nicht dies oder jenes. Höre denn, lass dich zu Boden! Weisst du von Rahels Ketônet passîm?"

"Ein Gewandstück von Mami? Etwa ein Festkleid? Ah, ich verstehe, willst du mir aus ihrem Kleide . . ."

"Höre, Joseph! Du verstehst nicht. Lass dich belehren. Da ich gedient um Rahel sieben Jahre, und der Tag herankam, dass ich sie empfangen sollte im Herrn, sprach Laban zu mir: 'Einen Schleier will ich ihr schenken, dass sich die Braut verschleiere und sich der Nana heilige und sei eine Geweihte. Längst habe ich,' sprach er, 'die Augendecke gekauft von einem Wandernden und sie in der Truhe verwahrt, denn sie ist kostbar. Einer Königstochter soll sie gehört haben vor Zeiten und soll gewesen sein das Jungfrauengewand eines Fürstenkindes, was da ist glaubhaft zu sagen, so kunstfertig wie das Gewirk bestickt ist über und über mit allerlei Zeichen der Götzen. Sie aber soll ihr Haupt darein hüllen und soll sein wie der Enitu eine und wie eine Himmelsbraut im Bettgemach des Turmes Etenemanki.' So oder ähnlich der Teufel zu mir. Und er log nicht mit diesen Worten, denn Rahel erhielt das Gewand, und war eine Pracht sondergleichen damit, da wir zur Hochzeit sassen, und ich küsste das Bild der Ischtar. Da ich aber der Braut die Blüte gereicht, hob ich ihr den Schleier, dass ich sie sähe mit sehenden Händen. Lea war's, die der Teufel listig hatte eingelassen ins Bettgemach, so dass ich nur meiner Meinung nach glücklich war, nicht aber in Wahrheit, — wer sollte nicht irre werden im Haupte, wenn er dahinein sich verliert, darum übergeh' ich's. Aber besonnen war ich im vermeintlichen Glück und legte gefaltet das heilige Gewirk auf den Stuhl, der da stand, und sprach zur Braut die Worte: 'Wir wollen ihn vererben durch die Geschlechter, und sollen ihn tragen die Lieblinge unter den Zahllosen'."

"Trug auch Mami das Tuch zu ihrer Stunde?"

"Es ist kein Tuch, es ist eine Pracht. Es ist ein Stück zu freiem Gebrauch, knöchellang, mit Ärmeln, dass der Mensch nach seinem Geschmack und nach seiner Schönheit damit verfahre. Mami? Sie trug's und behielt's. Ein-und aufgepackt hat sie's treulich, als wir dahin fuhren und brachen die staubigen Riegel und prellten Laban den Teufel. Immer hat's uns begleitet, und wei Laban es sorglich verwahrte von langer Hand in seiner Truhe, so auch wir."

Josephs Augen gingen im Zelte umher und nach den Kästen. Er fragte:
"Ist es uns nahe?"
"Nicht allzu fern."
"Und mein Herr will's mir schenken?"
"Zugedacht hab' ich's dem Kinde."
"Zugesagt und verheissen!"

"Aber für später! Nicht für den Augenblick gleich!" rief in Unruhe Jaakob. "Nimm Vernunft an, Kind und lass dir vorerst genügen an der Verheissung! Siehe, die Dinge sind in der Schwebe, und es hat der Herr sich ihretwegen noch nicht entschieden in meinem Herzen. Dein Bruder Re'uben kam zu Falle, und ich war genötigt, ihn der Erstgeburt zu entkleiden. Bist nun du an der Reihe, dass ich dich damit bekleide und gebe dir hin die Ketônet? Man kônnte antworten: Nein, denn nach Re'uben erschien Juda und erschienen Lewi und Schimeon. Man könnte antworten: Ja, denn da Leas Erstling fiel und verflucht ward, folgt Rahels Erstling. Das ist strittig und ungeklärt; wir müssen warten und nach den Zeichen sehen, wie es sich kläre. Kleide ich dich aber ein, so möchten die Brüder es fälschlich deuten, im Sinne des Segens und der Erwählung, und sich im Eifer erheben wider dich und mich."

"Wider dich?" fragte Joseph im stärksten Erstaunen . . . "Ich glaube fast, ich traue den eigenen Ohren nicht mehr! Bist du nicht der Herr? Kannst du nicht aufstehen, falls sie murren, und deine Worte hochfahren lassen und zu ihnen sprechen: 'Ich gönne, wem ich gönne, und erbarme, wes ich erbarme! Wer seid ihr, dass ihr mir dazwischenredet? Eher denn euch alle will ich ihn mit dem Mantel bekleiden und mit seiner Mutter Ketônet passîm!' Übrigens traue ich meinen Ohren; sie sind jung und genau. Namentlich wenn das Väterchen spricht, spitze ich sie zu feinster Schärfe. Sagtest du einst zur Braut: 'Es sollen den Schleier tragen die Erstlinge unter den Zahllosen'? Sondern he? Sondern he? Sondern he? Wer, sagtest du, solle ihn tragen?"

"Lass das, Unhold! Geh und schmeichle mir nicht, dass nicht deine Narrheit übergehe von dir auf mich!"

"Väterchen, ich möchte ihn sehen!"

"Sehen? Sehen ist nicht haben. Aber sehen ist haben wollen. Sei mir verständig!"

"Soll ich nicht sehen, was mein ist und mir verheissen? Also machen wir's: Ich kauere hier, gefesselt, rühre mich nicht von der Stelle. Du aber gehst und weist mir das Festkleid, nimmst es und hältst es vor dich, wie im Gewölbe der Kaufmann zu Hebron dem Käufer die Ware zeigt und lässt an sich hinabhängen das Gewebe vor den Augen des Lüsternen. Der aber ist arm und kann's nicht kaufen. Da verbirgt der Kaufmann es wieder."

"Sei es im Namen des Herrn," sagte Jaakob. "Wiewohl es für Dritte wohl aussähe, als sprängest du mit mir um. Bleib, wo du bist! Sitze auf deinen Bein, die Hände im Rücken! Du sollst sehen, was vielleicht einmal dein sein soll, unter Umständen!"

"Was schon mein ist!" rief Joseph ihm nach. "Und was ich nur noch nicht habe!"

Er rieb mit den Knöcheln die Augen, machte sich zum Schauen bereit. Jaakob ging zur gewölbten Truhe, löste die Riegel und schlug den Deckel zurück. Mancherlei Wärmendes nahm er heraus, das obenauf und tiefer lag, Mäntel und Decken, Schurze, Kopftücher, Hemden, und liess es gefaltet zu Boden fallen auf einen Haufen. Er fand den Schleier, wo er ihn wusste, nahm ihn, wandte sich, liess ihn aus den Falten fallen und spreizte ihn auseinander.

Der Knabe staunte. Er zog die Luft ein durch seinen offenen, lachenden Mund. Die Metallstickereien glitzerten im Lampenlicht. Silber- und Goldblitze überblendeten zwischen den unruhigen Armen des Alten zuweilen den stilleren Farbenschein, den Purpur, das Weiss, Olivengrün, Rosa und Schwarz der Zeichen und Bilder, der Sterne, Tauben, Bäume, Götter, Engel, Menschen und Tiere im bläulichen Nebel des Grundgewebes.

"Ihr himmlischen Lichter!" stiess Joseph hervor. "Wie schön ist das! Väterchen Kaufmann, was zeigst du dem Kunden da in deinem Gewölbe? Das ist Gilgamesch mit dem Löwen im Arm, ich erkenn' ihn von Weitem! Und dort kämpft, wie ich sehe, Einer mit einem Greifen und schwingt die Keule. Warte, warte! Ihr Zebaoth, was für Getier! Das sind die Buhlen der Göttin, Ross, Fledermaus, Wolf und der Bunte Vogel! Lass mich doch sehen — doch sehen! Ich kenn's nicht, ich unterscheid's nicht. Die armen Augen brennen dem Kinde vom Schauen über den trennenden Raum. Ist das das Skorpion-Menschenpaar mit den Stachelschwänzen? Gewiss bin ich nicht, doch scheint es mir so, wenn auch begreiflicherweise die Augen mir etwas tränen. Warte, Kaufmann, ich rutsche näher auf meinem Bein, die Hände im Rücken. O ihr Elohim, nahebei verschönt es sich noch, und alles wird deutlich! Was tun die bärtigen Geister am Baum? Sie befruchten ihn. . . Und was steht geschrieben? 'Ausgezogen — hab ich — mein Kleid, soll ich's — wieder anziehen?' Wunderbar! Immer die Nana mit Taube, Sonne und Mond. . . Ich muss mich erheben! Ich muss aufstehen, Kaufmann, ich sehe das Obere nicht: die Dattelpalme, aus der eine Göttin die Arme streckt mit Speise und Trank. . . Ich darfs doch berühren? Das kostet nichts, hoffe ich, wenn ich's schonend aufhebe mit der Hand, zu spüren, wie leicht und schwer es ist, wenn man's wiegt, wie schwer und wie leicht im Gemische. . . Kaufmann, ich bin arm, ich kann es nicht kaufen. Kaufmann, schenk' es mir! Du hast so viel Ware, — lass mir den Schleier! Leih ihn mir, sei so gut, dass ich ihn an mir den Leuten zeige zu Ehren deines Gewölbes! Nein? Durchaus nicht? Oder schwankst du vielleicht? Schwankst du ein ganz klein wenig und möchtest in aller Strenge auch weider, dass ich ihn trage? Nein, ich irre mich, du schwankst vom Halten und Spreizen. Viel zu lange schon mühst du dich. . . Gib! Wie trägt man's, wie schlägt man's? So? Und so? Und etwa noch so? Wie gefällt dir's? Bin ich ein Schäfervogel im bunten Rock? Mamis Schleiergewand—wie steht es dem Sohne?"

Natürlich sah er aus wie ein Gott. Der Effekt war vernünftigerweise zu erwarten und der geheime Wunsch, ihn hervorzubringen, dem Widerstand Jaakobs nicht zuträglich gewesen. Kaum hatte Joseph mit Methoden, deren Schlauheit und Anmut man am besten tut ruhig anzuerkennen, das Kleid aus den Händen des Alten in seine hinüberspielt, als es auch schon, mit drei, vier Griffen und Würfen, deren Sicherheit eine natürliche Anlage zur Selbstkostümierung bewies, auf freie und günstige Art seiner Person angetan gewesen war, — ihm das Haupt bedeckte, die Schultern umwand, an seiner jungen Gestalt in Falten herabwallte, aus denen die Silbertauben blitzten, die Buntstickereien glühten, und deren langer Fall ihn grösser als sonst erscheinen liess. Grösser? Hätte es dabei nur sein Bewenden gehabt! Aber der Prunkschleier stand ihm auf eine Weise zu Gesicht, dass es schwer gefallen wäre, seinem Ruf unter den Leuten noch irgendwelchen mässigenden Widerpart zu bieten, er machte ihn dermassen hübsch und schön, dass es schon nicht mehr geheuer war und tatsächlich ans Göttliche grenzte. Das Schlimmste war, dass seine Ähnlichkeit mit der Mutter, in Stirn, Braue, Mundbildung, Blick nie so sehr in die Augen gesprungen war, als dank dieser Gewandung,— dem Jaakob in die Augen, so dass sie ihm übergingen und er nicht anders meinte, als sähe er Rahel in Labans Saal am Tag der Erfüllung.

Lächelnd stand im Knaben die Muttergöttin vor ihm und fragte:

"Ich habe mein Kleid angezogen, — soll ich's wieder ausziehen?"

"Nein, behalt' es, behalt' es!" sagte der Vater; und während der Gott entsprang, hob jener Stirn und Hände, und seine Lippen bewegten sich im Gebet.

BERLIN — THOMAS MANN

EARLY MANHOOD

I shall be greatly obliged if you will add to your many tributes to Rabindranath Tagore these words from myself, wishing him a most happy birthday and future and many fruitful years of poetry bringing new delight and new understanding into the world.

OXFORD

JOHN MASEFIELD

TO RABINDRANATH TAGORE

(*Whom of all poets I love best, for none has spoken of God as he did*)

Through all our earthly ways there gleams a thread—
We follow it by inward inspiration,—
That leads from gloom and from inertia dead
To the free space and light of Initiation.

Thus Theseus from Cretan monster fled
Through Ariadne's thread brought to salvation,
Thus we, from birth to birth still higher led,
We wander through the cycles of creation,

Till we attain the perfect state divine,
The consciousness that God in us does shine
And that we move in Him like constellations,

Yet keeping each our colours and vibrations,
Till we unite in those high spheres above
A white, a radiant nebula of love.

TOKYO

INA METAXA

RABINDRANATH'S PLACE IN INDIAN LITERATURE

WHEN Rabindranath got the Nobel Prize, India suddenly and with a pleasant surprise became conscious after a long and disturbing night that she, who had witnessed so many vicissitudes—political and cultural, since the dawn of the Vedic singers, had still something to say, something to contribute to the New Culture which was being fashioned with such energy and *éclat* by the younger nations—specially of Europe and America. It merely marked the end of an epoch of a long period of gestation rather than indicate any sudden outburst of creative energy on the part of a submerged people whose spiritual growth had become arrested in course of time. Civilisations also seem to move in cycles—up and down like the hub of a wheel, or as Kalidasa expresses it, *nicair gacchaty upari ca dasa cakra-nemi-kramena.* People could hardly understand the significance of Vivekananda's journey to the West. The daring of a solitary and resourceless monk to preach India's age-old message of spiritual harmony and brotherhood of man to the powerful nations of England and America verged on the borders of recklessness ; but Vivekananda was only the harbinger of the dawn that was breaking on the Himalayan peaks and after the inevitable darkness of fatigue and exhaustion was already flooding the valleys of Hindustan with its light of song and devotion. Rabindranath mirrored and epitomised the soul of India as no other poet had done since Kalidasa. The only figure comparable to him in recent times was the great Goethe who symbolised the Germany that was to be. The most striking thing about both Goethe and Rabindranath is of course their versatility and their singular mastery over the music of words. And yet, these are by no means the most important features of their intellectual constitution. India had so perfected the art of musical and literary expression through centuries of intensive cultivation, that verbal mastery of the highest quality had ceased to be something novel and uncommon. Sanskrit, the mother of languages, had been transformed from the direct and simple tongue of the early singers of the Vedic hymns into an elegant and singularly supple and musical language of the aristocracy. Its medieval offsprings—the vernaculars—the languages that are spoken to-day, did not take long to imbibe the accustomed cadence and music of the mother-tongue, and at least one of them, the language of the *Braj*—the language in which the blind poet *Suradas* sang his passionate rhapsodies to the divine Radha and Krishna and which is spoken round about Mathura, had not only rivalled, but surpassed the Sanskrit in sheer artistry of form and verbal rhythm. Bengali had almost unconsciously glided from the elegant and alliterative melodies of Jayadeva's Sanskrit *Gita-Govinda,* into the beautiful and enchanting songs of Chandidasa and Vidyapati of the 15th century. Facile expression had therefore long ceased to be a virtue or an uncommon accomplishment.

With us poetry and song have been inseparable even as in the case of the early folk-songs of Europe, and the medium of song or lyrical poetry has been perfected to an extent that cannot be imagined outside India. It was in fact the principal channel through which literary and spiritual culture filtered down, without literacy, from the fountain source to the lowliest, throughout the length and breadth of the country. Thus are Tulasidas and Kabir known and sung wherever a little Hindi is understood. The literary culture of Hindustan is perhaps unique in the world and is not to be inferred and measured by the stupendous illiteracy of the people; for long before the invention of writing were the songs of the sacred Vedas transmitted and kept intact through the medium of an oral tradition for centuries on end and nowhere else in the world is it possible to see such intimate contact of understanding between the poet and the people as in India. Popular culture in an old country such as ours is something quite apart from popular literacy and there is in fact no doubt that modern education has, instead of widening the sphere of that culture, generally contracted it and certainly not always improved its quality.

Rabindranath's singular felicity of expression, which strikes the foreign reader so forcibly, is merely a common feature of the intensive development of linguistic art in this country. His mysticism and humanity—the elusive and universal character of his poetry, are parts of his cultural inheritance. Where however he is different from and surpasses his predecessors is the range of his interests, the variety of the media which he has used for the expression of his genius, and the dramatic quality of his major contributions. This latter characteristic is specially prominent in his short stories and dramatic pieces, where poetry becomes vibrant with conflicting emotions and pours forth in a torrent of impassioned eloquence. All the graces of Tagore's poetic art blend in a singularly effective amalgam to bring out and lay bare the varying and often contradictory elements of the human heart. I know of no more poignant and effective example of the dramatist's art than the short dialogue between Karna and Kunti.

Rabindranath like Tolstoy is always in sympathy with his *dramatis personae* and hence every character unfolds itself with the same naturalness and grace even as a flower. His essentially devout nature, his flaming sense of right, his passionate feeling for the poor and the exploited, his deep love for his country and righteous indignation for the wrongs done to and suffered by her, never obtrude themselves in his great dramas—such as *Chitra, Karna and Kunti,* his hitherto untranslated *Natir Puja.* Barring Bhasa—the master dramatist whom even Kalidasa paid his homage, there is hardly any other figure in the entire range of Indian literature who has had the dramatic quality of Tagore. But then, Rabindranath is also a consummate actor, a superb musician and an artist of rare susceptibility for graphic rhythm and plastic form. The world has rarely seen such an extraordinary and lavish combination of gifts and Rabindranath has used them freely and unstintingly. A characteristic feature of all his literary contributions is the creation of an appropriate atmosphere as a stage or a conductor for his poetic outpourings and this is achieved with the unerring instinct and swift precision of a great painter. It is only recently that Tagore himself came to realize his capacity for graphic form and with his amazing essays in this field of sheer form and rhythm, one is naturally tempted to apply the language of linear art as an instrument of appraising, for picking out the essential qualities of his literary contributions. Personally—and it may be the experience of most Indians, I have always felt that it is in the plays and short stories rather than in his elaborate poetic compositions that Tagore's varied genius has manifested itself in all its wealth of imagery, pointed imagination, acute understanding of the human nature, its essential sympathy with its weaknesses and its eternal urge for the ideal. And here, one hardly realizes whether it is the *milieu* as such or the doings of the human actors which matter most; so surely and inseparably are the atmosphere, the colour and the characters blended by the Master in a single harmony. And yet, this has always been the quality, the supreme achievement of our classical poets like Kalidasa and Bhavabhuti. The Indian mind approaches Nature spontaneously and as it were, by instinct, in its universal aspect, almost as a child reaches out to its mother; and this feeling dominates every phase of all truly Indian art, whether it be literary, graphic or plastic.

As a poet Rabindranath's place is naturally with our great Vaishnavite singers, to whom he is never tired of acknowledging his indebtedness. But then, the essential quality of Vaishnavism—the complete surrender of self, in fact the total loss, or shall I call it, absorption of the individual self into the universal and supreme Reality, is not peculiar to India, but is the unmistakable hall-mark of humanity wherever it has felt the immanence of God and the utter insignificance of our petty human achievements. If Tagore, as a playwright, is a compeer and in the direct line of descent of the classical writers, such as Bhasa, Kalidasa and Bhavabhuti, as a singer, he is of the family of the medieval *Bhaktas*—whose rhapsodies were but the humble, inadequate expression of their inner feeling, sometimes in terms of affection, sometimes in terms of reproach, but always in a mood of passionate surge to reach and hold fast to the ever-elusive, all pervading Reality. Devotion—and not poetry, the inner identity and not the external form were what mattered. But then, what great poetry is possible without the uttermost sincerity, without the inner harmony of the spirit? Without these poetry becomes merely an essay in verbal jugglery, a matter of skilled manipulation rather than a searching into the depths of the human soul, an attempt to soar high and free.

Twenty years ago who could have dreamt that Mother India—poor, not merely in material goods but veritably poor in spirit, distracted and diffident, had any future but slow and certain death, for she had ceased to be creative for the past two hundred years and more, and it appeared that the magnificent mausoleum of the Taj was not merely the memorial of undying love, but unwittingly the last monument to the achievements of an old country which had a past, but no future? The hope and confidence that are the keynote of the present were not even felt; so dismal was the outlook. Rabindranath and Mohandas Gandhi—each an artist in his own sphere and indubitably among the world's immortals, could hardly be conceived as a possibility. It did not then seem at all possible that the downward cycle had almost finished its course and that India was once again on the upward march, that she—the mother of so many cultures, the witness of so many conquests of Dharma—of Righteousness in every part of the world, was once again alive and awakened, and that she too had a part to play in the future, commensurate with her past. Gandhi and Tagore are thus the sons of the radiant, the ever youthful Mother, whose future none can now foretell. Is there any doubt that *c'est le printemps qui sonne*?

NAINITAL, INDIA

NANALAL C. MEHTA

ON behalf of the Anglo-Indians, a community having a common birthright in the land of India, I offer our sincerest and highest congratulations on the coming birth-anniversary of the Poet. Being sons of the soil, the Anglo-Indians rejoice to think that a true son of the soil has raised the name of India to deserve the honour of the nations around, by contributing to the world's peace, in bringing near to us the Divine, Who, as has been said, "hath made of one blood all nations of men to dwell on the face of the earth."

CALCUTTA

H. W. B. MORENO

THE Indian and the German peoples are children of the same mother. But they were separated in their childhood and sent to very distant countries, and thousands of years have elapsed in which they have had no sort of intercourse and no knowledge of each other. During the whole of the middle ages nought but some fabulous accounts of India reached Germany. After the sea-route to India had been discovered, some Europeans went to India and returned home with a fuller and truer knowledge of its inhabitants, their beliefs and rites, their customs and social order. Most of them were missionaries whose interest was chiefly in religion. They went to southern India, and if they learned anything of Indian languages, it was Tamil, not Sanskrit. The first of them was a Dutchman, Abraham Roger, who lived at Pulicat and Batavia and died in 1649. After his death his work *The Open Door to Hidden Heathendom* was published; it was translated into German in 1663. It contained the first specimen of Indian literature: two hundred stanzas of Bhartrihari (the *Vairagya* and the *Niti Satakas*, that about love being excluded), but it met with no serious interest. The next to follow Roger were chiefly Portuguese and Frenchmen—we even meet with a German among them. But it was not before the close of the 18th century, after the establishment of the British dominion, that the classical language of India became accessible to European scholars, and now Englishmen had the lead. At this time there appeared in rapid succession a series of classical works of Indian literature, and we must own that the Brahman helpers who advised the Europeans and led them to an understanding of the poems made an excellent choice. So we came to know the *Bhagavad-gita* 1785, *Hitopadesa* 1787, *Gita-govinda*, *Bhagavata-purana* 1788, *Sakuntala* 1789, *Manava Dharma-sastra* 1796; at the same time the first edition of a Sanskrit original was printed in Europe: *Ritu-samhara* 1792.

In Germany it was *Sakuntala* which decided the victory of Indian poetry, and the man who was the first to feel its beauty and the first herald of its fame was the great inspirer of our classical period, the listener to the voices of various nations: Herder. He had already given a somewhat dim ideal picture of the Indian people in his chief work *Ideas on a Philosophy of the History of Mankind* (Third Part, 1787). Now George Forster, the circumnavigator of the world and revolutionary, sent him his translation of the English Sakuntala on the 2nd May, 1791. Herder received the gift with enthusiasm, and in the following year he gave his impression in the fourth collection of his *Scattered Leaves* (*Zerstreute Blätter*). These three Letters *On an Oriental Drama* were for a long time the best appreciation the poem met with in Germany. Before him, immediately on reading it, Goethe had expressed his admiration in the few lines which praise *Sakuntala* as the sum-total of poetic perfection. He retained this love for it all his life and gave expression to it more than once. As late as in 1930, when the French scholar de Chézy sent him the first edition of the original with a French translation, he thanked him in an enthusiastic letter which sounds like an enlarged paraphrase of that epigram:

> When I first became acquainted with this unfathomable work, it aroused such enthusiasm in me, it attracted me so that I could not forbear studying it; I even felt impelled to the impossible task of acquiring it for the German stage. Through these endeavours, fruitless though they were, I became so intimately familiar with this most precious work, it has marked such an epoch in my life, it has become so entirely my own that I have not once looked either at the English or at the German text these thirty years. . . . . . It is only now that I realise the overwhelming impression that work has made on me at an earlier age. Here the poet appears in his highest function, as the representative of the most natural state, of the most refined form of life, of the purest moral striving, of the worthiest majesty and the most solemn contemplation of God; at the same time he is lord and master of his creation to so great an extent that he may venture vulgar and ludicrous contrasts which yet must be regarded as necessary links of the whole organisation . . . . . I will break off and only repeat the statement: that your *Sakuntala* must be reckoned among the most beautiful of the stars which make my nights more splendid than my day.

This love was even shared by Schiller who otherwise took little interest in Indian literature. He admired especially the picture of the heroine as a model of tender womanliness deeming it far superior to the best female figures of Greek tragedy. And he too tried to adjust it for the use of the German stage, but he found it unsuited through its extreme delicacy and its want of dramatic movement.

In their love for *Sakuntala* Herder and Goethe were in perfect agreement. In other respects there was a great difference in their attitude towards India. Herder was gradually becoming old and moralising. The moral purity and tenderness of *Sakuntala* had captivated him. And so it was the rich treasure of Indian gnomic and didactic poetry that appealed to him most. In the same volume of his *Scattered Leaves* which contained his letters on *Sakuntala* and which was almost entirely dedicated to the Orient, he offered his *Thoughts of some Brahmans*, a selection of gnomic stanzas in free translation gathered from *Bhagavad-gita, Hitopadesa* and *Bhartrihari.* That was his contribution to the adoption of Indian literature by Germany; it has not been fruitless, as many of these excellent verses have found their way into reading books for schools.

Goethe, on the other hand, felt as a poet and an artist. He was delighted by the harmonious beauty and lyrical intensity of the masterpieces of epics and *kavya*, but he did not care for *Hitopadesa* and philosophy, and he declined an interest in Indian mythology and sculpture. Up to the epoch-making year 1791 he had not been completely ignorant about India. In his youth he had read some of the travellers' accounts which were then current, such as Dapper and Sonnerat, had gathered from them the story of Rama and other epic tales, and being very fond of telling fairy-tales from his earliest childhood, when even on his mother's lap he vied with her in fabulous invention, he annexed them to this store, and the master-monkey Hannemann (as he found the name spelt, looking rather German) in particular delighted his youthful public. But the first deep impression was made by *Sakuntala.* And this bore fruit in his poetry. His *Faust* begins with a Prelude on the Theatre in which the director, the poet and the humorist discuss their different views on dramatic poetry. It was written in the year 1797, and it was long being noticed that the idea was suggested by the Prologue of *Sakuntala.* As it seems, the first to see the connection was Heinrich Heine, the poet who in a few lines has shaped that picture of India which lives in each German soul where a detailed knowledge of India is lacking:

Am Ganges duftet's und leuchtet's,
Und Riesenbäume blühn,
Und schöne, stille Menschen
Vor Lotosblumen knien.

The same year 1797 saw the birth of Goethe's first Indian ballad *The God and the Bayadere.* Goethe gave the story as he found it in his source, the account of an old traveller (Sonnerat?), and I do not know its origin. Vishnu in one of his avatars meets a bayadere (*deva-dasi,* nautch-girl), enters her house and is well received. In the morning she finds him dead at her side, and she is so filled with his love that she feels herself his wife and throws herself on the funeral pile to die after him. Then the God arises from the flame and takes her with him into his heaven. Goethe unvoluntarily gives the story a slight Christian note ("God rejoices over penitent sinners"), but his principal aim is to demonstrate the deep human meaning of the Indian tale: the apotheosis of faithfulness unto death in a woman from whom it is neither demanded nor expected.

But however strong and fruitful this love for India was, it was at first but an episode. On the whole, India could not have a similar importance for Goethe as Greece had, just because of the relationship of the Indian and the German minds. Both have a tendency towards formlessness and boundlessness, towards inwardness and transcendentalism. It is from a feeling of this want that the German mind seeks compensation in the study and discipleship of those nations which are especially gifted in the direction of clarity and finish of form—in the first place the ancient Greeks, and to some degree the Romanic nations, especially the French. In this school Goethe and Schiller had attained their definite style, so that their classical poetry may be regarded as the latest and highest phase of renaissance poetry. It is evident that this striving after perfect form and measure must make them ill-disposed towards Indian literature, in which they perceived the very want of discipline which they themselves were striving to overcome. And so, when after the deliverance of Germany Goethe took refuge in the East from the repugnant world which surrounded him, steeped himself in Eastern poetry and gave expression to his personal feelings in

Oriental costume, India had no part in this "West-Eastern Divan." Yet at the very time he was working at it, he found his way back to his previous love, and the poem that led him back was the finest piece of *kavya*, the *Megha-duta* (again Kalidasa!), translated into English by Horace Wilson, which he received in March, 1817 and welcomed as "a great treasure." We find allusions to it in a poem of 1821, and then, in due course, follows Goethe's second and sublimest Indian ballad *The Pariah*. (1824. Just before *The Pariah* had been introduced to the French and the German stages). The poem illustrates the truth that before God no human distinction of rank and worth can stand, that all states, all classes of society are alike near his heart and have the same claim on his mercy. The principal poem is encompassed by two prayers which refer to the former ballad. The bayaderes having got their divine representative, the pariah claims the same favour for himself, and it is granted him by the miraculous event that forms the subject of the "legend." This Goethe has taken from the same traveller, but here we can trace it back to the *Mahabharata*.

At this time the interest in India was widespread and consolidated in Germany. The very reason which to some extent made Goethe stand aloof gave the romantic poets a predilection for India, but they did not content themselves with glorifying it in poetry, they laid the foundation of a real science of India. The brothers Schlegel, the fathers of romanticism, were also the fathers of German Indology; and here, as elsewhere, Friedrich opened up the way by dint of intuition (in his book *On the Language and Wisdom of the Indians*, 1808), while August Wilhelm developed an Indian philology on the model of classical philology and became the first professor at the newly founded university of Bonn 1818. Bopp followed suit in Berlin; both produced a series of excellent editions, most of them with a Latin translation. Goethe followed them in their work with benevolent interest and appropriated what was congenial to him. So he was deeply impressed by the *Gita-govinda*, though he came to know it only from a very defective secondhand translation. Moreover, some fragments of the *Mahabharata* (the story of Nala) and the *Ramayana* gained his approbation. And so, what he appreciated and enjoyed, were specimens of epical and classical literature, chiefly love-poetry. (Vedic literature was at that time still an inaccessible world).

It is little more than a century since the Germans began to take their share in exploring India. But if they came last, they were certainly not the least, and I venture to say that no other people has done more for the investigation and appreciation of Indian language and literature, religion and philosophy. But as a spiritual communion must constitute a reciprocity of giving and taking, the other half of the work remains still to be done: India's discovery of Germany and her acceptance of her spiritual treasure. That will be the task of the next century.

When the Indian genius first found its way into Germany, it was through the medium of foreign travellers and English officers; India herself had no active part in this process. Now she comes to us embodied in a living man, the bearer of her message. With him a new stage in this intercourse has begun. And not only the form, but the contents have changed. Rabindranath Tagore is not the messenger of India alone, but the announcer and prophet of a new humanity in which the best and deepest aspirations of the Eastern and the Western man are united. This he presents to our eyes in his teaching, in his work, in his person. Herder and Goethe laid the foundation of a universal literature in the German language (the term is Goethe's), in which the voices of all nations were to mingle.. Rabindranath Tagore initiates a universal culture in which all nations will co-operate, each bringing its own gift in brotherly union. In this sense we all feel ourselves to be his disciples and bow to him in deep veneration.

HAMBURG — HEINRICH MEYER-BENFEY

SOME would wonder why I am an optimist. Pessimism is right if one considers only the destiny of an individual. Optimism is inevitable if one is able to feel the eternal truth of the human will. An enormous tree, even if told that it will be dried up and dead some few hundred years hence, cannot but sing its own joyous song, praising life and growing upwards towards the heavens.

TOKYO — J. MUSHAKOJI

SUR notre pauvre terre, toujours gluante des mêmes iniquités et des mêmes basesses, Tagore m'apparaît comme une de ces lumineuses figures, un de ces douloureux missionnaires de fraternité qui dominent les ténèbres et les haïnes, forcent le degoût et la honte chez les hommes qui s'égorgent.

PARIS — MARC ELMER

A BENEDICTION

The German poet says—

Wer den Dichter will verstehen
Muss in Dichter's Lande gehen:

'One who wishes to understand a poet must go to the poet's land.'

I had the pleasure, not only of seeing, and meeting, and hearing, and reading, and talking with, the poet in whose honour I write these few words, but also had the pleasure of going to and sleeping for one night at his Santiniketan, which is his *land* of lands. I remember with pleasure now—though at the time when the event happened it gave me much pain—that one night I had to shed my own blood for him—not strictly *for* him, but *after* him. A few years ago, the Ripon Club of the Parsees of Bombay gave in his honour, when he was in Bombay, a dinner, presided over by Sir Jamsetjee Jejeebhoy, the fifth Baronet. At the close of the dinner, when he departed, I followed him and the Honorary Secretary of the Club, and the swing door shut up after them rushed back in a manner which cut my hand. Instead of going home, I went to a chemist and druggist's shop in the neighbourhood to get my hand dressed. It is a custom on this side of India, especially in Kathiawar, that on great occasions relating to the ruling Princes,—occasions like those of accession to the throne, or marriage—the Prime Minister, or an honoured member of a noble family, puts a cut on the thumb of his hand and marks with the oozing blood, the forehead of his royal master, as a symbol of sacrifice on his part, which symbol is now taken as that of a good omen. I had no occasion or opportunity to apply the blood oozing from my hand to the forehead of the poet, who, in his own way, in his line, is a prince or a prince of princes. But I vividly remember that occasion now with pleasure, and take the dropping of the blood as my poor and humble sacrifice to his intellectual forehead, the poems flowing from which brighten and illuminate, smooth and sweeten the thoughts of many a son and daughter of India. Again, I had once the pleasure of delivering a lecture on a poem of the poet at the Bai Bhikhaiji Bengali School in Bombay.

The first time I saw the poet, I was immediately impressed with his look. Every inch, he looked like one of the *Rishis* of the olden times, who were both poets and prophets or seers. The Persian word for a poet is *Sha'ir* which, coming from an Arabic root, means 'a finder, a seer'. So great Poets of the East were both *Sha'irs* and Seers, Poets and Prophets. The Persian word for a Prophet is *Paigham-bar,* literally 'a bearer of message (from God).' Dr. Rabindranath Tagore has given us a number of messages,—messages which have soothed and solaced many a heart of his countrymen. Now, some of his readers in the different parts of the world are expected to send messages in honour of this Messenger of Messengers. The humble message of this poor pen, whose holder has seen him, heard him, read him, talked with him, dined with him, and even offered a blood sacrifice in his honour, is simply this:

'O Ahura Mazda! Give him a healthy life, a long life, so that he may long continue to send his messages to his countrymen, in whose poetic eyes the whole world is one country.'

And may I be allowed to pray in the words of my own Prophet:

Afrīnāmi tava, nara, vohu-jiti, us-jiti, daréghém-jiti.

'O Brave Man! I pray that you may live a good life, that you may live an exalted life, that you may live a long life.'

I pray in the words of our Pazend *Tan-durusti* (Prayer of Blessings):

Tan-durusti, dēr zīvashni,
Khoreh anghat ashahidār,
Yazdān-i minōyān, Yazdān-i getiyān, haft Ameshāspandān hameh berasād

'May you have Health of Body, may you have a Long Life.
May you have Righteous Splendour.
May the Yazatas of the unseen world, the Yazatas of this physical world, and the seven Divine Powers always come to your help.'

BOMBAY JIVANJI JAMSHEDJI MODI

MY elder brother, who can reach into the lofty heights of the Eternal, often stoops down to dry a tear; He is himself like the transparent glittering drop suspended on the eyelash of a child, still full of sorrow, but already dimly smiling.

SOERAKARTA, JAVA MANGKOENEGORO VII

THE POET DURING THE SWADESHI MOVEMENT (1906)

TAGORE IN CHICAGO

"POETRY: A Magazine of Verse" had the honour of being the first occidental publication to print Tagore's poems in English. His six *Gitanjali* poems, appearing in *Poetry* for December 1912, preceded by a few weeks the London India Society's private edition, which, though dated 1912, was not distributed until 1913.

Poetry, published in Chicago, was far away from India and even from London, where the Bengali poet had been sojourning; and its founder and editor had never heard of Tagore. But Ezra Pound, our foreign correspondent, had met him in London, and had induced him to permit the sending of some of the *Gitanjali* poems to the new little poets' magazine.

I remember how excited we were when they arrived. Devotional poetry is rarely of value considered as poetry, but these were beautiful devotional poems, and the religious feeling they expressed was a tribute to the universal God of all races and creeds.

A few days after the December number appeared, *The Chicago Tribune*, taking Tagore's poems for its text, devoted an editorial to *Poetry's* international aspirations, and soon we were amazed to receive a letter signed by a younger Tagore in the University of Illinois, saying: 'My father is visiting me here, and would like a few copies of the magazine containing his poems.'

This was news indeed—the distinguished oriental poet, whom I had supposed to be at home in India, if not still in London, was for a time our neighbour in my own state! I wrote to him at once, inviting him to Chicago; and Mrs. William Vaughan Moody, widow of the poet, seconded the invitation with an offer of her generous hospitality.

Soon after New Year's Day Mr. Tagore arrived with his son and exquisite little daughter-in-law, and during that winter the visit was repeated three or four times. This was a year before his Nobel Prize award and all its attendant publicity. So we were able to get acquainted with the poet without interference from the world's curiosity. We used to spend evenings around Mrs. Moody's fire listening to the chanting of poems in Bengali, or the recitation of their English equivalents, and feeling as if we were seated at the feet of some ancient wise man of the East, generous in his revelation of beauty. He talked also about his native country and the meaning of that huge word 'India,' and about his hope for more friendly consideration from the governing powers of the world.

Thus I came to think of Rabindranath Tagore as a friend; and although years have passed since I last saw him, I still feel something warm and intimate in his rich personality which makes and holds friends in every country he has visited. On this, his seventieth birthday, I would salute him first as a friend, even before I pay tribute to the distinguished poet, long dear to the hearts of his countrymen, whom now all the world delights to honor, since his art and its message of beauty are for all the world.

CHICAGO HARRIET MONROE

TAGORE AS A POLITICAL THINKER

TAGORE'S contributions to political thought have not received adequate attention as compared with his contributions to literature and art. His purely political writings do not also form any very considerable part of his total literary output. But they are enough to bring out the originality and definiteness of some of his political theories and notions, especially in their application to India. His first political writings appeared more than twenty-five years ago during those stirring times of 1905 and 1906, when Bengal, and, to some extent the whole of India, were thrown into a state of great political excitement, due to Lord Curzon's partition of Bengal, executed against the unanimous wishes of a great people. Those were the days when the mere muttering of *Bande Mataram* by tender striplings was visited with the punishment of their expulsion from Government Schools, under the new regime of resolute government inaugurated in the newly created province of Eastern Bengal and Assam by its first Governor, Sir Bampfylde Fuller. The reply which Bengal gave to these iniquitous circulars of Messrs. Carlyle and Risley was the establishment of her first National College at Calcutta under the principalship of Sri Aurobindo Ghose with national schools affiliated to it at different centres, and controlled by a Governing Body with Sir Rashbehary Ghose as its President, and Sir Gooroo Dass Bannerjee as one of its most active members. There was, however, going on behind the scenes a deep national movement which was preparing the ground upon which these new institutions were to take root. Of this movement, Tagore assumed his natural leadership, assisted by the organising ability and the practical commonsense of one of Bengal's greatest sons, Srijut Hirendra Nath Datta.

As boys were being expelled from different Government Schools for the sin of singing the national song of *Bande Mataram,* national schools were springing up to receive them. When their claim to recognition was refused by the Calcutta University, the senior students of the University who were appearing at the Degree Examinations at once organised a boycott of University Examinations by way of protest. The present writer was then going in for the P.R.S. examination and became one of the ringleaders of this Boycott Movement, along with Professors Rabindra Narayan Ghosh, Nripendra Nath Banerji and several others who were all candidates for the M.A. Examination in 1905. It was very difficult to keep up the boycott against overwhelming difficulties. It was only the consummate leadership of Tagore which enabled the young men to keep their eyes fixed on their goal and ideal. Tagore used to meet them, almost every evening, in the rooms of the then Metropolitan Institution, and gave expression to the new-born spirit of freedom inspiring the youth of Bengal by the composition of what are called his national songs, which rank very high in both the poetry and music of Tagore. Every evening would he come to the meeting with songs composed for the occasion and either sing them himself or have them sung for purposes of instruction by one of his prominent disciples, the late Ajit Kumar Chakravarti. Very shortly he came out into the open to deliver a series of powerful polemics and threw himself heart and soul into political pamphleteering, just as Milton did under similar circumstances, leaving aside his lyre. Learned papers followed in quick succession and were delivered to audiences beyond computation at overflow meetings. The most important and classical of these writings are entitled *Swadeshi Samaj*, *Saphalatar Sadupaya*, *Avastha-O-Vyavastha*, *Brahman*, *Atyukti*, and the like.

The political philosophy expounded in these writings is not the product of the poet's imagination, but is severely scientific, original, and well-founded in history, though, perhaps, Tagore might have worked with a general vision of that history without its details and documents. Quite recently, Tagore has given to Mahatma Gandhi the credit for giving to the world for the first time a new technique for political revolutions by which a people in servitude might win its freedom by the methods of bloodless warfare, of Non-Violent Civil Resistance. And yet, more than twenty-five years ago, Tagore himself gave the first adequate exposition of the principle of political evolution by which a self-governing society can checkmate an aggressive State by shutting itself up within the walls of Non-co-operation. Tagore has, for the first time, pointed out how in the distinctive political evolution of India the State and Society have operated as separate and co-ordinating entities, each with its defined sphere of work and jurisdiction, so that each knew of its limits of interference. India has believed in the eighteenth century European doctrine of *laissez faire, laissez passer* in imposing the utmost possible limits upon State-interference so as to give to the people the largest liberty in the management of their own vital concerns. India has not believed in any system of centralisation or over-government, but has always stood for the self-government of the Group formed on all possible principles of association, functional or local. India has thus, through the ages, built up a vast subterranean democracy, limiting the absolutism of her many political autocracies functioning at the top. It was this inherent native democracy of India, the democracy centred in her innumerable villages and social groups, which has helped India to preserve her soul against the many political revolutions affecting her body-politic in the different periods of her chequered history. In the words of Sir George Birdwood:

> India has undergone more religious and political revolutions than any other country in the world, but the village communities remain in full municipal vigour all over the peninsula. Scythian, Greek, Saracen, Afghan, Moghul, and Maratha have come down from its mountains, and Portuguese, Dutch, English, French and Dane up out of its seas and set up their successive dominations in the land ; but the religious trades-union villages have remained as little affected by their coming and going as a rock by the rising and falling of the tide.

It was this live democracy of India that is indeed responsible, not merely for the conservation of her culture, but even for the flowering of that culture during the darkest days of her political history under the first batch of her Moslem rulers. Indeed, it would appear that when the tyranny of Moslem rule was at its worst, the indigenous culture of India, far from being choked by the political powers, was asserting itself best and evolving out of its prolific vitality new means of self-expression. During these days of political confusion, India saw some of her greatest religious leaders, like Basava, Ramanuja and Madhava in the South; Ramanand, Kabir, Chaitanya, Vallabhacharya and Nanak in the North; men of letters like Bhavabhuti, Sri-Harsha, Rajasekhara, Jayadeva, Kahlana, Sayanacharya or Vedantadesikachar of the South; Vidyapati, Chandidasa and Mirabai, Tulasidasa and Dadu and Tukaram; or legists like Kulluka, Jimutavahana, Vijnanesvara, Vachaspati Misra and Raghunandana. The fact is that India has never trusted and given herself up wholly to politics, nor is she prepared to surrender to the State all that rightfully belongs to the sphere of the individual, or of that civilised society which is at the foundation of the State itself.

And yet, India has been thinking in terms of an essential democracy since the beginning of recorded time. Even the Vedas, which are acknowledged to be the oldest literary text of humanity, hail the democratic institutions called the *Sabha* and the *Samiti* as the twin creations of Prajapati, implying that they are coëval with civilised society. These popular bodies were already the organic parts of the earliest Indian Constitution. The position of the Sovereign in the Hindu State belongs to what is called the *Dharma,* while the Austinian sovereign is described as *Danda,* the Executive, which enforces the *Dharma.* The Austinian Sovereign in Hindu polity is not thus the source of Law, but rather its sanction and support. The sources of Law are enumerated as *Sruti* (Veda), *Smriti, Sishtachara* (approved customs), and decisions of the *Parishad* on doubtful points (judge-made law). The Law or *Dharma* was, on principle, not uniform for all conditions, nor centralised. It varied with groups and communities which legislated for themselves. The State, whether Monarchy or Democracy, stood for the self-government of the Group. The groups which were recognised for self-government by the State were known and arranged in an ascending order as follows: *Kula* (Clan), *Jati* (Caste), *Sreni* (Guild), *Samuha* (Corporation), *Sangha* (Community), *Puga* and *Gana* (Village Republic). These were self-governing as regards legislation, justice, and executive functions, within their own spheres. The State, subserving the ends of *Dharma,* believed in the free and natural grouping of individuals and encouraged all kinds of association, voluntary, local, or functional. Thus India became a land of self-governing groups and communities, of local self-rule, limiting the absolutism of the Central Government.

The structure of this indigenous Hindu *Swaraj* is a consistent structure in all its strata and layers, from top to bottom. If any section of it were taken anywhere, it would show the same features of self-rule. There was no place in it for distinctions

THE POET (1912)

By the Courtesy of the Gainsborough Studio, London

between advanced and backward communities in respect of the privileges of self-rule to which all were admitted equally, without any question of qualifications. The machinery of government existed for man, and not man for the machinery. It was so designed and devised that the more backward a community, the more was their share of self-government, and of its blessings. Some of the *Smritis* or Hindu Law-Books boldly lay down that 'foresters are to be judged by foresters, merchants by merchants, soldiers by soldiers, and villagers by their co-villagers.' The Hindu Polity did not believe in building up *Swaraj* only at the top. It built it up from its foundation in a uniform structure. It went boldly to the villages and built them up as self-contained republics, giving full scope to the growth of those social issues upon which the unified national democracy functioning for the whole country as a unit must ultimately rest.

It is to this native and nascent democracy of India that Tagore calls us back as the only means by which India can recover her lost soul against the invasion of Western methods which suit the West better than the East and are the outcome of different conditions of life and history. The future of India must be worked out as far as possible in accordance with the established traditions of her long and glorious past, and must not be shaped after the experiments of the West, like Socialism, Communism and all their varied brood. Tagore is our first Preacher of the Gospel of Non-co-operation whereby a Great Society, rich in its innate idealism and culture, in the resources of the soul, but rendered moribund in the deadening grip of political servitude, can achieve its freedom to preserve itself by the compelling methods of organised Non-violence and Bloodless Revolution. The miniature picture of such a society recovering its lost life and liberty is graphically presented by the Poet in his masterly discourse on *Swadeshi Samaj.* The freedom of India will be within her grasp if such vital centres of life and light, these local and social democracies, were to spring up in their hundreds and thousands all over the country as visible exhibitions of what *Satyagraha* and *Ahimsa,* Truth and Non-violence, can achieve against the unyielding obstinacy of an alien autocracy.

THE UNIVERSITY, LUCKNOW

RADHA KUMUD MOOKERJI

NEED AND NO NEED

AH! Fortune's slaves shed blood and tears;
Whips tear their backs, curses their ears!

He felt no need of friend or roof,
Silken array or weather-proof,
Being so taken up with thought,
He to himself seemed all but naught.

Neither child nor mate did she require,
Nor rooms full of eyes which could but admire,
Being deep as joy in . . and fused with . . love
Heaven flowed through her around and above.

Of hand to hold, of arms to embrace,
Of thoughts . . of words . . bewinged with grace,
Of long life or of other place,
What need has Iris-flower of these,
Having colour and form for ecstasies?

Well may we weep, who, plunged in need,
Both for ourselves and others, bleed!

LONDON

T. STURGE MOORE

TAGORE, THE SUPREME COMPOSER

THE world knows Tagore through literature and philosophy. Yet his genius is essentially musical. The rhythm of music supports his philosophy, its melody permeates his prose, and its harmony orchestrates the numerous manifestations of his genius. Music completes his personality and thus perfects his art-forms. But this is not all. The Poet is the most original composer of music that India has ever known. In number and richness, no less than in the delicacy and suggestiveness of valuable moods, his songs form an excellent and inexhaustible repertoire for his people. We in Bengal get the best and the most of him through his songs. Even a bird's eye view of the perspective of musical traditions in Hindustan throws the musical achievements of Tagore in high relief.

Hindustani music has two broad types, one of the Court, and another of the People. The court-patronage of princes had always mingled with the religious ardour of the people to maintain the continuity and enrich the quality of our music. Whenever classical or court-music was becoming dry, formal, and sophisticated, it would gain fresh accession of life from the music of the countryside. Such accessions of vigour had occurred in the Pathan and the Mughal periods of Indian History. Usually, they came in the wake of the Bhakti-cult, which was always bringing together different races, creeds, and cultures into its democratic fold. Even far into the middle of the 19th Century, the two types of music were being blended into new forms, *e.g.*, Tappa and Thumri. The changes in folk-music were naturally more slow and imperceptible. None the less they were real. But with the consolidation of British rule, the middle class, consisting of the educated and professional people on the one hand and of traders and commercial people on the other, began to displace the patrons of the art, the aristocrats of the soil, from their station in society. The new class were the pioneers of British rule, products of English education and profiteers of Anglo-Indian trade. They owed no account to culture. National traditions retired into the semi-feudal states which alone could be called Indian India. The landed gentry, in their humble way, kept the flame burning. This displacement was most apparent in Bengal which was the seat of the foreign culture, foreign government, and foreign trade. The noblemen shut themselves in against the vitalising influence of a contact with the new order of civilisation which the foreign government had clumsily introduced. Being on a perpetual defensive, the natural guardians of national culture could only insist on a punctilious observance of forms and rituals. Thus it was that all artistic creation, specially its flower, music, was languishing in this period of sheltered existence and mistrust on the part of the natural upholders of native traditions, and of indiscriminate imitation of foreign culture by those who battened on foreign rule and trade. At this crisis of Indian

Culture, the Tagore family took the lead in the movement of creative assimilation that had been initiated by Rajah Ram Mohun Roy. The movement was not eclectic, a mere mechanical mixture of the best of both cultures. Old restrictions were discarded, old ideals were re-valued, and new forms accepted and evolved. The great work was well divided between the members of the Tagore household. The Poet was the supreme artist in a family of artists. He had been accustomed to the intricacies of classical music, the best exponents of which had then gravitated to the new city in search of patronage by the newly rich. He had steeped himself equally in the folk-music of the country-side in course of his constant excursions. His family-surroundings, specially the sympathetic guidance of his brother, Jyotirindranath, were congenial to the spirit of invention. In such a context, and with such equipments, the Poet was eminently fitted to synthesise the classical and the folk-types of our music into a unique style. His urge of creation was furnished by the need of all life. He was the inheritor of the best of Indian and Western culture, he interpreted freedom and joy of life as continuous initiative in the creation of human values, he was the child of the new city and of the old village. In him were combined the sense of values of the aristocrat and the simplicity, directness and universality of the child of the soil. No wonder that his songs are sung in the most exclusive drawing-rooms, in the crowded market-places, and in the countryside of Bengal.

And he plays on the whole gamut of human feelings with equal skill. The myriad tones of religious emotion and love, of feeling for nature and man are all touched surely and truly in his songs. He has not only struck the relevant emotions in the schedule of the psychologist, he has produced and communicated new combinations of feelings which have enriched the life of the devotee, the lover, the poet, the humanist, the tiller of the soil and the vendor in the market-place. His songs have made us feel in a new way, a richer way. They have entered into our unconscious and conscious cerebration. They have passed into the parlance of the soul. Each word, by its appropriateness, creates an eddy in the confused tide of emotions, each phrase, by its precision, separates the currents, and the whole piece canalises the stream of a novel emotion. There are many such streams which are gathered in the dominant phase of the development of his personality. In one book of songs, love, in another, nature, in a third, devotion is the theme. And when a particular phase of emotion in a piece corresponds to that of the singer, the expression becomes spontaneous and beautiful. His songs, thus rendered, do not demand an artificial situation to which the singer has to respond by the display of sheer technical skill. From the human point of view, the exposition of Classical Indian music is a *tour de force ;* for expression is there a matter of technique, and emotions, as we understand them, are conspicuous by their absence. Herein lies an original trait of the Poet's music. Rabindranath, even in his adaptations from the classical style, evokes feelings through his language the adequacy and equality of status of which to the new musical form is so complete that it creates automatically an atmosphere for spontaneous expression. His songs are excellent poems and bear recital. The same cannot be said of most classical pieces. He is a magician of the language, and his songs are composed with due regard to the musical value of words and phrases. The texture of his verse, *i.e.*, its assonance and rhythm, its proper arrangements of vowels and consonants, its beginnings, pauses, and ends are all in tune with its music. The poetic value never jars with, in fact, almost invariably supports the musical value. To him words come clothed in music and the two are inseparable. It is by such happy combinations that emotions are generated and reinforced.

All emotions are ultimately human emotions in the sense that they suffuse the moods and feelings of the artist who creates or recreates, and of the artist who appreciates. In verbal arrangement, the meaning, which must be common to all, establishes a more or less immediate contact between the two. In a musical arrangement the connection is remote on account of the absence of meaning. But when a particular verbal sequence is in perfect accord with the sequence of notes, the remoteness tends to disappear, and all is well for the emotional osmosis or contagion. The glory of our classical music is its formal autonomy quarantined against the contagion of emotions as we understand them. Tagore has abolished this quarantine of formalities and humanised our music.

Naturally, the technique of the process of humanisation has to be simple and direct. Hence Tagore's technique is severely economical. In his characteristic songs his technical affinity is rather to the folk than to the court-music. His words and melodies are familiar and yet beautiful. The elaborate flourishes which distinguish the later developments of Indian music under sheltered court-patronage have no place here. But the features of the so-called earlier classical type, *viz.*, 'Dhrupad.' which, in reality, was the folk-music of Gwalior and its neighbouring areas, are retained throughout. The rigour and dignity of its composition, its division into four movements, its linear quality or 'Mirh,' its modulation or 'Murchhana,' its 'Gamak' or sudden changes, and its freedom from flourishes or 'Tans' are very well preserved in the earlier compositions. Though the classical purity of melodies is somewhat 'obscured' in certain songs by a slight shifting of stress between the important notes, the spirit is the same as ever. The rhythmic division of the earlier pieces is generally of Dhrupad ; its slow, simple, majestic and dignified movement is never obstructed or quickened in ill-conceived haste. But experiments are being made concurrently. Generally, they are either blendings of melodies and rhythms, rare or familiar, or adaptations of certain forms of folk-music. Even certain familiar forms of instrumental music, *e.g.*, *Sitar*, are commandeered. At this period, he is not above adopting a few forms of European music, chiefly the operatic. He even seeks to introduce harmony. His surging need for freedom creates new melodies and rhythms, and liberates songs from their bond-slavery to beats. The result of these technical experiments and innovations has been the creation of a unique style of Indian music which is a thing of joy to all but the prejudiced. Through his experiments many old techniques have survived, and many beautiful ones have emerged. The purist may sing his songs with the developments that he thinks he must needs introduce, he may sing without them, as the romanticist does in the way indicated by the composer, and yet in both cases he will be free. And the ordinary man renders them to the best of his abilities by imposing his own feelings on them or by being emotionally charged by them. Such a variety of repertoire cannot please all alike, yet all can draw on it with profit and joy.

Our music is not dead. It has grown, and grown by the usual procedure of adaptation and assimilation. The history of our classical music is full of instances of wholesale incorporations from local or folk-types, and personal contributions of eminent artists. Provincial 'Raginis,' styles, even personal variations have well-appointed niches in our Pantheon. And for one variety of Bilas Khan or Dhondi, for five of Miyan Tansen, Tagore has a dozen. 'Bangali' is a 'Ragini,' so is 'Gurjari' or 'Deshi.' The objection to the novelty of Tagore's creations in the face of the logic of history is thus meaningless and rather late in the day. It is just possible that the objection is too early, for the romantic of to-day becomes the classic of to-morrow. Besides, when Tagore's creations are of such excellent musical value by themselves, it is safe to prophesy that the life of Hindustani music is assured in his hands. Nobody in the history of our music is the creator of so many beautiful varieties of Bhairavi, Todi, Khambaj, Mallar, Kedar, Behag, Bahar, to take a few names. And the new melodies which cannot be labelled are a legion. Tagore is in the main line of traditions, urban and rural, but he stands where sophistication ends and creative freedom begins. To one who takes a historical and a creative view of culture, and whose ears are open to melodies other than the simply familiar and customary, Tagore's songs mark a new lease of life and herald in a new era for Hindustani music. Once again, music is free, full of joy and related to human personality in indissoluble ties.

THE UNIVERSITY,
LUCKNOW

DHURJATI PRASAD MUKERJI

SANCTITY AND SOCIETY

THE course of social evolution clearly shows that religion has been an indispensable instrument which has aided man in his struggles of life ; it has elicited attitudes and modes of behaviour which have offered man easy guidance in adjusting himself both to his environment and group. Religion in the highest minds, where it is not conventional or institutional, has kept alive in society a faith in certain ultimate values which have guaranteed social progress towards higher levels. Such religious experience is familiarly known as mysticism. To many people mysticism however suggests aberration rather than normal growth of personality. This attitude is mainly due to a tendency often manifest among the psychologists to view religious experience from a wrong perspective. Thus from James to Leuba what is for the most part religious disease has been examined, though not without sympathy, and the result has been that religion is either discredited or reduced to an illusion. In all imaginative experience there are higher and lower levels ; and as we do not condemn all art or poetry simply because there are found bad specimens we should not decry mysticism by examining only its inferior or misguided phases. A study of normal mystical experiences shows that the religious person with his greater sanity and freedom orders his life better, and attains greater heights and depths of personality than the ordinary person. So far as society is concerned, he is also a greater asset in as much as being a better judge of what human nature really needs he discovers the source of social values. In the religious person, social values re-incarnate themselves ; in him the conflict of social ideals is completely resolved. It is he who leads society towards that full harmony and complete concord, which he obtains from his experience of God.

It is in the intimacies of relationships with a personal divinity that mystics satisfy instincts of self-assertion, sex or paternal impulses, and develop a loyalty which Professor Royce describes as a principle fit to be made the basis of a universal moral code. The spirit of true loyalty is of its very essence a complete synthesis of the moral and of the religious interests. Now this loyalty springs from different relations between God and the mystic, such, for instance, as when the mystic regards himself as God's servant, as God's friend or comrade, as God's son or, again, as elect bride ; and therefore results in his different ethical attitudes towards society and the environment. And, indeed, the loyalty entails a gradual organisation of the emotions so that there is less psychic conflict, and man develops a permanent organised attitude which is most in keeping with his social behaviour. Thus the danger that an emotional abandon precludes social obligations is avoided. All religions emphasise different kinds of loyalty, and historical traditions, myths or legends give direction and aim to such loyalties.

The mystic chooses different emotional approaches to God such as the attitude of calm resignation, of consecrated service, of loving companionship, of paternal tenderness, or of passionate conjugal love; or rather his particular attitude towards God expresses the fundamental needs of his own nature. As he empties his sub-consciousness, perhaps another attitude comes easily and thus the denizens of heaven are but means for the fulfilment of his baulked desires and interests. It is to these that his incipient responses are directed. As men come in touch with physical objects only through their responses, their adaptive behaviour in relation to his symbols and ideal constructions brings home to them the sense of their physical presence. Gods and angels, and their friends and companions, like their adversaries such as demons and spirits, thus make their presence felt and these change their mood or behaviour to suit the impulses and interests that have created them. This is the phenomenon of communion in which the mystic is convinced of an impressive presence, more concretely real than what his eyes see, his ears hear or his hands touch. Poulain refers to this experience as follows: "There is a profound difference between thinking of a person and feeling him near us, and so when we feel that some one is near us, we say that we have an experimental knowledge of his presence. In the mystic state, God is not satisfied merely to help us to think of Him, and to remind us of His Presence. In a word, He makes us feel that we really enter into communication with Him." Now the difference between religious communion and dream or reverie which similarly proceeds from man's satisfaction in an ideal world of fundamental tendencies of human nature, such as self-assertion, the needs for paternal fondness, for affection and love, etc., is that divine beings blend together as large a number of impulses as possible and hence are more stable and recur much oftener. Thus the mystic exhibits an organised or stable system of behaviour. This is facilitated by the fact that the mystic concentrates his attention on the religious object or its attributes, and with effort directs all his impulses and interests along one channel. For this reason the object of worship not only gives greater consolation and joy but it also reveals itself to the consciousness with much greater beauty and power than, for instance, the figures in a day-dream or reverie, and hence the sense of its presence is more overwhelming. While the dream or reverie spins out in an endless series of images, thoughts and feelings eliciting behaviour without order and system, the mystic's vision is composed of more or less stable realities, which are true, good and beautiful, engendering certain permanent attitudes. Such stable attitudes exhibited in the diverse relations of the mystic to God as, for instance, His son, His servant, His comrade, or again, as His chosen bride, organise all his emotions and sentiments into a harmonious pattern, and thus his family, his kindred, his group come to possess a rich spiritual interest and significance for him. The various emotional approaches to God engender the romance and spirituality of motherhood, fatherhood, comradeship, or sex and weave in fine and delicate texture the pattern of social bonds. Religion thus becomes a search for the very substance of values, which have significance not merely for the mystic's own joy and complete living but also for the world of man. The *Maha-Nirvana Tantra* frankly declares: "The image of God conceived by the mind is as helpless in securing one's salvation as a kingdom obtained in dream is in securing for him the kingship. Those who worship earthen, wooden or stone images as gods labour in vain, as without knowledge of Reality salvation cannot be obtained." When the centre of mysticism is an ideal realised in a person, such as a supreme historic figure like Christ or the Buddha or a semi-historical figure like Rama-Chandra or Krishna portrayed in epics and legends full of ethical suggestions, the loyalty to God also binds man to the service of God in the world. Thus God not only vivifies the mystic's heart and satisfies his subconscious desires, giving him a peace that passeth all understanding, but also serves to establish a new kinship of man with fellow-man and the forces of nature. Such a life is possible only with strenuous effort. Indeed, the mystic consciously and deliberately seeks an experience of ultimate values and it is his sense of difference between different kinds of values which rescues society from maladjustment and conflict of attitudes. It is the mystic who lives a most self-conscious life, and it is his synthesis of ends and purposes in an ideal plane, which brings about social harmony and is thus an essential condition of the stability and complex evolution of society.

A religion of feeling through ecstatic experience which represents religion in its most acute, intense and living stage accordingly offers a far better solution of the ills of life than philosophy and metaphysics. The infinite worth of Man is stressed and, what is more, men move fellow-men as objects of their worship. Man achieves a cosmic gregariousness and life is regarded as a cosmic drama of loving finite spirits all reciprocating in their mutual relation the infinite love of God. It is well-known how the ancient monistic philosophy of the Vedanta was transformed in India by religious mysticism which laid stress upon a community of souls in the unity of the absolute life. The monistic position was not entirely given up. It was maintained that God is infinite and at the same time a person, but the limitation of personality does not apply to the case of God, whose infinitude of power can be felt by every finite being. Love demands a sympathetic and synthetic response. Thus the finite being is as much a requirement for God as God for the finite being. This idea is neatly expressed in a Bengalee folk-song which reiterates that there is no salvation, because love sees the equal reality and necessity of both the divine and the finite, and holds each other in sweet, eternal communion. Rabindranath Tagore has translated the song as follows: "It goes on blossoming for ages, the soul lotus, in which I am bound, as well as thou, without escape. There is no end to the opening of its petals, and the honey in it has such sweetness that thou like an enchanted bee canst never desert it, and therefore thou art bound, and I am, and salvation is nowhere."

THE UNIVERSITY, LUCKNOW

RADHA KAMAL MUKHERJEE

A CHORUS FROM THE *PROMETHEUS BOUND* OF AESCHYLUS

[All living things and the whole world of nature suffer in pity for Prometheus, the crucified champion of mankind.]

We sigh, O Prometheus, for the doom that lieth o'er thee;
    Our soft-eyed rivers flow sobbing to the main
Through a mist of tears, lifted as in sacrifice before thee;

    And dew is on my cheek for the world and its pain.
'Tis the new law of Zeus hath ordained this desolation;
And his sceptre, it is stern and unbent by supplication
    To the remnant of the old Gods' reign.

For the whole Earth groaneth with travail of compassion;
    And shapes of old beauty, which none before could see,
And powers of old greatness, are aching with thy passion,
    For thee and for thy brethren, and the pride that used to be.

The multitudes afar, that in Asia have their dwelling
And sit in holy places, with strange tears are welling;
    And the lips of them that perish pine for thee.

Yea, the Amazons, the dwellers beyond Phasis,
    Who love not, who battle without fear;
And the hordes that wander in fierce places
    At the world's rim, the Scythians of the Mere:
And hard men, of Araby the flower,
    Where the high crags of Caucasus advance,
They groan in their mountain-builded tower,
    Amid great wrath and flashing of the lance.

The breakers of the sea clash and roar
Together, and the gulfs thereof are sore
With longing; there is murmur of hearts aching
    In Hades and the Cavern of the Deep,
And the torrents of the hills, white-breaking,
    For pity of thy pain weep and weep.

OXFORD

GILBERT MURRAY

FOR those who have grown up in the Tagore tradition in India it is a little difficult to measure the great influence it has exercised on them and on the country. I cannot venture to do so. But I wish to pay my deep homage to one who has been as a beacon light to all of us, ever pointing to the finer and nobler aspects of life and never allowing us to fall into the ruts which kill individuals as well as nations. Nationalism, specially when it urges us to fight for freedom, is noble and life-giving. But often it becomes a narrow creed, and limits and encompasses its votaries and makes them forget the many-sidedness of life. But Rabindranath Tagore has given to our nationalism the outlook of internationalism and has enriched it with art and music and the magic of his words, so that it has become the full-blooded emblem of India's awakened spirit.

ALLAHABAD

JAWAHARLAL NEHRU

PEACE

Dark in its channel which the grasses hide,
With living speed through marsh and desert flowing,
Thirty feet deep its waters curl and slide,
Almost without a whisper going.

Quiet things come and lap it with soft tongue,
Footstep by footstep through the silence creeping,
And starry leopards shine its reeds among,
When all but they and stars are sleeping.

It has no name among the streams of earth,
No proud explorer has its bearings given ;
Only the sun and moon watched at its birth,
And it has sucked the breasts of heaven.

In peace assured, these perilous lands between,
It will its waters to some deep deliver ;
And had I been what I too might have been,
Then had my peace been like a river.

CENTRAL AFRICA

HENRY W. NEVINSON

TO RABINDRANATH TAGORE

What a bird and flower leave unsung,
Thou shalt at once take up: symphony born, not fashioned.
Oh, to have thy song without art's rebellion,
To see thy life gaining a simple force that is itself creation,
Oh, to be forgotten by the tyranny of intellect!

Thou biddest the minuet, chanson and fancies to be stopped,
The revels and masquerade to be closed;
Thou steppest down from a high throne
To sit by people in simple garb and speech.
In simplicity
Thou hast thine own emancipation;
Let us be sure of our true selves.
There is no imagination where there is no reality;
To see life plain
Is a discovery or sensation.

I read in thee the problem of life and the world,
The twist of tears and joy,
The depth of space, the amplitude of time,
The circle of the universe in perfection;
I read in thee our obedience to exigencies and law,
The real knowledge
That makes the inevitable turn to a song.
Exigency is only change of rhythm;
Feeling the harmony
Makes us strict to the law.

Thy song looms above time and space,
A quality of psychical life not troubled by eternity or fashion;—
The real touch;—
The surprise.
Thy song is nothing but thyself.

I see before myself the busy feet of the wind,
Suggesting humanity and law.
The wind hastens
To the shadow whose passion lies;
Shall we go abroad and start anew, O wind,
To build again a better life and song?

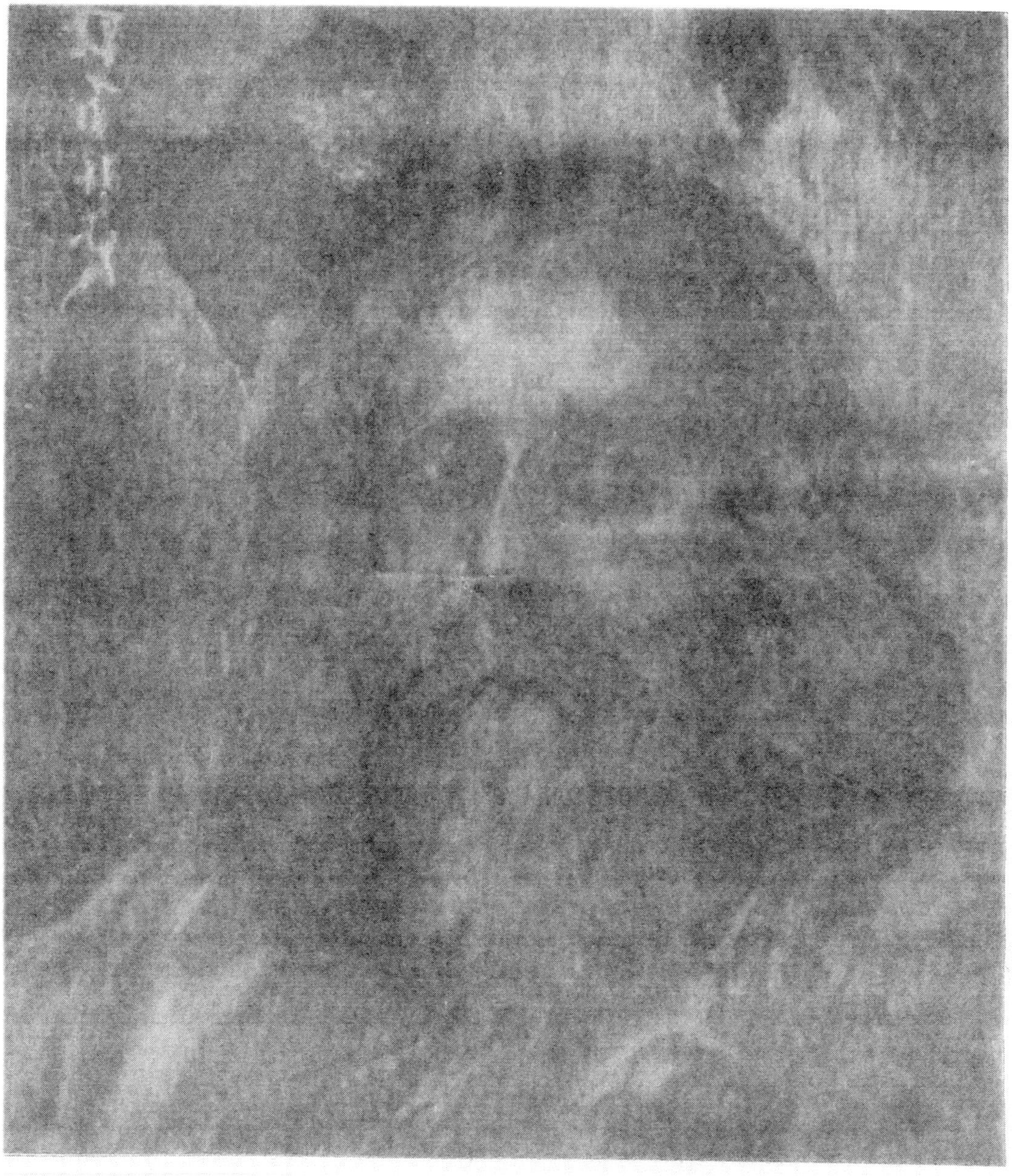

Thou, a light born of dream and hope,
Thou, singer of life's thrill,
Let thy magic of meditation,
Thy witchery of song, play
On the vastness of silence!

TOKYO

YONE NOGUCHI

VORREDE ZU DEM BUCHE "TAGORE'S BEKENNTNIS"

als Gruss an den Dichter und Weisen

IM Sommer 1930 besuchte Rabindranath Tagore unsere Philipps-Universität in Marburg und hielt uns den Vortrag uber *seine* Religion. Tief eindrucksvoll war uns diese hohe Erscheinung edelen Ariertumes aus dem Osten in ihrer Verbindung von Schlichtheit mit feinster Würde, von künstlerischer Formung mit geistigem Gehalte, von umfassender Humanität mit individuellster Prägung. Er gab Zeugnis von "seiner Religion." Was uns dabei den tiefsten Eindruck machte, war, dass er weder religionswissenschaftliche Theorien vor uns ausbreiten, noch ein abgekürztes System indischer Glaubensweise vortragen, sondern rein sein persönliches Erleben darlegen und uns daran teilhaben lassen wollte— sein ganz persönliches, das von dieser Person und ihrer besonderen Art gar nicht abgezogen und allgemein gemacht werden kann, das aber eben durch seine Eigenart und Unmittelbarkeit und durch die Kraft seines Selbstausdruckes uns packen und uns vor die Frage stellen kann, was denn wir von religiöser Erfahrung wissen und Eigenes haben und ob wir etwas haben.

Um deswillen nehme ich mir die Freiheit, dieses Bekenntnis Tagore's bekanntzumachen. Ich gedenke nicht, aus ihm Kapital zu schlagen für meine eigene Theologie, noch es einzuordnen in meine religionstheoretischen Fächer. Ich fühle erneut den sphärenweiten Unterschied zwischen indischem Upanishadengeiste und dem Geiste, der vom Boden Palästinas aus durch die Welt gegangen ist, und den Unterschied der Religion des Dichters von der Religion biblischen Prophetentumes, die die meine ist. Aber noch mehr fühlte ich und fühlten andere, die mit mir ihrer christlichen Sonderart bewusst waren, die belebende Kraft der Berührung mit tiefem persönlichen Erfahren und den erfrischenden Reiz, der von ihr auf das eigene Wesen geheimnisvoll weckend ausging.

Tagore weiss und bekennt sich frei von fremdher aufgedrängter und nur übernommener Fühlensweise. Dennoch beruft er sich suf das Blut seiner vedischen Vorfahren, das in seinen Adern fliesst, und auf die gleiche Weise des Erfahrens und Deutens der Welt mit jenen. Und in der Tat wurzelt seine Art tief in seinem eigenen indischen Boden und trägt seine Farbe. Man hat ihn aus englischen Dichtern interpretieren wollen: man weiss nicht, dass er, wenn schon in moderner Weise doch selber in gewissem Sinne Fortsetzer einer speziell bengalischen Dichterschule und-tradition ist, um deren Bekanntmachung er selber die grössten Verdienste hat. Aber noch mehr: in der Tat lebt altes Upanishadengut in seinen Werken. Als ich ihn bei seiner vorigen Reise durch Deutschland besuchte und in einem sehr persönlichen Zwiegespräche fragte, ob eine der alten heiligen Schriften Indiens eine besondere Bedeutung für ihn gehabt habe und welche das sei, gab er eine Antwort, die ich vermutet hatte. Er erzählte, dass sein Vater unter den Upanishaden die *Isa-Upanishad* besonders geschätzt habe, ihre Worte oft zitiert habe, sie mit ihm gelesen habe, und dass der Geist gerade dieser feinen kleinen Schrift ihn selber am tiefsten bewegt habe. Es ist ein Schauspiel von hohem Interesse, zu sehen, wie hier in der Tat uraltes religiöses Erleben sich erneuert in einer modernen Seele, und es ist dann noch lehrreicher, zu sehen, wie sich altes Erbgut in einem Heutigen zugleich auch wandelt, und wie es in einem Menschen ungewöhnlich individueller Eigenart sich ganz individuell gestaltet.

MARBURG — RUDOLF OTTO

MESSAGE FROM BURMA

ON behalf of Burma and the Burmese Buddhist Community, I welcome the Seventieth Birth Anniversary of one of India's greatest sons, Dr. Rabindranath Tagore. Through his services to humanity in manifold spheres he has given us honour, and we honour him. We are proud of him and we are grateful for all that he has done for us. As a messenger of peace and a missionary of human brotherhood, he has travelled far and wide, and he has worked strenuously to bind the East and the West together with the golden tie of Love. His life and ideals will long inspire all workers in the cause of humanity.

Every thing spoken about him would be inadequate, if a word is not said about his Visva-Bharati, the premier international educational centre of the East. It is only a man like him who can bring together so many distinguished workers of different countries of the world and harness their activities in the common cause of cultural progress of all mankind and establishment of brotherhood and peace on earth. Dr. Rabindranath Tagore is now old in age—though not in spirit. I wish him peace and all happiness and bless him in the holy language of the Buddhists—

Bhavatu sabbamañgalaṁ rakkhantu sabbadevatā,
Sabba-Buddhānubhāvena sadā satthī bhavantu te:
Sabba-Dhammānubhāvena sadā satthī bhavantu te:
Sabba-Sañghānubhāvena sadā satthī bhavantu te.

(BHIKKHU OTTAMA)

TO RABINDRANATH TAGORE

I drink from you,
You fountain of the mountain,
You who gush up, rush down,
And wash smoothly the curb, marbly and verdant.
(Oh, your limpid garland, your festoons!
Oh, a moment of sun-glow!)
After a day of ample work, bending my form,
I soak my lips of ardent thirst in you,
In your crepuscular water immersed the Zenith's profundity,
In your abundant water delicious, clear and transparent.
Above your full flow
Lies the pale gold of the peace after a storm,
And from the rosy peak to peak, far away,
God's flag of truce is trailing and waving.
The thousand preperceptions swell your bosom,
Especially at the end of a day.
You give yourself to the sacred dark of the night,
Resounding with your songs the eve full of expectations.
I drank from you, delicious fountain in the twilight,
You who conceive already the dawn of to-morrow.
And kneeling on the mosses sombre and soft,
I quaff and swill your pulsation of Life
Full of expectancy and birth,
Full of maternal joys of Creation.

TOKYO KIHACHI OZAKI

Many happy returns.

TOKYO BARON OKURA

University of the Philippines extends heartiest greetings and best wishes.

MANILA RAFAEL PALMA

RABINDRANATH AND BENGAL

WHEN the British brought to us the inspiration and message of the modern European culture, through the new English schools and colleges, established under their auspices, Bengal unconsciously took to this culture, not as something alien to its history and genius, but as a thing that had an inherent affinity with these. This new European culture was pre-eminently the product of the French Illumination with its ideal of freedom, equality and fraternity. These ideals were not foreign to the history and spirit of Bengalee culture ; only the terms and expressions and the social implications of the gospel of the French Revolution brought to us by our British masters were new. The spirit was the same ; only the expression was different. This expression was certainly more rational and thorough than what we had known before, in our own culture and history. The movement of revolt resulting from the introduction of English education and European culture in Bengal was therefore *formal* and not real. The reality behind it was an attempt on the part of the spirit of Bengal to go back to itself and not to go out to Europe. From the very beginning the modern movement in Bengal, though in its outer expression a movement of revolt against existing religious faiths and social institutions, was really in its soul and essence a movement of revival and return. Raja Ram Mohan Roy was the Father of the new Renaissance in Bengal. To understand Rabindranath we must understand Bengal as interpreted and represented by the Raja.

Rabindranath's inheritances from Raja Ram Mohan were more direct and intimate than those from the general thought and culture of his race and province. The Raja was an intimate friend of Rabindranath's grand-father Dwaraka Nath Tagore, who was one of the trustees of the Raja's Brahmo Samaj. Rabindranath's father Devendra Nath succeeded the Raja in the leadership of the Brahmo Samaj Movement. Owing to these intimate associations Rabindranath grew up from his very birth under the influences of the Brahmo Samaj or more correctly of that wing of it of which his father was the Leader and Minister.

Nor can we ignore Rabindranath's inheritances from his own family, the Tagores. The Tagores of Calcutta have been the greatest representatives of the composite Bengalee culture that developed under Moslem rule in Bengal. It was the composite culture which developed among us under the influence of the Moslem court. Rabindranath's grand-father, Dwaraka Nath, was the first Bengalee Hindu (except Raja Ram Mohan) to cross the 'black waters' in defiance of orthodox Hindu interdiction and visited England and France, where he was received as a 'Prince' by the highest classes of society. Rabindranath inherited the undeniable aristocratic mind and manners, in the best sense of the terms, from his family. He is a democrat by education, but really an aristocrat by nature, in the highest sense of the term.

Raja Ram Mohan had, however, one great limitation. He was not able to appreciate or assimilate the thought and art of Bengal Vaishnavism. The Raja's theology was unmistakably filiated to the Sankara-Vedanta School more than to the Vaishnava School of his own province. It was really no fault of the Raja. The Vaishnavas of Bengal were feebly posted in the philosophy of their own denomination. The movement of Sri Chaitanya Mahaprabhu committed a great blunder by adopting the popular Krishna legend as vehicle both of their religion and their art. It helped certainly to popularise the externals of the Vaishnava propaganda in Bengal. But, on the other hand, this Krishna legend overwhelmed the rational theology and the emotional spirituality of our Vaishnavic cult and culture to such an extent that these became a bye-word among the higher classes of the Bengalee Hindu community, dominated by the rival Sakti Cult. The theology of the Sakti Cult was clearly based upon the Sankara-Vedanta Monism. The central note of the Sakti culture is the Cult of the Mother, or the Universal Mother, or Mahamaya, or the creative energy of Brahman. The popular image-worship of the Sakti Cult has been openly regarded as symbolic only and designed for the education of the unillumined. When the Truth is realised and the devotee becomes conscious of his identity with Brahman, all these lower cults and cultures drop off like the slough of the snakes. The exuberant emotionalism of this Mother Cult was also protected by the very conception of the Divine Mother from those vulgar sensualities by which Vaishnavic piety and art in Bengal were notoriously overwhelmed at the hands of the unillumined crowd. All these have been responsible for Raja Ram Mohan's lack of understanding and appreciation of the theology and art of Bengal Vaishnavism. In fact, the Movement of Sri Chaitanya needed the message of Raja Ram Mohan for its highest self-fulfilment. Unfortunately, the Brahmo Samaj under Rabindranath's father Devendra Nath failed to realise this essential aspect of its own mission. It strove to take back modern India to the Upanishads, condemning the subsequent evolution of Hindu thought and culture of what is called the Pauranic Age as evidences of degeneration and arrested development.

Rabindranath's theology is inspired by the teachings of his own father. Rabindranath's God is the God of the Upanishads. His father's faith was a living faith in a Personal God. It was Faith and not really philosophy or theology. The Upanishads proclaim the immanence of God. Whatever is, is Brahman. Side by side with this they also declare what may be called the transcendence of God. Brahman is in everything, yet Brahman is in nothing. He permeates all, and stands beyond all. The philosophy of the Upanishads is really the philosophy of the Unknown and the Unknowable.

Art, like that of Rabindranath's, could not possibly grow on a soil like this. Fortunately, however, Rabindranath's philosophy like the theology of his father is really not agnostic but essentially theistic. And in the development of this theistic art, Rabindranath has drawn, though unconsciously, to a very large extent upon the realisations of Vaishnavic art. Vaishnavic art of Bengal or more accurately the Vaishnavic lyrics have developed around the Radha-Krishna legend. Rabindranath has not followed the Vaishnava poets of Bengal in this. But the reality behind the Radha-Krishna legend is the reality of universal human experience. In his religious creations Rabindranath has more or less worked upon these universal human experiences without any specific human materials or symbols. Such materials and symbols would not appeal to the modern mind, either in India or any other country. But the modern man feels exhausted by the barrenness of logical deductions and inductions and philosophical abstractions and generalisations of modern thought. It has been groping after a Personal God, established by philosophy, and capable of being tested and enjoyed by poetry. Rabindranath's *Gitanjali* gave to the modern man just the thing which, consciously or unconsciously, and more unconsciously than consciously, he was hankering after. It is real without being sensuous, and ideal without being abstract.

But the depth, the grandeur, the power and the superb beauty of Rabindranath's creations can never be brought out in translations. One must read and study them in the original to appraise the genius and art of Rabindranath correctly. No other Indian province could produce a Rabindranath. No Indian vernacular except the Bengalee could supply the material for his art-creations. The wealth of diction, the music of sound, that characterise Rabindranath's poems, are the special contribution of his mother-tongue. Rabindranath had mastered both the spirit and the form of the Vaishnava lyrics of Bengal in his early youth. His *Bhanusinher Padavali* or Poems of Bhanusinha are the clearest possible evidences of it. M. Madhusudan Datta also tried his hand in composing modern lyrics after the manner of the mediaeval Vaishnavas, but he failed woefully, because he never made himself familiar with Vaishnava lyrics as Rabindranath had done. Madhusudan's diction is more classical. His vocabulary is far more Sanskrit than Bengalee. Rabindranath, however, is intensely a Bengalee in both. Rabindranath has demonstrated as much by his poetic creations as by his prose style the great wealth of the Bengalee language. True it is that Bengal had no prose literature worthy of the name before Raja Ram Mohan Roy. But the material for building up a high-class literature, both in prose and poetry, have been present even in our mediaeval Bengalee lexicon. These materials were waiting a master builder. That builder came in Rabindranath. And the greatest contribution of Rabindranath is this, namely, that he has secured a place for his provincial thought and literature in the world-thought and world-literature of our day.

He has built upon our old foundations. Our old Vaishnava art, though unsurpassed in its own line, was, however, narrow in its outlook. The four *rasas* with which Bengal Vaishnava lyrics deal do not exhaust the whole range of man's emotional life and experience. These four *rasas*, namely, (*i*) the romance of the servitor and master or subject and king, or sons and daughters and parents relation, called the *dasya rasa*, (*ii*) the romance of friendship, (*iii*) the romance of the parental affection, and (*iv*) the romance of the man and woman or the hero and heroine relation in poetry and drama, which have been delineated with unrivalled skill by our Vaishnava poets, do not exhaust the whole range of man's romantic experience. These *rasas* are romances of our domestic and communal life. The modern man lives an almost infinitely larger life to-day. His relations expand far beyond his family or his community, or even his own country. He is bound up to-day in a net of relations, economic and commercial, political and cultural, that covers the whole of humanity. These many-sided relations are not without their own romances. These romantic experiences of the modern man are not included in or exhausted by the four old Vaishnavic *rasas*. Yet the general characteristic of *rasa* or romance is present in all these relations, as they are in the old Vaishnavic delineation. Rabindranath has lifted our old lyrics from the narrow groove in which they are confined by our Vaishnava poets. The romantic love of one's own country, the yearning for national freedom, the passion for Universal Humanity—these are the special creations in our national lyrics of Rabindranath. By these he has helped to universalise what was special and particular in the poetic creations of his predecessors. Rabindranath therefore is not only the poet of modern Bengal but he is equally the poet, in a special sense, of the modern man all the world over.

He is also the prophet of the new age. His denunciation of modern nationalism marks him out as the prophet of that Internationalism towards which the whole world is unmistakably advancing. The word of the history and evolution of the last century, as Lord Morley once pointed out, was nationalism. That nationalism has already done its work. The word of the history and evolution of the present century is Internationalism. And Rabindranath stands in the very forefront of the prophets of this internationalism.

In all this Rabindranath is, above all, a Bengalee. In his philosophy he has worked to bring the ancient theosophy of the Upanishads to the modern man. In his poetic creations he has brought the realisations of the mediaeval Vaishnava and Sakta worshippers of Bengal to the most advanced modern plane. In his protest against the spirit of current nationalism, which has been a call to universal war, and in his message of that Universal Humanity wherein every national group must seek and find the highest fulfilment of their legitimate national freedom, which must replace current competitions by universal co-operation—Rabindranath has tried to fulfil the mission of that Universal Religion for which Raja Ram Mohan strove. In all these he represents, in a very special measure, the genius and culture of his own people and province.

CALCUTTA

BIPIN CHANDRA PAL

AN RABINDRANATH TAGORE

Welche Botschaft kann uns das gwaltige Indien sagen?
Es gibt keine grössere, als seinen Verzicht auf jede Gewalt ausser der das Geistes.
Und welche Predigt kann Indien uns geben, die wir der Mahnung bedürftig sind?
Keine eindringlichere, als den Gesang der Freiheit in wohllautenden Strophen, mit denen uns der Sänger entzüchte als er Gast in unserem Lande war und wir kamen, um ihn zu sehen.
Wir werden uns seiner hohen Gestalt und seines strahlendes Gesichtes erinnern.
Denn wir sind aus der Vorstellungskraft und aus der unendlichen Macht desselben Schöpfers hervorgegangen.

FRANKFURT-AM-MAIN

ALFONS PACQUET

FROM THE Y. M. C. A.

On behalf of the National Council of the Y.M.C.A.'s of India, Burma, and Ceylon, and for myself personally, I send our felicitations, on the occasion of the 70th birthday of the Poet. We thank God for his long life and for his great service to the people of India in the realms of Religion, Education and Literature. There are few people who have not received inspiration and enlightenment from his works and from his personality. He has raised India high in the estimation of the world, and we pray God that He may spare him yet for many years of health and strength in order that he may continue his great work.

CALCUTTA

H. A. POPLEY

TAGORE AND THE LITERATURE OF THE SOUTH

IT is unnecessary to emphasise that, at least so far as Hindu India is concerned, there is, in spite of much apparent diversity, a unity of culture which transcends provincial boundaries and ethnological divisions. The widespread influence of religious, cultural and social movements even in medieval India, when communications were not so easy as at the present time and contact between peoples was more difficult, has been recognised to be a matter of unique significance. The Saiva Siddhanta of the Tamils has had repercussions even in far off Kashmir. The philosophical speculations of Sankara affected the thought and religious life of the whole of India. The Vaishnava movement which originated with Ramanuja penetrated far and wide and was responsible for an outburst of literary and religious activity such as India has but seldom witnessed. In our own day, owing to the complexity of national life and the emphasis attached to political movements, this re-unification of Indian thought has not been properly understood. But it is undoubted that the work of such reformers and thinkers as Raja Rammohun Roy, Swami Vivekananda and Swami Dayananda has profoundly modified the thought and life of not merely the provinces and areas they worked in but the whole of Hindu India. The modernism of the Madras Presidency acknowledges its inspiration from Brahmo thought.

If in religious and social activity this unity is still a living fact, it is much more so in the realm of literature and art. The different languages of India, whether they be Prakritic or Dravidian in origin, have all been nourished by the traditions of Sanskrit. The result is that the humanism of these literatures is fundamentally the same. Their forms of thought, their general attitude towards life and the culture they reflect are not in any way different. The modern influences that are shaping their development are also the same. They are in fact the many voices of a single living civilisation. In consequence, a literary movement of importance in one language imperceptibly affects and inspires the development of all others. This fact, which should have been obvious but for the political pre-occupations of modern India, only became clear with the rise of Rabindranath Tagore as a world-poet.

That Tagore should have become naturalised or adopted in the literatures of North India was perhaps inevitable. After all Vidyapati, Kabir, Mirabai, Tulasidas and Nanak have become the poets not merely of Maithili, Hindi or Panjabi but of India. In the same manner, because of his being the most outstanding exponent of Indian humanism, Tagore was bound to become not merely the laureate of Bengali, but equally of Hindi and other North Indian languages. His direct influence, however, has not stopped as in the case of Kabir and others with the Vindhyas. If to-day a Malayali or Tamilian were asked as to who was the leading literary force in their respective languages, the answer would undoubtedly be Tagore. It is not that the writings of Tagore have found widespread popularity among the masses in the Tamil country or in Malabar. It is undoubtedly true that his works are popular with all classes. But it is not this popularity which gives him his predominant influence in the artistic creations of the South. It is the new life he represents, the new force to which he has given expression, the new humanism of which he is the prophet in India. Tagore represents a creative literary force which has shown to the vernaculars of the South the prospect of a new life freed from the leaden weight of encrusted tradition.

The unique example of this influence of Tagore in a Southern language is the case of the great Malayalam poet Vallathol. A poet of rare genius and a scholar of great repute in Sanskrit, Vallathol was till 1914 a blind votary of the classical tradition who wrote verses as acrobatic feats in words. He had written a *Mahakavya* in the manner of *Sisupala-vadha* of Magha, translated the whole of Valmiki's *Ramayana* and devoted himself entirely to the cultivation of unreality in art. His works had no relation to the intellectual or emotional life of the people for whom he wrote. In 1913 the new light of Tagore dawned on him. The transformation in him was slow, but within the next five years Vallathol had become what no other poet of Malabar had ever been, the leader of an intellectual and artistic movement embracing not merely literature but music, art and dancing. He began to be influenced by the new life that surged around him and became in fact identified with every movement meant for the emancipation of Indian thought. But his main interest lay always in the regeneration of art in its varied forms. That movement which had its origin in Vallathol has so grown in momentum that it can legitimately be said to represent the intellectual renaissance of Malabar.

Vallathol's poetry also underwent a fundamental transformation. No longer was he interested in elaborating puerile conceits with the help of a highly complicated technique or in fulfilling rigidly the canons laid down by the rhetoricians of Sanskrit; instead, he began to give exquisite and sensitive expression to the life of his own people, to their spiritual aspirations and to their artistic impulses. Nor was this influence confined to him. The younger generation, already up in arms against the rigid and unreal classicism of the poets and writers of the time, hailed him as their leader, with the result that the Malayalam language to-day is being directed by the unseen hand of Tagore and the forces he has set in motion.

It is significant that this movement which has naturalised Tagore in the South has not been confined to literature. The Malabar renaissance is perhaps better studied in the extraordinary revival of drama and dancing. Here also Vallathol is the leader and chief protagonist. When once the vision came to him of the unity of all arts and the inter-dependence of their interpretation, it became clear that, if Malabar was to develop a culture of its own, it must revive the fast dying traditions of its arts. Himself a dramatist and actor, he has devoted the last ten years of his life with single-minded devotion to this purpose. The *Kerala Kala Mandalam* which he has founded is an institution which strives to revitalise the arts of Kerala and to give new and modern direction to her creative impulses. It has already achieved remarkable results in regard to a special and unique form of classical dancing and drama known as *Katha Kali*. *Katha Kali* was once the national art of Kerala. Owing mainly to the decadence of taste following upon the soulless education of our colleges, it was fast dying out, both as a profession and as an art. Vallathol has not merely rescued it from almost complete oblivion but re-established it in popular favour. He established under the auspices of the *Kerala Kala Mandalam* a training school for *Katha Kali* actors and recruited to the profession young men of education and social standing. It is perhaps interesting to note that Tagore was so impressed by this development that he sent one of his own students for training in the School under Vallathol.

The popularity of 'the Tagore School' in the literatures of South India is by no means a passing fashion; in fact it has held the field for over 15 years now. It is true that much of what has been produced under the impetus of this movement has nothing in common with the poetry of Tagore. None the less they are in the main the outcome of the forces generated by the personality of Tagore and are in varying degrees the reflections of the same inspiration and light which came first to him among the writers of modern India. Tagore is a world-poet in the universality of his appeal, in the message which it conveys to all without difference of race, colour or creed; but to us he is essentially the poet of India, the inspired singer of songs who has shown a new way in literature, who has opened up new vistas of life and thought. The literatures of the South have drawn freely from his inspiration and their life has been rendered more varied, rich and beautiful by his influence. Thus he has once again unified the intellectual life of India, in the same manner, if not to the same extent, as Sankara, Ramanuja and Chaitanya and the other saints of earlier days.

BHOPAL — K. M. PANIKKAR

FROM V. O. K. S.

My Warmest Greetings to Rabindranath Tagore.

Dear Poet, I wish you continued happy years of creative work, benefiting India and humanity. Cultural workers of U. S. S. R. wish all success to your great educational work for renascent India.

MOSCOW PETROV

EDUCATION IN SOVIET RUSSIA

MANY a time, in the course of uncounted centuries of the history of mankind, the dream of 'the golden age', of general happiness and of the reign of justice has flashed upon the mind of poets and visionaries who rose above their time and above the narrow interest of class. Such visions served as materials for the poets who are allowed to dream as long as they are not called for action and fight for a better order.

Thus a new class grew up and organised itself with the aim of creating a new society based on justice, and guaranteeing the untramelled and unchecked progress of humanity. This burning passion moved them to greatest struggles and noblest sacrifices.

The most wide-awake and advanced section are waging a ceaseless war for the triumph of a better life. But what are its characteristics? A man belonging to this new order is 'one who lives a full life, completely developed, and ever ready to do everything'; he is a man of maximum creative activity; free and joyous, he consecrates his work to the welfare of the great whole. He is the true soldier, ever disciplined and enthusiastic, keen on sweeping away all class distinctions and aspiring to construct the future society; he is a man of real culture, a culture which looks with contempt on idlers, exploiters and oppressors of the working people, a culture which makes a man a true comrade and a reliable friend of all oppressed and exploited human beings and equipped with all the resources of human science, art and technology.

There are many impediments in the path of the attainment of this aim, the principal being the legacies of the old order. Therefore, our first task is to get rid of old habits and old customs of ownership. We are trying also to sweep away the religious superstitions; and to fight the interested class within the Church who are the pillars of exploitation and allies of the oppressers of all the wide world.

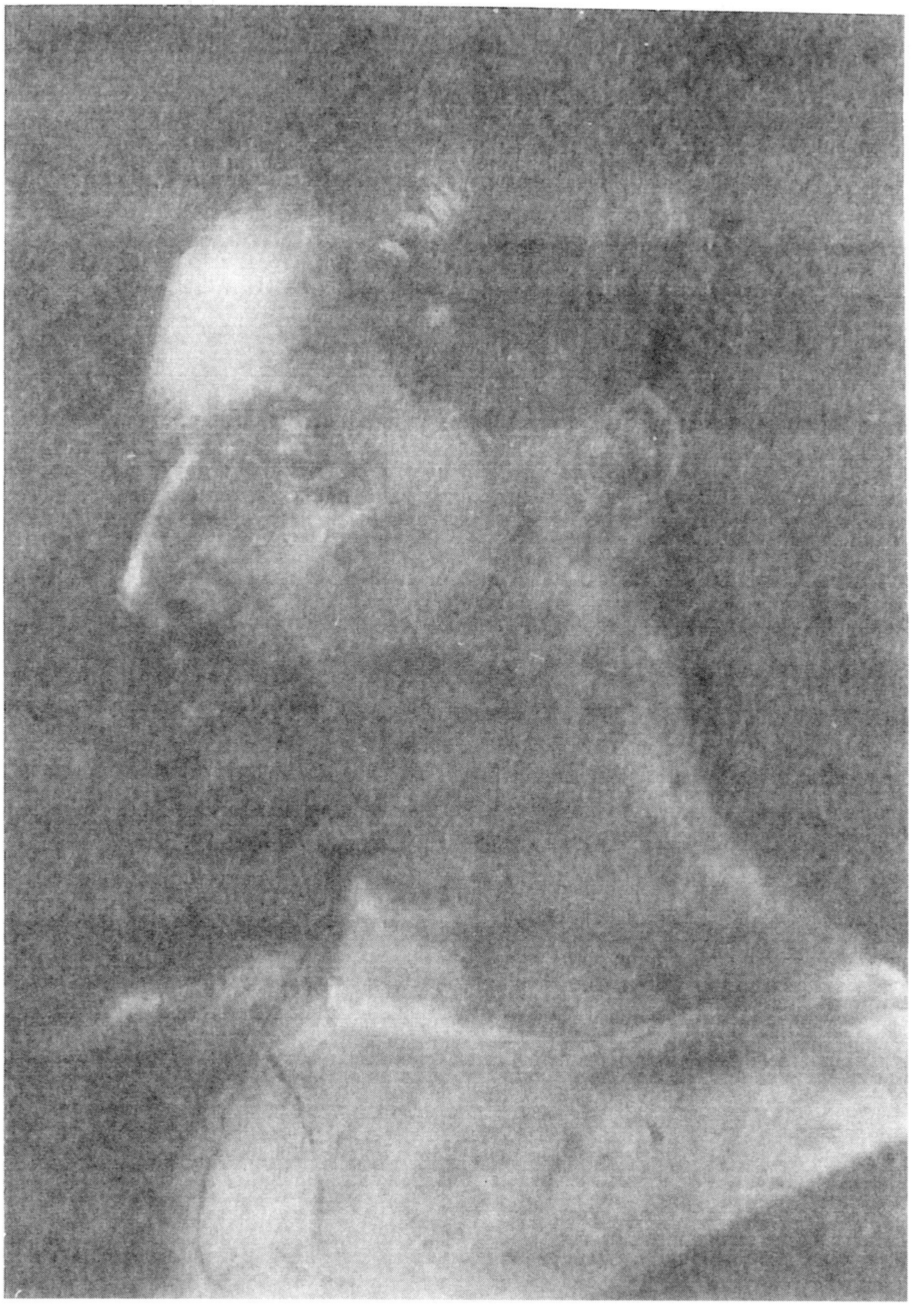

A PORTRAIT IN PASTEL

By Dr. Abanindranath Tagore, C. I. E.

By the Courtesy of
Sir J. C. Bose, C. I. E.

The vast multitudes are for the first time being attended to by innumerable education organisations. In 1931, over twenty-two millions of illiterate adults are under instruction; fourteen millions are studying in primary schools, while huge crowds are flocking to the lower, the middle and higher professional schools. Thousands of libraries, museums, picture houses, and theatres have been built and are working as educational agencies. Lastly, there are about four millions of children pioneers who are our partners in this great movement and acting as a tremendous educational factor in the creation of the new society.

The Soviet system of education and upbringing is also being carefully adapted to the varied requirements of the national culture of our two hundred nations living in U.S.S.R. New alphabets are being created, new types of schools are being constructed, national language, national literature and art are being encouraged everywhere in the same old Russia which for many ages was a synonym for savagery, stupidity and superstitions. And in this transition from the capitalistic to collectivist régime, we hope to bring about a fundamental reconstruction of the whole order through literature and science, art and education.

No less striking and original is the method of Soviet education; it has definitely broken with the passive methods and has made the people an active collaborator of his teacher. The methods of the Dalton plan, purified of their bourgeois individualistic character, are freely used.

But the most characteristic trait of our education is the inseparable connection between culture and its collective utilisation which we called Politechniquism. There is no fatal break between mental and physical work—one of the most degrading traits of capitalistic society. Hence Politechniquism occupies one of the most important places in our fight for the destruction of class distinctions. Getting acquainted in theory and practice with all the main branches of industries, the young generation gets used from their teens to a common fight and a common programme of reconstruction.

These hosts of men and women, old and young, of these vast countries are made to acquire and appreciate all that is precious in the old culture. They remember the words of their leader Lenin, who advised them 'to acquire and to utilise all that was valuable in the two thousand year old history of the development of human thought and culture.' Thus they learn gradually to realise the unity and homogeneity of the workers of the world over, gaining thereby a truly international education.

MOSCOW

ALBERT E. PINKEVITCH

BUDDHISM AND CHRISTIANITY

WHEN we in the West hear the name Rabindranath Tagore, we think at once of the marriage of Poetry and Religion: Poetry ennobled by spiritual content, Religion adorned with the irresistible appeal of Beauty. The combined product thus emerging is a symbolism and a mysticism which speaks directly to man's heart and mind, and which draws its strength from all of the great religions. It may, therefore, be not inappropriate, in a volume such as this, to devote a few pages to a comparison of two of the greatest of these religions and their respective contributions to man's spiritual needs.

What at first seems an insuperable difficulty in making such a comparison as I propose is the fact that neither Buddhism nor Christianity is capable of exact definition. Only a part of any great religion is to be found in its teachings; and even if, in our study, we should confine ourselves to the *teachings* of Buddhism and Christianity, we should find that these have varied and evolved and assumed innumerable forms in the many centuries of gradual growth that both have gone through. And if we confine our attention to the religions as they exist to-day, we are confronted with the great division in Christianity between Protestantism and Catholicism, and the even more striking contrast between Southern Buddhism and Northern. In spite of all this, however, I am willing to assent to the general agreement that Buddhism means something and that Christianity means something; and if this is really the case, some sort of significant comparison ought to be possible.

Let us, then, consider some of the more important characteristics which these great and noble religions have in common. Among the first that springs to one's mind is the attack they both make upon the sins of the flesh and upon selfishness, which they both regard as the root of all evil. Corresponding to this negation of sin, there goes in both religions a positive emphasis upon pity for the suffering and love for all. And here we must note that the love and pity of Buddhism has a wider extension than that of Christianity: for the Christian teaching limits this interest to humanity, while Buddhism takes within the fold of its sympathy and tenderness every form of sentient animal life. Within the human realm both religions carry the ideal of love to the extreme limits of accepting death in the service of others, of returning good for evil, and of loving one's enemy as one's self.

In contrast to the moral systems of some of the other great religions, these two pierce beneath the surface of man's acts and its consequences to man's will and his motives. While others look upon the outer appearances, Buddhism and Christianity look upon the heart. Both of them consider the inner life of man his true life, and both seek to cultivate it in their followers. And if we turn from the inward side of ethics to the outer, to the fundamental principle of righteousness, I think it could be shown (though I confess not without considerable argument) that both religions, in the last analysis, identify the good life with the rational life, the life that can be justified by reason, the life that gives itself to the production of the greatest amount of genuine spiritual values in oneself and in others.

The effect of both religions upon their loyal and obedient followers is a peace that passeth understanding and a joy that the world can neither give nor take away. There is, to be sure, some difference between them here. The characteristic state of the Buddhist saint is peace: that of the Christian saint is joy. Yet the Christian certainly has peace, and no one can read the ecstatic expressions of many Buddhists who have followed in the footsteps of their Master without realizing that a certain quiet and lasting joy is theirs.

It is in their effects upon the moral and hedonic lives of their followers that the two religions are most at one. Yet in their cosmic teachings they are not wholly divided. At least we may say this much: both of them tend to be pessimistic about a mere cross section of the world—the world of sin and selfishness—but both are essentially optimistic about Reality as a whole. For both of them the Universe, taken in its entirety, is essentially moral. The moral laws are the fundamental laws of being. Mahayana or Northern Buddhism would, moreover, go farther with Christianity than this: for the loving and mighty Amida Buddha, the central figure of many of its sects, is much the same kind of personal deity as the Christian God.

But with these similarities there go certain equally interesting, though not equally important, divergencies. Buddhism, like Christianity, emphasizes the will, but in the cultivation of the moral life it lays more stress than does Protestant Christianity upon discipline, training, habit formation. The perfection of one's own inner moral character is something which one must be working at all the time by conscious and systematic processes. Consequent upon this, there is in Buddhist morality a certain stiffness and self-consciousness, and a corresponding lack of that spontaneous abandon in the service of a great cause which is the very aroma of so much of the noblest Christian morality. The follower of the Buddha must be very intent on his every act, word, and thought, lest carelessness sully his carefully cultivated character; but while this is also often true of second-hand Christians, one who has been with Jesus is so devoted to a larger self than his petty one that he thinks but little of his own precious moral character, and with Wilberforce may for long periods forget that he has a soul. Noble deeds spring from him as spontaneously and beautifully as roses from a rose plant, and with as little deliberation.

Both Christianity and Buddhism teach the individual to seek his own moral perfecting and the welfare of society: but Hinayana Buddhism certainly stresses the individual, while Mahayana Buddhism and Christianity stress (at least in theory) the social. The Buddhism of the Founder as it is preserved (and doubtless considerably changed) in the Canon has a decidedly monastic coloring, and while it is positive as well as negative, stresses the negative virtues more than does Christianity. This, and a certain moral self-centredness, follow almost inevitably from the most important of the Four Noble Truths namely, that the great source of sorrow is desire. To kill out desire is thus one of the great aims of Hinayana Buddhism, for only thus can sorrow be avoided. And in this connection is to be seen another contrast between Christianity and the Hinayana, *viz.*, in the attitudes they take toward sorrow. Hinayana Buddhism is almost morbidly afraid of it. At all events it wishes to play safe. Christianity has something of the typical Western willingness to take a chance, and if worst comes to worst, it will not fear sorrow but make use of it. It is not without significance that of these two religions one has chosen as its supreme symbol and ideal the figure of a sage plunged in deep meditation and perfect calm: the other the form of a young man dying upon a cross, in which supreme suffering is present, but present to be overcome by love. I should hasten to add that in the matters here discussed, Mahayana or Northern Buddhism takes a position much more like that of Christianity. The typical Mahayana saint acquires merit in order to present it, vicariously, to others, and he would be willing even to sin if thereby he could help any other sentient creature in the moral pilgrimage.

In their attitudes toward cosmic or metaphysical matters there is, as I have said, more contrast between the two religions than on questions of ethics. And briefly put, Christianity is essentially theistic, the Hinayana agnostic, and the Mahayana monistic or pantheistic. Personality is not highly prized in Buddhism. If it exist at all, it is something to be ultimately got over, something to be at last surrendered for the prize of entering into a larger spiritual unity. And while Amida Buddha is presented to the religious imagination in personal terms, back of the personal Amida, as back of all the Buddhas in their particular aspects, stands the impersonal Divine as such, the Buddha Nature which is in us all.

Partly as a result of this less personal and more inclusive view of the Divine, partly as a result of its carelessness of history and of particular finite events, Buddhism is less dependent upon historical facts, is freer from authority, and better able to adapt itself to all sorts of scientific discoveries and changing philosophical conceptions than is Christianity. This elasticity, this adaptability toward many kinds of philosophical ideals and toward many kinds of human superstitions and human needs has made it and its mother, Hinduism, unique among the religions of the world.

One more similarity and contrast let me note before closing this comparison. These two religions possess the inestimable advantage of having for their Founders perhaps the two noblest figures in history. In many ways their aims and their characters closely resembled each other. Yet here, too, and in the effect which the thought of them has upon their followers, there are contrasts as well as similarities. Jesus is the intense and even youthful lover of the soul: Gotama the calm and thoughtful sage. In Jesus' presence one feels the infinite love of God; in Gotama's the depth of supernal wisdom. Each makes his great appeal, but each to a separate type of mind. To many the thought of the Buddha is cold and uninspiring, while the influence of falling in love with Jesus has been the source of more transformation of the moral life than any other single thing in history. Yet there is also a type of mind to which the very youth and intensity and personal charm of Jesus is something of a detraction, and for which the supreme inspiration is the image of the great saint and sage of India. A similar contrast persists if we turn our eyes from the two historical figures, and focus them upon the philosophical figures into which Christian and Buddhist thoughts have transformed Jesus and Gotama. The Logos of Christianity is the Second Person of the Trinity, but He is a person still, the living Christ, interested in you and me as individuals. The Eternal Buddha is the Absolute Mind inclusive of all that is, of which you and I are eternally aspects or parts; for the Buddha Nature is in all things.

The contrasts I have pointed out between the two religions make it plain, I think, that the followers of each of them are mistaken when they assert (as they so often do) that their own religion contains all the values of both. The truth is that each of them has its own peculiar genius, each has its own contribution to make. And this not merely because they represent different forms of philosophy but also because there are many different kinds of people in this world, and each of the great religions makes its appeal only to certain types. Not all human bodies need the same kind of physical food, and not all human souls need the same kind of spiritual food. I think it probable that Christianity is adapted to the needs of more people than Buddhism—though this is only a guess. But I feel sure that there are many men and women, both in Buddhist lands and in Christian lands, who find, or would find, in the less personal, more cosmic attitude of Buddhism, a form of spiritual nourishment which would appeal more to their imagination, satisfy more fully their emotional needs, feed more lastingly their souls than anything which Christianity as ordinarily interpreted has to give.

If the conclusions to which we have come are justified, it would seem to be manifest that this old world of ours needs both Christianity and Buddhism, that it would be poorer if deprived of either one of them. For I am convinced not only that both these religions have contributed much and still contribute much of inestimable value to the life of man, but that if either of them should die out of the world, the peculiar and characteristic contributions which it makes could never be exactly replaced. The contribution to man's life which the historical religions are making in these centuries that we are living through, and probably in all those to come, consists not in abstract conceptions of ethics or metaphysics. Such conceptions they doubtless possess and teach, but these if forgotten could be restored by man's abstract intellect. What religion does is to translate the abstract into the concrete, reason into life, to make the ideals of ethics into burning motives of human conduct, to transform philosophical concepts into beckoning vistas and shining inspirations, to make the Eternal Word become Flesh. This miracle of incarnation religion achieves very largely by its appeal to the imagination and through the use of symbols. To many a man for whom the Stern Daughter of the Voice of God has little lure, the loving Buddha and the living Christ will speak in irresistible tones. The personal touch within the realm of the imagination still has an immense power over most of those brought up in the Buddhist or the Christian tradition. The power of tradition in this matter is inestimable, and once the tradition is broken it can never be restored.

The great loss which the race would suffer should these traditions cease will be better appreciated if we think for a moment of the force possessed by religious symbols. Much of the magic by which the great religions incarnate truth into life, they owe to the peculiar power of ancient symbols over the imagination and the emotions. Let one compare the effect of some abstract ethical or metaphysical teaching with the influence of the crucifix or the thought of the Madonna on a good Catholic or of the Buddha image or the Goddess of Mercy on a good Buddhist, and he will see what I mean. And what is true of these great symbols is only in less degree true of the many lesser symbols, visual and verbal, of both these religions. For most men and women the great truths of philosophy become living and compelling guides only when handed on by a revered tradition and clothed in traditional symbols. For such symbols and such traditions carry with them the immense force of the Community and the austere grandeur of the Past, and thus they get a grip on the mind of the young child which he never wholly loses. They get this power over the mind, however, only if they begin their action while the mind is still very young. The full power of religious tradition and of religious symbols can never be felt save by one who has thus breathed them in with his earliest breath, they speak with the assurance and authority of the sacred Past, of the great days from which they sprang. This old world of ours will probably have to get on with the stock of religious symbols and traditions it already possesses. Those which it loses will be forever irreplaceable. I cannot but think Emerson too optimistic when he sings:

> 'One accent of the Holy Ghost
> This careless world has never lost.'

I may be wrong in this so far as my judgment of the Past is concerned, but at any rate I feel sure of two things: that much of the spiritual heritage of mankind is at stake; and that those who out of religious zeal in any camp seek to destroy any of the great religions of man are sinning against the Holy Ghost.

The world's need to-day is not the destruction of the old faiths and the old symbols, but the deepening of them. And for the answer to this need we turn, not primarily to the priests or to the scholars, but to the men of insight, who can teach us to unite the love of Beauty with the love of God. And so we come back to the point from which we started, and to the Poet to whom this volume is a tribute.

WILLIAMSTOWN, MASS., U.S.A. JAMES BISSETT PRATT

TAGORE AS AN INTERNATIONAL FIGURE

THE multiplicity of human dialects is a barrier to international appreciation even in the field of the exact sciences. This is so in spite of the fact that a little knowledge goes a long way in following the language of a scientific paper. To appreciate humour or pathos or to appraise literary merit in a work is a very different matter. Science uses language merely to convey information. Literature makes with words a garment which half covers and half displays the subtleties of human thought. It follows that international fame in the field of letters and in the field of science stand on a wholly different footing. It is unbelievable that a great scientific discovery could to-day be made in one country and remain long unknown to the rest of the world. But it is perfectly possible for a great man of letters or a great philosopher to remain entirely unknown outside his own country. For a whole millennium, Europe knew nothing of Kalidasa or Sankaracharya. It discovered Tagore when he chose to translate some of the *Gitanjali* poems 'to while away the time.' The discovery was complete when Sweden crowned with the Nobel award his 'profoundly sensitive, fresh and beautiful poetry, and the consummate skill with which he introduced his poetic thought in English guise to the literature of the West.'

It would be wrong, however, to assume that Tagore's great international fame rests only on such of his writings as have found their way into other languages from the original Bengali. It would be more correct to say that it is the rare charm of his personality and his human qualities which have won for him the high place he holds in the esteem and affection of mankind. In the course of his extensive travels, he has left behind him everywhere personal memories which are cherished and treasured. His simplicity and dignity, his varied gifts in literature, art and music, and his fine sense for all that is true and good and beautiful are some of the hall-marks of his greatness which are patent to all. That the world claims him to-day as one of the greatest of living men admits of no manner of doubt.

THE UNIVERSITY,
CALCUTTA

CHANDRASEKHARA VENKATA RAMAN

POET, PATRIOT AND PROPHET

IT is a very happy event that we are celebrating to-day, the seventieth birthday of our distinguished countryman, Rabindranath Tagore; for in this unfortunate land of ours, where so many of our most gifted men have been cut off before they reached their maturity, we deem it an especial grace that our country's pride, the world-renowned Rabindranath, should have been spared to us so long and should still be able to uplift and inspire us with his marvellous poesy and wonderful idealism; and it is the heart-felt prayer of all of us, his admiring countrymen, that Providence do spare him for us yet for many a year to come, to delight us all with the fragrance of his rare personality.

It has been also a happy idea that in order to celebrate the septuagenary of the birth of our Poet, a volume of symposia is being brought out which will contain tributes in honour of the great Poet from East and West alike. But I cannot say that it has been an equally happy inspiration on the part of the organizers of this commemorating volume to have asked me, a prosaic Chemist, a mere man of science, to pay my humble mite of tribute to the great Poet, perhaps the greatest Man of Imagination now living: not that I yield to anyone in my admiration for our great countryman, but only that what I may have to say about him will be merely commonplace. For I can only admire and revere Tagore's wonderful personality, and immensely enjoy his writings; and am quite content with that admiration and reverence and enjoyment; I have neither the desire nor the temerity to play the role of the critic or the assayer. And I shall accordingly content myself with giving expression to that feeling of admiration for the Poet that surges within my breast.

I think I can make bold to assert that it is impossible for any foreigner to realise what Tagore means to Bengal. Tagore's age now is three score years and ten, and he began to sing and enchant from when he was in his teens, and before he was thirty he had already made his mark as one of Bengal's leading Poets—so that it is for a period of half a century and more that Bengal has known and enjoyed and marvelled at her inimitable Bard. Go where you will, in the most outlying areas of Bengal's far-flung frontiers, in the deepest recesses of Bengal's most insignificant hamlets, you will hear the enthralling strains of Rabindranath hummed by the village swain and the rustic maiden. Many of these innocent village folks do not know whose songs they are, but they know the words and the tunes of the songs well enough, and burst into them spontaneously when emotion seizes them. Tagore's songs and lyrics have entered into the very texture of the life of modern Bengal, and have coloured the very outlook of modern Bengali society in all its strata, high and low alike. It is indeed difficult at the present day to visualize Bengal without Rabindranath's inspiration.

There are many reasons for this. The first and foremost reason to my mind appears to be this, that steeped as Rabindranath is in the best elements of Western culture, he is still essentially the scion of the great Vaishnavic Bards of Bengal, that immortal band of singers from Jayadeva through Vidyapati and Chandidas to Jnanadas and Govindadas who raised the emotion of Bengal to the pinnacle of religious exaltation and swept her off her feet with entrancing melodies woven round the eternal loves of Radha and Krishna on the storied banks of the sacred Yamuna—and for all his Western veneer Rabindranath is at heart the child of that tradition which stirred Bengal's emotional depths as nothing else ever did. And thus it is that Tagore's love songs, Tagore's religious songs—and many of them, true to Vaishnavic type, are both—have carried by storm the heart of Bengal. On the top of this ever-responsive chord in the Bengali heart, Tagore has won Bengal by touching another chord also dear to her, and that has been his enthusiasm for the natural scenery of our countryside, his poetic idealisation of the beauties of rural Bengal, his intimate sympathy with the simple joys and sorrows of the average Bengali household—these have endeared him and made the humblest Bengalis feel him as one of their very own, despite the fact that Rabindranath belongs to one of the most exclusive and aristocratic families of Bengal, cultured, city-bred and prosperous. This spirit of oneness and identification with the Bengali home that breathes through his inimitable short stories, this fervour for Mother Bengal which inspires his immortal song:

আমার সোনার বাংলা, আমি তোমায় ভালবাসি।
চিরদিন তোমার আকাশ, তোমার বাতাস,
আমার প্রাণে বাজায় বাঁশী ॥

or the song—

সার্থক জনম আমার জন্মেছি এই দেশে,
সার্থক জনম মাগো তোমায় ভালবেসে ॥

and other equally famous songs will keep the memory of Bengal's Poet ever green and fresh in the heart of Bengal, even when his more intellectual productions may have been forgotten, except by the learned few.

This brings us to another aspect of Rabindranath's personality. His worship of the motherland did not exhaust itself in mere sentimental effusions over her natural beauties or her glorious past—his patriotism had a more virile and constructive aspect. And this explains why when there surged over Bengal in 1905 the waves of an awakened self-consciousness and nationalism, Rabindranath was found in the very forefront of the national movement, inspiring it with his soul-stirring national songs, stabilizing the emotional excitement with his thoughtful discourses, instinct with the spirit of constructive nationalism, elevating the movement out of the rut of sordid materialism and blind race-hatred by the momentum of his catholic idealism. When the beautiful *Rakhi-bandhan* ceremony was instituted to affirm the unity of Bengal inspite of official *fiats*, it was Rabindranath who pronounced its *mantra*.

বাংলার মাটী, বাংলার জল,
বাংলার বায়ু, বাংলার ফল,
পুণ্য হউক, পুণ্য হউক,
পুণ্য হউক, হে ভগবান্ ।

If Surendranath Banerjea represented the practical side, and Bipin Chandra Pal and Aravinda Ghosh the passionate side, Rabindranath Tagore incarnated the idealistic side of the new Indian nationalism. When in course of a few years out of the fumes of the *Swadeshi* movement emerged the spectre of terrorism, Rabindranath uttered his solemn voice of warning, pointing out that this new phenomenon was alien to the spirit of Indian culture and would lead the country to a morass from which it would be difficult to emerge unscathed. It was in those stirring days that the masculine prose of Rabindranath's pen burst forth in its splendid virility, and almost eclipsed the Poet himself. And I can say with the deepest conviction that the patriotic young man of the present day cannot do better than study the magnificent discourses of Rabindranath of a quarter of a century ago, his *Swadeshi Samaj*, his *Desha-nayak*, his *Samasya*, his *Path O Patheya* and other pieces now published in the collections *Raja-Praja, Swadesh, Samaj* and *Samuha* ; if the young man does it he will equip himself far more effectively for political life than by idly imbibing the inane froth that issues out of the daily press to-day.

But in the heyday of national resurgence few people are in a mood to listen to sober reason or to regulate their conduct by idealistic standards ; and so Rabindranath felt himself more and more isolated from the main currents of the active nationalist movement, and came to realise that a Poet can indeed inspire Nationalism but can hardly hope to control it when once started on its impetuous career—a Poet's place is not in the rough and tumble of political struggle, but the Poet's soul, like a star, must dwell apart. And so, disillusioned and disappointed at the turn things were taking, Tagore withdrew unto himself and began to develop the third phase of his moral unfoldment. Growing sick of the aggressive and exclusive type of nationalism, he began to pine after international fellowship, to realize the essential solidarity of mankind, and to preach the gospel of universal humanity. The small educational experiment that he had been conducting at Santiniketan in Bolpur developed under the stress of this idea into the Visva-bharati, an international university which would give the widest scope to human culture, both of the East and the West, and would offer a meeting-ground of world-renowned savants of all races and climes. This drew out Rabindranath the educationist ; and in his own peculiar domain—on the poetic plane—it gave us the Rabindranath of the *Gitanjali*. The spirit of catholicity, of idealism, of universal humanism that pervaded the series of poems at once arrested the attention of the civilized world, and the award of the Nobel Prize for

Literature in 1913 was the natural sequel. From being the Bard of Bengal, from being the prophet of Indian Nationalism, Rabindranath now emerged as a world-figure, a seer and an apostle of international fellowship and human solidarity. Curiously enough, the very year after Rabindranath appeared on the world's stage with a new message of love and fellowship, there burst upon the world the greatest cataclysm of recent history, the Great World-War. The war dragged on its weary length from year's end to year's end, drawing into its vortex more and yet more countries, until after well-nigh five years of unexampled carnage some sort of peace was patched up at Versailles by a shattered and war-weary world. The Great War was the *reductio ad absurdum* of the doctrine of aggressive nationalism and rampant Chauvinism against the danger of which Tagore had raised his warning voice in Bengal many years before. And so to the war-weary world the message of Tagore, the gospel of love and fellowship and co-operation, fell like a soothing balm, like a healing enchantment, and was felt to be the only evangel of hope for suffering humanity. And all Europe and America felt, when this Eastern sage appeared in their midst with his gospel of hope and faith and charity and they vied with one another to do him honour, that once again the ancient words had come true, *Ex Oriente Lux.*

And we, his admiring and loving countrymen, felt elated and proud that our Rabindranath, our own darling poet, whose songs had nourished and inspired generations of our young men and women, the prophet and poet of our own nascent nationalism, had at last met with his due recognition at the hands of the entire civilized world, and had been acclaimed as one of the seers of universal humanity, as one of the band of the Elect whose names are jewels that "on the stretched fore-finger of time sparkle for ever." And our feelings were those beautifully expressed in our own Oriental adage: **कुलं पवित्रं जननी कृतार्था,** and it is this feeling that permeates us still—the feeling of national pride, the feeling of intense thankfulness that even in these days when our hapless land is beset with so many perils and is confronted with so many difficulties and is suffering from so many ills, our mother-land has still been able to produce a son like Rabindranath, worthy to sit side by side with Valmiki, with Vyasa, with Kalidasa, the glorious bards of this ancient land, and worthy to rank with the World's Immortals. These are my feelings on this solemn occasion and I can say no more, and can only close with the prayer—the ancient prayer of our Aryan sages—

जिजीविषेत् शतं समाः ॥

UNIVERSITY COLLEGE OF SCIENCE,
CALCUTTA

PRAPHULLA CHANDRA RAY

YEARS ago I happened to be a guest at a dinner given by some university men in New York, and the conversation turned on the political servitude of India. I argued that the crucifixion of India's political body had enabled her to discover and develop her soul and evidenced Tagore's *Gitanjali* as proof, to which a professor of philosophy retorted:—'That means I have got a sensation because somebody has given me a knock on the head and I gladly resign myself to foreign knocks because of the sensations they evoke.' I replied that the natural gift of Negroes (and our untouchables) for music was probably due to their sufferings, and quoted: 'Our sweetest songs are those that tell of saddest thought.' Jesus Christ was a man of sorrows and a nation of sorrows may yet be the source of a gospel of international salvation. It was a few days after this dinner that the award of the Nobel Prize for Literature to Rabindranath Tagore was announced, and I triumphantly pointed to it as a startling justification of my contention.

About the year 1908, the chief vogue of Tagore in the Andhra Desa was as the stirring laureate of Indian nationalism. The country can never forget the way in which he inspired and roused us to active patriotism. But the call of the universal was to his sensitive soul a living command; he has since then progressed from Nationalism to Humanity, subordinating all particularisms to the higher Absolute Values, without however impugning their relative and temporary validity. This phase marks his highest reach as poet and seer and has revolutionised the spirit and tone of the best modern Andhra Poetry.

Tagore's powerful condemnation of the state as a soulless machine and the patriotism that grounds itself on 'My country right or wrong' to the negation of moral ideals, has stirred the conscience of the world, horrified at its own terrible doings in the Great War. His call to regulate life on the principle of humanity has been taken up by Romain Rolland and other western thinkers. But the subject nations of the East have not found much consolation in that doctrine, since obviously it is only the imperialist nations that could take the initiative and illustrate the new direction. Japan, ever fearful that the fate of the other Oriental nations may yet befall her, and China struggling fitfully for nationhood have derided it as the philosophy of defeatism. India with her longing for freedom, still feeble and ineffective, has not been able to accept this dispensation. 'Religion is not for empty bellies,' said the divine Ramakrishna Paramahamsa. In similar wise humanitarian ardour is not for slaves, nor internationalism for those who are no nation. The higher should be a synthesis or federation of nationalities and if race and colour barriers are in process of time dissolved, there may be a growth into world-state through absorption and assimilation.

But have not the Imperialist Powers made a hopeful response to this ideal of human federation? I think they have. The League of Nations is the embodiment, in however feeble and tentative a form, of this higher spirit of international co-operation. The oldest of the races, India, through the intuition of her imaginative genius, Tagore, invoked the idea, and the youngest of the nations, America, through her President, Woodrow Wilson, organised it into institutional shape and potency. What a miracle of ideal co-operation! More than any other poet of the world, Tagore shines forth as the laureate of humanity.

It does not mean that he is not a patriot, or that he is one of those artistic or scientific exquisites who profess to be above patriotism chiefly for pleasing the Government, or that he condemns nationalism and the state as evils *per se* to be destroyed root and branch. The noble heart that flung his knighthood in contempt back into the hands that gave it to him because they had become blood-stained at Jallianwallah Bagh, the generous soul that more recently emerged from its ecstatic retirement to bemoan the Chittagong happenings and resent the Hijli shootings, cannot for a moment be thought to be a less ardent patriot than Das, Nehru, or Ansari. What he condemns is the claim (alas, widely conceded) of the state to be an end in itself and a law unto itself, in brutal disregard of ethical standards, reducing itself to a non-moral animal impulse. Just as the family has in course of evolution been subordinated to society, and is no longer an interest overriding all other considerations, so must the state be subordinated to humanity. A nation should be just one member in the larger society of the family of nations and the Fatherhood of God must be implemented by the brotherhood of Man. And just as a family must be healthy and efficient in order to subserve successfully social ends, so must each nation be strong and efficient in order to fulfil its humanitarian functions properly. The state should be content to occupy the position of a means to world ends, instead of continuing to be a lawless exhibition of greed and force.

Is Gandhian Nationalism any different from this in essence and spirit? It seems to me that the Tagorean mirror contains a faithful reflection of the Gandhian universe. Or to put it differently, in its insistence on Truth and Non-violence, and the subordination of political ends and methods to moral laws, Gandhism may almost be said to be an organised form of Tagorism. India must be free, not that she may thereupon roam about like a beast of prey, but that she may the better subserve human brotherhood and culture. And she must achieve her freedom by means of Truth and Non-violence, historically speaking novelties never before tried; by invoking and never by inflicting suffering; by converting the enemy and getting him to be your friend instead of exterminating him; and melting his heart in the fire of world's pity and righteousness. And it follows as day the night that freedom thus won is bound to be used for spreading a regime of light and love, and not for perpetuating dark deeds of exploitation. Nor is it only blood that may not be shed. Uncompensated sweat too may not be, and the capitalism that has thriven on the ill paid sweat of the labouring masses must melt into co-operative effort. In fact even tears are forbidden ; for you must undergo your sufferings with a quiet, bravely and cheerfully, like martyrs. Then only will its transfigurative efforts be forthcoming.

I wonder if Soviet Russia is not in many of its aspects a true answer to Gandhian prayers, the organised and institutionalised form of his social and moral ideals. It is ready to disarm completely ; clan is its regulative category, not country ; it has abolished the exploitation of the masses ; it is a knight-errant ready to march against the many-headed Hydra of imperialism ; it is no respector of race and colour ; its patriotism is subordinate to the world-proletariat ; and it is universalistic in idea and intention. Only it is not prepared to lose its life by meekly practising non-violence against its enemies, a human weakness which may be forgiven.

But Gandhi is for the ascetic life, the life of minimum needs and requirements, since these could be more easily shared equally by all than the life rich in manifold pleasures and satisfactions. The perfect life is the ideal of Tagore, the primitive of Mahatma Gandhi. Community in fasting is more easily secured than community in feasting, and how could a man of heart feast in the midst of so much starvation? Such cultural and aesthetic (in the best sense of the term) life as the world has enjoyed so far has, it must be confessed, rested on the exploitation of the many by the few. Artistic and philosophic Greece rested on slavery, and indeed held that without slavery the best life would not be possible. Religious and philosophic India turned exploitation into its chief Dharma, and fashioned castes as well as outcasts for this purpose. European civilisation has divided society into capital and labour, into classes and masses. Every man of God, unless he be worshipping the Devil under that respectable pseudonym, must revolt against this iniquitous negation of human brotherhood. Gandhi's revolt, in despair at making all equally rich, would like them to be equally poor in material goods and exalted in spirit. He would have no machinery, no large industry, no palaces, but just neat little cottages and the restless *Charkha*. Tagore's intuition is the truer and it may yet be realised consistently with the demands of our conscience. Though as history has gone so far the ideal of the full life has not been consistent with the moral ideal of equalitarean co-operation, the great Russian experiment has shown that material prosperity and human equality could go together and that asceticism is not the indispensable basis of socialism. Its new social and economic order, its marvellous powers in education and the broad-casting of the amenities of civilisation, and its five-year plan, demonstrate the possibility of the communistic achievement of the perfect life, where light, love and joy will in widest commonalty be spread. Meanwhile until this divine consummation is reached by the world, Mahatma Gandhi as the great man of action, the reviver and inspirer of our jaded national will, and the organiser of mass action on a scale almost miraculous, will rightly hold the primacy in our affections as well as admiration. He is will; he is action; he is life; and there are more than idea and imagination.

I have had the honour of knowing Rabindranath Tagore in person, and can never forget the impression he made during his visit to Mysore in 1918. After completing his tour in South India he told me that nothing healthy could grow under the shadow of our temples. He revealed to us the beauty that Kalidasa and other ancient poets found in the forest where the hermits had their dwellings (*Tapovanas*). South Indian music was an intellectual exercise, barren of heart and soul. The music of Bengal penetrates the heart and quickens the soul. I can confirm the truth of this contrast by personal experience of both. If Bengal has a soul, fiery, reckless, and generous to a fault, part of the explanation may be found in its stirring, emotional music. And Tagore's creation of the Visva-Bharati! What perfect insight does it not show into the nature of university education, which should be research and creation and the development of personality, and not, as the government universities are, distributing channels for the scanty, muddy, slow, belated flow of western knowledge and discoveries.

Tagore's name will live as long as humanity lasts. To have been the glory of India is indeed a great triumph; but he is more, he is one of the lights of the world.

MADRAS

C. R. REDDY

A l'occasion du 70-ème Anniversaire de la Naissance de l'illustre Poète Rabindranath Tagore et de la publication de *The Golden Book of Tagore,* je suis heureux d'apporter l'hommage de mon admiration au grand écrivain, au delicat artiste qui a ciselé avec tant de finesse et d'harmonie *le Naufrage, le Jardinier d'Amour, la Fugitive, Mashi;* au grand Hindou qui a toujours defendu eloquemment les aspirations de son peuple; a l'homme dont les créations et les manifestations les plus diverses dans tous les domaines de la pensée, la hauteur et l'independance de caractère, rendront son nom immortel.

PARIS

ERNEST RENAULD

TAGORE THE SEER AND INTERPRETER

WHEN Zarathushtra (in one of the older books of the East) asked Ahura what his name was he gave two in reply, which are remarkable—the Seer or 'Discerner' and the 'Healer.' They would serve well, it has been said, to mark the functions which Rabindranath Tagore made his own in that later phase of his career, when the trouble of his days had made him more keenly alive to the needs of men and women in India all the world over. His temperament, his love of Nature, and the life of meditation that the Indian sun favours, might have led him to retire from the struggle for the new order. A sharper force drove him to look to the ailment of his time, and he became, instead of its ascetic, or its hermit in the wilderness, its Healer, its Discerner, and its Interpreter.

He did it by the simplest magic of heart and mind, such as poets and children know. When you talk to him, and walk in the sun with him, you learn the secret. You see how by the divination of the heart he learnt to join together two spirits, two faiths, two regions. India and Indian faith and divine philosophy have often seemed immensely far away from ours; not touched by the affectionate piety and the feeling as of a mother to her children, or the intimate faith of a St. Francis. But in Tagore you feel the humanity that was in the Son of Man, comforting the children of light in their awe of the Eternal. In him the spirits of the Upanishads reach the same threshold. It was natural that out of a living belief in the beauty of the earth, in sun and stars, and in the waters below, there should grow a living faith such as Rabindranath Tagore has expounded in *Sadhana*. The test of its truth for him is that, living by it, and dowered by Nature to enjoy life to the full, he has found the medicine to heal the troubles of his own day. He is able to speak so naturally to us in this country, because he came an early pilgrim to our shores. In youth he went like some of the old Buddhistic pilgrims on a long and arduous journey into our outer world, saw for himself the spectacle of our Western civilization, and what it was doing for good and evil; and he felt those forces of today which are affecting his own country, too, at times, and seeming to threaten the secret faith in which his songs were sung and his books sent into the world.

Thus he has been not only a seer, but the herald of the new Dawn that we hope means the New Day for our two allied regions and our two troubled civilizations.

LONDON

ERNEST RHYS

STRONGHOLDS OF CULTURE

IT may seem to some that the questions of Culture which preoccupied the human mind since times immemorial, are already strongholds. As if entire cities and countries accepted Culture. As if our times can in self-content look back upon those far far distant, those poor ones, who had neither telephones, nor radio and were even deprived of moving pictures. What a self-conceited error! And how few understand that Culture as such dwells only upon the summits, and the ways to these strongholds of the human ascent of spirit are as before unusually difficult, and who knows may be even still more difficult than in some previous epochs. Our ships are very swift. Somebody wanted to construct a ship of 100,000 tons. It would be instructive to know what were his intentions as to the quality of the cargo for shipment. Were not guns and opium meant for the sake of profit? Our houses are rising high. Somebody builds a house 100 storeys high—much higher than the Tower of Babel. However, often in living quarters there is room lacking either for a desk or a bookcase. Very roomy are our slaughter houses. Thanks to an unusual technique hundred thousand animals can be slaughtered, but at the same time in modesty and almost unknown remain the researches of scientists about vegetable vitamines. With all our so-called education few will innerly agree that a lemon or orange can replace a bloody beefsteak. Only recently even the seemingly learned physicians sent their patients to the slaughter houses that they should be able to drink the still warm blood. The very same physicians advised as the most curative means to devour like beasts raw bloody meat. But even in those countries where according to conditions of nature aborigines are compelled to use only raw meat since ancient times, they act wisely eating it either dried in air or in an extreme case they use it smoked.

Our mechanical technique applied all efforts to produce as many robots as possible. True, even robots often fell into mechanical madness and disturbed the traffic of the world. Somebody invented a mechanical salesman for shops and the next inventor enlivened the lips of the machine with the mechanical 'Thank you!' But in response to mechanization are born armies of unemployed. Is this the achievement of Culture?

Only recently we brought cannons into churches for benediction. However, any discussion on peace and religion became in Society something unbefitting and shameful. Should somebody dare instead of the ugly one-sided sport, instead of slander and calumny, to speak of the uplifting principles of Culture, the well brought-up people, with a shrug of their shoulders would whisper, 'How dull he is.' And if somebody upon entering a drawing room would dare to make a sacred sign of his own religion, he would simply be considered not only badly bred, but a crass bigot as well. The questions of religion and spirit, the questions of Culture are removed for the appeasing of ignorance into abstraction. If everything uplifting is made abstract, it means we are as if not responsible for it. In the best case people will excuse themselves through routine, everyday's work, which as if hinder them to turn to the uplifting foundations of the spirit. So often it is thought of, forgetting that everyday's labour is the benevolent *pranayama*. It creates energy, it brings us nearer to the cosmic rhythm, it helps us kindle the inner fires: these benevolent links with the spacial Agni. So often we find self-vindications! We are very far-fetching in avoiding responsibility, forgetting thus that the great responsibility for the condition of the entire planet is unavoidable there where human distinction is attained. Does not this distinction oblige one to apply all powers to find the corresponding rhythm of evolution? It obliges one to think how not to find oneself in the cosmic refuse. This is not abstraction. Verily, this is vivid reality as true as Existence itself! And do not we freely choose either disintegration or creation, negation or affirmation, creativeness or dealiness? Does not the entire history of humanity point out the highest bliss of creative thought in whatever form expressed and wherever manifested? The great examples of history display to us unusual creators of thought who either clad it in some material or broadly proclaimed it by spatial megaphone. If all is one, then is not all interrelated, as expressed since long in the wisdom? We reiterate the sacred hymns of the Bhagavad-Gita and the Psalms about the indestructibility, about all-conquering spirit, but often in chanting we lose the understanding that the expressed wisdom is given for immediate application.

Does not Culture imperatively demand this immediate application in life of all beautiful which we ourselves send into the exile of abstraction? The condition of the planet is such that either a true approach to evolution will be found or a spiritual savageness threatens. The great Agni will either awaken the most blissful force or will tensify the most wondrous energies or if not admitted by our spirit will turn to ashes of destruction the illusory Maya which we in self-conceit mistake for a basic stronghold. Either we shall once again realize the grandeur and immutable necessity of the Hierarchy of Bliss; or in savageness we shall reject every conception of Teacher and noble leadership of the Guru.

If the strongholds of Culture crown as always only the heights, withstanding all difficulties of a thorny and stony path, how then must we be grateful to all those who have taken upon themselves the strain of the leadership to Culture. And with what care must we safeguard the walls of these strongholds created by untiring every-day's labor. How we must bless those who kindle and sustain our enthusiasm. When we think of invincible energy, blessed enthusiasm, pure Culture, before me always rises the so dear to me image of Rabindranath Tagore. Great must be the potentiality of his spirit which prompts him to apply untiringly in life the foundations of true Culture. The songs of Tagore are inspired calls to Culture, they are his prayers about great Culture, his blessings to the seeker of the paths of ascent.

Synthetizing his immense activities, which ascend the very same mountain of Bliss and which penetrate into the narrowest alleys of life, could any one abstain from the feeling of inspiring joy? So blissful, so beautiful is the essence of the hymns, the calls and works of Tagore.

Verily Santiniketan is growing like the tree of Culture. We cannot judge how a powerful tree grows, why its branches are spreading in one or another order. Under the conditions of winds or other conditions of nature, we would find an explanation, but it is important for our spirit to realize that this tree is growing; or, according to the language of the stronghold, it is important that the walls are being strengthened. And we know that these walls are constructed in the name of Culture, and they exist only through Culture. Is it not sacredly-joyous, the feeling which overwhelms us, looking at the eternal snows of the Himalayas, saturated with the miraculously acting dust from the far-off worlds, to realize that now in our midst lives Rabindranath Tagore; that seven decades he glorifies and praises untiringly the Beautiful, and tirelessly he accumulates the eternal stones of Culture, erecting the stronghold of joy of the human spirit? This is so urgent! This is no undeferrably needed! Let us repeat untiringly about the necessity of the strongholds of Culture. Let us tirelessly proclaim this true pride of a nation and of the entire world.

The strongholds of Culture like magnets gather all which pertains to Culture, and, like anchors, keep the ships of spirit, which toss in the stormy ocean of the elements.

Tagore lives for the glory of Culture. Let Santiniketan stand as a guiding milestone for the growth of the human spirit, as a construction of the most needed, the most noble and most beautiful.

Vijaya Tagore! Vijaya Santiniketan!

URUSVATI, KULU,
HIMALAYAS

NICHOLAS ROERICH

কবি-রবি

স্নিগ্ধ রক্তরাগ রথে পূর্ব্ব অম্বরে
বাঙ্গলার ভালে যবে রবীন্দ্র উদয়,
উঠেছিল দিগ্বধূ গাহি জয় জয়,
হেরি তারে। তিনি আজ অর কর্মস্থলে,
মেলি আঁখি চাহে বঙ্গ আনন্দের ভরে,
এ কি আলো! এ কি গান! গীতি-জ্যোতির্ম্ময়
এ যে গো মায়াবী রবি, শুধু কবি নয়;
কোন বিধি সর্ব্ব দৈন্য ঘুচাবার তরে।
যত বেলা বাড়ে, ঊর্দ্ধ হতে ঊর্দ্ধতর
চলে তার আলোক রথ, ঝরে শতধারে
অমৃত নির্ঝর, বিশ্ব লোটে নভঃ পারে
হেরে মধ্যাকাশে রবি, অপূর্ব্ব ভাস্বর।
বঙ্গের, কি ভারতের কে কহিবে তারে?
রবি বিশ্বের কবি আজ কে না জানে?

শ্রীকামিনী রায়

[TRANSLATION]

In the rose flush of the eastern sky
When Rabindra rose as the morning sun,
The nymphs of heaven sang pæans of victory ;
Knowing him by his voice, Bengal opened her eyes
And cried in the gladness of her heart,
'What light! What song! song-lit—
'This is my own Sun, and the Gods have given him
'As a solace for my many ills.'
As the day grew, higher and higher wheeled
His chariot of light ; in a hundred streams
Flowed nectar ; the world, looking heaven-ward,
Saw the dazzling sun in the meridian ;—
Bengal's or India's, who can tell?
This day the world acclaims Rabi as its own poet.

CALCUTTA

KAMINI ROY

[TRANSLITERATION]

Kavi Ravi

Snigdha-rakta-rāg rathe pūrab ambare
bālâruṇ-rūpe jabe Ravīndra-uday,
uṭhechila dig-vadhū gāhi 'jay, jay' ;
heri tāre, cini tāre tār kaṇṭha-sware,
meli ā*n*khi kahe Vaṅga ānander bhare,
'e ki ālo ! e ki gān ! gīti-jyotirmmay
e je go āmāri Ravi, ār kāro nay ;
dilā Vidhi sarvva dainya bhulābār tare.'
jata velā bāḍe, ūrddhwa ha'te ūrddhwatar
cale tār ālo-rath, jhare śata-dhāre
amṛta barasā, viśwa cāhi nabhaḥ pāne
here madhyâkāśe ravi, apūrvva, bhāswar.
Vaṅger, ki Bhārater, ke kahibe tāre?
Ravi jagater kavi āj ke nā jāne?

Śrī Kāminī Rāy

WHAT can I say of Rabindranath? Homage has been paid him by the East and by the West. Wherever he has passed—and what lands has he not visited?—garlands have been hung about his neck and men and women have taken the dust from his feet.

Few men have lived to know such fame as he has won. His books are read in every tongue; throughout India his songs are sung. In Europe and America his name stands for India herself, and like Einstein's, it stands for tolerance, for mutual understanding among the peoples of the earth.

I had the privilege of knowing Rabindranath when Tagore was a name familiar only in Bengal. As he is now he was then; as he was then he is now.

His heart was young at 50; at 70 his heart is young still. For beneath his ripe wisdom lies, deep-seated, a rich wit, a laughing humour, genial, most human.

To strive for perfection is natural to exceptional men, but others are suspicious of those who assume perfection. That mantle Rabindranath has never worn; his sense of values, his humour, would not permit him to be measured for such a garment. For he shares the qualities and the failings to which man is heir. To be more, or less than a man, Rabindranath would never aim.

Hence his songs and stories stir our hearts as do great folk-songs, telling, as they do, of the joys and sorrows of every man and of every woman. Through Rabindranath, India's humblest villagers speak to the world. To be the flute of God and to be the flute of men likewise, what nobler end can a poet achieve?

LONDON

WILLIAM ROTHENSTEIN

THE ROMAN CAMPAGNA—MIDSUMMER

A wide and silent emptiness of space,
A void of breath, a taste of woes to come,
Surrounding Roman pride to mock it dumb,
Extends about in isolated waste.

It sprawls, a clumsy tortured mass of dust
Choking beneath a sun whose brazen glare
Has stilled all hopeful life and stripped it bare
Of hope, and superposed a crumbled crust.

For nothing lives in this unhealthy spot.
Shimmering waves of dancing death alone,
Beneath the fitful gusts that slowly moan,
Can move and be in an atmosphere so hot.

But when the twilight brings repose to pain
The gasping, tortured earth outstretched by heat,
Returns, relieved, to primal state. The beat
Of purple hazes sweeps across the plain.

As shades appear from out the ground and sky
And penetrate the land, illusion grows
And peoples all that plain with all its woes,
Its centuries of conflict long gone by.

And strong is felt that supernatural awe
That darkness brings to vast, unpeopled spots
Shrouded by shadows hiding that which rots,
Which waits for dawn, misunderstanding law.

LONDON

ARNOLD RUBIN

HEARTIEST greetings to Tagore on his Seventieth Birthday! He has contributed as much as any man living to the most important work of our time, namely, the promotion of understanding between different races. Of what he has done for India it is not for me to speak, but of what he has done for Europe and America in the way of softening of prejudices and the removal of misconceptions I can speak, and I know that on this account he is worthy of the highest honour.

HARTING, PETERSFIELD,
ENGLAND

BERTRAND RUSSELL

॥ श्रीः ॥

न कर्हिचित् किल प्राची प्रतीच्या संगमिष्यति।
पुरस्ताद्वै रविस्तूद्यन् प्रतीचीमप्यरोचयत्॥
दक्षिणामप्युदीचीं च व्यभासयदुरुक्रमः।
तत् पूज्यसे रवीन्द्र त्वमुत्तरस्यां विशेषतः॥

DEPARTMENT OF SANSKRIT,
THE UNIVERSITY, HELSINGFORS, FINLAND

J. N. REUTER

It gives me great pleasure to greet Rabindranath Tagore on his seventieth birthday with my admiration and my best wishes.

BOSTON, U.S.A

EDWIN ARLINGTON ROBINSON

THE POET (1926)

After a Photograph by Suse Byk

FIRST LOVE

What treasure would I not have poured
At the white feet when love had power,
If beauty that I had adored
Were tender to me for an hour.

I pass these burning memories by
And run to find a child who lay
On the warm earth, made tender by
A love breathed up from the dark clay.

How may I win that love again?
All I could bring to earth it owns.
What sacrifice must be, what pain
To be at league with these grey stones!

DUBLIN

A. E.
(GEORGE RUSSELL)

FOUR meetings with the Poet Rabindranath Tagore are bright in my memory. The first was at his house in Calcutta. I had come to India in the Autumn of 1917 on the business of a University Commission. I was anxious, before coming to any conclusions about the future government and growth of the University of Calcutta, to learn as much as I could about the talents and temperament of the students in Bengal. No one helped me more, few so much, as the Poet in a talk which he allowed me to have with him early in 1918. In our conversation I asked what place is taken by music, poetry, and painting in the home-nurture and school-training of a young Bengali. In order that my colleagues and I might understand the beauty of Indian music, he arranged a recital in the historic mansion of the Tagore family. He himself sang in the small choir. He had planned a programme in two parts. The first part was confined to older music. The second was made up of modern compositions, including some of his own. The intensity of his feeling, his absorption in his art, made an ineffaceable impression on my mind. Just as a lover of European painting can feel his eyes and thoughts being opened to the rhythm and significant conventions of Eastern art under the gentle teaching of one who knows the beauty of both ; so, under the influence of the Poet and under the spell of his skill, our ears and minds became sensitive to the cadence and harmonies of Indian music.

The second meeting was at Santiniketan. We had been asked to visit the Poet and to see his school. When we reached Bolpur, we felt the exhilaration of the air. We saw the stately trees sacred with the associations of at least two honoured lives. Exquisite in the glow of sunrise lay the contours of the country-side. And then the Poet, tender and gracious, took his little class of bright-eyed boys. So, a hundred years earlier, came to Yverdun those who were privileged to see and hear Pestalozzi.

Twelve years had passed before the third meeting. The Poet was in Oxford. C. F. Andrews brought a message that the Poet would show me his drawings. I was thrilled by their colour and design. He told me how he had found this new means of self-expression: how, almost absent-mindedly, he had made patterns with his pen: how coloured inks had diversified the decorations: how, stage by stage, his draughtsmanship had become more deliberate: and how in Paris painters and critics had hailed the beauty and freshness of his art.

A few days afterwards I met him for the fourth time. He was to lecture at Manchester College. The great hall was thronged. On the dais the Poet sat like a prophet. He gave his message, and those who heard him will never forget.

As I brood over what Rabindranath Tagore has been to India, how he loves her, how he has spent himself in her service, I am haunted by another name, an English name, and by the sense of a dim but deep resemblance between the Poet and one whose tone of mind and temper have made him beloved by many of his fellow-countrymen for nearly three hundred years. It is true indeed that no two great men are alike. And how different in outward seeming are Oxfordshire in the first part of the seventeenth century, and Bengal in the first part of the twentieth. Yet, in spite of this, the English name recurs as I ponder over the life-work of Rabindranath Tagore. And the name is Lucius Cary, Viscount Falkland.

OXFORD — MICHAEL E. SADLER

AN INTERNATIONALIST'S RELIGION

OUR Friend Rabindranath Tagore is an International Personality. He belongs to all nations and all countries. Therefore on the occasion of his Seventieth Birthday I present an International Interpretation of Islam as a contribution to the Commemoration Volume:—

"Worship One Supreme Being, there is none like unto Him. Love God and His people. Honour and respect the Prophets, old and new, of all the religions. Peace be on all and Blessings of Allah. All the people are children of God, without any distinction of colour, race and country. Sympathise with all and be kind. Always keep your Faith above the world. Do good to all and look for no returns. Trust in Allah, the Creator, the Provider, the Forgiver, the Protector, the Constant Companion and the Best Friend."

QADIAN, PANJAB, INDIA — MUFTI MOHAMMAD SADIQ

INDIA AND TAGORE

IN the beginning India was the source of human knowledge. Pythagoras was saturated from that source.

The structure of philosophy was moulded from the soil of India and the soul of India was blown therein. Greece dressed it with the equipage of wisdom.

The glittering star of wisdom rose from India and, before all, enlightened Iran and, through the illuminated Persia the Greeks traced out its Indian *foyer*. As we already know, before the time of Alexander, and afterwards, the Greeks got the human wisdom of India from its translation made into Iranian language.

Yes, for many centuries the light-casting India was the teacher of humanity. But even the Gods themselves do not always remain in the same condition.

Then the West raised itself in front of the East and Western knowledge professed to be more efficient in saving humanity.

The West suckled the offspring of humanity, but could not make the child rosy-cheeked and healthy.

The fruit of the Western civilization is fragrant and gaudy, but in the taste of humanity it has no pleasing savour and some say that it ruins the health.

Eyes were anxiously looking in every direction, and the human soul was in quest of its lost Beloved.

All of a sudden, from the East, yea from the everlasting East, rose the resplendent sun greeting our eyes. India once more sent her divine Poet-herald out to the World.

The five rivers of sugar and honey streamed from India to the extremities of the Universe. A delightful breeze blew from the banks of the Ganges, charming our souls. Songs of love found their way into the East and the West. The conflicting hearts were reconciled, and the anxious eyes received the rays of happiness and joy. Bitterness got transformed into sweetness. Humanity rediscovered its beloved Poet in Rabindranath.

O Tagore! though you are just going on to the seventieth year of your age, nevertheless, be sure your resplendent teachings and thoughts have infused such vital strength that all bonds and barriers of the unknown and obscure future have been broken, and we have been taken now seven-thousand-years ahead.

Behold, Master, I, on behalf of Persia and the Persians, who are your admirers, salute thee! O the Sun of the Orient! Long live thy soul.

TEHRAN RAHIMZADEH SAFAVI

POETRY AND SCIENCE

WHEN man came to this world in the distant pleistocene age, he must have felt utterly helpless in a world of giant reptiles, and colossal mammals. He had neither their strength, nor the fleetness of foot possessed by certain other weaker animals. The first cycle of his existence must have been spent in caves, and there he must have developed the two precious gifts of speech and brain with which he was endowed.

He must have peeped out in herds for collecting food and water and must have stolen an occasional glance at inscrutable Nature ; the smiling Earth teeming with fruit, flower, and game ; the life-giving Sun in all his majesty ; the Moon with her soothing rays ; Rain, and Cloud, with occasional thunders ; and lastly, the blue firmament with its inlaid stars and their mysterious motions. And occasionally, he must have noticed a forest-fire consuming whole landscapes. Some man of brain, a Prometheus, must have learnt the art of making fire from these natural fires, and this gave man such a preponderating power over beasts that he was no longer afraid of them, but could come out of caves, live in the open, and hold his own against the beasts.

The development of other arts followed—the art of farming, hunting, cattle and sheep raising, as well as of metal working. But these peaceful developments must have been interfered with by the outburst of savage passions on the part of individuals or groups. The strong lazy man will always like to shirk work, and try to deprive his fellowmen of the fruits of their labour. The nomad who has to eke out a miserable existence out of steppes or deserts, is always ready to fall upon the peaceful agriculturist and carry away his cattle and grain. Ancient history is the story of conflict between nomads and settled agricultural communities—*e.g.*, the perpetual conflicts between Iran and Turan, between the Chinese and the Hiung-nu, between Egypt and the desert-folk from Libya and Asia, between India and Central Asia.

The services of the Man of Speech must have been very early needed in these struggles. As orator, he incited them to fight for the defence of hearth and home ; as musician, he sang the praise of the warriors, and stirred up the heart of young men to a love of fight and adventure.

In an age when the art of writing was unknown, or ill-developed, the poet's service to the community was far more valuable. The poet must say something in pithy, soul-stirring strains, which the community would not allow to be forgotten. He sings of virtue and valour, of love and beauty, of sacrifice and splendour, and raises a picture which makes a lasting impression on the finer faculties of the youthful mind. He is the seer, because he sees the hidden secrets of Nature ; in some countries, the poet and the prophet are synonymous, because they deliver messages of the future good world. He is the Logos, because through him the Cosmic Will speaks to mankind.

Now man has gained considerable mastery over Nature, and Science has proved that the old world picture on which some poets based their strains, is utterly inadequate and misleading. More than two thousand years ago, Aristophanes poured his scorn on Homer and Hesiod because they sang the praises of a group of gods of questionable moral character dispensing justice from the top of a little hillock in Thessaly. People now make light of Dante who thought in terms of a medieval cosmos, of an earth which is the centre of the Universe, with the Creator's attention specially focussed on certain gentlemen with a capitalistic frame of mind. In India, too, there are Hindus who make light of Hindu deities. The Bolshevik, a successor of the Zoroastrian, because Capital is his Ahriman, and Labour is his Ahura Mazda, pours scorn on the whole group of medieval poets, since many of them sang the virtues of the hated Bourgeoisie.

Is the poet's profession then gone? Will he be extinct like the dodo in the modern age of machines, or shall he be succeeded by cinema knights, and heroes of the boxing ring? I think not.—We live in an age of Babel. It has been now more necessary than ever to build a Tower to Heaven by co-operative efforts, but we do not understand each other. The Politician, the Economist, the Capitalist and the Military man are all talking in jarring tones, while the groan of oppressed and exploited nationalities is still unrelieved. Nations and groups are still bent on fighting like wild beasts over the spoils of the earth.

But the Man of Brains feels that the fight is unnecessary, for if this spacious Earth be properly exploited with the aid of modern science, there will be enough food and sustenance for every mortal soul, and even luxuries will be forthcoming. But the Man of Science is crude in his expressions and cannot rouse people's heart to the same height of emotion as the Poet.

Some poets are unconscious of the beauties of the modern scientific world-picture. Their cosmos is still Olympian, their moral code is scriptural, their economics is bourgeoise. Of modern science, they are cognisant only of the worst side, of poison gas, chemical warfare, and the soul-killing machine. They are not aware of the beauties of the Einstein conception of the Cosmos, the blending of time and space, a blending of the creeds of Chronos and of Zeus Pater; they do not realize that the scientist has turned away from the creed of inelastic codified religions to the worship of the inner spirit of Nature. Unlike the ancients, he does not worship the lifeless symbol, but the very Spirit. His place of worship is not the sacrificial altar, but the laboratory or the observatory. Only Goethe, amongst the great poets, turned for a long time to the pursuit of science, but in his time, the natural and biological sciences were only in the beginning.

Our Rabindranath, in our beautiful mother-tongue, has always sung of the True, the Good, and the Beautiful. In course of his long life (may it be longer still), the surging events of the times have always found a ready response in his poetical heart. Sometimes like Homer, he sings in irresistible strains of the prowess of an old hero, then he passes into a deeper mood, and sings of piety and devotion like an old Hebrew prophet. Sometimes like Aeschylus he repaints an old story in more gorgeous colours of morality and virtue; and again, like Aristophanes, he pours scorn on the still lingering old world superstitions with simply crushing effect. Sometimes like the old master Kalidasa, he picks up words like a jeweller, and pieces them together with the finest effect, then he relapses into the simple unaffected art of the country poet. His career reads like a poetical Odyssey, and he is the old, yet the ever young poet. In him the art of speech has reached its perfection.

But we, scientific men, beg to bring one complaint against him. His great powers have not yet been used in the exposition of science—of the synoptic world-picture of to-day, of the beauties of the world explored by the physical, the biological and the anthropological sciences.

May we not hope that, like his illustrious predecessor Goethe, he will turn for a while to modern science, and give expression in his inimitable poetry to the Hope behind the invading despair and the Harmony behind the modern Babel of jarring voices.

THE UNIVERSITY,
ALLAHABAD

MEGHNAD SAHA

WHAT can I say which would be a suitable tribute to the Truth which the great Poet has proclaimed in his songs to the East and the West? He has delivered in these new times the ancient message of righteous living in sweet simplicity—the message which is from time to time delivered by devotees and poets in this land of Rishis.

SIMLA, INDIA

JOGENDRA SINGH

GREETINGS FROM RAJPUTANA

HAIL! Rishi of Modern India: the Land of Chivalry, Rajputana, tenders its greetings to you on your seventieth birthday. Hail! the embodiment and the true representative of all that is high and noble in the Culture of India. You embody not only the spiritual culture of Ancient India, but have given it a beautiful expression, in language as inimitable, as sublime, as soul-stirring as the spirit of that culture, carrying a message of joy of life in nature. Your work illustrates not only the depth of that culture but also its all-embracing universality, thus vindicating not only the glory and greatness of Aryan Culture but its triumph over modern thought and modern feeling which the world is slowly recognising and realising.

A great poet is a great seer. You, the greatest poet of Asia of modern times, are also its greatest seer. You have the vision to find the joy of life in every thing that lives and lives eternally, though it assumes new shapes and new forms, thus illustrating the eternal nature of Truth and proving that Truth is Joy and Joy is Truth.

The highest representative of true Indian Culture, your exposition of it in the various cultural centres of the West and the Far East has had favourable repercussions, and has placed India, the source of that culture, in a new light, rehabilitating it in the minds of leaders of thought in every country, giving it a high place in the hierarchy of nations. Your genius has the quality of universality, and it is because of this unique quality, which no one else in the East or the West is known at the present time to possess in such a striking degree, that you are the first and so far the only true interpreter of Eastern Thought and Culture to the West. Indian Culture and Art have found their supreme expression in you, and because of this you are best fitted not only truly and satisfactorily to interpret the East to the West but co-ordinate the best in both in a new whole.

You are a great poet and a great philosopher, imbued with the true spirit of philosophy. You are a novelist. As a teller of short stories you are unrivalled in the world. The pathos in them stirs the soul deeply. You are a dramatist and an essayist. As an educationist you belong to the highest order, as your vision sees through the barriers which baffle even trained minds, and your imagination reaches the furthest flights of human nature. Your realisation of the essential elements of human nature transcends colour, dogma or nationality.

Your consummate art, apart from its literary expression, shows itself in your drawings and paintings and your histrionic gifts and musical compositions. Your superb mind shows its high qualities in whatever department of mental activity it finds occasion to work. As a poet, a philosopher, a patriot and a philanthropist you have achieved world-wide fame and brought honour to the country which has given you birth, and through which, as your countrymen are proud to recognise, you are serving Humanity.

AJMER, RAJPUTANA, INDIA

HAR BILAS SARDA

PERHAPS our chief ground for gratitude to Rabindranath Tagore is that he has bridged the gulf that divides East and West. He is not only a supreme representative of the culture of his own people, but has entered into the very heart of ours. That is an extraordinary achievement for which we owe him in equal measure admiration and thanks.

MANCHESTER

C. P. SCOTT

MASTER,

You know probably not much of my country—this northern land in which at times we are subjected to unbroken light and again to unbroken darkness. Let this, therefore, be to you only a warm hand-clasp, intended to convey to you the significant fact that in spite of the greatest outward dissimilarities, our widely-separated birth-places are linked together by one deep and decisive similarity. In both of them beats the same human heart ; in both the inexplicable something, for which we know of no other name than human-ness, beams from human eyes. This essence of human-ness recognizes its own wherever found. I cannot help feeling deeply that it unites us and our distant countries.

HELSINKI (HELSINGFORS),
FINLAND

F. E. SILLANPÄÄ

'Arise ye little glancing wings and sing your infant joy,
    For everything that lives is holy.'
'Verily from the Everlasting Joy do all objects have their birth.'
'None could live or move if the energy of the all-pervading joy did not fill the sky.'
'In what manner do we accept this world, which is a perfect gift of joy?'
'Gladness is the one criterion of truth.'

Thus the One Voice speaks through many voices: through William Blake as through the ancient Upanishads, and through the poet who in these latter days reports and interprets their great message.

'Ist Er in Werdenlust
Schaffender Freude nah.'

So East and West alike proclaim.

Among the gifts which Rabindranath Tagore has brought us, we may surely count his power to recall those who even in our action-driven West have entered into the secret places. Again and again, Blake comes to mind, as we read the early essays, *Sadhana,* or the poems of love, human or divine. There is the same honour for the 'luminous imagination,'—that creative force, in which, Blake says, all things exist; the same large freedom in a love that casts off bonds. Above all, we find a like profound insight into a Humanity that is divine.

'Thou art a Man; God is no more:
Thine own humanity learn to adore.'

Might not this couplet of Blake's serve as motto to Tagore's last noble book, *The Religion of Man*? 'The idea of the humanity of our God, or the divinity of Man the Eternal, is the main subject of this book,' says Rabindranath.

One could proceed far with such comparisons with Blake. But other associations crowd the mind. In that compelling drama, *The King of the Dark Chamber,* is it Tagore who reports the words of the unseen King, to his bride who may touch him but not behold,—or is it St. John of the Cross? When at the close of the play the old Initiate, the penitent bride, the conquered enemy, meet on the way seeking the Unknown God, pursued and pursuer, have we not metaphor cognate to *The Hound of Heaven*? Delighting in Tagore's early love poems, we perceive for what good reason he was called the Shelley of India. How natural that it should have been Yeats who in 1912 introduced him to the European public! (Yeats by the way compares him to Thomas à Kempis). We can recede far into the thought of the West and still find parallels. *The Religion of Man* reiterates earnest witness that Reality means escape from separateness: so old Boethius, 'Know thou then that unity and goodness are the same.' In Tagore's exquisite praises of the divine revelation conveyed by natural beauty, can be found almost a transcript of passages from St. Bonaventura's *Itinerarium Mentis in Deum.*

In the pure full stream of mysticism flowing from St. Francis may indeed perhaps be recognized the closest analogue to Tagore. There are passages from Capuchin sermons of the seventeenth century which sound like commentaries on the penetrating ecstasies of *Gitanjali.* The movement inspired by the saint who sang the Lauds of the Creatures is, at its most distinctive, as free as Tagore himself from the asceticism which in West as in East has often betrayed men into ingratitude. Neither Tagore nor the greater Franciscans ever confuse the complete surrender of greed and claim for which they both stand, with denial of natural good ; alike they find in such surrender pushed to the limit, the entrance into fullness of life and joy.

Yet if Tagore shares the perceptions of the Western soul on its highest levels, one hastens to rejoice that he has nothing in common with its more cynical moods. With what refreshing scorn he castigates the 'chuckle of an exultant disillusionment' that is 'becoming contagious,' while 'the knights-errant of the cult of arson are abroad, setting fire to our time-honoured altars of worship'! As he repudiates the crass pseudo-realism of the pessimist, so he transcends the scientific materialism even among us now obsolescent. With what spirit he maintains that not in detail of process but in marvel of result we are to look for ultimate reality! The lad who recoiled disgusted from a dissected windpipe, came to incorporate in his thought all that Western science has taught concerning the advance of physical life. Yet he puts the scientific concepts of the West at the service of the mystic wisdom of the East. 'I could not bear the artizan to occupy the throne that was for the artist who concealed the machinery and revealed the creation in its ineffable unity.' Eloquently he reminds us that 'in the secret chamber within the heart' 'the fire of Nature's workshop is transformed into lamps of a festival, the noise of her factory is heard like music. The iron chain of cause and effect sounds heavily outside in Nature, but in the human heart its unalloyed delight seems to sound as it were like the golden strings of a harp.'

In such absorption of European culture by a temperament distinctively Eastern, Tagore's greatest originality may perhaps be found. Might it be surmised that by a rhythm of compensation, Western mysticism at its best owes much to an Oriental strain, while conversely the mysticism of the East gains new richness when it accepts the gifts of Europe? This fusion of elements is characteristic of Tagore, as it is of a great spirit from Japan, Kagawa. The genius of these men has triumphed over Separation. It has broken down the invisible barriers which divide race from race. Tagore can bring home to us with balanced appreciation the gifts, with the perils, for which two civilizations stand: the 'best ideal in the West, the great truth of fight,'—a 'holy spirit,' which yet at its worst 'breeds unappeasable greed for material gain, and leads to unmeaning slavery to things'; and the Eastern 'inner concentration of mind' where 'the peace of the extinguished desire may become the peace of death; and the inner world in which we would dwell become a world of incoherent dreams.' If there is value in the stormy approach of East and West which we are now experiencing, it may be because the clash of these contending ideals shall become a marriage whence a more adequate ideal than either shall be born. Such marriage is foreshadowed in the writings of Tagore.

The poet is especially useful to us because he separates himself from the 'time-honoured tradition' of those negative Hindu schools whose aim is 'to reach a condition wherein mind becomes perfectly blank, losing all its activities.' When he says that this discipline 'may be valuable as a great psychological experience, but all the same it is not religion,' we sigh with relief. Tagore has always disclaimed, too completely it would seem, the title of philosopher; but it is true that his teaching springs from that living experience which underlies the plane of thought. The very claim of life has turned him from the quest for vacancy; it has led to his asserting that conscious union in love with 'the Eternal Person manifested in all persons' is our central aspiration. As we share such aspiration, as we advance toward such union, antagonisms of race and nation will vanish. The poet severed relations with active politics in 1907. But in the deeper regions of psychical life, he is doing much to draw civilizations together. All the nations, says he, are breaking their shells; and he helps in the process. It is fitting that we bring tribute of gratitude to one who so sets us inwardly free from the prison of false nationalism as from that of the personal self; who in his own work illustrates the possibility of fecund marriage between East and West; and who enables us to see with clearer vision, in the energy, often so disconcerting, of this bewildering universe, 'the Play of Love.'

WELLESLEY, MASS., U.S.A. VIDA D. SCUDDER

PURE Art is sincere and disinterested no less than the 'Will to Good,' but in appraising either or in laying down the norm, it would be 'pathological' to appeal to any emotion other than the emotion of contemplating the beautiful or the good. No doubt, all emotions are proper plastic stuff for constructions in aesthetics as well as ethics; but as building material, experience in all its forms is intrinsically valuable,—ideation, imagination, instinct, no less than emotion. But none of these enter into the norm.

What *does* enter into the norm and test of Poetry is not emotional 'exaltation,' imaginative 'transfiguration' or disinterested 'criticism,' but in and through them all, the creation of a Personality with an individual scheme of life, an individual outlook on the universe.

Judged by the above criterion, Tagore's poetic achievement is characteristically complete. His early poems are an exercise in emotional 'exaltation.' To this he soon added the art of imaginative 'transfiguration' (as in *Urvasi*). In his maturer achievement, he developed the criticism of life without sacrificing either exaltation or transfiguration. Finally in his consummate later art, he has summed up all these elements and achieved the supreme mastery,—the creation of a Personality with an individual scheme of life, an individual outlook on the Universe.

BOMBAY

BRAJENDRANATH SEAL

RABINDRANATH AND THE UNIVERSITIES OF INDIA

RESPONDING to the kind invitation of the sponsors of the *Golden Book of Tagore* to contribute to its pages, it strikes me that my own tribute of praise to the poet on the occasion of the seventieth anniversary of his birth may best take the form of an exhortation to the Universities in India to show greater recognition to his writings. It is true that limitations of language will prevent most of the Universities outside Bengal from making any effective and wide-spread approach to his work in the original, but by his eminence as poet, Rabindranath has such a strong claim on the nation and translations are beginning to play such an important part in literary culture to-day, that his volumes should figure even in their renderings in a foreign language on the syllabuses of our boards of studies, side by side with the best classics of Western literature.

It was my privilege, years ago, as the head of the department of English Studies at the Benares Hindu University, to make a beginning in the direction, by introducing the works of Rabindranath into the courses of studies in English, the *Gardener* appearing on the list for the highest examination in the University, some of his novels and stories taking their places in the earlier courses. It is significant that even in the national atmosphere of that centre of learning in the ancient city of Benares, there were not wanting people who shook their wise heads in doubt and expressed their misgivings about the experiment which had not yet been tried in any other University in India. The University had, however, had no reason to regret the innovation, and the example has since been followed more than once by other educational authorities in the country, in the United Provinces as well as in the rest of India. If it has not become more popular, one can only attribute it sometimes to the inferiority-complex of our own people, or again, to the want of self-confidence in the judgment of contemporary literature which has not yet passed into the well-worn dignity of acknowledged classics. It is possible that narrow prejudices have also sometimes contributed to this result.

While the highest achievement of English Literature must be always inseparably associated with aspects of British life and civilisation, it is no ordinary handicap to the young student in India that the English classics placed in his hands invariably deal with a world with which he is not very familiar. This applies not merely to differences of natural surroundings, but also to strange variations in social institutions, folklore and tradition and general outlook on life and its problems. It is difficult for him to go into ecstasies over the skylark and the daffodil; but he could understand the language of the "little *kokil* singing on the *sirish* bough" and he has recollections of the lotus opening to the morning sun in the village tank. He has no knowledge of heather blooming on the highlands of Scotland, but he has often run along the smiling rice fields of his own native land. He has not seen fairies dancing on the village green at midnight, nor has the nightmare frightened him out of his wits in his sleep, though he has perhaps fled away in breathless excitement from the *bhut* sitting on the wayside tree, or recoiled with horror from the possibility of an ascetic's 'wrath.' It may be, he has heard his parents cursing their *karma*, but he is certainly puzzled at the idea of being born with an initial equipment of vicarious sin.

It is alright to argue that highest literature transcends all considerations of local interest and is universal in its appeal, but there is the obstinate fact that, except in the abstract regions of philosophical speculation, literary masterpieces are built, in considerable measure, with the brick and mortar of our daily experience made out of the world which is in our immediate neighbourhood. It would, therefore, undoubtedly make English literature more real to the Indian student if it could deal, at least in some instances, with the ideas and objects of his own atmosphere. There is hardly a writer better suited to serve this purpose than Rabindranath Tagore, whose background is Indian to the core, in spite of his constant withdrawal to fascinating worlds of idealism and romance independent of climes and people, and his works sum up some of the finest aspirations of the Indian life and civilisation of to-day.

It should not be imagined for a moment from what has been said, that this plea for the wider introduction of Rabindranath's works into the curricula of our Universities is based only on the Indian interest of their material. As a professor of English, always anxious to keep up the highest standards of literary appreciation in our Universities, I should have hesitated to indulge in this exhortation, even on the ceremonial occasion of the birthday anniversary, if I did not feel convinced that the works furnished ample material for useful study and stimulating exposition in the class-room. In the delicate artistic and emotional susceptibilities of his lyrical poems, in the placid and mysterious depths of his plays, in the variety of human experience in his novels and short stories and in the profundities of his philosophical writings, there is the widest scope for the student and professor of literature to co-operate with happy results. I am not unaware of the fact that a cynic has remarked that the surest way of making a literary masterpiece dull and uninspiring is to prescribe it for a University examination ; but I think better of the teachers of this generation. And with all its dangers, it should be pleasant for the poet himself to feel that he is in such effective and intimate touch with the future citizens of the nation. As for the students themselves, it must be no ordinary inspiration to know that they are reading the works of a writer who is one of the noblest exponents of their national life and civilisation and whose literary achievements have brought great prestige to India and the East.

CAWNPORE

P. SESHADRI

IN 1928 I visited India and had the honour of being received as guest in Santiniketan. On the return journey across the Pacific I wrote down the impressions of my Indian visit for the Munich periodical *Zeitwende*. My contribution to the *Golden Book of Tagore* is a translation of the last paragraph of this article, since I believe that the hope expressed therein corresponds to the aspirations of our celebrated friend:

"It is our heartfelt wish that India soon will see economic improvement and a fulfilment of its political hopes. This wish is due, not to ill-will toward England, but to a conviction that mankind will gain when our gifted Indian cousins, who in early times so surpassed us, can once again take their merited place in the world partnership of culture with the result that their speculative, transcendental outlook may counteract the expediency and materialism of the occident."

THE UNIVERSITY, MUNICH — ARNOLD SOMMERFELD

I had the pleasure of hearing Rabindranath Tagore over the radio. He was in New York and I was in California, but it was as if he was in the room. After having listened to him, I, a Socialist, wanted to write him a letter, pleading with him to open his mind to one aspect of the modern problem. It seems to me that the evils of modern times which he deplores—of materialism, ugliness, and greed—are not caused by the use of machinery, but by the fact that the machinery is in private hands and used for private profit, and for the exploitation of all members of the community except those who happen to own the machinery. I expect a wholly different kind of civilization when machinery is socially owned and used for the social welfare. I believe that it will then no longer be the enemy of the soul of man, and will no longer have to be challenged by poets and moralists. I plead with a great poet and moralist of India to lend his precious gifts to the service of the movement to socialize and thus to humanize industry.

PASADENA, CALIFORNIA, U.S.A. — UPTON SINCLAIR

A PORTRAIT IN PENCIL (1917)

By Mr. Mukul Dey, A. R. C. A., Principal, Govt. School of Art, Calcutta

A TRIBUTE

I

IT was a monsoon evening in Simla in 1910. Foamy vapour floated in the valleys and shrouded the summits.

* * * * * * *

Some one in the house that I was approaching was singing. The notes were low and plaintive. The voice—quite evidently a woman's—was mellow and resonant.

Presently I recognized it. The singer was none other than Srimati Sarala Devi Chaudhurani, a guest in the same house in which I was staying.

As I entered the room I saw Sarala Devi sitting at a harmonium, her jet-black hair streaming over her shoulders. At my request she sang the song again. It was in the Bengali—a sister of my own mother-tongue, Panjabi. For long the two had been parted, but they nevertheless retained much of their common heritage.

After she had finished she slowly repeated the words and explained to me the meaning of those that I did not understand. It was an ode to Mother Ind, composed by her uncle—Rabindranath Tagore. Freely translated it ran:

Who is it that constantly approaches and retires
With eyes overflowing with tears?
Who is looking toward us with vain hopes?
She is my Mother! She is my Mother!
In the dark house what sad-faced one has prepared the meals for us?
Whose is the food that no longer pleases our palates?
It is our Mother's! Oh! It is our poor Mother's!

Thus it was that I, who had just returned to India after many years of world-wandering, caught the first gleam of the Poet's golden soul shining through the lattice-work of his words.

II

A few months later I was staying at Baroda.

A stream of callers was coming and going at all hours. Among them was a Bengali of refined manners and cultivated taste, but lately returned from Oxford. His Highness had met him while in England and had appointed him to the Baroda Service.

I soon found that he was a devotee of Tagore. He knew many of Rabindranath's poems by heart. The Poet's works occupied a place of honour in the little home that he had fitted up for himself.

As we sat in the cool of the evening on the roofless verandah on the first floor of the *Chimanbagh* looking out upon a marble swimming bath rimmed with tall, slender palms, over which hung a huge *pipal* (ficus religiosa) tree, I would get him to read poem after poem to me. He needed no coaxing. Many were the hours we spent in this fashion. I was never tired of listening to this invocation to the Motherland:

Thou who dost charm the heart of all the world,
Thou land gleaming with the golden glory of the sun,
Thou mother of our fathers and mothers,
The soles of whose feet are washed by the waters of the blue sea,
Whose green skirts are fluttered by the breeze,
Whose forehead, the Himalayas, is kissed by the skies.
Who wearest the diamond diadem of the snows;
It was in thy hermitages that the first hymns were sung.
Words of wisdom, religion, poetry, history, first
Were preached in thy forest temples.
Thou art blessed, the eternal dispenser of good,
Thou dost distribute food from land to land,
The Ganges and the Jumna are the milk of mercy flowing from thy breasts.

III

Tagore's Art had from the very beginning cast a spell over me. My whole being seemed to vibrate in unison with the tunes he piped. The music of his measures enthralled me. So did his imagery. I marvelled at the economy of material he used in weaving the fabric of his dreams—and at the simplicity of that material.

His verse led the mind—imperceptibly but inevitably—out of the maze of the senses into the realm of the spirit. At least it did mine.

There was nothing parochial about his message. It was not for one people, but for all peoples.

Even Rabindranath's love for the Motherland was not selfish or exclusive. A native of any country, reading his patriotic lays, could translate them in terms of his own land and be thrilled with the sense of national pride with which they inspired him.

He sang of the beauties with which the Creator had adorned our India—of the cultural heritage that her sons and daughters had accumulated through centuries untold. He lamented the depressed state into which she had fallen—bemoaned the fact that she had become a weight upon mankind instead of continuing to be a contributor to the common store of knowledge. Politics interested him only as a lever to lift his people from the quicksands of despond on to the firm ground of parity with other races, where alone they could live in amity with others, freely exchanging gifts of the mind and the spirit.

It was a great pity, I felt, that all this artistry—all this spirituality—should be lost upon the great wide world—upon even India outside Bengal.

Why was it, I wondered, that he with his universal message, was little known except in the province of his birth. The only explanation that satisfied me was that he employed a medium that was not understood beyond the bounds of Bengal.

Would he have done better had he adopted English as the vehicle of his thoughts? He had been familiar with that language from his boyhood upwards.

I dismissed the idea almost as soon as it was formed in my mind. With effort he may no doubt have been able to twine the tendrils of his fancy round a foreign frame: but they clambered naturally over the home-made trellis.

Years later I learnt that somewhere in the late nineties of the last century Professor (later Sir) Jagadis Chunder Bose—another gifted son of India—had tried to introduce the Poet to the West. He had translated some of Tagore's stories into English. They fell into the hands of the Prince Kropotkin—then a refugee in England—who admired them so much that he sent them to an American publisher. Judging by what happened, that publisher must have lacked money-sense as well as imagination: for he returned the manuscript on the plea that the author was totally unknown to the reading public of the United States.

IV

The day dawned finally when the whole world acclaimed Rabindranath Tagore. The publication of an English rendering of his *Gitanjali* was followed by the award of the Nobel prize for literature..

The lilt that characterized Tagore's original composition was wanting in the English version. Some of the wistfulness had fled from his fancy. As Ramananda Chatterjee, the Editor of this book, who, in his unostentatious way, has done more to make the Poet's writings available in English than perhaps all others combined, once wrote to me, "The flavour—the aroma—of the original is lost in the translation, however carefully done."

Despite all disadvantages, Rabindranath's genius shone. His similes were quaint—his imagery potent. Yet he was no prodigal with words.

The English take delight in depicting themselves as a dull nation. So adept are they at creating illusions that this fiction has supplanted the actual fact. This is all the more amazing because no people in the world possess a richer, vaster store-house of imaginative literature than they. Tagore's genius (as Englished) made a deep impression upon the cultured classes in the British Isles.

I was living in London at the time, having gone thither from Baroda by way of Bombay and Cairo, during the summer of 1911. Writers in the British Press, with which I was connected, lionized him—as is their wont after some one else has discovered the lion for them.

Tagore's vogue spread from year to year. Edition after edition of the *Gitanjali* was called for. The demand for other compositions of the Poet led to the publication of *Sadhana* and other works—poetical and prose.

V

Judging by my knowledge of the Continent (imperfect and inadequate as it is) the religious element of Tagore's thought has been better appreciated there than perhaps in the British Isles. Srimati Sarojini Naidu told me, in 1919, that during her visit to Norway she had found complete sets of Tagore's works in humble homes in remote villages in the "Land of the Midnight Sun."

The United States of America especially responded to Tagore's message. America is supposed to be highly objective. But objectivity has produced a reaction there. It has bred an intellectual, idealistic class, largely consisting of women, longing for spirituality. I doubt if there is any place, outside Bengal, where the Poet is more deeply venerated.

VI

Tagore's message of goodwill came, moreover, at the psychological moment. The world was beginning to groan under the weight of armaments. The miseries engendered by the war and the disillusionment that came in its wake, had sickened Europe and America unto the very soul.

Politically-minded men were advocating certain ways to achieve permanent peace. They would have the governments of the world federate in a society of nations—a world league—and through that organization bring about, by stages, the reduction of armaments. The ultimate aim was the outlawry of war.

The more daring among these thinkers postulated a "world state." The idea was not new. Auguste Comte for one, had visualized a "planetary government" fifty years earlier.

But the world had not passed out of the stage of little-mindedness. The national ideal rested, in most cases, upon a "superiority complex." Each nation insisted upon being on the top. The doctrine of *uber alles*—of "ruling the waves"—was dominant. Talk of a real super-state, therefore, frightened many nationalists.

Tagore blazed a new trail—the trail of cultural co-operation. It was broad, smooth and safe. No one need be frightened of it.

He saw that no nation was or at least could afford to be—self-sufficing. As he explained to me, on one occasion, subjectivity needed the corrective of objectivity—especially we in India. But, on the other hand, the objective people of the occident would be entirely lost without the corrective of subjectivity.

VII

My first meeting with Tagore took place somewhere in 1919. The moment was fraught with shame and humiliation for all Indians.

In the spring of 1918 some bureaucrats in the Panjab—the province of my birth—backed up by bayonets, had scented a revolt. Barbarism broke the chain with which it had been tethered to the post of civilization. Bombs were thrown from the air on unarmed civilians and actually fell in the compound of a school in Gujranwala. Fire was opened upon a large assemblage peacefully listening to a publicist lecturing in an open space (the Jalianwala Bagh) in Amritsar, surrounded by high walls which imprisoned the unfortunate sufferers and placed them completely at the mercy of the guns trained upon them. Respectable citizens were made to crawl on their stomachs through a narrow, dark alley in that city.

Edwin Samuel Montagu, then at the helm of the India Office, sought to visit the culprits with exemplary punishment, but failed to influence his colleagues of His Majesty's Government to do so. He was assailed by the Imperialists for even the weak action he had persuaded that Government to sanction.

The sensitive soul of the Poet felt deeply the humiliation that had been heaped upon his—and my—people. In token of his shame he had stripped himself of the Knighthood that the British Sovereign had conferred upon him some time earlier.

Shortly after this he came to London. I took the earliest opportunity to call upon him at the apartment that he occupied near Kensington Gardens.

Hardly had I seated myself, when the door opened and the Poet entered the room. A tall black Astrakhan cap was set on his grey, flowing, wavy locks. A kindly, patriarchal expression irradiated his face. Beneath his long, strong nose a moustache accentuated but did not hide his sensitive mouth. His beard was snow-white but for a few stray black strands. He wore a loose Cashmere coat over a long shirt that came down to his knees, white stockings and slippers heavily embroidered with gold thread.

A fine figure of a man. Well groomed. It was easy to imagine that in his youth he must have set the fashion for the aristocratic young Bengalis of his day.

He looked—and talked—like a *Rishi*—benign and friendly. By the way conversation flowed, he might have known me all my life. There was nothing to suggest that he was meeting me for the first time. There was no awkwardness—no standoffishness—no pose.

Before I knew it, we were discussing the horrors of the martial law regime in the Panjab. At the memory of it gloom spread over his face like a soft grey veil of tulle. His voice fell. A note of sorrow crept into it. It vibrated with emotion.

There was not a trace of anger. He did not utter a single word of wrath. His gaze seemed to be turned inwards. His mind was intent upon the degradation that had befallen our people. He seemed particularly oppressed with the thought that India should have fallen so low that men of another land, in her pay, should have dared to heap such indignities upon her. No passionate protest could possibly have been more stirring than his super-sensitive spirit crushed under his sense of shame.

Deeply touched, I asked him if I might cable the purport of our talk to some of the newspapers with which I was connected. He told me that, before leaving the Motherland, he had given expression to his feelings: but he would not stand in my way.

I pulled out a pencil and drafted a few lines on the back of an envelope that I found in one of my pockets and read them to him.

Then the artist came to the front—for the first time. I had interpreted him correctly. His meaning was there. But not quite his language. He had me read the draft to him again. As we went through it—sentence by sentence—clause by clause—he would stop me and ask me to alter a word here—a phrase there.

I was glad that it happened that way. It gave me (or so at least I fancied) some idea of the manner in which he must ensure that his writings, translated into English, would convey the same spirit that he had infused into the original Bengali.

VIII

Tagore carries to the public platform the quiet dignity that distinguished him in private. That impression rises uppermost in my mind among the recollections of a meeting that I attended, before which he read a paper.

The subject—"The Forest Universities of India"—that he chose for his discourse was characteristic of him. It was a clear-cut exposition of the *Gurukulas* of old—where lads drawn from palace and from mud-hut alike sat on terms of equality near to Nature's heart, at the feet of men who had dedicated themselves to the service of the Goddess of Learning.

The Poet's voice was thin (he had not been in good health for some time). The hall in which he spoke was large. Every inch of it was crowded.

Surveying the audience from a seat near the rostrum I could see that many persons could not hear what Rabindranath was saying. Yet there were no cries of: "Speak up, please." No noise. No shuffling about or nervous coughing. There was something about the lecturer that held even those outside the orbit of his voice spell-bound.

Yet he hardly looked up from the sheets on which his address was written. His tones were level, seldom raised to emphasize a passage. There was no gesticulation. Only some magnetic current, hidden from sight, was at work.

Tagore's treatment of the subject interested me. He talked of things that made our blood flow faster. His sense of restraint prevented him from assuming a "holier-than-thou" attitude. Therein lay his charm as a speaker.

LAHORE — ST. NIHAL SINGH

I have read Tagore's *Religion of Man* with deep interest. This great prose-poem on God and Man is a wonderful blend of Western Science and Eastern Spirituality, and the result is a rare feast for those who care for the spiritual view of the world. It is in every way a fine achievement—perhaps the best work Tagore has yet written.

HOUSE OF ASSEMBLY,
CAPE TOWN, SOUTH AFRICA

J. C. SMUTS

FROM THE SPANISH ACADEMY

Leyendo *Pájaros Perdidos*.

"El vestido de los hechos aprieta demasiado a la verdad.
Cuanto mas holgada está vestida de ficciones!"

Qué hermosa la amplia vestidura de la *Poesía*! Qué misteriosamente realza con sus majestuosos pliegues la eterna excelsitud de la Verdad! . . . . Cuan admirable la desnudez divina! Cuan radiante se transparenta en la apretada túnica de la *Historia*!

"Si de noche lloras por el sol, no verás las estrellas."

En tu noche triste contempla los lejanos mundos siderales; no llores por que te falta el sol, vivificador del mundo tuyo. Y cuando vuelva ese sol, apagando para ti las estrellas una a una, piensa que ellas siguen inflamando de luz mundos mas gigantes que el tuyo.

ACADEMIA ESPANOLA,
MADRID

R. MENENDEZ PIDAL

TAGORE'S DRAWINGS

TAGORE'S drawings constrain us to pause and ask ourselves anew, what is the purpose of drawing, of painting, of art generally. Is it to be a pretty toy to amuse and flatter us, or is it to convey the deepest feelings from soul to soul?

The popular artist, like the popular preacher, is careful never to offend our prejudices, or to call us to make any great mental or spiritual effort, while the true poet or painter asks us to see what we have not yet seen.

The drawings of Rabindranath Tagore prove that the poet, though a master of the use of words, feels that certain things can be better expressed, or perhaps only expressed in the language of line, tone and colour.

These things are not outward facts such as those of anatomy and perspective, and the rules that can be taught in Academies, which become too often a hindrance to the freedom and vitality of the imagination. Tagore's drawings are, as I see them, the work of a powerful imagination seeing things in line and colour as the best Oriental sees them, with that sense of rhythm and pattern that we find in Persian or Indian textiles and craft work. The colour sense is indeed superb.

But there is much more than this ; there is a deep feeling and apprehension of the spiritual life and being, of men and animals, expressed in their features, their movements, their outward forms, lines and colours.

Can one explain all this in words? Can one say this drawing means this, or that one means such and such? Assuredly no, for if any one could say it, the poet himself could do so, and if he could say it then why draw or colour? We look and look silently, and immerse ourselves in these pictures, and thus here and there if we are humble enough, deep answers unto deep.

BIRMINGHAM JOSEPH SOUTHALL

THE INBORN CRITERION

THE invitation to contribute to this volume reached me, in far away America, when I had in my hands the new book which gives to the world a brilliant expression of Tagore's mind. I refer, of course, to his Hibbert Lectures, *The Religion of Man,* in which, as might be expected, one finds the imaginative artistry of a poet, the penetration of a philosophic mind, the ardour of a soul which has "touched the infinite" and possesses an "inner source of divine wisdom." In the reading of this book, which so happily supplements the volumes from Tagore's pen already accessible to the English-speaking world, I have found an illumination which has brought into clearer relief and more significant relationship such fragments of knowledge as I have of ancient and modern India. But it has done more; it has suggested that East and West, separated though they have been, are sundered only (to borrow imagery used by Tagore in a quite different connection) as half of a poetic couplet may be torn away from the other half. It is in "a state of suspense" while the other line, with which it rhymes and which could give it fulness, is "smudged by the mist away in some undecipherable distance." How otherwise do I seem, as I read one page, to be listening to Plato, who found in mathematics a vestibule to knowledge of the Real World, and as I read the next to be listening to Bergson, who builds a metaphysical system on biological data; at one moment to be looking over the shoulder of Marcus Aurelius while he writes those words which demonstrate the highest reach of "the unassisted virtue of man," and at another to be standing in a crowd of English villagers while George Fox describes the Inner Light and the peace of communion with God?

Such parallels, and many others, are suggested to my mind, and yet the words of Tagore are wholly consistent, as it seems to me, with his inheritance, his environment, his achievements as an Indian poet and teacher. How can this be? The explanation is one which is hard to express only because we all suffer from the defects of our education, in which the imagination was not stimulated to visualize the people of distant lands. True, we of the West were led as far eastward as Rome, Greece, Judea, but this was to study not the living but the dead; the Greeks and Romans were hidden behind menacing walls built of grammar books; the Jews, even the great prophets, were known only through early Christian documents and were therefore obscured by prejudice. That great civilizations had existed in India before Athens and Jerusalem were even rude rock fortresses, that during ages which were "dark" in Europe men had journeyed overland from China to India to attend universities, that in our own time India possesses anything more than bejewelled rajahs, clever elephants, famished villagers, and *Jungle Book* animals, were not mentioned to us.

The truth Tagore so clearly expresses to-day is one that some Westerners have proclaimed but which transcends all distinctions between East and West because it is a truth about man as man. Let me now select but one aspect of it for emphatic mention. Tagore speaks of an "inner faculty" of our own, which helps us to find our relationship with the supreme self of man ; elsewhere he calls this "an inner source of divine wisdom," or an "inborn criterion of the real." This is, of course, closely related to the keen sensitiveness which he tells us characterized his mind from infancy. He is occasionally made intensely conscious of an all-pervading personality "answering to the personality of man." The experience of this inborn criterion is not unlike the "intimate feeling a father has for his son," in which he "touches an ultimate truth," the truth of their relationship. But it goes further, for in immediate realization it grasps the "grand unity of relationship" in the universe. At such times he has "touched the infinite." Vision, not knowledge, intuition rather than logic, has brought this experience. Such consciousness of God "contradicts the trivialities of our daily life, and upsets the arrangements made for securing our personal exclusiveness behind the walls of individual habits and superficial conventions. . . . It invokes unexpectedly in the midst of a self-centred life a supreme sacrifice."

Further yet Tagore goes in characterizing this experience of what he variously calls the universal in man, the supreme personality, or God. The consciousness of God comes to us as a call and we dedicate our lives in response, consecrating ourselves to the service of mankind, of truth, of beauty. In other words, in this experience not only is man reaching out to God, but God is meeting man. "Somewhere in the arrangement of this world there seems to be a great concern for giving us delight." Over and above all that we can learn of matter and its arrangement, or of the forces into which science has resolved matter, "there is a message conveyed through the magic touch of personality."

We are reminded of the "divine sign" to which Socrates listened and which he obeyed at the cost of his life ; of the voice Jesus heard as he came up out of the water of the Jordan after he had indicated his association with John by undergoing baptism ; of the voices which directed and guided Joan of Arc ; of the visions which moved John Bunyan now to fear and now to hope ; of the affirmative mysticism of George Fox and many other Quakers, who saw "an infinite ocean of light and love, which flowed over the ocean of darkness" and in that vision saw "the infinite love of God."

To-day, in our Western world, there are many who are seekers for the experience around which the whole of Tagore's interpretation of life is centered. The Religious

Society of Friends continues to bear its testimony to the principle that all religious practices, statements of belief, cherished customs, and methods of organization depend for their validity and vitality upon the personal experience of the individual who finds God to be a guiding, enriching, and constraining force in life. Many others are aware that life has not yet brought them its greatest joys because their lives are fragmentary, incomplete, detached in self-centered satisfactions. They have heard that there is a Truth which meets man more than half-way in his search but so far the only truth they know is one which seems almost reluctant to be discovered. They have heard that there is an illumination of life, not merely of the next step but of the distant goal, or at least of a path which "shineth more and more unto the perfect day." They have been told that there is Power, and that this is not a power they can put to use for their own profit but a power that will use them, even in their weakness. They have seen a few souls consecrated to the loving life and they have discovered that Love is not simply the nebulous ideal of a few affable souls who are blinded to life's conflicts. And they would like to experience such truth, such illumination, such power, such love. They would like to discover for themselves that God is really so active in meeting man that those who ally themselves with the universal welfare of man, in a great act of faith overcoming the obstacles and barriers of ancient prejudice, transcend the limits of mortality and live in the infinite.

To help some of these seekers to find the truth which can bring them liberation of spirit will seem a more holy cause, perhaps a less difficult task, to those of us in the West who have been privileged to come under the influence of Rabindranath Tagore.

DARTMOUTH COLLEGE, U.S.A. HAROLD E. B. SPEIGHT

"A TRUE CITIZEN OF THE WORLD"

WHEN I was last in India—some four years ago—I was talking about Tagore to one of his own Bengali countrymen and he said to me, "You English can never know what a great and wonderful poet he is in his own language. You read him when he writes in your language, and you read translations of his poems, but that cannot tell you what he is to us." Then he broke into a chant and sang me a poem, music and words both by the poet—and "how," he said, "can you translate that?"

Of course a fatal handicap for me, but on the other hand I was able to assure my Bengali friend that the Poet wrote beautifully for us in our language, and that by his writing he had done more than any man living to bridge the gap which is supposed to divide the mind of the East from the mind of the West. Tagore is always an Indian patriot and he has rightly resented what is wounding to the pride or self-respect of his countrymen, but his thoughts travel beyond patriotism to the unity of the spirit in which alone there can be peace and reconciliation for nations or individuals. In this he had been a true citizen of the world, teaching not an Eastern or an Indian doctrine, but the one human truth of which mankind everywhere stands in urgent need to-day.

As an Englishman I like to remember that he is within our fold ; and if I were thinking of a test of British-Indian policy to-day, I know of none better than that the solution, whatever it may be, should be one which would enable Rabindranath Tagore and men like him to feel that they are living a free and self-respecting life in their own home-land.

The visit I paid to Santiniketan in 1926 left me with an ineffaceable memory of a personality at once gracious and fervent, imaginative and practical. Many men have dreamed dreams, but few have so steadily applied themselves to showing by example and practice what it is possible to do in their own time and generation. Tagore commands our respect and admiration not only by his writings but by a life of disinterested and self-sacrificing work for his ideals.

I can only echo the thoughts of thousands of admirers in wishing that he may have many years of happy life and influence before him and that he may find time to visit us again. For we too take a pride in him and have need of him.

CHANTREY PLACE, MARDEN,
KENT, ENGLAND

J. A. SPENDER

WHY NEED WE EVER GROW OLD?

OLD age is not a matter of years. Counting by years, some of the oldest men in the world have not reached what is called middle life. They are old because they are old in soul. The soul is the true measure.

As soon as the freshness and interest is gone out of one's life, he is old.

As soon as one wants the years or the days to hurry by, or as he begins to think and talk about 'killing time,' he is getting old.

As soon as a man makes up his mind that the deepest human motive is selfishness, or that every man has his price, he is old ; his heart is withered.

As soon as a man begins to suspect everybody's sincerity, he is old ; his soul is wrinkled, whatever may be the appearance of his cheek. I know of nothing more dreadful than such premature and unnatural old age as comes from living selfishly and on the surface of life, until all that is noblest and deepest has faded away and has come to seem an unreality.

The man who lacks faith, whether faith in truth, or in justice, or in his fellow-man, or in himself, or in God, is aging in heart ; weakness and decrepitude are creeping into his soul.

There are still other marks of real old age—old age of the heart and mind. As soon as the tender green of the grass or the gold of the dandelion or the witchery of the falling snowflake ceases to be a joy to one, he is aging.

He who habitually looks backward, instead of forward, is old ; no matter if he has seen only twenty years of time.

He who is interested in nothing new, is old.

He who sees Eden in the past, and who thinks the former times were better than these, is old.

He who distrusts the young, and thinks the great men are all dying off, with none to take their place, is old.

He who is timid and afraid to undertake new enterprises, is old.

The pessimist is old. The sceptic and the cynic are old. The habitual fault-finder and complainer is old.

The man or woman or child who looks habitually on the dark side of things, and always thinks it is going to rain or snow or storm, is old.

The person, no matter how young he may be in years, who has made up his mind that he is unlucky, and that 'when his bread and butter falls on the floor it always falls butter side down,' is already old.

He who does not care for children is old. He to whom the laughter of children is not music, is old. If a man has children and does not play with them and enjoy the play, he is old, and may well ask himself, 'Am I really their father? Am I not their grand-father?'

He who does not enjoy humour, and whose face seldom smiles, is old.

He who never has time to stop and hear a bird sing, or to admire a sweet flower, is old.

He to whom a rupee is of more value than an uplifting thought, is very old and very poor.

Thus we see that old age of the mind and heart—the only kind that any of us need much to dread—has little to do with years. It is well nigh as likely to come at forty or thirty or twenty, as at seventy or eighty. In comparison with this kind of old age how little is to be feared the aging of the body! For in the oldest body may dwell the youngest spirit.

Another serious mistake often made regarding old age—the old age of years I mean—is to think of it as necessarily an idle or inactive or unproductive period in life. The truth is, some of the very best work of the world has been done and is being done to-day by persons far on in years. Take away from history the great achievements of men above sixty, or seventy, or eighty, and the world would suffer an irreparable loss. Writes Longfellow, in his *Morituri Salutamus,* a poem composed in his old age:

'Cato learned Greek at eighty; Sophocles
Wrote his grand *Oedipus,* and Simonides
Bore off the prize of verse from his compeers
When each had numbered more than four score years.
And Theophrastus at four score and ten,
Had but begun his *Characters of Men;*
Goethe, at Weimar, toiling to the last,
Completed *Faust* when eighty years were passed.'

This is scarcely a beginning of the long and splendid list of achievements of men far on in life.

The artistic and literary genius of Michel-Angelo was little if at all dimmed at the age of eighty-three, as is shown by the exquisite sonnets, the fine architectural drawings and the noble models for sculpture produced by him at that advanced age.

Linnaeus was still a devoted botanist at seventy-seven, and exclaimed, 'I am happier in my work than the King of Persia!'

Humboldt kept young to ninety in scientific studies and publishing the results of his scientific investigations.

Gladstone was holding the office of Prime Minister of Great Britain at eighty-three, and fighting one of the most strenuous political battles of his life, that over Irish Home Rule; and at eighty-seven he was addressing great meetings all up and down England to arouse public sentiment in favour of the suffering Armenians.

Sir Moses Montefiore, the distinguished Jewish philanthropist, carried on his works of beneficence almost to the time of his death at the great age of one hundred and one, and made the last of his seven notable journeys to the Orient in the interest of the Jewish people when he was nearly ninety.

James Martineau continued his literary productivity until beyond ninety, and gave to the world his three greatest books after he was eighty.

Victor Hugo continued to write on with wonderful freshness and power almost to the time of his death at eighty-three, and declared at the last, 'I have not yet given expression to a hundredth part of what is in me.'

Tennyson gave to the world his exquisite 'Crossing the Bar' at eighty.

At eighty-five and beyond, Edward Everett Hale was Chaplain of the United States Senate, he was at the same time a writer wielding a pen prolific and powerful beyond almost any other in the nation, and a leader in nearly every great movement for reform and for educational, social and religious progress in the country.

At far beyond eighty Count Tolstoy was writing with vigour, penetration and power surpassed by no author of modern Europe.

General William Booth, the head of the Salvation Army, continued until beyond eighty to tour about the world with as much spirit and to push forward the work of the Army in all lands with as much energy as he had shown thirty years earlier.

Nor are achievements in advanced age confined to men. Women have their full part.

Queen Victoria carried the heavy responsibilities of her high position until the age of eighty-two.

Mary Somerville published her able and valuable work on Molecular and Microscopical Science at the age of eighty-nine.

The Baroness Burdett-Coutts continued her active and far-reaching work in charities and philanthropy until almost the time of her death at the age of ninety-three.

Mrs. Julia Ward Howe maintained until past ninety her keen interest in the progress of the world and vigorous literary and philanthropic activity. She spent a part of her ninety-first birthday reading Greek and a part pleading before a Boston Scientific Commission for pure milk for babies. She said, 'The deeper I drink of the cup of life the sweeter it grows—the sugar at the bottom.'

Thus we see that age is a relative term. The point in life at which people begin to regard themselves old is largely a matter of custom. If a foolish custom fixes the time of the coming on of old age as at seventy or sixty or even fifty, the majority of people are likely, simply because others do so, weakly and foolishly to consent, creep into a corner, and regard their active years as over. Thus one-third of life, and what should be the best third, is lost. We want a new psychology which will make men and women everywhere think of old age as beginning at least twenty or thirty years later than they have been imagining.

POUGHKEEPSIE, N.Y., U.S.A. JABEZ T. SUNDERLAND

DEAR TAGORE,

I think most often of you, not as the poet of *Balaka* or *Chitrangada* or *Naivedya* or as the writer whose short stories have so opened up his country's life to us, but as the patriot whose passionate love for 'Banga-Lakshmi' has not prevented him from being just to our 'Inga-Lakshmi' (if Mother Sarasvati will forgive such an outrage on Sanskrit rules of union). I never forget that your generosity has been conspicuous under cruel provocation. A great writer, you have been greater still in this magnanimity.

At Santiniketan you have made yourself a local habitation and green body that your thoughts will live and work in, after your physical body has died. If any foreigner desires to know how lovely is the heritage that India has received from her *Rishis* and forest teachers, let him go to Santiniketan and be gathered into the arms of that friendliness which knows no distinction of creed or nationality. And if he wakes at dawn he will think he has died in sleep and passed to the *Nandan*-groves, with the daughters of the gods visible before him as they pick up the blooms that darkness has dropped.

I saw three maidens gather in a heap
Such snowy harvest as the wood-nymphs reap,
Sephali fallen through the hours of sleep.
A double task to my enraptured sight!
They wove a garland to salute the Light,
And 'filled the Basket of Farewell to Night'.

OXFORD EDWARD THOMPSON

BUST BY MR. JACOB EPSTEIN

By Courtesy of Birmingham City Corporation

PROFESSOR Gilbert Murray said in a speech to the Indian Students' Union this year, 'Dogma divides, but religious experience unites.' I think I was never more conscious of this than when I had the privilege some years ago of meeting Rabindranath Tagore in his hotel in London, and he talked to me of the aim and work of the Drama and of Religion. It was an hour I shall never forget as long as I live, for he gave me a glimpse of the very things I had been striving to find and understand as a Christian through the eyes of a great mind of another race. I remember coming away feeling that extraordinary sense of unity that one does occasionally realize—the deep underlying unity of the Great Faiths of the human peoples. Deep down we are brothers, whatever our race and creed. I had felt this before when reading the works of Dr. Tagore, but I never had so clear a vision of it as on that early morning when he talked to me as to one of his pupils. I am immensely grateful to him for what his plays and poems have shown me—also it is because of his teaching that I have been privileged with the friendship of many Indians. For this and for that vision of oneness I am always thankful for Rabindranath Tagore.

LONDON

SYBIL THORNDIKE

THE WOOD

Near my house is a wood full of wonders,
Dearer to my heart than many a dear friend.
With each season it puts on some new beauty.
In May between its old birches and oaks
Bluebells spread into lawns and wind in lanes.
Then splendour after splendour of scarlet and purple
Great rhododendrons open their lordly flowers,
While among them, yellow or pink or ivory-white,
Feminine azaleas delicately unfold.
But soon these glories are all withered and fallen,
And once more it is a loveliness of green leaves
Embowering cool repose in its cool shades.
Slowly the summer passes ; over the hazels
Sweet honeysuckles ramble; the nuts ripen;
Birch-leaves change to amber, the ferns to gold.
But days shorten ; stern winter is coming:
With wind and rain sweeping the oaks, it lays
Their branching grandeur bare against the sky.
Lovelier in its severity then seems
Their naked beauty than all their green pride.
Why then, with such bountiful companionship
Ever at hand to enchant or to console,
Do I not stay content, but week by week,
With a heart restless and thankless, must be still
Fleeing from a known happiness to towns
And people whose souls I know not, nor they mine?
Alas, being not a tree, but a mere man,
What is better I see and praise, what is worse I follow.

DORKING, ENGLAND

R. C. TREVELYAN

May the Poet's message continue to bring peace and harmony to a troubled and distracted world.

NANKING

HSÜ TSE-MOU

SUCCESSION

The little clock upon the table ticking
Tells of a world where measured moments pass.
Outside, the grass
Pursues its rhythm in undivided time,
The trees move strangely to their secret rime.
Sudden the dreamy cat has ceased his licking
And waits paw-poised upon the quiet air;
Discerning there,
As the sharp instants fast
Fall from the dying present to the past,
The grave pulsations of that greater flood
Moving towards a bourne not understood
Wherefrom, as scudding waves from the seas rest,
Our life lifts up its crest.

LONDON

EVELYN UNDERHILL

DIVIDED CLAY

What are you, flesh, that you must have towers of thought,
    Sky-snatching dreams, empires of perfect love?
You have five escapes from the house in which you are caught;
    Five sure ways of delight and five are enough.

What troubles you, flesh, that you twist in your nightmare and shout
    For things which, having, you hate, and lacking, but make you ill?
Is it for words or the ghost of a word that you wear yourself out,
    Driving your grave that walks to the grave that lies still?

How shall your eyes take meaning or measure of Truth?
    Will Faith ever feed, Virtue comfort or keep you warm?
What bewilders you, flesh, that you wait for these phantoms to soothe
    You who are greater than spirit, you who are action and form?

Then go your way, flesh, to your doom, for you cannot be guided,
    Whose earliest breath is "I might," and whose last is "I must."
Ride on the tops of the world, self-deceived, self-divided,
    And cry your impossible cry, you mouthful of dust.

NEW YORK

LOUIS UNTERMEYER

THE BRASS POT

"THERE is need of drinking-water. Fetch some, like a dear girl, from the far pond, Ushasi,[1]" said her mother.

To herself Ushasi's mother sighed, "Ah! Daughter of my heart, to-morrow where wilt thou be?"

Ushasi, with the docility of a Bengali daughter, lifted from its stand the great brass water vessel, heavy even when empty. Holding it by the neck in the crook of her arm, she rested its bulk on her thin hip, thrust out to bear the weight, as in future she would carry her children in their infancy, astride on her side. Bare-headed and bare-footed she stepped along the narrow path that led to the pool where the gathered rain water was pure and not yet choked with water-weeds, threading her way past the standing crops of bright green paddy, the tall coral-coloured stems of the jute plant, like a miniature forest, and the patches of feathery lentil shoots. The waving greenery of the lentils was not more tender or graceful than the light-moving figure of the girl who passed, without seeing them, the familiar beauties of her father's fields.

In the vast, stretching plain, lovely in all its monsoon plenitude of ripening food under a sky, wide-horizoned as in mid-ocean, that glowed with the splendours of sunset, Ushasi looked scarcely larger or more significant than the white paddy-birds that hopped and flew along the rim of the rice-fields. But behind the wistful eyes and dreaming brow a whole world of human sadness revolved until her head ached wearily and her heart felt big with pain.

Ushasi was a bride of three years' standing, and to-morrow her girlhood in her father's house was to come to a final end, and she was to be handed on to her *Swasur-bari* (father-in-law's house) and to become a wife in reality.

It was not, however, any thought of wifehood that occupied her mind, nor even of the husband, to her but one of a shadowy crowd of strangers among whom she must henceforth live. What filled her thoughts was the natural childlike dread of separating from all that was familiar and dear, and venturing alone into the Unknown.

[1] Ushasi = *Dawn*.

"Oh! How can I leave Mother and Father and Granny, and Big Brother and Khooki,[2]" she asked aloud of her own reflection in the clear water pool. "Who will love my pigeons, and Toong-Toong the white calf, and how will the cow give her milk if I am not there to talk to her at milking time?"

Far away, against the copper-coloured west, above the sea of green, a dark smudge showed where the smoke of the great city of Calcutta drifted in the monsoon breeze. The sight stirred fresh regrets. Ushasi had never been there. Her farthest journeyings had been on foot to other village homesteads, or by *shalti*, the primitive canoe in which the flood waters of the rainy season may be traversed to distant fairs and markets. To her rustic imagination Calcutta was the scene of countless wonders, chief among which was the "Magic-house," as the Museum was familiarly called, a place of pilgrimage and the subject of fabulous tales among those villagers who had once beheld its mysteries.

"First Grand-father was to take me there, and now he is dead; then Father, when he had any money to spare, but my wedding expenses and dowry have used up all the money; then *Mama*,[3] and he has gone away to the city for work and never comes; so now every chance has gone. *Swasur-bari* is so far away, and no one there will care much about me or ever think of taking me to the Magic-house. I shall have to cover my head and veil my face and stay quiet. I shall be a bird in a cage, nothing more!"

She stooped down and dipped the brass pot into the pond, the ripples breaking up her still reflection. The pot came up, heavy as lead like her troubled child's heart. The great beautiful eyes filled with tears as she thought:

"No, no, I shall never see the Magic-house, nor have any amusement any more. Well do I know it."

The tears overflowed and splashed unheeded into the wide mouth of the vessel as she bent over it.

That evening Ushasi's household drank the water she had fetched with their evening meal, little knowing it had been salted with the tears of the girl who sat among them so quietly waiting for to-morrow, her day of destiny.

CALCUTTA

MARGARET M. URQUHART

[2] *Baby-Sister.*

[3] Mama—*Maternal Uncle.*

THE POET AND THE PROPHET

IT is true of the great men of all time that they have served their generation both as poets and as prophets, and no higher honour can be paid to any writer than a recognition that in his work he has combined these two activities. The underlying motive in both poet and prophet is the same,—a sense of the unity of all life; but in the poet the sense of unity is more direct, whereas in the prophet it is mediated through a sense of the Divine purposes working for the perfecting of humanity, especially in respect of ethical need. It would be true to say of Dr. Rabindranath that he united both these phases of spiritual activity, and, further that, seeing it is not given to even the greatest of men to expend the energy of his soul equally in all directions, his emphasis is rather on the aesthetic attitude to human life than upon the prophetic.

He carries with him into his teaching the ancient Indian philosophy of "one-pointedness," but his stress is upon the positive rather than the negative aspects of the doctrine of unity. If he admits the negative at all, it is in the direction of a transformation of ordinary values rather than a denial of all values. No affirmation of the spirituality of the universe must be allowed to deprive the universe of meaning. If our hands are filled with the merchandise of the markets of the world, if in getting and in spending we have laid waste our souls, the remedy is not in a withdrawal from the ordinary life of humanity, but in a discovery of that region where divine and human activity may meet, in a crossing of "the bridge leading to the immortal being." The world is a product of the divine activity, to which with reverence we must ascribe the deepest truth, and of which we must find out the motive, and make that motive our own, allying our human energy with the divine, realising that "the same stream of life which runs through my veins night and day, runs through the world and dances in rhythmic measure." The doctrine of the unreality of the finite finds no favour in Dr. Rabindranath's eyes. "Who so steeped in untruth as to dare to call all this untrue—this great world of men, this civilisation of expanding humanity, this eternal effort of man? He who can think of this immensity of achievement as an immense fraud, can he truly believe in God, who is the truth?"

So, as the artist and the poet, he goes forth to discover God in the infinite variety of nature, realising with Bacon that "there is nothing in which nature so much triumpheth as in dissimilitude" and inspiring us with courage to "knock at every open door" of understanding and appreciation. He contrasts Greek and Indian civilisation, and thinks that the latter is more helpful to this movement of the soul. The former was "nurtured within city walls," whereas the latter found its natural home in the forests and took its character from this environment of immediate accessibility to nature and sensitiveness to all her moods and varying aspects. But in the sweep of his poetic and reverential conception he brings man back from the forests, and sets him in the midst of ordinary life, "where the tiller is tilling the hard ground and where the pathmaker is breaking stones." Both in the variety of nature and in the experiences of humanity he wishes to find the actual and significant working of God.

Yet with all his interest in the particularity of nature our poet refuses to lose sight of the central spiritual unity or to relapse into the determinism of mere naturalism and materialism. This is a danger which is never far away from the artistic appreciation of the details of nature or even from the scientific interpretation of it. The poet may find himself overwhelmed by the world towards whose beauty he is so reverential, unless he can recognise the dual aspect of nature. Dr. Rabindranath shows in a paragraph of *Sadhana* how vividly he is conscious of this distinction. "It indeed seems to be wonderful", he says, "that nature has these two aspects at one and the same time, and so antithetical—one being of thraldom and the other of freedom. In the same form of sound, colour, and taste two contrary notes are heard, one of necessity and the other of joy. Outwardly nature is busy and restless, inwardly she is all silence and peace, she has toil on one side and leisure on the other. You see her bondage only when you see her from without, but within her heart is a limitless beauty." (*Sadhana,* 103). And he arrives at the position of the seer of the *Upanishad,* "From joy does spring all this creation, by joy is it maintained, towards joy does it progress, and into joy does it enter." Here is the ultimate motive of creation, as the artist understands it and becomes a worshipper as he understands. The world is the outcome of the divine joy, and we share this joy as we rise above conceptions of mere law and utility, when, for example, we behold a flower not as a stage on the way to fruit, but as a revelation of beauty and a mirror of the mind of God. It is the intention of God that we should share this joy, for joy in its essence involves duality. When we rejoice we wish others to share our joy, and if there are no others present with us, we, as it were, tell our joy to a second self. Thus also and in far fuller measure it is with God. The divine joy issues in the divine love.

Thus is the poet conscious of God, and the prophetic attitude must come as a deepening of the poetic. In seeking for this deepening we are reminded of the position of Lotze, who finds the motive of creation in "the expansive love which urges Him to communicate his holiness to other beings." The emphasis upon the ethical motive may lead to a certain strenuousness and seriousness for which the dominance of the motive of joy does not seem to leave quite sufficient room. The lightheartedness of the poet does not harmonise completely with the prophet's sense of the tragedy of humanity, and the struggle with the evil of the world does not readily reach the rest and peace that is at the heart of things. But the difference is temporary, and not essential and eternal. Perhaps a reversal of the order of the divine motives might reconcile the two points of view. If in our analysis of fundamental motives joy is given the first place, this seems to explain the world of the optimist,—I do not mean of the merely superficial optimist, but even of the man who, conscious of sorrow and of evil, is yet able to conceive of these as being due to partial views and to regard himself and others with similar experience as redeemable through greater enlightenment. But if, instead of speaking of joy as issuing in love or finding dualistic expression through love, we place love as the fundamental divine motive, and think of love as (after experiencing and dealing with and triumphing over the sorrow and evil of the world) resulting in joy, we seem to reach a deeper conception. The thought of joy by itself as dominating the heart of God is apt to produce a too exclusively artistic attitude towards God and to induce the idea of the divine impatience or even petulance towards those who are so foolish as not to sacrifice the lower to the higher values or rise to the appreciation of the beauty in which the divine joy finds expression. Rather are we forced by the tragedy of the world to crave for pity at the heart of God, born of the realisation that man may use his freedom not merely frivolously or foolishly but in deliberate antagonism to the divine purposes. He requires not merely to be enlightened but to be redeemed, and because of the evil to which he has surrendered his soul, he is so involved in the struggle towards the good that he is hardly conscious of the peace and rest of attainment. Unity with the divine has so degenerated into disunion that he requires for remedy the deeper conception of of restored communion.

Yet, as has been said, there is no ultimate discrepancy. Despite the poignancy of the ethical struggle, there is always, where that struggle is sincere, something of fruition even in the midst of the struggle. For man there is no happiness higher than the joy of the redeemed, and in the heart of God—in heaven—there is "*joy* over one sinner that repenteth."

SCOTTISH CHURCH COLLEGE,
CALCUTTA

W. S. URQUHART

J'adresse à l'illustre Poète l'hommage et les vœux très fervents que mon âme occidentale m'inspire pour sa personne et sa grande œuvre.

Je garde de lui le plus vénérable souvenir.

ACADEMIE FRANCAISE,
PARIS

PAUL VALÉRY

TAGORE AND A BURNING PROBLEM

THE poet-statesman, who has the rare merit of thinking every way, has discovered and has been emphasising, what is not recognised clearly and vividly by our thinkers and leaders, that political *Swarajya* alone cannot make India free. An intense admirer of ancient India and of her unique institutions, it is he who has discovered and revealed in unmistakable accents that certain things have crept into our social organisation that have made India incapable of self-defence and coping with modern civilisation. This phenomenon has a two-fold aspect. Firstly, it relates to the innumerable castes, subcastes and outcasts that make up and divide the Hindu society. Secondly, it refers to the relations between the Hindus and the other Indians whose religion is not Hinduism. It refers especially to the Hindu-Muslim relations. Of these two aspects of the social problem, the second is the more tough and growing more and more dangerous to the country at large. The poet has, naturally enough, suggested as the solution of the problem, constructive work from within by ourselves and for ourselves. This suggestion is being sincerely adopted by all the true political reformers of the country, and it may be asserted that the problem under the first aspect is being fast solved while in the meanwhile its existence is by no means a menace to the political advancement of India. The solution recommended by the poet as regards the second aspect of the problem is 'the moral power of love and vision of spiritual unity.' True, this is the best solution and we, Hindus, must recognise our duty to start it and to set an example. But every day events convince us that this source of solution needs a supplemental source. This is not visible yet. I do prayerfully hope that our poet-statesman would be spared for us for many a long year. Three score and ten is but the commencement of old age, low as the average age is in India. We must ever remember that several English judges asserted that they were at their best between their sixty-fifth and eightieth years. A poet-statesman may well add ten more years to this estimate. Well, India sadly wants the supplemental source of solution of this unique problem. The tragedy at Chittagong, not to mention other places, made him issue a very distressing but inspiring dirge. It is but natural that the country should look forward for more light and safe, effective guidance from him in view of getting rid of this strange phenomenon, so peculiar to our unhappy India. The coming political constitution, however perfect, cannot solve this problem. The necessity is imperious, therefore, for all the patriots and politicians of the country to pool their ideas and ideals and discover a real and permanent source for the solution of this ugly and dangerous problem. And I venture to think that efforts in this vital direction are best made under the auspices of the divine poet. And we cannot think of our pilgrimage towards our destiny in the family of free and great nations of the world unless and until we shall have solved this problem.

It is a misfortune of my life that I do not have the proud privilege of a close personal acquaintance with the poet. But I have ever found consolation in talks with my friend, Mr. C. F. Andrews, an intense admirer and a devoted friend of his ; and this, added to the desultory study of his works, reveals the noble and lovable nature of the man, and it is easy for me, therefore, ever gratefully to admire the immortal Indian and to wish him health and long life, if only for the sake of our country at this crisis of her history, as well as of humanity at large. For he is singing and practising the rare part of a glowing patriot and philanthropist at the same time.

This verse from *Bhagavad-gita* is pre-eminently applicable to him if to any: 'He from whom the world doth not shrink away, and who doth not shrink away from the world, freed from the anxieties of joy, anger and fear, he is dear to Me.'

C. VIJIARAGHAVACHARIAR

SALEM,
MADRAS PRESIDENCY, INDIA

CHAMPIONS OF LOVE

THE Wheel of Life, as we find it pictured in a fragmentary fresco of Ajanta or painted in glaring colors in the monasteries of Tibet, has in its centre three animals, a dove (or cock), a snake and a hog, which symbolise the three consuming evils—lust, hate and error. Such is the Buddhist view of mundane existence. If we behold the hopeless state of confusion presented by this sadly struggling world of men or look back on the still darker days of the great war, is there not much reason to believe that, indeed, the Buddhist gloomy view is fully justified and that human life is governed by those three animals?

We need only call to mind the spectacle of civilised nations striving to exterminate each other with every weapon which modern science placed in their hands. And sadder still: we have seen their feelings of hatred being kindled by a campaign of ruthless slander carried on as relentlessly as the internecine strife of the contending hosts.

This, surely, is the most alarming element in this desperate state of affairs that the sentiments of deep aversion between large communities of human beings still subsist and are continued to be stirred up by the powers of evil, so that at any moment the smouldering fire may burst out again into a conflagration as terrible and destructive as the one we have witnessed.

It would be a comfort, were we allowed to suppose that this aversion is merely artificial. But alas! this would be an illusion. The facts are against such an assumption. That gulf, on the contrary, which separates not only nations and races, but also religious and social groups belonging to one and the same nation and race, is largely and perhaps fundamentally natural and due to natural causes. It is found even among the most primitive tribes, which possess neither press nor newspapers.

What then is the antidote against that deadly poison which threatens to consume the whole world of the living? It is Universal Love. It is sympathy fostered by knowledge and true culture. This is the great task of the leaders of mankind—prophets and saints, poets and artists, statesmen and scholars—to promote that feeling of mutual understanding and goodwill which is inspired by Universal Love. Love is the heavenly champion whose mission it is to slay the beasts of evil.

Among those leaders of men we greet the Poet of India, whose songs have comforted and rejoiced not only his own people but the peoples of the East and the West, and whose noble mission it has been to unite the disunited through the power of Divine Love.

THE UNIVERSITY,
LEYDEN, HOLLAND

J. PH. VOGEL

V.O.K.S. FIRST PIONEERS' COMMUNE

To

RABINDRANATH TAGORE

DEAR POET,

The First Pioneers' Commune still remember the evening they spent with you, and send you their warm greetings on your seventieth birthday.

We remember well your national song which you sang to us.

Since your departure life has carried us ahead and the country has taken giant strides towards socialism.

Almost every day we see a new industrial plant or a factory cropping up to carry out the Five-year Plan which, not very long ago, was ridiculed by our hostile critics as a fantasy.

But the enthusiasm of the nation works miracles. Not adults alone are taking part in the building up but also four millions of children who have declared that they are not only builders of the future but also of the present. Our communes are fighting on all fronts of National Labour, shoulder to shoulder with other blocs.

We work at the metallurgical factory "Sickle and Hammer". This factory belonged formerly to the French capitalistic group Goujon. There are yet amongst us workers unenlightened enough who drink, get drunk and stay away from work. We are trying to redeem them: We use our most powerful means—the Social Contract. We promise to study well at school and we take their word not to idle about any more. Numerous idlers have given their word not to fly from work any more but to take an active part in the national reconstruction.

There is another sad legacy of the old order—Illiteracy. There are still millions of illiterate people in the country and we have been enlisted to fight illiteracy. We, in our school, teach fifty such people. Besides that, we are doing cultural work in connexion with the "Red Corner" in the Library. We also help in introducing technical education among the masses. Thus we are educating ourselves politically and preparing for the great constructive work of the nation.

We wish you all happiness and hope to meet you again in our free socialistic country.

Greetings from the First Pioneers' Commune.

MOSCOW

CIRCLE

How may the universe forget?
Stars never set,
They wind about the sky above, below,
As little glittering shuttles come and go.

How may the circle fail?
We see the dreams exhale,
Like mist wreaths, upward, building into cloud
The castles that we thought so real, so proud ;
Fading into another vaguer shape,
We think their souls escape.

Yet done is never done.
One after one
Our dreams rebuild the things we say are gone.
Space shapes Madonnas on
Out of the shapeless mist of vanished things :
The circle swings,
The tiny circle widening again
Till once more there are men.

NEW YORK MARGARET WIDDEMER

RABINDRANATH'S VISIT TO MUNICH

THE visit of the great Indian poet and philosopher to Munich has left an indelible memory in the heart of all who had the good fortune to come into contact with him at that time, and that out of two reasons. At a time of utter confusion, when the German nation has not yet been able to overcome the grave moral and spiritual injuries sustained by Germany during the war and when perfected personalities are becoming more and more rare, it is really gratifying to meet a man who can give perfect expression to the noble harmony of his own inner self. Besides, we should not forget that Rabindranath Tagore came to Munich just at a time when, from here, the first successful attempts had been made towards forming happy and promising relations with the academic world of India. This academic interrelation could not be better expressed symbolically than by the performance of *Post-Office* by the German students and of *Chitra* in the original Bengali language by the Indian stipendiaries of the Deutsche Akademie. It was really astonishing to see that the German audience, who could but guess at the meaning of the words that were spoken on the stage, were so enraptured that the performance of *Chitra* had to be repeated not only in Munich but also in other towns of Germany.

Formerly we have honoured in Rabindranath Tagore the universal poet and philosopher only, but his visit to Munich last year revealed to us quite a new and charming side of his personality. The rhythm of his soul found new expression in enchanting pictures which fill us with awe and wonder—an absolutely new departure so late in life! Goethe's immortal words 'eternal urge and unceasing exertion' (ewig strebend sich bemühen) have been actually realized in this man and it is a very significant accident that, soon after Rabindranath's seventieth birth-day anniversary, the world is going to celebrate the hundredth death anniversary of the great German poet, who, though already dead three generations ago, is to-day more alive than ever.

Unfortunately, it is not possible for us Germans to appear before the Master and according to the graceful Indian custom place a garland of blooming blossoms round his neck, as his countrymen did, when he alighted from the train in Munich. But words which fulfil themselves in deeds are less transitory than the blossoms of the spring. These are the respectful words and these the good wishes which I bring forward before the Master in the name of his friends and admirers in Munich, and I hope, as often as the eyes of him, for whom they were written, fall on them, they may assume the glory and lustre of actual life.

MUNICH — THEODOR VON WINTERSTEIN

TO RABINDRANATH TAGORE

DEAR POET,

Everything I have thought or written, since living in your country, has been influenced by India, and especially by you. 'The steps that I heard in my play-room shall echo from star to star!'

For your kindness to me I can never be sufficiently grateful. It was when you were very ill that you sat up all one night reading *Bengal Lancer,* and wrote a review that gave the endorsement of your prevailing name to reminiscences which might well have been almost still-born. I shall never forget that, nor my hour of pride when I saw that the foremost man of letters of our day had approved my writing. It would have been so easy to find fault with a stranger's presentment of India: it was generous of you to look on the lights rather than the shadows of my book.

But beyond your personal kindness, I see in you a guide and a *Guru.* Even if I have never known you, I would revere you as an interpreter, not of India only, but of the Universe.

Thank you for what you are, dear Poet, even more than for what you have done for me. May I be privileged to see you again, and often; and may you enjoy health and happiness to give the fruits of your genius to the world, and continue the service you render to Art, to India, and to Youth.

RYE, SUSSEX,
ENGLAND

F. YEATS BROWN

Dear Tagore,

They wrote me sometime ago to ask me to contribute to your *Golden Book*. I forgot and then Rothenstein wrote to me, but his letter, delayed in the post, only reached me two days ago. I have been travelling about, and shall be for some days yet, and when I am settled enough to think, it may be too late. I, therefore, want to tell you that I am still your most loyal student and admirer. Your poems, as you know, came to me as a great excitement; and of recent years I have found wisdom and beauty, or both, in your prose—*The Home and the World,* your short stories and your *Reminiscences*.

Since we met I have married. I have now two children, a boy and a girl, and feel more knitted into life; and life, when I think of it as separated from all that is not itself, from all that is complicated and mechanical, takes to my imagination an Asiatic form. That form I found first in your books and afterwards in certain Chinese poetry and Japanese prose writers. What an excitement it was the first reading of your poems, which seemed to come out of the fields and the rivers and have their changelessness!

Yours sincerely,

DUBLIN

W. B. YEATS

FÜR RABINDRANATH TAGORE

Zwischen Weinen, Lust und Lachen
Sind wir willenlos gestellt,
Traümend meinen wir zu wachen,
Doch der Traum ist Wahn, nicht Welt.

Bloss ein Spiel der stummen Dinge
Mühen wir uns, Sinn zu sein,
Aber Schlaf mit schwarzem Ringe
Schliesst den Traum des Traümens ein.

Zwischen ihm, dem wir entstammen
Und dem Schlaf, der uns erharrt
Zuckt in bilderhaften Flammen
Unser Schein von Gegenwart.

SALZBURG

STEFAN ZWEIG

[TRANSLATION]

Between weeping, joy, and laughter
We are set, having no wills of our own ;
Dreaming, we think we are awake.
Forsooth, the dream is an illusion, not the world.

A mere sport of dumb things,
We take pains to rise to thought ;
But sleep with a black ring
Locks up the dream of dreaming.

Between Him from whom we are descended
And sleep that awaits us,
Oscillates in image-building flames
Our appearance of the Present.

OFFERINGS

RABINDRANATH TAGORE'S MUSIC

WHEN the request to write a contribution to the Poet's *Golden Book* reached me, it struck me that in no way could I better pay my homage than by writing about music, the poet's music, so little known in Europe, about the character of which such strange errors persist even in India. Still, the idea of a poet composing his own music is by no means unknown in India, neither in classical, nor in folk music. As far as the former is concerned, we find mentioned in the old Sanskrit texts the artist called Vāg-geya-kāraka—the maker of words and melody. So in the 'Saṅgīta-darpaṇa,' III, śl. 57:

vāg-varṇa-samudāyas tu mātur ity ucyate budhāiḥ,
geyaṁ dhātu, dvayoḥ kartā prokto vāg-geya-kārakaḥ:

'The complete group of rhetorical figures such as words and varṇa is called mātu by the wise, that which is sung dhātu. The composer of both is called vāg-geya-kāraka.'

The good Vāg-geya-kāraka tops the list of artists.

When we turn towards the field of popular music, we find this phenomenon in a still stronger degree. The great mystics of the middle ages, pre-eminently men from the people singing for the people, in their outbursts of ecstasy created both words and music; and even in our days we find the *Bāuls* of Bengal—just limiting ourselves to Tagore's native province—who, in their best utterings, create words and music together.

Now, why is it that in the case of Rabindranath Tagore so comparatively few amongst those of his educated fellow-countrymen who are trained in classical music fully appreciate this music and do justice to it, whereas it appears from different reliable sources that the common people often take to his songs, words and melody?

I think we may safely attribute this fact to the vogue for what is now called 'classical' music, *viz.*, *ustādī* music, the art developed and produced mostly by Muhammadan singers, presenting a combination of what was living from olden times in India, with the kindred music imported by the Muhammadan conquerors, mainly from Persia.

This art undoubtedly came to a brilliant and wonderful development at the time of the great Mughal emperors, but it did not escape degeneration when that glorious period came to an end. One of the signs of this degeneration undoubtedly was the loss of sense of proportion and construction, betrayed by a well-nigh unparalleled growth of detail. The sense of the words became often smothered under flourish, whereas in the classical Sanskrit treatises the giving of a clear sense is still mentioned as of great virtue. The music-loving connoisseurs and artists, of the last two or three generations at least, have become so accustomed to this form of art-music that it is now almost impossible for them to appreciate a kind of music in which the word and the melody have equal importance, and where consequently the unbridled passion for flourish is mercilessly checked.

Protest was raised in large circles. This music was decried as un-Indian, Europeanised, etc. Still the music of Rabindranath Tagore is neither Europeanised nor un-Indian. On the contrary, it is solidly rooted in its own soil, that of his native province,

Bengal. The strong personality of the poet, however, has stamped it with an unmistakable character of its own. It is undeniable that at a certain time there really has been European influence. Rabindranath Tagore himself amply describes it in his 'Reminiscences,' and fully acknowledges the part English music played in the creation of his first stage-work, *Vālmīki Pratibhā*.

The fact that the house of the Tagores never closed its doors against foreign influence is sufficiently known, and it is certain that Maharshi Devendranath Tagore encouraged the study of Western music as well as that of the classical Indian styles for the restoration of which his near relative, Raja Sourindra Mohan Tagore, so valiantly fought.

Consequently the young Rabindranath Tagore must have heard both in his ancestral home, but even at that time the charm of Western music was not strong upon him. Whereas he describes the sense of disappointment he experienced when learning some English (Irish) melodies, the rapture enjoyed at the trips on the river with his brother Jyotirindranath,—when they varied their *rāgas* and *rāgiṇīs* along with the course of the day—is still strong when he relates this episode so many years after. As a matter of fact harmony, so essential to our present Western music, still baffles the poet and leads him astray. Consequently the influence of Western music is of passing importance in the totality of Tagore's musical creations.

Not Western music, nor even classical Indian music, was destined to bring his genius to its full development. It was the folk-music of Bengal that stirred the depths of his nature with such wonderful results. Only the fact that the educated classes of his country who live in towns have lost contact with the real folk-life accounts for the discredit of his music in the appreciation of so many who love and admire his poems.

As a young man even Tagore himself did not realise the importance of the culture of the common people. It was not until his wise father had entrusted him with the management of the East Bengal estates that Rabindranath became fully aware of the treasures of his own country.

East Bengal and later West Bengal: *Bāul* songs—*Kīrtan* music. Hear how in the *Bāul* songs, and in the closely related boat-men songs, the highest mystical truths are expressed in words so simple as to be clear to every one, sung to melodies as simple in structure as the words, and thus enhancing the spiritual appeal. Hear how the *Kīrtan* music sings the glories of the love of Krishna and Rādhā with a glow of devotion ; lyrical words, not smothered by a deluge of flourish, however intricate melody and rhythm may be.

Neither *Bāul* nor *Kīrtan* singers employ the classical *rāgas.* Both use notes and intervals as suited, not as prescribed. *Bāuls* do not mention *rāgas* even. *Kīrtan* music has kept names of classical *rāgas,* once used perhaps, but long since converted into new structures.

Nothing could be more congenial to Rabindranath Tagore's nature than this attitude towards the rigidity of classical rules. He is ever the breaker of bonds and fettering traditions, but never the destroyer of their true basis. Knowing the old *rāgas* perfectly well, he too had the right to use and change them as his own inspiration told him to do.

Had not the old mystics created their own *rāgas,* the *Bāuls* their own tunes, and had not *Kīrtan* adapted the old forms to its new needs?

His perfect balance of words and melody, and his simplicity and conciseness of construction, are contributions to the whole of Indian music that cannot be underrated easily.

It is characteristic of the genius of Rabindranath Tagore that he has, as if by instinct, found the *Dhrūpad* the only form in ancient Indian music that could serve as a basis for his creations. From long before the Muhammadan conquest even up to our present days, this form of Indian music, regarded as most sacred, continued to exist, in which the words had and have their importance. Still the holy character implied the use of very difficult time and very dignified *rāgas.* The poet has succeeded in keeping the essential features of construction, but nevertheless has made the form supple and clear, fit for the direct appeal even to the heart of the simple peasant.

This happy combination of the *Dhrūpad* and folk-music is the strongest feature of the musical *œuvre* of Tagore.

It had been the tendency in Europe to see the figure of Tagore as a more or less isolated phenomenon, but his real greatness can only be realised when one sees him against the background of the culture of his own country.

There are three things by which an Indian musician can realise his intention: words, melody and rhythm. By the repetition of the essential words at the end of a strophe an often exquisite effect is reached. Certain intervals enhance the spiritual meaning of the words. One could give dozens of examples of that fact, but two will be sufficient here:

There is the amazed question expressed by a leap of a major third from the *'sa'* on the last syllable of *sundara* in the song that begins with *Ekadā ki jāni kon punyera phale, o go sundara* (Once, by what fruit of merit, O thou beautiful?)

Then there is the exquisite change from the regularly used minor third to the major in one song from the drama *Naṭīr Pūjā* (The Dancing-girl's Worship). The words are *Pathe jete ḍekechile more* (Going on the path thou hadst called me), with the sudden brightening of the major third on the first syllable of *more,* a gleam of light, drowned immediately again by the returning of the minor interval, in keeping with the general sentiment of the poem.

This phenomenon is by no means unknown in Indian music, but Rabindranath Tagore has used it, restoring its proper significance.

Lastly, there is the unsurpassed use of slight rhythmical variations, even in the repetition of the same melodical phrases, giving an entirely different character to the music.

In the same song *O go sundara* we find in the first stanza *ghum-bhāṅgā cokhe dharāra legeche bhālo* (to the sleep-broken eyes of the earth appeared beautiful, *viz.,* the first tender light of dawn) where the leap of a fourth from the *'pa'* to the upper *'sa',* in quavers, still suggests something of the heaviness of the sleep.

When towards the end of the song the words *piche piche tava uḍāye caluk tabe* (ever after thee let me be swept, *viz.,* by the evening breeze) occur, this same melodical phrase is used, but the urge is made felt by this leap of a fourth in semi-quavers.

Instances of this kind are to be found over and over again. So when in *kār cokher cāwār hāwāy dolāy man* the unequal rhythm two plus four is suddenly left for the rocking three plus three at *dolāy man* (rocks thy heart), only to return immediately after these words.

This is by no means a conscious process, but the result of an intuitive realisation of the deepest meaning of the words. It is for that reason that the songs of Tagore are complete in themselves. Nobody but the poet himself can realise the full meaning of both music and words, and create the necessary details. Changes in melody, rhythm or words can therefore be but deteriorations. The usual Indian freedom for changes within the song becomes absurd in this case. It is as if one had a painting by some great artist and one started changing its design and colours!

The only attitude for approaching the music of Tagore is the one natural towards any creation of a great artist, *viz.*, open-minded and with the desire to realise the thing as it is. Nobody will be disappointed at the riches that are revealed to him by this process, even though some songs may appeal to one more than others. It is certain that one will experience the truth of what Tagore himself says concerning the melody of songs, speaking about how he composed a very well known poem of his *I know thee, O Woman of strange lands* ('Reminiscences,' page 206):

'Had not the tune been there I know not what shape the rest of the poem might have taken, but the magic of the melody revealed to me the stranger in all her loveliness. It is she, said my soul, who comes and goes, a messenger in this world from the shore of the ocean of mystery. It is she of whom we now and again catch glimpses in the dewy autumn mornings, in the scented nights of spring, in the inmost recesses of our heart—and sometimes we strain skywards to hear her song. To the door of this world-charming stranger the melody, as I say, wafted me, and so to her the rest of the words are addressed.

'Long after this, in a street in Bolpur, a mendicant *Bāul* was singing as he walked along:

How does the unknown bird flit in and out the cage?
O, could I but catch it, I'd ring its feet with my love.

I found this *Bāul* to be saying the very same thing. The unknown bird sometimes surrenders itself within the bars of the cage to whisper tidings of the boundless unknown beyond. The heart would fain hold it near to itself, but cannot.

'What but the melody of song can tell us of the goings and comings of the unknown bird?'

SANTINIKETAN,
INDIA

A. A. BAKE

THE OMNISCIENT BEING IN INDIAN ART

Sīmār mājhe, asīm! tumi
bājāo āpan sur—
āmār mājhe tomār prakāś
tāi eta madhur.

An earnest longing to realise the Infinite in the finite, an unceasing endeavour to explore the limits of the Limitless, is one of the dominant notes of Rabindranath Tagore's lyrics. The ancient Indian artist who undertook to give shape to the human conception of the divine, to carve the image of the Omniscient Being, possessing limitless, infinite knowledge, union with whom or transformation into whose likeness is the goal of spiritual life, was inspired by the same longing, though using a different vocabulary. Who is the Omniscient Being possessing limitless knowledge? He is the Jina (Tīrthaṅkara) of the Jaina, the Buddha of the Bauddha, the Śiva of the Śaiva, the Viṣṇu of the Vaiṣṇava. The *kevala-jñāna* of the Jina, the *sambodhi* of the Buddha, the *ātma-jñāna* of Śiva or Viṣṇu, are but the different names of the highest, unlimited, infinite knowledge conceived in different ways by the different sectaries. Ancient Indian artists use the same plastic language for giving shape to these conceptions and thereby reveal the basic unity of all Indian creeds. A brief analysis of this language will be attempted in this note.

In the *Kalpa-sūtra* of the Śvetāmbara Jainas it is said of the last Jina Mahāvīra's attainment of the *kevala-jñāna* :—

"During the thirteenth year, in the second month of summer, ... outside of the town Jhṛmbhaka-grāma on the bank of the river Ṛjupālikā, ... in a squatting position with joined heels, ... being engaged in deep meditation (*jhāṇ'aṁtariyā = dhyānāntarikā*), reached the highest knowledge and intuition, called *kevala* which is infinite, supreme, unobstructed, unimpeded, complete and full (120)."[1]

About Mahāvīra's death it is said in the same work :—

"At the time of early morning, in the town of Pāpā, and in King Hastipāla's office of the writers, (Mahāvīra) single and alone, sitting in the *samparyaṅka* posture . . . . died . . . . freed from all pains."[2]

Saṁpaliaṁkaṇisaṇṇa in the original is explained by the commentator thus :—

Saṁgata-paryaṅkaḥ padmâsanaṁ tatra niṣaṇṇa upaviṣṭaḥ[3]

"Sitting cross-legged on the hams is the lotus posture ; one seated in that posture."

[1] English translation by Jacobi, *Sacred Books of the East*, Vol. XXII, p. 263.
[2] *Sacred Books of the East*, XXII, p. 269.
[3] *The Kalpa-sūtra of Bhadrabāhu* edited by H. Jacobi, Leipzig, 1879, p. 114.

According to Pali and Sanskrit Buddhist texts Siddhârtha (the future Gautama Buddha), when quite young, performed the first *dhyāna* sitting cross-legged under a *jambu* (rose-apple) tree in a village inhabited by the ploughmen. Again, when, as a monk, he found austerities useless, seated in the same posture under a Pipal tree at Uruvelā near Gaya he performed in succession the four *dhyānas* that led to *sambodhi,* perfect knowledge, and thereby became a Buddha, 'the omniscient one'. In the Pali Vinaya (*Mahāvagga* I, 1) it is said:—

"At that time the blessed Buddha dwelt at Uruvelā, on the bank of river Nerañjarā, at the foot of the Bodhi tree, just after he had become Sambuddha. And the blessed Buddha *sat cross-legged* (*pallañkena nisīdi*) at the foot of the Bodhi tree uninterruptedly during seven days, enjoying the bliss of emancipation."[4]

From these extracts it is evident that the way to gain *kevala* knowledge or *bodhi* which characterises the Omniscient Being, is the performance of *dhyāna,* meditation, called *yoga* or *dhyāna-yoga* in the Brahmanic texts, seated in a set posture with joined heels or cross-legged called in the Pali Buddhist texts as *pallañkaṁ* (*paryañkam*) *ābhujitvā.* The posture is thus defined in the Pali Nikāyas:—

"Sits (*nisīdati*) cross-legged (*pallañkaṁ ābhujitvā*), holding the body erect (*ujuṁ kāyaṁ paṇidhāya*), and sets up his memory in front of (the object of thought) (*parimukhaṁ satiṁ upaṭṭhāvetvā*)."

The *āsana* or posture of the yogin defined in the *Śvetâśvatara Upaniṣad* (II. 8-10), the *Vedānta-sūtras* (IV. 1, 4-11) and the *Bhagavad-gīta* (VI. 11-13) is evidently the same cross-legged posture. A graphic description of it is found in Kālidāsa's *Kumāra-sambhava* (III. 45-50),[5] wherein the poet pictures Śiva engaged in performing *dhyāna* seated cross-legged (*paryañka-bandha*) on an altar under a *Devadāru* (oak) tree, like Gautama under the Pipal tree at Uruvelā. The scholiast Mallinātha (on *Kumāra* III, 45) quotes a stanza attributed to Vaśiṣṭha, wherein the posture is named *Vīrâsana,* 'hero's posture'. All seated images of the Jinas and almost all seated images of the Buddhas show this *paryañka-bandha* posture.

Broadly speaking, the Jinas of the Jainas and the Buddhas of the Bauddhas correspond to the *Puruṣas,* spirits or souls, who, according to the orthodox Sāṁkhya and Yoga systems, have obtained *Kaivalya,* final isolation, emancipation, through the attainment of the highest knowledge, while Śiva of the Śaivas and Viṣṇu of the Vaiṣṇavas correspond to the *Īśvara,* Lord, of the Yoga system of Patañjali, who is but one of the *Puruṣas* (*puruṣa-viśeṣa*) who has never been subject to the law of *karman* and rebirths and whose omniscience is unlimited (*niratiśaya*).[6] Like the *Īśvara,* Viṣṇu or Śiva has not attained this unlimited omniscience by practising *yoga,* but it is the essence of his being. Images of Śiva and Viṣṇu in full *paryañka-bandha* posture are rare. But the most important feature of this posture, the pose of the eyes fixed on the tip of the nose, is found in all

[4] Translated by Rhys Davids and H. Oldenberg, *Sacred Books of the East,* Vol. XIII, pp. 73-74.
[5] For this reference I am indebted to Mr. Sudhanya Kumar Sarkar.
[6] *Yoga-darśana* or *Pātañjala-darśana,* I. 24-25.

PLATE I

THE BUDDHA-BODHISATTVA FROM KATRA

(Curzon Museum, Mathura)

PLATE II

THE BUDDHA-BODHISATTVA OF THE YEAR 64
FROM BODH-GAYA

(Indian Museum, Calcutta)

PLATE III

AVALOKITESVARA FROM SARNATH

(Indian Museum, Calcutta)

[After Copyright Photographs, Archaeological Survey, India]

their images whether seated or standing. The significance of this pose of the eyes is discussed by Śaṅkara in his comment on the *Bhagavad-gītā* VI. 13. The stanza runs :—

samaṁ kāya-śiro-grīvaṁ dhārayann acalaṁ sthiraḥ,
samprekṣya nāsikâgraṁ svaṁ diśaś cânavalokayan.

"Holding the body, the head, and the neck erect, immobile and steady, fixing the gaze on the tip of his nose and not looking in other directions."

Commenting on the first part of the second line of this stanza, Śaṅkara writes :—

"(As if) observing one's tip of the nose. Here 'as if' (*iva*) should be considered as understood. The observation of the tip of one's own nose is not provided. What then (is provided) ? The mechanical direction of the sight of the eyes (to the tip of the nose is provided). This also has been provided for the concentration of the mind. If the observation of the tip of the nose be provided, the mind would concentrate itself on that and not on the 'self.' The concentration of the mind on the 'self' (in *yoga*) is provided in (the text), 'Fixing the mind on self' (*Bhagavad-gītā,* VI. 25). Therefore by adding the word *iva,* 'as if,' though omitted, *samprekṣya* is to be understood as denoting the mechanical direction of the eyes' sight (but not observation)."

This pose of the eyes which indicates *samādhi,* rapt concentration, characterises not only the images of the Jina, the Buddha and other omniscient beings seated cross-legged, but also their images seated in other postures, as well as their standing images. So eyes fixed on the tip of the nose must be recognised as the common factor of all varieties of *yoga* posture, and in an image the mark of limitless omniscience.

The earliest representations of deities seated in the *yoga* posture are found on seals unearthed at Mohen-jo-Daro in Sind and at Harappa in the Panjab. In a note on excavations at Mohen-jo-Daro in 1924-25 Sir John Marshall writes :—

"On a tablet of blue faience which has just come to light is depicted a figure seated cross-legged (like Buddha on a throne) with a kneeling worshipper to right and left and behind the worshipper a snake (*nāga*), while at the back is a legend in the pictographic script of the period. Now, it is possible that the seated figure is nothing more than a royal personage, but the presence of the kneeling devotees and particularly of the *nāgas* certainly suggests that the central figure was intended to represent a deity rather than a king."[7]

The pose of the eyes is not noted here, and it cannot be expected that in a figure carved on a small seal it should be clearly marked. But a fragment of a bearded statuette of stone and paste found at Mohen-jo-Daro, of which one of the inlaid eyes and the nose are well preserved, clearly shows eyes fixed on the tip of the nose.[8] Like the figure on the seal seated cross-legged this statuette was probably also intended for worship. What this posture denoted in the Chalcolithic period it is now difficult to say. Though a gap

[7] *A. S. I., A. R.,* 1924-25, p. 61.

[8] *A. S. I., A. R.,* 1925-26, p. 90, pl. XLII (*a*) ; Coomaraswamy, *History of Indian and Indonesian Art,* London, 1927, p. 3, pl. I ; *Memoirs A. S. I.,* No. 41, p. 25, pl. I (*b*).

of nearly three thousand years separates these figures in *yoga* posture from our earliest known images in the same posture, it is impossible to suppose that the tradition was wholly lost.

The earliest known Jina images seated cross-legged in meditation are found on tablets of homage recovered from the Kaṅkālī Ṭīlā at Mathura and now deposited in the Lucknow Provincial Museum. Two of these tables[9] bear votive inscriptions in Brāhmī characters that closely resemble the characters used in the Brāhmī inscriptions of the time of the Mahākṣatrapa Śōḍāsa who reigned about the beginning of the Christian era. The figures of the Jina on these tablets are crude in workmanship and the posture is not correctly rendered. The accession of Kanishka about a century later gave a strong impetus to the manufacture of the Buddha images in Gandhara and Bauddha and Jaina images at Mathura. The flowing hair, the musculature of the limbs, and the drapery arranged in naturalistic folds that distinguish most of the Buddhas of the Gandhara school are Hellenistic in style. The craftsmen of Mathura of the Kushan period produced three different types of images of the Buddhas and the Jinas (other than Ṛṣabha), the latter being distinguished from the former by total absence of drapery. These types are: (1) shaven head with a top-knot of hair curling like a shell (so far found in the Buddha images only) and plain drapery sticking to the body; (2) head with short hair in ringlets curling to the right and in the images of the Buddha drapery arranged in naturalistic folds in the Gandhara style; (3) head with hair arranged in conventionalised waves and in the images of the Buddha drapery arranged in the Gandhara style.[10]

As the craftsmen of Mathura borrowed the style of drapery of the images of Buddha of types (2) and (3), and probably the arrangement of hair of type (3), from the school of Gandhara, the Gandharan (Indo-Greek) craftsmen borrowed in their turn from Mathura arrangement of hair in ringlets which only a comparatively small number of images of the Buddha produced in Gandhara show.[11] It was the image of the Buddha resulting from the combination of types (1) and (2) (plain drapery sticking to the body or drapery with folds marked by conventional superficial lines, and hair arranged in ringlets on the head) that carried on the *dig-vijaya* or conquest of the Buddhist world outside Mathura and Gandhara.

From the second century B.C. onward there flourished in Central and Eastern India a school of art which was non-representational so far as the Buddhas and the Jinas were concerned, but which represented them by symbols such as empty throne, foot-prints, the wheel of law and so forth. From the beginning of the reign of Kanishka (the votive inscription on the colossal Bodhisattva at Sarnath dedicated by the monk Bala is dated in the year 3 of his reign) we find images of Gautama Buddha of Mathura stone and work-

[9] V. A. Smith, *The Jaina Stupa and other Antiquities of Mathura*, Allahabad, 1901, plates VII and X; Coomaraswamy, *History, &c.*, plate XIX, Fig. 71.

[10] Vogel recognises types (1) and (2), and of type (1) he writes, "These images cannot be immediately derived from any known class of images in Gandhara"; it is "d'un type local." (*A. S. I., A. R.*, 1909-10, p. 66; *La Sculpture de Mathura, Ars Asiatica*, XV, Paris, 1930, p. 39).

[11] *Bachhofer, Early Indian Sculpture*, Paris, 1929, Vol. I, p. 106.

manship imported to centres of Buddhism in Central and Eastern India like Sanchi, Bodh-Gaya, Sarnath and Śrāvastī. It is possible to follow the development of the Gupta type of the image of the Buddha from the Kushan type of the Mathura school step by step in the specimens deposited in the Museums at Mathura and Sarnath. But between images of the Buddhas and the Jinas produced by the Mathura school in the Kushan period (second century A.D.), and images produced at Mathura and elsewhere in the Gupta period (A.D. 350-500) there is a vast difference. Let us take one of the best products of the Mathura school of the Kushan period, the inscribed Buddha-Bodhisattva statuette from Katra in the Mathura Museum, reproduced on plate I, for comparison. This image is carved with considerable skill and does not lack vitality. But the eyes, though half-shut, are not correctly posed, and the face is devoid of expression. The Kushan art of Mathura is a dead art of repetition.

With the establishment of the Gupta empire in the fourth century A.D. a miracle happened in the field of art. The dead suddenly began to pulsate with vigorous spiritual life. This transformation is first illustrated by an image of the Buddha-Bodhisattva of red sandstone of Mathura discovered by Cunningham at Bodh-Gaya and exhibited in the Indian Museum, (plate II). The votive inscription on the base of this image is dated in the year (*Saṁvat*) 64 which should be assigned to the Gupta era and corresponds to 383-384 A.D.[12] So close is the typological resemblance that a comparison of this image with the Katra image suggests that it (3′ 11″ × 3′ 1″) is but a mechanical enlargement of the

[12] *A. S. I., A. R.*, 1922-23, p. 169. Cunningham took the year 64 to represent 464 of the Seleukidan era equivalent to 152 A.D. by omitting hundreds (*Mahābodhi*, London, 1892, p. 53). Foucher recognizes *Saṁvat* 64 as a year of the Śaka era equivalent to 143 A.D. (*L'art Gréco-Bouddhique du Gandhara*, Tome II, Paris, 1922, p. 681). The assignment of the year 64 to the Gupta era has been accepted by Dr. Coomaraswamy (*History of Indian and Indonesien Art*, p. 85; *Rūpam*, 1930, Nos. 42-44, p. 8) and Dr. Scherman (*Sonderabdruck des Münchner Jahrbuches der Bildenden Kunst*, 1928, Bd. V. Heft 3, p. 148, note 34). Dr. Stella Kramrisch, who recognises the Bodh-Gaya image as the starting point of the Gupta art, takes *Saṁvat* 64 to be a year of the Kalacuri era equivalent to 312 A.D. (*Wiener Beitrage zur Kunst und Kulturgeschichte Asiens, Band* V, 6. 15). No epigraph dated in the early centuries of the Kalacuri era has yet been discovered around Mathura and Bodh-Gaya (*Epigraphia Indica*, Vol. V, Appendix p. 55). Bachhofer follows Foucher (*Early Indian Sculpture*, p. 104). Not only the style of the Bodh-Gaya image, but the form of the letters of the inscription renders the ascription of the date to the Śaka era impossible. These letters differ from the letters of the Kushan inscriptions on the one hand, and agree with those of the Gupta inscriptions on the other, in the following particulars :—

(1) Excessive elongation of the vertical of *ka* and *ra* and the right hand vertical of *a*.

(2) The division of the original vertical of *ṇa* and of its upper bar.

(3) The transformation of the lower triangular half of *ma* into a horizontal line projecting to the left of the letter.

(4) The left limb of the *la* turned sharply downwards.

(5) *Ha* with hook-like shape, the base-stroke turned to the left as in the horizontal base-stroke of *ha* in the Allahabad pillar inscription of Samudra-gupta.

But, as compared to the Allahabad pillar inscription of Samudra-gupta, this inscription retains *na* and *ta* of the archaic type. In an inscription on a pillar (recently discovered at Mathura) dated in the year 61 of the Gupta era (380-381 A.D.) in the reign of the Emperor Chandra-gupta II the angular Kushan forms of *ga, na, pa, ma, la, śa, sa, ha* are retained side by side with the Gupta form of *ṇa*. But any inscription dated in the Kushan era of Kanishka containing Gupta type of letters is unknown. Therefore the occurrence of a considerable number of Gupta letters in any inscription justifies the assignment of it to the Gupta period.

latter (2′ 3¼″ × 1′ 8″). But a closer examination reveals a great difference. Hair in ringlets covers the head and a fleshy protuberance takes the place of the spiral top-knot. The Kushan formula of showing the half shut eyes gives place to a more realistic representation. Though the left eye of this image is destroyed the face retains its wonderful expressiveness. The right eye fixed on the tip of the nose reveals a mind concentrated on something within. That something is *sambodhi* or *kevala-jñāna,* infinite, limitless, perfect knowledge. Civilized man, oppressed by the limitations that limited knowledge imposes upon his activities, has ever conceived the vision of a Being with limitless knowledge as his guide and goal, but never has he succeeded in giving that vision a plastic form as convincing as in India in the Gupta period.

The bulky torso and the heavy limbs of the Bodh-Gaya image and other images produced at Mathura in the Gupta period accord ill with the expression of the face. The refinement of the type was carried out by the sculptors of Benares who carved images of the Buddha and the Mahāyāna deities for the monastery at Mṛga-dāva (Sarnath). A masterpiece of Gupta art from Sarnath, an image of the Mahāyāna god Avalokiteśvara (3′ 7¼″ high), exhibited in the Indian Museum, is reproduced in plate III. In the modelling of the body of this figure delicacy is combined with breadth, and in its face beauty of form is combined with profound depth of expression. The Gupta artist had to work under certain disadvantages. Stiffness is more or less inherent in the posture of *dhyāna,* and in modelling the body the artist could not draw inspiration directly from nature, but had to show the marks of the *mahāpuruṣa* (superman) which involved the adoption of a rigid formula. But within these limitations the Gupta artist achieved perfection. This art, born in a workshop of Mathura in the second half of the fourth century A.D., thrived for eight centuries, though gradually losing spontaneity and freshness and gradually overwhelmed by details. Sculpture fell into a state of atrophy after the Muhammadan conquest at the end of the twelfth century A.D. There was a revival of Hindu painting four centuries later. The theme of this art is the *līlā,* sport, of Kṛṣṇa and Śiva, performed, not in an absent-minded fashion while engaged in *dhyāna-yoga* as in the Gupta and the post-Gupta reliefs, but with open watchful eyes. The lyrics of Rabindranath Tagore once again fill our minds with the same longing for the realisation of the *Aśeṣa,* the Limitless, like the images of the Omniscient Being fashioned in the Gupta period :

śeṣer madhye aśeṣ āche—
ei kathā-ṭi, mane
āj-ke āmār gāner śeṣe
jāgche kṣaṇe kṣaṇe.

CALCUTTA

RAMAPRASAD CHANDA

THE GODS OF INDIA*

THE Vedas and Epics set forth several distinct cosmologies and myths of creation, and present us with a pantheon tantalisingly confused, with many functional doublets and a successive emergence of new names of the supreme and other deities, major and minor, only clarified here and there by an intuition that all these represent concepts of human origin imposed upon an ultimate ineffable One. Apart from this philosophic or mystic scission of the Gordian knot, is it possible to find a rational order in the actual theology? Obviously, this cannot be done by a tabulation of family relationships, functions, and myths, for the former are shifting and unconstant, and the latter never exclusively attached to any one individual. If at all, it can only be done by means of an historical untangling of the twisted threads.

Some light first appears when it is realised that Vedic theology presents us with a mixture of two conflicting types of divinity, Asuras and Devas, typically represented by Varuṇa and Indra. In the conflict, the Devas are nominally victorious; and yet it is not Indra, but Viṣṇu (whose name is unimportant in the Vedas) who emerges as the great king of righteousness, cosmic ruler, and ultimate ideal. This Viṣṇu, alike in majesty and moral grandeur, and in matters of mythology and iconographic formulation, is more like Varuṇa, himself the noblest conception of the Vedas, than any other of the older gods. Thus, in brief, Varuṇa is lord of holy order, and Viṣṇu, particularly as conceived in the person of Rāma, embodies the Hindu concept of righteousness; and are not *ṛta* and *dharma* one and the same eternal Law? Both Varuṇa and Viṣṇu are types of the ideal king upon whose virtue (*vīrya,* 'mana') depend the fall of rain in due season and the fruitfulness of the earth. The actual creation proceeds from a tree that springs from Varuṇa's navel as he rests upon the primeval Waters; and in turn, from a demiurge who is lotus-born from a stem that springs from Viṣṇu's navel as he too lies recumbent on the Waters at the commencement of a new cycle of creation. Varuṇa and Viṣṇu are each of the colour of the firmament. The identity of Varuṇa and Viṣṇu is actually asserted in the *Agni Purāṇa.*

Has the conception, then, of the Great King of the Universe persisted dominant from a time before the Vedas to the present day? It is true that Varuṇa, *under this name,* declined to a lesser status as god of the sea, and that it is customary to differentiate sharply the Epic from the Vedic mythology. In reality, the continuity is veiled only thinly by changes of name. There is a succession of cosmic progenitive deities, Prajāpati, Viśvakarman, the Unborn, the Self-Existent, Brahmā, Nārāyaṇa, and of related types, Tvaṣṭṛ, Dakṣa, whose names are for the most part epithets; and with these are connected many of the myths and conceptions elsewhere attached to Varuṇa and Viṣṇu. These epithets do

*Much of the detailed evidence for the point of view here expressed, together with references to other recent literature on the subject, will be found in my *Yakṣas,* and *Yakṣas* Part II, Washington 1928 and 1931.

not represent new deities, but are designations reflecting the imagination of successive periods, and usurping the place of older names which of necessity therefore retained only a more limited application or connotation. That at any one time a given deity has countless names and epithets is a familiar fact of Indian, and indeed of other mythologies: we recognize, for example, the identity of Kubera and Vaiśravaṇa, even that of Kubera and Jambhala, or Kubera and Pañcika ; and it is no less proper to recognize an identity in any deity whose names and epithets are distributed along the line of time, when the evidence of persistent character and myths is available.

Somewhat similarly the Asura deity Agni, originally a great cosmic principle, becomes merely the god of fire and messenger of the gods, while much of his character and myths are inherited by the red god, the 'blue-throated' Śiva-Rudra.

To take another case, a feature typical of Hindu theology is the conception of the supreme deity as Two-in-One—Puruṣa and Prakṛti, Śiva-Śakti, Lakṣmī-Nārāyaṇa, etc. This concept of polar types, Supreme Male and Mother-Mate, appears from the beginning in Varuṇa and Aditi. Are not Aditi, Iḍā, Vāk, Gaurī, Lakṣmī, in fact the Devī in every aspect one and the same? So too with lesser genii: the Gandharvas and Apsarases, originally the 'people' of Varuṇa and Soma, powerful and even dread progenitive deities, soon come to be no more than the musicians and dancers of Indra's court, but their original character and functions are carried on by the Yakṣas and Yakṣīs. Yakṣa was once a term of high respect, and there is no Indian deity, however exalted, who is not in one place or another referred to by this title ; nor even in later times are the Yakṣas anywhere clearly distinguished from other deities and spirits, all of whom, except only the Supreme Cosmic God, have once been men and will in due course be reborn as men.

Again, the oldest cosmology is a belief in the origin of life in the Waters, and its perpetuation and renewal by means of the *soma* or *rasa,* an Essence in the Waters that falls from heaven in rain and is the basis of all propagation and increase. This cosmology has for its iconography the Plant Style as we find it when Indian art is first extensively preserved in permanent material, and as this so-called 'decorative' art has persisted to the present day.

Thus Hinduism emerges, not as a post-Vedic development, a theistic declension from the lofty visions of the Upaniṣads, but as something handed on from a prehistoric past, ever-changing and yet ever essentially itself, raised at various times by devotional ecstasy and philosophic speculation to heights beyond the grasp of thought, and yet preserving in its popular aspects the most archaic rites and animistic imagery.

Behind Varuṇa and Aditi, Ahura Mazda and Anāhita, lie Tammuz and Ištar. All goes back to early cultures dependent on agriculture and irrigation ; ultimately to a time when theology was hardly yet conceived, but welfare seemed to depend on a mysterious energy underlying all the operations of life, an energy scarcely personified, but which could be instigated by rites of sacrifice and sympathetic magic. A 'god' then implied, not a known person, but a dramatisation of a man's direct experience of forest or river, cloud or mountain, birth or death. A combination of many such experiences induced the view that behind them lay a person or persons whose character might be inferred from that of the manifestations themselves, and who could be pleased or displeased ; and hence arose theology and worship, distinct from magic. It is the peculiar value of India to the student of humanity that we find here not only an agelong historical continuity extending from prehistoric times to the present day, but even at the present day every essential stage of the development, from the worship of the vegetative powers to the knowledge of the Self that is 'Not so.' At all times the gods have assumed the forms imagined by their worshippers ; their lineaments are a function of the relation between the worshipper and the object of his devotion. Nothing has been rejected, but all finds its place in a gradated synthesis of elements adapted to every mental age ; and here only therefore has the true meaning of tolerance been understood, here only could it have been said, believed, and acted upon that true teaching consists not in imparting a new kind of truth, but in assisting men to understand still better their own kind of truth.

MUSEUM OF FINE ARTS,
BOSTON, U.S.A.

ANANDA K. COOMARASWAMY

MARKS OF THE GREAT BEING: MAHAPURUSA-LAKSANA

THAT the world originated from Man, created out of himself or as a result of his dismemberment, is a belief recorded in some of the oldest sacred writings in India. By creation or by sacrifice, Man is transmuted into the Universe. This Man is the Superman, the Great Being, the Mahāpuruṣa. To conform with his action his body is impressed with insignia of the cosmos, while at the same time it incorporates standards of human perfection and others for which no canon of beauty has laid down the rules, but which have the sanction of remotest antiquity, to such an extent that their meaning had been as much taken for granted as it had become obscure even in the earliest texts that mention them.

Brahmanical as well as Buddhistic writings enumerate the marks of the Mahāpuruṣa ; yet such marks that can be rendered in plastic terms are almost exclusively confined to the image of Buddha. They are there in their proper places, from the days when the first image of Buddha was created, about the middle of the first century B.C. This may appear strange, because the Mahāpuruṣa-lakṣaṇa, the marks of the Great Being, are connected with the Brahmans, and with the art of soothsaying, as one of their special activities ; they were, however, appropriated by the Buddhistic texts.

The Buddha being looked upon as the Mahāpuruṣa is endowed with his marks. The Brahmanical pantheon, on the other hand, is represented by many divinities, none of whom, however, as rendered by the sculptors, claim to embody the Mahāpuruṣa. And yet, being divinities, some of them have a few marks that are their prerogatives, or other signs closely related to them. The question then arises how this came about.

The notion of the Great Being had shaped itself in the mind of the Aryan invaders of India. But while at that time there existed images of gods, they belonged to those people whom the Northern invaders had found in the country and to whose artistic genius they gradually had to open their doors. Their own conceptions of divinity, on the other hand, were supra-visual. A comparison of the earliest images of Buddha with those of Brahmanical gods of the same age shows the visualised results of speculation in the first, and a spontaneous naturalism in the latter instance. (Cf. for example the Śiva-liṅgam from Guḍimallam).

Buddhism at first had been reluctant to allow the fashioning of any likeness of the Exalted One. Yet, using the art of the country that was teeming with figures of all beings, it had to succumb to the creative onrush of the pre-Aryan people. The critical moment fell into the first century B.C. when those conditions seem to have been agreed upon, under which it was permissible to make an image of the Blessed One. Those conditions were that he should be rendered in the likeness of the Mahāpuruṣa endowed with his signs and differing altogether from the gods of those outside Buddhism. Thus in the fashioning of the Buddha image a survival of Aryan formulæ of vision becomes imprinted on bodily appearance, the latter being the vital share the pre-Aryans have in it.

The 32 marks of the Superman to the greater part refer to an ideal beauty of the body on the basis of normal human appearance. A few, however, transgress the ordinary human figure, not in the sense of the ideal, nor in that of the supernatural. They are formulated in the past tense of the corresponding feature of the present day appearance. They refer to one or the other characteristic trait of pre-historic man and have no further meaning. 'Standing and without bending he can touch his knees with either hand, he evenly touches the earth with the entire surface of the foot, he has projecting heels.' Such are the physiognomical peculiarities that can be, and are rendered by the sculptor and painter, whereas that the number of his teeth is forty, as laid down in the texts, points to the same direction. The golden age, the glorification of the past, satisfy in a wider sense that longing for a better state which the regret of having fallen away from it keeps the more poignant,—the more sharply some of those past qualities or features are still remembered. In this respect the Mahāpuruṣa is not the omnipresent but the past-present human, without an allusion to his transcendental nature.

Not of historical and descriptive origin, but cosmical and symbolical 'wheels appear thousand spoked on the soles of his feet.' The artist, however, goes further than the texts. He imprints palms as well as soles with the mark of the wheel. He goes still further and places behind the head the wheel we call halo. These sun-wheels, of necessity, are small when carried on hands and feet, and there is not much scope for elaborate and loving decoration. Yet even then the spokes are so indicated that the wheel appears transformed into a lotus with open petals.

Spokes of the wheel, rays of the sun, petals of the lotus are interchangeable with the Indian craftsman from an early date. When Buddhist art knew of no icon of the Buddha as yet, the disc of the sun-lotus wheel is one of the most frequent devices that decorate the carved railings of the early Buddhist Stupas. There (at Bhārhut) these round medallions of large size are filled with concentric circles of radiantly luscious lotus petals, or a disc formed by rays is centre of the lotus medallion and background at the same time, or a human bust, or the lotus-sun device occupies the centre and around it in concentric rings animals, phantastic or real, or floral creepers, or chains of jewellery are displayed,—the life, in short, and the precious beauty of this world. The plastic rendering of the sun-wheel, that was to adorn palms and soles and to surround the head of the Buddha image, was prior to the conception of the latter. It is an ancient Northern symbol that stands for nature manifested as an expression of the supreme source of life. This is called *Hvarenah* in the Avesta. This lotus-like sun (and water) wheel, surrounded by a ring of strutting animals, moreover, may be found on one of the silver vases from Maikop in South Russia of the 3rd millenium B.C. (Strzygowski, Asiens Bildende Kunst, p. 98). When in the efflorescence of Indian art in the Gupta period, the Buddha image (images of the fifth and sixth centuries A.D.) did attain fulness of spiritual penetration and of sensuous loveliness, the large halo that surrounds its head unfolds in concentric rings the wealth of floral creepers and the precision of wrought chains of jewelry.

The wheel lakṣaṇa of the Mahāpuruṣa impressed on soles and palms of the Buddha (predominantly in the earlier images) is based on a recollection dim but mighty. The artist gave wider scope to it than the texts. The halo that surrounds the head of the Buddha as centre of light and life spiritual had been a familiar decorative device in ancient India, but its ancestry points back into a far-away past in the North.

Another and one of the most important and controversial marks of the Buddha image and of the Superman is the *uṣṇīṣa*. Invariably the sculptors fashioned it as a protuberance on the top of the head or else as a head taperingly drawn into height. (For the latter, *cf. Buddha from Amarāvatī, 3rd century A.D.* in W. Cohn's *Buddha in der Kunst des Ostens*, pl. 19 ; or the Mankuwaḍ image of mid-sixth century).

This cranial abnormality is a condition *sine qua non* of all the Indian and further Indian Buddha images. It appears, with the rest of the skull covered by ringlets of locks, in the majority of Buddha images, but it is fashioned already prior to the earliest Buddha images in a pillar figure from Bodh-gayā of the early 1st century B.C., where, however, a fillet-like device lines this peculiar coiffure against the forehead, suggestive of a wig ; wig-like too is the head-dress of considerable height, consisting of a mass of short ringlets distributed over the entire wig, including the *uṣṇīṣa* on top, in a relief from Gandhāra, showing the Bodhisattva (Coomaraswamy, *History of Indian and Indonesian Art*, fig. 93). These are the only instances of a kind of *uṣṇīṣa* not on the head of Buddha himself.

Ancient as well modern interpreters of the *uṣṇīṣa* in literature, considerably differ in their conclusions. The images, however, clearly show that the *uṣṇīṣa* is an excrescence of the head itself ; whether the hair covers it in carefully arranged waves, whether the long hair is twisted and coiled about it, whether cut short, it encompasses skull and *uṣṇīṣa* or the heightened skull in parallel rows of conventionalised curls. What does this cranial protuberance, the *uṣṇīṣa* of the Mahāpuruṣa, mean on the head of the Buddha?

A distinction of almost all Indian divinities, excepting the Buddha, is to wear high crowns or else to have matted locks piled up into an intricate and high edifice. To add to the height of the divinity by a high crown or high coiffure and to make this addition just above the head is a means by which their loftiness is enhanced. In this respect, the *uṣṇīṣa* of the Buddha has a similar aim. Yet a further component, however, has to be considered. In Mohen-jo-daro (3rd millenium B.C.) some of the heads show a peculiar formation of skull which seems over-high on top. At the present, in some parts of Burma the infant's head is swathed and so compressed as to make it grow in height, in preference to all other extension, following the belief that the child hereby may become clever in later life. In the Far East, although not before the Ming dynasty, the popular god of Longevity is endowed with an absurdly high head.

The high cranium, be it as an ethnical characteristic or an individual occurrence only, had been understood by the Brahman sooth-sayers as seat of an exalted mind. In a popular form this belief in Burma is alive to the present day ; in the Far East, the notions incorporated in the high skull rose from people's opinion into the world of art not before, however, the Buddha image that hitherto had been inconceivable without the *uṣṇīṣa* had been bereft of that attribute of his by the artists of the 12th century and later, who in their paintings frequently rendered a round and bald patch, in lieu of the *uṣṇīṣa*, surrounded by shaggy black hair. The supernormal shape of the Buddha's head then only had been dispensed with and was replaced by the tonsure of the monk.

The *uṣṇīṣa*, it follows, pre-existent to the image of the Buddha and interpreted as seat of an exalted mind, or of a special faculty of mind, had to be one of the marks of the Great Being, and therefore of the Buddha, when his image came to be made. It is probable that, to suggest this loftiness of mind, wigs may have been worn with the *uṣṇīṣa* (*Cf.* Bodhī-gayā pillar figure and Gandhāra relief whereas later on all other Indian divinities precluded from the possession of an *uṣṇīṣa* like that of the Buddha were by compensation endowed with high crown or coiffure.

The ūṛnā, a hairy mole between the eyebrows, another of the 32 lakṣaṇa of Mahāpuruṣa, is shown in a large number of Buddha figures as a small hemisphere, either carved in the same material as the image itself or inset in a more precious material. It is not accidental that a number of images, though never that of the Buddha, show the middle of the forehead marked by the third eye, whereas to this day devotees have the middle of their forehead occupied by their respective sectarian marks (*tilaka*), while women of the Northern half of India and people of both sexes in the South favour an auspicious mark painted with vermilion or applied with cut beetle wings where the Buddha has the vestige of the 'third eye', *i.e.*, the sense organ of a lost faculty of perception. The ūṛṇā seems to be the version specifically selected for the image of the Buddha. The texts speaking of a hairy mole had altogether become out of touch with the original meaning.

Although not amongst the 32 lakṣaṇa of the Mahāpuruṣa, one further peculiarity is indispensable to every Buddha image. These are, what is called 'elongated ear-lobes.' The current interpretation is, that the Buddha when leaving the world gave up the heavy earrings worn by royalty while the disfigurement of the lengthened ear-lobes persisted. Yet not only are the ear-lobes elongated but the entire ear is expanded beyond its normal length. Such an ear denotes a capacity of hearing, different from that of mortals. The greatness of what it is capable of, and what it does hear cannot be taken in by ordinary ears. The transcendental origin of *that* sound is hinted at by his large ears.

Such are the conspicuous marks of the Buddha image, of the Great Being. They were kept alive in the creative memory of the craftsman long after their meaning had become obsolete in literature. For the artist who visualizes the divinity of the image he is about to give form to, cannot but make use of the human body as a simile for his God-vision. As he transmutes the whole body into a vessel of contents superhuman, whose shape is moulded by these contents, dim reminiscences of the past and attributes of the Superman regain their meaning.

THE UNIVERSITY, CALCUTTA

STELLA KRAMRISCH

INDIANS IN ASIA MINOR?

THE oldest evidence of Aryan tribes in Asia Minor is derived from Kassite records, particularly from some words preserved in a glossary containing the Babylonians' equivalents of a few Kassite words.[1] Further evidence of some Aryan element in Mesopotamia is given by the names of the Mitanni kings in the Tell-el-Amarna letters.[2] But the material then at our disposal was scanty, it could not lead to any decisive result and the problem remained unsolved. A new start was taken when in the year 1907 Professor H. Winckler[3] brought to light a treaty (dating from the 14th century B.C.) between the Hittite king Šubbiluliuma and the Mitanni king Mattiwaza, where more than one hundred deities are invoked as witnesses to the treaty and where after the Babylonian deities, Anu and Antum, Enlil and Ninlil we read the following in the Mitanni version of king Mattiwaza:

ilāni Mi-it-ra-aš-šil ilāni A-ru-na-aš-šil In-da-ra ilāni Na-sa-at-ti-ya-an-na.

In the Hittite version of king Šubbiluliuma the same gods are invoked, only instead of *A-ru-na* is to be read *U-ru-wa-na* and instead of *In-da-ra* we read *In-dar.*

No doubt it was very strange to meet in Mesopotamia in the 14th century B. C. in a list of deities the names of Vedic gods Mitra, Varuṇa, Indra and Nāsatya, which clearly sound either Aryan or Indian, but not Iranian, since the name Nāsatya in accordance to the Iranian phonology would require the form Nāoñhaithya[4]. Therefore Ed. Meyer and with him most Indologists were of the opinion that those Indo-European people who came to Mesopotamia in the 15th century or before that time were either Aryans or proto-Iranians.[5] A small group differed. Professor Jacobi maintained that the gods mentioned in the inscription were identical in form with Vedic gods and that the religion of the tribe who imported them into Mesopotamia was essentially the same as Vedic religion as far at least as concerns mythology.[6] The existence of Vedic gods in Mesopotamia in the 14th century B.C. seemed to agree wonderfully with his theory on the antiquity of the Veda and he was convinced that the excavations at Boghaz-köi were giving "an entirely new aspect to the whole question of the antiquity of Indian civilisation." Some scholars[7] again

[1] *Cf. F. Delitzsch,* 'Die Sprache der Kossäer' 1884; J. Scheftelowitz, K. Z. XXXVIII (1905), p. 270.

[2] *I. A. Knuatzon,* 'Die zwei Arzawa-Briefe, die ältesten Urkunden in indogermanischer Sprache,' Leipzig, 1902.

[3] *H. Winckler,* 'Mitteilungen der Deutschen Orient. Gesellschaft,' December, 1907, p. 51. Since that time the documents in question have been often published, translated and commented upon. *Cf.* particularly *E. F. Weidner,* 'Politische Dokumente aus Kleinasien,' Boghazköi-Studien 7 (1922), pp. 32 and 54.

[4] *Cf. Chr. Bartholomæ,* 'Altiranisches Wörterbuch', *sub voce.*

[5] *Ed. Meyer,* 'Sitzungsberichte der k. preussischen Akademie der Wissenschaften,' 1908, p. 14ff.; Kuhn's Zeitschrift, 42 (1909), p. 24.

[6] *H. Jacobi,* JRAS., 1909, p. 721, 1910, p. 456.

[7] *Cf. Paul Kretschmer* in a very instructive article 'Varuṇa und Urgeschichte der Inder' W. Z. K. M. XXXIII (1926), p. 1., K. Z. 55, p. 78; *B. Hrozny',* 'Die Länder Charri and Mitanni und die ältesten Inder,' Archiv orientální I (1929), pp. 91—110.

thought that the language from which the names of the Mitanni chieftains and the names of gods were taken was pre-Indian, which view was supported by another document found in Boghaz-köi containing terms on horse-training and some numerals, *viz.*, *nā* (or *nawa*, Sanskrit *nava*), *satta* (Skt. *sapta*), *panza* (Skt. *pañca*), and particularly *aika* (Skt. *eka*), the Iranian form being *aiva*.[8]

From all this it has been deduced that an extreme branch of proto-Indians, migrating to India, settled sometime in the second millennium B.C. in Mesopotamia and made for itself a prominent place among the Mitanni people.

I do not agree with this view either, and venture to offer a different explanation. I am, of course, quite aware that genuine and reliable material is extremely scanty, *viz.*, we have but (a) few names of kings, (b) of gods, and (c) a few numerals: (a) *Šauššatar ; Artatama* (= *Skt. Ṛtadhāmā*?) ; *Šutarna ; Dušratta ; Mattiwaza* (= *Skt. Mativāja*?) ; (b) *Mitra ; Aruna, Uruwana ; Indara ; Nāsatiyanna* ; (c) *aika ; tera* (*t(r)iera*) ; *panza ; satta ; na* (*nawa*). These words evidently belong to the same language. The script does not represent the real sound of the words—it does not distinguish the aspirates and long vowels.

The vocabulary is undoubtedly Aryan. The stage of the language to which the words belong could not have been Iranian, as the sibilants of several words (*Cf. Nasatiyanna, satta*, the prefix *su-*) indicate. It could not have been Indian either, as the name of the king *Dušratta* clearly shows ; in Sanskrit, this would be *Dūratha*. But I think it cannot have been proto-Iranian or proto-Indian either. It seems to me that the name of the king *Šauššatar* is a patronymic of the known Aryan type derived from *su-satar*[9] that may be connected with the Skt. root *śa-*'to sharpen, to excite.' Such compounds are, it is true, not very common in Sanskrit, but they are not impossible ; *cf.* Vedic *su-mātṛ* 'having a handsome mother,' *su-sanitṛ* 'a great dispenser.' Now both in Sanskrit and Iranian (and also Old Slavonic) the *ṛ*-stems have lost their *r* in the nom. sg. ; *cf.* Skt. *mātā* 'mother,' *pitā* 'father,' *śāstā* 'ruler,' Avestan *mātā, pitā, dātā* 'Creator,' Old Persian *brātā* 'brother,' Old Slavonic *mati* 'mother,' Lithuanian *motė* 'wife.' The *r* is retained by the western (*centum*) languages, *cf.* Latin *mater, pater, frater*, Greek *mētēr, patēr*.

Therefore it seems to me that the language of the Mitanni chieftains is neither proto-Indian nor proto-Iranian, but represents with those two a third, yet unknown branch of the Aryan group.

CZECH UNIVERSITY, PRAGUE, CZECHOSLOVAKIA V. LESNY

[8] *P. Jensen*, 'Indische Zahlwörter in keilschrifthittitischen Texten', Sitzb. der preus. Akad. der Wis. 1919, p. 367; *E. Forrer*, 'Die Inschriften und Sprachen des Hatti-reiches,' Z.D.M.G. 76 (1922), p. 174; *Sten Konow*, 'The Aryan gods of the Mitanni people', Kristiania, 1921; *A. B. Keith*, 'The Early History of the Indo-Iranians,' *Bhandarkar Commemorative Essays*, 1917, p. 81, *The Indian Historical Quarterly*, I (1925), p. 16, The Religion and Philosophy of the Veda and Upanishads,' 1925, p. 5; *Walter Porzig*, 'Kleinasiatisch-Indische Beziehungen, ZII. 5 (1927), p. 264.

[9] The double *š* is of little consequence in this case, *cf.* Mattiwaza—Skt. Mativāja (equation proposed by Walter Porzig, Z.I.-I., 5 (1927), p. 264).

UN ANCÊTRE DE TAGORE DANS LA LITTÉRATURE JAVANAISE

JE suis heureux de dédier cette étude au glorieux descendant de *Bhatta Nârâyana*, à mon cher et grand ami Rabindranath Tagore. C'est de sa bouche que j'ai appris, à Santiniketan, à l'occasion de la représentation d'un acte du *Venîsamhâra*, que le nom de *Bhatta Nârâyana* figure dans la liste rituelle de ses ancêtres. Et ce mémoire, composé à son intention pour célèbrer le 70e anniversaire de sa naissance, évoque avec plus d'intensité que jamais dans ma mémoire les jours heureux que nous avons, ma femme et moi, passés près de lui entre octobre 1921 et août 1922. Appelé par son choix à inaugurer l'enseignement de l'orientalisme à la manière occidentale dans l'Université de Visva-Bhâratî qu'l fondait à ce moment, j'y ai appris beaucoup plus que je n'y ai enseigné. Par *Gurudev*, comme nous l'appelons là-bas, par l'élite de savants et de disciples qui se sont groupés autour de lui et qui vivent de son inspiration, j'ai connu dans sa réalité vivante cette âme de l'Inde que l'étude des textes m'avait appris à admirer ; c'est seulement à Santiniketan, au contact du Maître et de son entourage, que j'ai pu apprécier dans leur charme incomparable cette dignité de la tenue, cette noblesse des sentiments, cette exaltation contenue de la pensée qui se combinent sans effort avec une gaieté malicieuse, une fanta isie spirituelle, une douceur exquise, et cette communion perpétuelle avec la nature qui donne à la vie journalière une teinte délicieuse d'éclogue virgilienne. L'homme qui a su créer et animer de sa puissante personnalité cet *Asram* est bien l'héritier authentique de ces anciens *rsi*'s qui, retirés dans leurs ermitages, concentrés dans leurs méditations sans se détacher de la vie, ont légué à l'Inde ces trésors de sagesse qui ont fait sa gloire.

A la fin du Xe siècle J.-C. règne sur la partie orientale de Java un grand prince, Srî Dharmmavaṁśa tĕguh Anantavikramadeva. Rival et souvent adversaire du royaume de Śrîvijaya (Palembang) qui avait créé dans l'île de Sumatra un magnifique foyer de culture indienne, Dharmmavaṁśa donne à l'étude des textes sanscrits un vigoureux essor. Sur son ordre, le MahâBhârata est traduit en langue javanaise. L'ouvrage n'existe plus aujourd'hui à Java même ; mais la petite île de Bali, dernier asile de la civilisation indienne dans l'Archipel, en a conservé quelques sections. Friederich, à qui il faut toujours remonter quand il s'agit de Bali, fut le premier à les signaler, dans son précieux mémoire sur Bali (Verhandel. Batav. Gen. XXII, 1849). Kern, en 1871, a publié, d'après une copie préparée par Van der Tuuk, la table des matières (Anukramaṇikâ) du MahâBhârata javanais (Bijdr. T.L.V.-kunde van N.I., 3e Volg. dl. VI, 1871) ; six ans plus tard, il a donné une notice sur l'Âdiparva, où il a reproduit le Pauṣyacarita, texte javanais (kavi) et traduction (Verhand. K. Acad. Wet., afd. Lett. dl. XI, 1877). Depuis, Juynboll a édité l'Âśramavâsa, le Mausala et le Mahâprasthâna (1893), l'Âdiparva (1906), et le Virâṭaparva (1912).

Le traducteur javanais a incorporé dans sa version, comme une garantie d'authenticité et de fidélité, certains vers, ou fragments de vers, de l'original sanscrit, dont il a donné la glose littérale. En outre, il avait placé en tête de chacun des parva's des stances sanscrites, dont le texte s'est fâcheusemant altéré de copiste en copiste. Kern a déjà fait connaître la stance initiale de l'Âdiparva, mais il n'a pu en restituer que les trois premiers quarts. J'ai pu moi-même pendant mon court séjour à Bali (juin 1928), prendre copie des stances qui ouvrent les quatre parva's conservés, l'Âdi, le Virâṭa, le Bhîṣma et l'Âśramavâsa. Je publie ici ces vers, dans l'espoir qu'is pourront provoquer des recherches intéressantes; un d'entre eux tout au moins pose un probléme curieux, comme on va le voir. Je donne le texte tel qu'il figure dans le manuscrit avec les confusions de caractères si fréquentes dans les mss. balinais (la prononciation n'y distingue ni les sifflantes, ni les aspirées, ni les dentales et les cérébrales), et avec les coupures baroques introduites souvent à l'intérieur des mots ; j'indiquerai ensuite les restitutions probables.

ÂDIPARVA

Ms. (1) jayati paraśarasûnus satya vâdi hrĕdayaṁ-nandâ no byâsaḥ-parasya sukârti-pathayi tvâ-vâmadâ saṁkya sakâla jagatĕm-siva miti.

[Var. du ms. de Kern.........paraśarassûnus......sukârtthiyitvâ...saka jugatĕm.]

Kern a bien reconnu une âryâ, et il a restitué :

jayati parâśarasûnus Satyavatîhṛdayanandano Byâsaḥ
parasya sukhârtthaheto............................

(2) srotanjali putara vayavĕm-vitabhavân bhâratâ kyâhĕm-mrĕśa dukta mahâ bhavâtem vrĕsṇi-krĕsṇa dvaipâyana midem dadyât suphala jagatâdhayaḥ—paśupati paṇḍita krĕsṇa jagat va macitam-sarva slokĕm pavâya mânaḥ—kavi muktaḥ paraśâryaḥ vivrĕttâ nyeti.

Je reviendrai plus loin sur ces vers.

VIRÂṬAPARVA

Ms. (1) satreyo yastapa syanḍakâri pura vanâṣṭarṣa lâsâni tevai-puṁgâ yukto palese viśala pasula niryâ punaḥ kanya kartha — — âpâdharmma pratikâra janana kuśalo yasta morâtma putraḥ-krĕsṇâ dvaipâyânâ kyâstha jayati bhagavân śrotryânĕm viśesaḥ.

Le vers est clairement une sragdharâ, et même fort correct au point de vue métrique, sauf au second pâda pratikâra à rectifier en pratîkâra ; néanmoins la restitution est souvent douteuse ou embarrassante[1] :

śâktreyo yas tapasy andhakaripuravanaṣṭa ⏑ — — ⏑ devaiḥ
puṁsâ yuktopalebhe vimala ⏑ ⏑ ⏑ — yâ punaḥ kanyakâtvam.
âpaddharmapratîkârajananakuśalo yas tayor âtmaputraḥ
kṛṣṇadvaipâyanâkhyaḥ sa jayati bhagavân śrotriyâṇâṁ viśeṣaḥ :

Ms. (2) yasmâ chra (*var.* chro) meti guṇa sâlikâ deyâ-sârddhâna varṣa śata rohinâssite (*var.* spite)-ya (*var.* yad) dhairya varṣâ mita karâstu sâ-śrî dharmma vaṁśa d-guh anantavikramaḥ

[1] Pour ce vers et les variantes, cf. outre l'édition du Virâṭaparvan de Juynboll, l'ouvrage en danois de K. Wulff, Den oldjavanske Wirâṭaparvan, Copenhague 1917, p. 226-233.

On reconnaît une indravaṁśâ à peine altérée. Le dernier pâda, de lecture certaine, garantit le mètre ; il faut toutefois, contrairement à la prosodie sanscrite, laisser l'a final de vaṁśa bref devant le mot javanais dgu (dĕgu) qui fait partie du nom royal. Le second pâda semble exprimer une date avec les mots varṣa śata ; en ce cas il faudrait y retrouver 918 śaka, date fournie par le texte même en javanais (kavi), mais je ne vois pas comment on peut y réussir. On peut essayer de restaurer ainsi :

yasmât sravante guṇaśâlikâdayaḥ
sârddhâ ⏑ varṣaśata rohiṇî site :
yaddhairyavarṣâmita-karâs tu saḥ
śrîdharmmavaṁśa dguh anantavikramaḥ.

BHÎṢMAPARVA

Ms. (1) krĕsṇâñgambhoda pañktiḥ kila kapila jatâ tâlikî veṣṭamâna-dhûlipreñkadvalâkâ pravitiśaya valâ stotrâ pâjanya ghoṣa-yasya jñâna pravarṣeḥ suka yati janatâ nîla kaṇṭa pravahân-tamvan devyâ sasajñamyata manukrĕtaye mâtrayâ tadvânânâm.

Le mètre est la sragdharâ, presque entièrement correct ; l'ensemble se restitue assez facilement :

kṛṣṇâñgâmbhodapañktiḥ kila kapilajaṭâveṣṭamâno
dhûlipreñkhadbalâkâniratiśayabalastotraparjanyaghoṣaḥ :
yasya jñânapravarṣaḥ sukhayati janatânîlakaṇṭhapravâhân
taṁ vande vyâsasaṁjñâyutam anukṛtaye mâtrayâ tatpadânâm.

Ms. : api ca (2) yas śrî darayaca patiḥ kalu loka phalaḥ-tasyammano hari pada trayam eti samrat-śri dharmmavaṁśad-guh anantu maddhyam-sajñan nrĕpaḥ pranida dhâti savikramântam.

Vasantatilakâ métriquement correcte, mais avec une lacune au 3e pâda ; la restitution offre peu de difficultés. C'est ici encore un éloge du roi Śrî Dharmmavaṁśa dĕguh Anantavikrama :

yaś śrîdharo narapatiḥ khalu lokapâlas
tasyâ(?)manoharapadatrayam eti saṁjñâ :
śrîdharmmavaṁśa d-guh [tadâdim ?] anantamadhyâm
saṁjñâṁ nṛpaḥ praṇidadhâti savikramântâm.

ĀŚRAMAVÂSAPARVA

Ms. : aśvamaḥ piñgâlâ jana padvâkâla-paprañgu pâṇḍhava krĕsṇatva kvadanaḥ-sarvva śloka padhartha vinokta kavi-mukta sarvva gasâla mi vrĕnonati.

Cette stance, d'un type métrique indéfinissable, présente au premier aspect un certain nombre de mots ou d'éléments déjà rencontrés dans la seconde partie de la soi-disant stance qui suit le vers initial de l'Âdiparva. En effet, nous avons de part et d'autre : krĕsṇa. . . tva. . . sarvaśloka (ślokĕm). . . kavi mukta. . . vivrĕttânyeti (mivrĕnonati). Le rapprochement des deux morceaux permet de reconnaître une des stances de bénédiction conservées en sanscrit par un des manuscrits grantha, le G2 de l'édition Sukthankar. G2 lit au vers 13, mètre mattamayûrâ, après une série de namaskâra :

abhraśyâmaḥ piñgajaṭâbaddhakalâpaḥ
prâṁśur daṇḍî kṛṣṇamṛgatvakparidhânaḥ
sâkṣâl lokân pâvayamânaḥ kavimukhyaḥ
pârâśaryaḥ parvasu rûpaṁ vivṛṇotu.

L'Âśramavâsa javanais (Âś.) a fait aśvamaḥ de abhraśyâmaḥ, piñgâlâ jana de piñgajaṭâ, padvâkâlâ de baddhakalâpaḥ ; paprañgu pâṇḍhava (Âś.) et paśupati paṇḍita de l'Âdiparva (Âd.) sont l'un et l'autre des altérations de l'original prâṁśur daṇḍî ; krĕsṇa tvakvadanaḥ (Âś.) et krĕsṇa jagatvamacitam (Âd.) sont l'un et l'autre des altérations de kṛṣṇamṛgatvak-paridhânaḥ ; sarvaślokapadhartha vinoktakavi mukta (Âś.) et sarvaślokĕm pavâyamânaḥ kavi muktaḥ (Âd.) ramènent tous deux à sâkṣâl lokân pâvayamânaḥ kavimukhyaḥ ; enfin paraśâryaḥ vivrĕttânyeti (Âd.) et sarvagaśala mivrĕnonati (Âś.) sont des débris du dernier pâda : pârâśaryaḥ parvasu rûpaṁ vivṛṇotu.

Nous sommes donc ramenés à une recension de l'Inde méridionale ; rien de plus naturel ; depuis les Pallavas jusqu'aux Coḷas, l'Archipel et le Sud de l'Inde sont unis par des rapports fréquents.

Je reviens maintenant aux stances initiales de l'Âdiparva. Kern ne s'est essayé, comme je l'ai dit, à restituer que la première, et seulement en partie. Pour les deux suivantes, il se contente de déclarer que 'dans les deux vers sanscrits qui suivent, il y a peu de chose à reconnaître en dehors des noms propres *Bhâratâkhyam* et *Kṛṣṇa Dvaipâyana*. Ce qui est clair, du moins, c'est que le contenu de ces deux vers, maintenant méconaissable, est en fait d'accord avec MahâBhârata I, 17-19 (Calc. ed.).' Nous pouvons aujourd'hui pousser plus loin.

Tout d'abord il semble impossible de croire que les stances en l'honneur de Vyâsa qui ouvrent les quatre parvan's jusqu'ici accessibles, soient réellement l'œuvre du traducteur javanais ; les stances en l'honneur de son patron royal Dharmmavaṁśa qui n'ont pas pu naturellement être empruntées à des ouvrages d'origine indienne trahissent une gaucherie de facture qui les distingue fâcheusement des autres ; quelle que doive être la part de responsabilité des copistes dans l'état corrompu du texte, la maladresse et l'indigence de l'auteur n'éclatent que trop visiblement. En outre, nous savons maintenant, grâce à la précieuse édition critique du MahâBhârata donnée par l'Institut Bhandarkar de Poona, que le premier hémistiche de la stance initiale—

jayati Parâśarasûnus Satyavatîhṛdayanandano Vyâsaḥ

se lit au début de la recension cachemirienne de l'épopée (ms. K3) ; le second hémistiche est, à dire vrai, tout différent :

yasyâsyakamalakośe vâñmayam amṛtam pibati lokaḥ.

Nous sommes sans doute en présence d'un de ces exercices de *pâda-pûraṇa* si goûtés des versificateurs hindous ; une portion de vers étant donnée le poète doit la complèter par une invention de son cru. Personne ne sera disposé, je pense, à croire que la recension cachemirienne du MahâBhârata est allée chercher à Java, dans une traduction en vieux javanais du Xe siècle, un hémistiche d'adoration à Vyâsa pour le placer en tête du MahâBhârata. On est donc forcé d'admettre que le traducteur javanais a emprunté à l'Inde cet hémistiche ; l'état désespéré du second hémistiche dans le texte javanais ne permet pas de discerner avec quelque vraisemblance s'il est une invention du traducteur javanais ou s'il est copié d'un original indien. En tout cas, c'est un fait digne de considération que le rapport s'établisse entre le MahâBhârata de Java et la recension cachemirienne. J'ai déjà montré, à propos du Râmâyaṇa (Journ. As. 1918, 1, 135) que c'est aussi à la recension cachemirienne de ce poème que remonte l'imitation du Digvarṇana introduite dans un sûtra bouddhique. La valeur des textes du Cachemire se trouve donc fortement établie ; en outre, dans le cas du Râmâyaṇa, le texte cachemirien semble le mieux informé sur les îles de l'Archipel. La traduction javanaise montre, d'autre part, que le texte d'un parvan du MahâBhârata connu au Xe siècle à Java était celui du Cachemire. Toute une série d'autres indices semblent marquer des relations directes entre le Nord-Ouest de l'Inde et les pays d'outre-mer à l'Orient.

Le second vers va nous reporter dans une autre direction. Kern y avait reconnu les mots *bhâratâkhyam* et *Kṛṣṇa Dvaipâyana ;* mais on peut en outre lire avec assurance au début les mots *śrotrâñjali.* Ce sont là des repères suffisants pour être tenté d'y retrouver, puisqu'il s'agit d'une glorification de Vyâsa, le vers d'hommage qui ouvre le drame fameux du Veṇîsaṁhâra, immédiatement après la nândî :

> śravaṇâñjaliputapeyaṁ viracitavân bhâratâkhyam amṛtaṁ yaḥ,
> tam aham arâgam atṛṣṇaṁ Kṛṣṇa-Dvaipayanaṁ vande.

L'accord est aussitôt évident. Soulignons les portions communes qui se retrouvent dans le texte javanais :

śrotranjali puta ra va*y*aveṁ *vita*bhav*ân bhâratâ kya*â*hĕm mr*ĕśa duk*ta mahâ* bhav*âtem vrĕsṇi krĕsṇa dvaipâyana m* ideṁ.

śrotrâñjali est une simple variante de *śravaṇâñjali ;* le mètre, âryâ, s'accommode aussi bien d'une lecture (‒ ‒ , spondée) que de l'autre (‿ ‿ ‒ anapèste). *puta* est identique à *puṭa ;* les mss. de Bali confondent totalement dentales et cérèbrales. *ravaya* se ramène aisément à *peya* dans cette écriture, où la voyelle *e,* tracée à gauche de l'akṣara (comme en bengali) se distingue difficilement du *ra. veṁvitabhavân* recouvre *viracitavân,* le *m* et le *c,* comme dans la plupart des écritures indiennes, se ressemblent ; le *bha* de *bhavân* a dû être introduit par la fausse science d'un scribe. *bhâratâkyahĕm* est, comme Kern l'avait deviné tout de suite, *bhâratâkhyam. mrĕśa* (*rĕ* est la notation du *ṛ* sanscrit) a conservé en partie a)*mṛ*(t)*a*(*m*) *; duk* s'est substitué à *yas,* j'ignore comment et pourquoi. Mais *tamahâ,* qui suit = *tam ahaṁ ; bhavâtem* correspond à *arâgam* ou à quelque autre lecture ; *vrĕsṇi* répond à *atṛṣṇam* ou à *akṛṣṇam,* variante de plusieurs mss. ; la forme du *v* s'accommode aussi bien à un *k* qu'à un *t.* Enfin *idem* couvre en partie *vaṁde.*

Donc c'est à l'auteur du Veṇîsaṁhâra, à Bhaṭṭa Nârâyaṇa, que le traducteur javanais a emprunté cet hommage à Vyâsa. D'autres réussiront quelque jour à retrouver l'origine des autres stances qu'il avait recopiées. Bhaṭṭa Nârâyaṇa est, suivant une tradition toujours admise, un des cinq brahmanes que le roi Âdiśûra avait appelés au Bengale pour y restaurer la pureté de la caste brahmanique. La date de Âdisûra a été fréquemment discutée ; déjà Wilson en 1827 (Hindu Theatre III, app. p. 27) assignait le Veṇîsamhâra au VIIIe ou IXe siècle ; nous pouvons désormais affirmer avec certitude qu'il est antérieur à la fin du Xe siècle. Les citations abondantes qui en sont données dans tous les traités de dramaturgie et de composition poétique prouvent la haute réputation de ce drame. Qu'un ouvrage composé au Bengale soit parvenu à l'Archipel, il n'y a pas lieu d'en être surpris ; les relations étaient régulières entre les deux pays. C'est à Tâmraliptî, le grand port du Bengale, que Yi-tsing s'embarque pour passer à Śrîvijaya (685). L'inscription de Kelurak (782) atteste qu'un des moines bouddhistes de la tradition du Bengale (Gauḍîdvîpagurukrama) était alors le chapelain royal d'un roi Śailendra de Java. L'inscription de Nâlandâ, dans la seconde moitié du IXe siècle (Ep. Ind. 1924, 310, 327) montre les Pâla's du Bengale engagés, sous les auspices de la religion, dans des relations politiques avec une dynastie de Sumatra (Suvarṇadvîpâdhipamahârâja). Vers l'époque même où le MahâBhârata est traduit en javanais, le célèbre Atîśa, qui devait jouer un rôle éclatant dans le bouddhisme au Tibet, vient du Bengale à l'Archipel, probablement à Sumatra (Suvarṇadvîpa), pour y compléter ses études sous la direction de Dharmmakîrtti, grand prêtre du pays (début du XIe siècle).

Si un drame indien, et particulièrement un drame fondé sur le MahâBhârata, était connu à Java sous le régne de Śrî Dharmmavaṁśa, l'hypothèse d'une influence indienne sur l'origine du théâtre d'ombres javanais, le wayang, gagne en vraisemblance. C'est justement sous le successeur de Dharmmavaṁśa, le grand roi Airlaṅga, que l'existence du wayang se manifeste comme un fait positif, en rapport avec la composition de l'Arjunavivâha, la première œuvre originale en javanais fondée sur le MahâBhârata (cf. Krom, Hindoe-Javaansche Geschiedenis, p. 47-48 et note, et p. 265). On sait quel lien étroit a subsisté au cours des siècles entre le wayang et la grande épopée hindoue.

COLLEGE DE FRANCE,
PARIS

SYLVAIN LÉVI

RABINDRANATH TAGORE THE HUMANIST

I

THE humanism of Rabindranath Tagore has two aspects: the actuality of individual joy and suffering in the concrete, with the reality of a world-culture of humanity as its background. Both give full scope for creation, one in the life of action, the other in the life of the spirit. Rabindranath has worked unwearingly to relieve the distress due to flood and famine, chronic poverty, ill-health, and want of education in his own villages of Bengal ; equally untiringly he has endeavoured to spread to the four corners of the world the message of the coming together of the races of mankind, of universal humanity. The Poet is not interested in the arid region of abstract principles ; uplift has no appeal for him. He does not believe in the cult of organized patriotism nor in that of an unfocussed cosmopolitanism. His is not the philosophy of negation, of barren renunciation, but a realization completely comprehensive. Rabindranath has placed his faith in the Kingdom of Man on earth, rich with the variety of human relationships. For him true freedom lies in the growth of personality from the life of the flesh to the life of the spirit which finds its supreme expression in the divinity of Man the Eternal.

II

Rabindranath was born in the atmosphere of the advent of new ideals in Bengal, ideals 'which at the same time were old, older than all the things of which that age was proud.'

That atmosphere was created mainly by Ram Mohun Roy. The Poet has repeatedly acknowledged that the first source of his inspiration was from that large-hearted man of gigantic intellect:

> Ram Mohun Roy was the first great man of our age with the comprehensiveness of mind to realize the fundamental unity of spirit in the Hindu, Moslem, and Christian cultures. He represented India in the fullness of truth based not upon rejection but on perfect comprehension. I follow him, though he is practically rejected by my countrymen.

That atmosphere was a confluence of three movements—intellectual, spiritual, national—all of which were revolutionary. The poet's father Debendranath was the great leader of that movement after Ram Mohun, a movement for the sake of which he suffered ostracism and braved social indignities. The Poet was thus born in a family which had to live its own life, and which made him seek guidance for his self-expression in his own inner standard of judgment.

It is, therefore, not at all surprising that the Poet's faith in his own country and in a culture of universal humanity transcending all barriers of time and place both find expression in his earliest writings. At the age of sixteen he discussed the promotion of material prosperity in Bengal, and the possibilities of building up a new civilization through the meeting of East and West in an essay entitled *Hope and Despair of Bengalis** published in the *Bhārati*. The titles of other essays such as *The Anglo-Saxons and their Literature, Dante and Beatrice, Petrarch and his Laura, Goethe's Loves, Anglo-Norman Literature* and *Tasso* reveal his wide interests at this period (1878-80).

This was the time of the awakening of national sentiments in Bengal, traces of the Poet's share in which are left in a number of patriotic songs of which '*To you have I dedicated my body and my spirit, my Motherland*' (1877) is probably the best known.

Along with the national movement occurred the neo-Hindu revival in Bengal. The sentimental obscurantism and the bellicose patriotism of this pseudo-religious movement repelled the Poet strongly, and with merciless logic and biting sarcasm he lashed the smug self-satisfaction and shallow boastings in scathing satire in *Boot-rations, Loud Speaking, Tongue-waving, The Agitation of Neo-Bengalis,* and in a small group of poems in the *Mānasi*: *Wild Hopes, Up-lift of Our Country, The Heroes of New Bengal,* and *The Propagation of Religion*. The anger of the Poet flamed up against the social thinking which glorified caste and child-marriage and the sophistry which discovered pseudo-scientific justifications of unintelligent customs and fantastic superstitions in such essays as *Moustache and Eggs, Superiority of Monkeys, Truth, Hindu Marriage* and in the poem *Love-making of a Newly-married Bengali Couple* (1882-88). The darkest pictures were, however, invariably relieved by a touch of humour.

Rabindranath was convinced that there could be no real political progress until social injustices were removed. He asked his countrymen if the freedom to which they aspired was one of external conditions. Was it merely a transferable commodity? Had they really acquired a true love of freedom? Had they faith in it?

> Unless we have true faith in freedom, knowing it to be creative, manfully taking all its risks, not only do we lose the right to claim freedom in politics, but we also lack the power to maintain it with all our strength. Men who contemptuously treat their own brothers and sisters as eternal babies, never to be trusted in the most trivial details of their personal lives,—coercing them at every step by the cruel threat of persecution into following a blind lane leading nowhere, often driving them into hypocrisy and into moral inertia,—will fail over and over again to rise to the height of their true and severe responsibility.

In all these discussions he maintained, however, a remarkable detachment of mind, and although he always showed an enthusiastic appreciation of the intellectual greatness and strength of character of the European nations, he vigorously denounced the habit of blind imitation, and emphasized the need for preserving much of permanent value in the traditional culture of the country. In an article written in 1883, on the occasion of the opening of the National Fund, he foreshadows, at the age of twenty-two, his later outlook on the political work of the country. He protested against political agitation being made the sole object of the proposed fund ; he felt that the only aim of such agitation was to influence an alien government and had no real connexion with the welfare of the country. This policy

*I have given everywhere a literal English translation of the original Bengali titles. The dates also refer to the Bengali writings unless otherwise mentioned.

of 'begging favours from the white masters' could only foster an infantile mentality of irresponsible criticism and a spirit of parasitic dependence on others. He distrusted rights which could be conferred or withdrawn at the sweet pleasure of the rulers. He realized that the use of English as the sole language of political work effectually isolated such work from the people ; he urged that a vigorous attempt be made to awaken the mind of the masses by spreading education, and to create a spirit of self-reliance by initiating welfare work by our own efforts. The patriotic songs of this period are inspired by the same spirit of independence ; in one the Poet implored his countrymen to throw away 'the salver of petitions and memorials.'

The appeal of a wider humanism was not lacking in the writings of this period. At the age of twenty, Rabindranath made an angry protest against the forcing of opium on the Chinese in an article, *The Traffic of Death in China* (1881). In another essay he said : The call of humanity is ever sounding. Have we nothing of permanent value to contribute to the future of human civilization? He pointed out that true freedom consists in subordinating selfish interests to the universal spirit of humanity, while isolation, even in independence, was bondage. In the *Song of Invitation* (1885) he called upon Bengal to take her place in the world of humanity. At the same time he made clear his dislike of a nebulous cosmopolitanism. In an essay on *A Plot of Land* (1884), he said : The universe is present in each and every small holding. To be able to know truly even a small plot of land is the only way of realizing the Universe. In an essay on *Ram Mohun Roy* (1884), he pointed out that the significance of a people lay in the individuality of its contribution to sum of human culture.

III

In 1891, Rabindranath took charge of the Tagore estates in North Bengal and went to Shileida, where he stayed for several years. He came into intimate contact with 'the poor, patient, submissive, family-loving, home-clinging, eternally exploited ryots of Bengal,' and gained a deep insight into their everyday life and needs. His passionate preoccupation in village welfare work which is such a marked feature of his latterday activities may be said to be a direct resultant of his stay among the peasants. He wrote at this time :

> I feel a great tenderness for the peasant folk—our ryots—big, helpless, infantile children of providence. I know not whether the socialistic ideal of a more equal distribution of wealth is attainable, but, if not, then such dispensation of Providence is indeed cruel, and man a truly unfortunate creature. For, if in this world misery must exist, so be it; but let some little loop-hole, some glimpses of possibility, at least, be left, which may serve to urge the nobler portion of humanity to hope and struggle unceasingly for its alleviation. . . . If there be any under-current along which the souls of men may have communication with one another then my sincere blessing will surely reach and serve them.

The relation between the rulers and the people increasingly engaged his attention at this time. In an essay on *Englishmen and Indians* (1893) he pointed out the lack of human touch in the British administration of India. The British rule was terribly efficient, but was purely mechanical and thoroughly impersonal. The rulers need never come into any personal contact with the people ; they might help or hinder their aspiration but only from a disdainful distance. And what might be a matter of mere policy to the rulers might pierce into the very core of life, might threaten the whole future of the governed but never touch the chord of humanity. This was his greatest condemnation of British rule in India.

In a large number of short notes and comments (1893-98) he showed how this mechanical administration was creating in the bureaucracy a mentality which looked upon the subject people as less than human, in dealings with whom the human code of honour and morality could be abrogated. It weakened the moral sense of the white man, and debased the humanity of the rulers as well as that of the governed. In *Remedy to Insults* and in *Digestion of Whipping* (1896) he suggested that the best interests of both Englishmen and Indians demanded that the former should be taught the lesson that the latter could not be insulted with impunity. The lynching of Negroes in the United States, the pogrom against Jews in Russia, or the atrocities in Belgian Congo did not escape his attention and called forth forcible protests (1898).

At the same time, he grew more and more dissatisfied with the activities of politicians which had protests as their sole aim, and proposed that the Indian National Congress, instead of passing resolutions for the benefit of Government, should take up a definite programme of constructive work in the country. The problem of education thus began to loom large in his mind. In *The Tortuosities of Education* (1892) he vigorously advocated making Bengali the medium of instruction and emphasized the need for making education fit in with the life of the people.

Amidst the growing perplexities of social, educational, and political problems, his mind slowly turned to the past in an endeavour to discover in the history of India a central ideal for regulating our life and work. In 1895 we find a small group of poems ; *Brāhman* (in *Chitrā*), *To Civilization, Forests, Forest-homes, Ancient India* (all in *Chaitāli*) in which the mind of the poet was evidently captivated by the Message of the Forest :

> The forest, unlike the desert or rock or sea, is living; it gives shelter and nourishment of life. In such surroundings the ancient forest-dwellers of India realized the spirit of harmony with the universe and emphasized in their minds the monistic aspects of truth. They sought the realization of their soul through union with all.

Shortly after this we have a series of studies in which Rabindranath emphasized that the history of India had not merely been one of the rise and fall of kingdoms, of fights for political supremacy. The history of our people was that of our social life and the pursuit of spiritual ideals.

> The Nation is the organized self-interest of a people where it is least human and least spiritual. The spirit of conflict and conquest is at the origin and in the centre of Western nationalism; its basis is not in social co-operation. It has evolved a perfect organization of power, but not of spiritual idealism.

He contrasted the political civilization of the West which is based on exclusiveness with the social civilization of India which is based on human relationship and co-operation.

He rejected the cult of nationalism very decisively, and in a series of essays and sermons (1898-1902) expounded the ideals of the social civilization which he considered to be the most valuable contribution of India. It was the peculiar gift of India to invest even utilitarian relations with human value. The ideal of Indian civilization was the unitary society which was maintained through the social regulation of differences on one hand, and the spiritual recognition of unity on the other. Rabindranath rejoiced in the fact that when Asoka was the Emperor of India, he sent messengers of peace and universal love, instead of conquering armies, to the different countries of the world. The Poet found the truth of India in the spiritual message of the Upanishads and of the Buddha.

The *Naivedya* poems of this period (1900-01) are permeated by an austere spiritual idealism. At the close of the 19th century, just before the outbreak of the South African War, he wrote with almost prophetic vision :

> The last sun of the century sets amidst the blood-red clouds of the West
> and the whirlwind of hatred.
> The naked passion of self-love of Nations, in its drunken delirium of greed,
> is dancing to the clash of steel and the howling verses of vengeance.

He knew that this was not the way of India :

> Keep watch, India.
> Be not ashamed, my brothers to stand before the proud and the powerful.
> Let your crown be of humility, your freedom the freedom of the soul.
> And know that what is huge is not great, and pride is not everlasting.

Rabindranath reminded his countrymen again and again :

> With the help of unrighteousness men do prosper.
> With the help of unrighteousness men do gain victories over their enemies.
> With the help of unrighteousness men do attain what they desire.
> But they perish at the root.

In order to give concrete form to his ideas he left Shileida and started the *Brahma-Vidyālaya* (as the school used to be called at that time) at Santiniketan in December, 1901, on the model of the forest-hermitages of ancient India. Rabindranath sent his invitation in the name of the One who was *Sāntam, Śivam, Advaitam* :

> The Peaceful, in the heart of all conflicts; the Good, who is revealed through all losses and sufferings; the One, in all diversities of creation.

IV

In 1904 the Swadeshi movement broke in tumult all over Bengal. To Rabindranath it came as a splendid opportunity for initiating a great movement for constructive work of which he had been dreaming so long : We must look after our own interests, carry out our own work, earn our own welfare, do everything ourselves.

Of our impoverished and helpless villages he said : It will not do merely to remove wants ; you can never remove them completely ; the far greater thing is to rouse the will of the people to remove their own wants.

He gave a complete scheme of constructive work in the presidential address to the Provincial Congress at Pabna (1907), and suggested that our young men should form themselves into bands of workers who would go round the villages ; give a new orientation to the village fairs (*melās*), bring together Hindus and Muslims in fruitful work ; confer with and help the villagers in starting schools, making roads, supplying drinking water and the like ; devise other ways and means in regard to all matters of general interest. In his address to the students (1905) he said :

> The down-trodden and the despised who have become callous to insults and oblivious of even the rights of their humanity must be taught the meaning of the word brother. Teach them to be strong and to protect themselves; for that is the only way. Take, each of you, charge of some village and organize it. Educate the villagers and show them how to put forward their united strength. Look not for fame or praise in this undertaking. Do not expect even the gratitude of those for whom you would give your life, but be prepared rather for their opposition.

His sympathy for the lowly and the despised has also found expression in his poems, for example, in the *Gitanjali* in '*My unfortunate land, you must come down in humiliation to the level of those whom you have despised.*'

Rabindranath threw himself heart and soul into the agitation against the Partition of Bengal. He gave lectures, wrote articles, composed a large number of songs such as '*My Golden Bengal,*' '*From the heart of Bengal, you have arisen in your glory, my Mother*' whose central theme was Bengal and which created a patriotic fervour never known before. He spread the use of the hand-loom, experimented with the *charka,* and actively participated in the organization of co-operative societies and cottage industries. It is interesting to note that in *Leader of the Country* (1905), he proposed that a single individual should be invested with full powers of leadership. In his opinion such a step would consolidate the discipline of the people in a personal allegiance to an individual man.

In his writings of this time he made it clear that he considered it a moral duty to fight evil. In fact, although he has no faith in force or violence, he has never given non-violence the status of a cult. His position in this respect is more akin to that of the Gita. For example, in an article written in 1903, he thought it right, under certain circumstances, to have recourse to force, provided this could he done without hatred or anger.

Throughout the Swadeshi movement his mind remained essentially creative and positive. In one of his letters we find :

> I remember the day, during the Swedeshi movement in Bengal, when a crowd of young students came to see me, and said that if I would ask them to leave their schools and colleges, they would instantly obey. I was emphatic in my refusal to do so, and they went away angry, doubting the sincerity of my love for my country.

This incident took place in the midst of his activities in connexion with the Bengal National Council of Education, which had been set up as an independent organization in opposition to the University of Calcutta. He was one of its founders, and he worked hard in its cause, made plans, raised money, gave courses of lectures to the students, but was not prepared to support a merely destructive boycott of the official university.

Politics was always a secondary thing with him. His views on the function of the Congress are significant. He said that even if all the political aims of the Congress failed completely, the Congress would still serve a most useful purpose if it succeeded in bringing the different provinces of India into closer personal contact. At the height of the Swadeshi movement he declared that the ultimate object of political work was to mould the mind of the people into one.

In the midst of his activities, as the excitement and the heat of the movement increased, Rabindranath suddenly retired to Santiniketan. The Hindu-Mahomedan problem and the clash of varying interests in India continued, however, to trouble his mind. In his novel *Gora* (1907-09) he laid more and more emphasis on the unifying principle which manifested itself throughout the whole course of the history of India:

> To India has been given her problem from the beginning of history—it is the race problem. Races ethnologically different have in this country come into close contact. This fact has been and still continues to be the most important one in our history. It is our mission to face it and prove our humanity by dealing with it in fullest truth. We have to recognize that the history of India does not belong to one particular race but to a process of creation to which the various races of the world contributed—the Dravidians and the Aryans, the ancient Greeks and the Persians, the Mahomedans of the West and those of Central Asia.

Just at this time violence made its first appearance in Indian politics. In an important essay on *The Way and its Fare* (1908), Rabindranath tried to stem the impatience which sought quick results through violence. He opposed recourse to violence, not by an appeal to an abstract moral maxim, but on the ground that it violated the truth and ultimate purpose of the history of India.

In the same essay he insisted upon the need for toleration in the face of opposition, and advised the lifting of the ban on British goods on the ground that the boycott movement was accentuating Hindu-Mahomeden differences and was encouraging race hatred. He described the conflict of ideals of this period at a later date in the novel *The Home and the World* (1915-16).

In *East and West* (1908) he said: In India, the history of humanity is seeking to achieve a definite synthesis. The history of India is not the history of Aryans or non-Aryans; it is not the history of the Hindus, nor that of only Hindus and Musalmans taken together. He declared:

> Now at last has come the turn of the English to become true to this history and bring to it the tribute of their life, and we neither have the right nor the power to exclude this people from the building of the destiny of India.

His vision of the meeting of humanity in India was now complete. It found magnificent expression in two *Gitanjali* poems (1910) begining with, *'I see before my eyes the rolling clouds of humanity,'* and *'On the sacred shores of the ocean of humanity of this India, Awake my heart.'*

V

The award of the Nobel prize in 1913 gave him the opportunity of establishing personal contacts with the different countries of the world. During the Great War he joined the intellectuals of the world in issuing a Manifesto against war. In 1916 he toured in Japan and America, and delivered the well-known lectures on *'Nationalism'* which contain his indictment of the modern Nations which had become organized as machinery of rapine and destruction. The contrast between the aggressive spirit of the modern West and the peaceful ideals of the ancient East became increasingly vivid. When he returned to his own country his thoughts naturally turned to the heritage of ancient India. He felt the need for an institution which would be a true centre of human culture.

In 1918 in his lectures on *'The Centre of Indian Culture'* he faced the two stupendous problems of India: the poverty of intellectual life and the poverty of material life. He proposed to start an institution which would be a centre of Indian learning for the co-ordinated study of the philosophy and literature, art and music of the various cultural streams of India: the Vedic, the Puranic, the Buddhist, the Jaina, the Islamic, the Sikh, and the Zoroastrian ; to which would be gradually added the Chinese, the Tibetan and the Japanese. This institution would also be a centre of the economic life of India.

> It must cultivate land, breed cattle, feed itself and its students; it must produce all necessaries, devising the best means and using the best materials, calling science to its aid. Such an institution must group round it all the neighbouring villages, and vitally unite them with itself in all its economic endeavours.

The Poet coined the word 'Visva-bharati' at this time *Viśva* in Sanskrit means the world in its universal aspect ; *Bhāratī* is wisdom and culture.* The Visva-bharati was to be the centre of learning for the whole world. Appropriately enough the following Sanskrit text was selected as the motto of the Visva-bharati :

Yatra Viśvam bhavaty eka-nīḍam:
'Where the whole world forms its one single nest.'

Since the days of the Swadeshi movement Rabindranath had kept himself aloof from political activities, devoting his energies to his institution at Santiniketam. In 1919, the Jalianwalla Bagh incident, however, brought him into a momentary contact with the political life of the country. He renounced his knighthood, "taking all consequences upon himself in giving voice to the protest of millions of his countrymen, surprised into a dumb anguish of terror." It was a protest recorded in the name of humanity, not in the hope of gaining concessions or to make political capital out of it. This was made clear by his emphatic refusal to support the movement for erecting a memorial at Jaliwanwalla Bagh.

After the end of the Great War, Rabindranath undertook a long tour in 1920-21 in Europe and the United States. He spoke everywhere on the need of the meeting of East and West in a common fellowship of learning and a common spiritual striving for the unity of the human races.

Western science was destined, through the mastery of the laws of nature, to liberate man from the bondage of matter. This was not all. Rabindranath was convinced that the West owed its greatness not only to its marvellous training of intellect and its readiness to suffer martyrdom for the cause of justice and truth but to its spirit of service devoted to the welfare of man. In his appeal to the peoples of the West, he said :

> The world to-day is offered to the West. She will destroy it, if she does not use it for a great creation of man. The materials for such a creation are in the hands of science; but the creative genius is in Man's spiritual ideal.

*There is an allusion to India (*Bhārata*) in the word *Bhārati*, which thus also represents the Spirit of India.

When he returned to India in 1921, the non-co-operation movement was at its highest. Although great pressure was put upon him from all sides, he steadfastly refused to join it. He was unable to accept the claim of a spiritual movement made in its behalf.

He could never agree to isolating India from the stream of world thought and progress. In the midst of an unprecedented political unrest and excitement, and against the whole force of the current of popular sentiment, he expounded his own views with great courage in two lectures, *The Call of Truth* and *The Meeting of Cultures* (1921). He said:

> It is a fact of unique importance in the history of the world to-day, that the human races have come together as they have never done before. . . . The mentality of the world has to be changed in order to meet the new environment of the modern age. Just as, hitherto, the collective egoism of the Nation has been cultivated in our schools, and has given rise to a nationalism which is vainglorious and exclusive, even so will it be necessary now to establish a new education on the basis not of nationalism, but of a wider relationship of humanity.
>
> It has been said in our scriptures: *'atithi devo bhava,'* asking us to realize that the Divine comes to us as our guest, claiming our homage. All that is great and true in humanity is ever waiting at our gate to be invited. It is not for us to question it about the country to which it belongs, but to receive it in our home and bring before it the best we have.
>
> Our wealth is truly proved by our ability to give, and Visva-bharati is to prove this on behalf of India. Our mission is to show that we have a place in the heart of the great world; that we fully acknowledge our obligation of offering it our hospitality.

Rabindranath founded the Visva-bharati in December, 1921, and proclaimed that Visva-bharati was India's invitation to the world, her offer of sacrifice to the highest truth of man.

VI

Since then he has carried the message of the Visva-bharati far and wide. In 1924 he visited China. In his address to his hosts, he reminded them of those days when India sent her messengers of peace and universal love who found their unity of heart with the people of China. The Poet hoped that the old relationship was still there, hidden in the heart of the people of the East, and his visit would reopen the channel of communication. Asia must seek strength in union, but not in competition with the West in selfishness or brutality.

In the autumn of the same year he went to South America at the invitation of Peru on the occasion of the Centenary of its independence, and visited Italy on his way back.

The growing strength of the cult of power with its increasing tendency towards the mechanization of institutions and the repression of personality stirred the Poet deeply. He gave voice to his protest in a number of lectures and essays, and also indirectly in two dramas of this period, *Waterfall* (1922) and *Red Oleanders* (1924).

The possibilities of acquiring money has increased tremendously in modern times. Production has assumed gigantic dimensions. This has led to an enormous number of men being used merely as material; so that human relationships have become utilitarian and men have been deprived of a large part of their humanity. Modern society has lost its integrity; its different sections have become detached and resolved into their elemental character of forces. Labour is a force; so also is Capital; so are the Government and the

People. The repressed personality of man is smouldering in the subconscious mind of the community, and has created a dangerous situation. Faced with the possibility of a disaster, the great Powers of the West are seeking for peace by concentrating their forces for mutual security. The Poet warned them, however, that the conflict of selfish interests was bound to grow more and more acute so long as their league was based on the desire for consolidating past injustice and putting off the reparation of wrongs.

Rabindranath does not believe in systems or organizations. All systems produce evil, sooner or later, when the psychology which is at the root of them goes wrong:

> Therefore I do not put my faith in any new institution, but in the individuals all over the world who think clearly, feel nobly, and act rightly, thus becoming the channels of moral truth.

In 1926 he again went to Europe and received a great welcome in Italy as an honoured guest. He was favourably impressed by the material prosperity of the country, but inspite of his delicate position in having accepted her hospitality, he was unable to accord his approval to a political ideal which had declared its loyalty to brute force as the motive power of civilization. He made an extensive tour in the contries of Western and Central Europe, and visited the Balkan States, Turkey and Egypt. In *The Rule of the Giant* (1926), one of the lectures delivered during this tour, he described the suppression of the human personality as the parent ill of the present age. He admitted the need for having organizations. These help to simplify the application of energy for attaining our purpose. They are our tools. But if this fact is forgotten, and huge and hungry organizations are allowed to overwhelm the individual man, then the life stuff of humanity will be eaten up. The only remedy was to restore the value of personality in human civilization.

> I believe in life, only when it is progressive; and in progress, only when it is in harmony with life. I preach the freedom of man from the servitude of the fetish of hugeness, the non-human. I refuse to be styled an enemy of enlightenment, because I do stand on the side of Jack the human, who defies the big, the gross, and wins victory at the end.

In 1927 Rabindranath visited the Malay States, Java, Bali, and Siam, and revived the ancient bond of India with these countries, which at one time were culturally integral parts of India. In 1929 he attended the Triennial Conference of the National Council of Education of Canada. He was the outstanding figure at the Conference, and he roused a wonderful enthusiasm wherever he went. The welcome given to him gradually became not only a personal homage to his greatness but also a testimony of good will from Canada to India itself. On his way home to India from Canada, he visited Indo-China. In 1930, in his seventieth year, he again undertook an extensive tour in the West, visiting England, France, Germany, Denmark, Russia and the United States.

The visit to Russia created a deep impression on his mind, and his *Letters from Russia* (1930-31) give a remarkable picture of the Soviet experiments in State Socialism. On the eve of his departure from Moscow he said:

> I wish to let you know how deeply I have been impressed by the amazing intensity of your energy in spreading education among the masses, I appreciate it all the more keenly because I belong to that country where millions of my fellow countrymen are denied the light that education can bring them. You have recognized the truth that in extirpating all social evils one has to go to the root, which can only be done through education.

But he remained a convinced individualist. Freedom of mind was essential for the reception of truth. Creative activity would cease in a world rendered completely sterile by a mechanical regularity of opinions. In his farewell message he told his hosts:

> I must ask you: Are you doing your ideal a service by arousing in the minds of those under your training, anger, class hatred and revengefulness against those not sharing your views? You are working in a great cause. Therefore you must be great in your mind, great in your mercy, your understanding, and your patience.

VII

The humanism of Rabindranath Tagore has its deeper source of inspiration in his Religion of Man which is the highest expression of his own spiritual experience.

The universe has significance only in terms of human values. Beauty has no existence apart from the appreciation of man. All values have their orgin in the mind of man. Even the truth of science is reached through the process of observation and reasoning which is human; its value as truth being a creation of the human mind. Science can only deal with such facts as man can know and understand, and the Absolute which is beyond the intellect of man can never be the subject matter of scientific investigations. The nature of the universe does not, however, depend upon the comprehension of the individual person. There exists a universal mind of humanity which transcends separate individual minds, and has an integrity of its own which is something more than the sum of its components. It endures beyond the life of the individual person. It is super-individual, it is the Universal Mind. The truth of science receives its validity by reference to the standards of judgement of this Universal Mind. Truth thus has its existence in the Universal Mind, and is independent of the comprehension of the peculiariaties of individual minds which are limited in space and time.

It is not merely a reasoning mind. It is also the ultimate ground of all other values. It is the Supreme Personality: "The God of this human universe whose mind we share in all true knowledge, love and service."

It is the Eternal Person manifested in all persons. It may be only one aspect of *Brahman,* the One in which is comprehended Man and the Human Universe. But this is the only aspect in which he can reveal himself to human beings.

> He is the infinite ideal of Man, towards whom men move in their collective growth, with whom they seek their union of love as individuals, in whom they find their ideal of father, friend, and beloved.

For Rabindranath this is not an abstract philosophical system; it is a matter of direct spiritual realization. In his Hibbert Lectures (1930-31) he has described his first experiences when he was working in the Tagore estates:

> On that morning in the village the facts of my life suddenly appeared to me in a luminous unity of truth. I felt sure that some Being who comprehended me and my world was seeking his best expression in all my experiences. To this Being I was responsible; for the creation in me is his as well as mine. I felt that I had found my religion at last, the Religion of Man, in which the infinite became defined in humanity and came close to me so as to need my love and co-operation.

This idea found expression in the group of poems addressed to *jivan devatā,* the Lord of Life. 'The idea of the humanity of our God, or the divinity of Man the Eternal' was the one theme which unfolded itself through all his religious experiences. Speaking of the time of starting the Santiniketan school, he said:

> I am sure that it was this idea of the divine Humanity unconsciously working in my mind, which compelled me to come out of the seclusion of my literary career and take my part in the world of practical activities.

The meeting of humanity now receives a new significance. It is the acknowledgment of the spiritual kinship of man which is universal. Rabindranath has said:

> So long men had been cultivating, almost with religious fervour, that mentality which is the product of racial isolation; poets proclaimed, in a loud pitch of bragging, the exploits of their popular fighters; money-makers felt neither pity nor shame in the unscrupulous dexterity of their pocket-picking; diplomats scattered lies in order to reap concessions from the devastated future of their own victims. Suddenly the walls that separated the different races are seen to have given way, and we find ourselves face to face.

And thus to all men:

> The God of humanity has arrived at the gates of the ruined temple of the tribe. Though he has not yet found his altar, I ask the men of simple faith, wherever they may be in the world, to bring their offering of sacrifice to him. I ask them to claim the right of manhood to be friends of men.
>
> I ask once again, let us, the dreamers of the East and the West, keep our faith firm in the Life that creates and not in the Machine that constructs.

ya eko' varṇo bahudhā śakti-yogāt
varṇān anekān nihitârtho dadhāti:
vicāiti cânte viśvam ādāu sa devaḥ,
sa no buddhyā śubhayā saṁyunaktu:

He who is One, and who dispenses the inherent needs of all peoples and all times, who is in the beginning and the end of all things, may He unite us with the bond of truth, of common fellowship, of righteousness.

CALCUTTA

PRASANTA CHANDRA MAHALANOBIS

INTUITION AND INTELLECT

IN this short paper it is my intention to indicate, rather dogmatically, my agreement with the view on which Rabindranath Tagore has frequently insisted, that there is greater emphasis in Western thought on critical intelligence and in the Eastern on creative intuition.

EASTERN EMPHASIS ON CREATIVE INTUITION

The alleged dialogue between Socrates and the Indian philosopher suggests that for the whole western tradition man is essentially a rational being, one who can think logically and act in a utilitarian manner. The western mind lays great stress on science, logic and humanism. Hindu thinkers as a class hold with great conviction that we possess a power more interior than intellect by which we become aware of the real in its intimate individuality and not merely in its superficial or discernible aspects. For the Hindus a system of philosophy is an insight, a *darśana*. It is the vision of truth and not a matter of logical argument and proof. They believe that the mind can be freed by gradual training from the influences of speculative intellect as well as past impressions and that it can unite itself with the object whose nature is then fully manifested.[1] They contend that we can control destiny by the power of truth. Knowledge means power. The lack of this knowledge is the root of all trouble. *Vidyā* is *mokṣa*: *avidyā* is *saṁsāṛa*. Intuitive realisation is the means to salvation. He who knows is saved directly and immediately, and by means of that knowledge. Intuitive insight is identical with freedom. "Whoever knows 'I am Brahman' becomes this all."[2] "He who knows that supreme Brahman becomes that Brahman itself."[3] We cannot know Brahman fully and truly, unless we partake of its essence, become one with it. To know God is to become divine, free from any outside influence likely to cause fear or sorrow. Brahman which symbolises the absolute reality means also holy knowledge, intuitive wisdom. Intuitive wisdom becomes personified as the first principle of the universe. He who knows it knows the essence of the cosmos. The acceptance of the authority of the Vedas by the different systems of Hindu thought is an admission that intuitive insight is a greater light in the abstruse problems of philosophy than logical understanding. Śaṅkara, for example, regards *anubhava* or integral experience as the highest kind of apprehension. While it may not be clear and distinct, it is sure and vivid. Buddha emphasises the importance of *bodhi* or enlightenment. His impatience with metaphysical subtleties is well known. The sophistries of the intellect were according to him hindrances to the higher life. Knowledge of reality is to be won by spiritual effort. One cannot think one's way into reality but

[1] *Vaiśeṣika Sūtra* (IX. 2.13): Different names are given to this apprehension which is not due to the senses or inference such as *prajñā, pratibhā, ārṣa-jñāna, siddha-darśana, yogi-pratyakṣa*; Jayanta's *Nyāya-mañjarī*, p. 178; *Bhāṣā-pariccheda*, 66.

[2] *Bṛhadāraṇyaka Upaniṣad*, 1.4.10 & 15.

[3] *Muṇḍaka Upaniṣad*, III 2.9.

only live into it. In early Buddhism *prajñā* or intuitive insight represents the highest activity of the human mind. The general tendency of Hindu and Buddhist thought is to take hold of the aspiration of the human soul after a higher life, and treat this fact as the key to the interpretation of the universe, and all critical philosophy took this into account.

WESTERN EMPHASIS ON CRITICAL INTELLIGENCE

While the dominant feature of Eastern thought is its insistence on creative intuition, the Western systems are generally characterised by a greater adherence to critical intelligence. This distinction is not to be pressed too closely. It is relative and not absolute. It describes the chief tendencies and there are in fact many exceptions. It is only a question of the distribution of emphasis.

If we may trust the Pythogorean tradition, the method and achievements of Greek philosophy were largely affected by the example of mathematics. Socrates is credited by Aristotle with two things, inductive arguments and universal definitions. Whatever is real must have a definable form. Things are in virtue of their forms. The classification of moral concepts is the first step to any improvement in practice. Suggested definitions are tested by Socrates with reference to actual facts. For Plato, geometry was the model science. Even God geometrises. Aristotle invented the science of logic. For him, man is pre-eminently a rational animal. Logic for the Greeks is not so much a science of discovery as one of proof. The civic life of the ancient Greeks centred round the assembly and the law courts, where intellectual subtlety and mental dexterity are most in demand. The great aim was to secure victory in debate, and the chief means to it was to master the technique of argument. More prominence was given to the expression and communication of thought than to its discovery and growth. There is an intimate relation between grammar and logic in Aristotle's *Organon*. The tendency to stereotype thought in conventional ways grew up. The canons of formal logic would be of excellent use, when all truths were discovered and nothing more remained to be known, but logic cannot dictate or set limits to the course of nature and progress of discovery.

I have no doubt that this summary description is quite inadequate to the complexity and richness of Greek thought. The non-mathematical side of Plato's teaching is perhaps his most important contribution. For Plato, noesis is the highest kind of knowledge, and supra-intellectual. He believed in what he called dialectic or the conversation of the soul with itself, which is not scientific knowledge. Aristotle speaks of the absolute self-knowledge of God, a pure activity which knows no law and no end outside itself. This is not the place to discuss the alleged influence of Eastern thought on the Orphic mysteries and Pythagoras and through them on Plato's philosophy. Pythagoras and Plato may owe to Indian thought more than the Hellenists are willing to admit.[1]

[1] The Dean of St. Paul's traces this mode of Plato's teaching to Asiatic thought. Professor Muirhead commenting on Dean Inge's *Platonic Tradition in English Religious Thought* (1926) says: "Beginning in Asia, this mystical faith swept over Greece and Southern Italy in the form of Orphism and Pythagoreanism. It found an intelligent sympathiser in Socrates, and under his inspiration

Speaking generally, however, it is not incorrect to hold that the Greeks attempted to give an explanation of the problem of certainty in terms of logical reason and failed to justify the logical postulates themselves.

Plotinus[2] and the New-Platonists were convinced that logical knowledge alone was inadequate. Neo-platonism, which originated in Alexandria, where Oriental modes of thought were not unknown, presented a more organic view and grounded logical processes on the certainty of immediate experience. But the post-scholastic philosophers fell back upon a purely rationalistic approach to certainty and the attempt to ground philosophy in science became more popular with the growth of natural sciences, which were actually engaged in pushing back the frontiers of knowledge through observation and experimental verification. Though the methodology of the sciences studied the processes by which beliefs grew and thoughts evolved, its actual interest was more in the grammar of discovery than the life of it. The latter by its very nature sets limits to logical exposition.

For Descartes, with whom modern European philosophy takes a new direction, truth means clearness and distinctness. Whatever can be expressed in mathematical form is clear and distinct. Descartes sets forth a system of universal concepts of reason, which are derived from a consideration of certain fundamental logical and mathematical relationships. In a famous sentence, he observes, "I was especially delighted with mathematics. I was astonished that foundations so strong and solid should have had no loftier superstructure raised on them." His conception of universal mathematics and faith that all things are mutually related, as the objects of geometry,[3] imply a strictly mechanical world. For Spinoza, even Ethics should be treated by the geometrical method. For Leibniz, again, the monads or perceiving minds differ in nothing other than the *form* of perception, for each monad resembles the others as regards the content of its perception. Each reflects the total universe from its own special angle. But the lowest monads, the plant and the animal ones, have dim and confused mode of perception. Divine cognition consists in completely distinct and adequate ideas. We human beings are in between. Our ideas of sense qualities are confused, those of logic and mathematics distinct. We attempt to transform the former into the latter kind, factual presentations into notions conceived by reason. The accomplishment of this ideal means for Leibniz the setting forth of a general system of the possible forms of thought and the universal laws of connection which these laws obey. Such a plan was outlined by Leibniz in his *General Characteristics,* which is the foundation, in a sense, of symbolic logic, which reached its great development in the works of Boole, and Peano, Frege and Russell.

Kant's fundamental aim was to lead philosophy into the safe road of science, and he inquired into the possibility of philosophy as a science with the intention of formulating

reached its highest expression in the Dialogues of Plato." *The Platonic Tradition in Anglo-Saxon Philosophy* (1931), p. 27.

[2] Plotinus accompanied Gordian's army in order that he may have an opportunity of studying Indian and Persian philosophy. Though Gordian's death in Mesopotamia stopped him half way, his enthusiasm for it is evident.

[3] *The Philosophical Works of Descartes,* Eng. Tr. by Haldane and Ross (1911), Vol. I, p. 92.

its conditions. The 'Nature' with which we deal in science and everyday life is due to the work of the understanding which arranged the multiplicity of sense in an orderly world according to a logic which Kant distinguished as synthetic from the traditional formal or analytic logic. His successors took over this logic of synthesis and utilised it for the purpose of resolving the imperfections of Kant's system. The tendency in Kant to postulate an intelligible world as the foundation of ethics is dismissed as irrelevant and the world of things in themselves declared a poetic fiction. In Hegel, logic ceases to be a mere theory of thought but becomes an account of reality. It is an abstract representation of an actual process by which the absolute spirit reveals itself as the universe in the different forms which the universe assumes to human consciousness, nature, history, society, art and religion. "What is rational is real, and what is real is rational."[1] Hegel's view of history as the manifestation of spirit in the threefold moments of thesis, antithesis and synthesis is an intellectual scheme which largely forced the facts into conformity with an *a priori* formula. Hegel's influence is continued in the later idealists. "No fact," says Edward Caird, "which is in its nature incapable of being explained or reduced to law, can be admitted to exist in the intelligible universe."[2] For the Hegelians, reality is essentially knowable in the logical way. While Bosanquet is more Hegelian in his outlook, Bradley is more Kantian. For Bradley, thought moves within the realm of relationships and can never grasp or positively determine the ultimate reality. The realists are the worshippers of logic and the scientific method. Faith in the logical intellect as the supreme instrument of knowledge has led the realistic thinkers to devote their major energies to the precise formulation of specialised problems. The Behaviourists insist on the close relation between thinking and talking and reduce thinking to a matter of language or expression. In the words of Max Müller, "To think is to speak low. To speak is to think aloud."

From the Socratic insistence on the concept to Russell's mathematical logic, the history of Western thought has been a supreme illustration of the primacy of the logical. Rationalism is deep in our bones and we feel secure about scientific knowledge and sceptical about religious faith. If "there is no higher faculty than those involved in ordinary knowledge," if 'the truth of religion' or the validity of religious experience is to be established, "as reasonable inference from discursive knowledge about the world, human history, the soul with its faculties and capacities, and above all from knowledge of the inter-connection between such items of knowledge,"[3] then it will be difficult for us to be certain about God. But the tradition of religion holds that those who have known God by acquaintance and not by hearsay, have known him not as a valid conclusion from logical reasoning but by the constraining authority of experience.

ANDHRA UNIVERSITY, WALTAIR — S. RADHAKRISHNAN

[1] Hegel: *The Philosophy of Right*: Eng. Tr. by Dyde (1896), p. xxvii.
[2] Hegel: p. 141. See also Ritchie: *Philosophical Studies*, p. 226; Watson: *The Interpretation of Religious Experience* (1912).
[3] Tennant: *Philosophical Theology*, Vol. I (1928), Ch. XII, p. 325 ff.

MUNDARI POETRY

THERE is no known people on earth so rude as to be devoid of poetry and song. The so-called 'savage' has neither the innate inferiority in mental capacity which uninformed popular opinion associates with him, nor the 'pre-logical' mind which Levy-Brühl and some other anthropologists attribute to him. The 'primitive' man is as much human as members of the most advanced communities, and, though his categories of thought may be different, his processes of thought and reasoning are the same as ours, and he too is moved by the same emotions as we are, and feels as often as, if not more often than, we do, the inner urge for giving artistic expression to the surging emotions of his soul. Poetry, like Religion, is, in fact, one of the earliest devices by which primitive man sought temporary relief from the troubles and anxieties which beset him and the burden of emotions that oppressed him.

The older belief in the comparatively recent evolution and brief duration of humanity and human civilization has now been dispelled by Science. Thanks to the revolutionary researches of Pre-historic Archæology, we now know that the antiquity of civilized man —'man who had invented language and was a first-class artist'—cannot be measured by centuries or even by millennia. Our comparatively primitive tribes have for countless generations been carrying on the same interminable struggle with the forces of Nature that the more advanced communities in more favourable environments have waged with better success. As a result of this age-long struggle with Nature, the so-called 'primitive' tribes, too, have succeeded in working out a form of civilization of their own, which though inferior in refinement and complexity to those of the more advanced communities, is not different in essence. The character and pattern of each civilization, its outlook on life, its fundamental beliefs and categories of thought, are determined by its particular environment and history, and are faithfully reflected in its Poetry as in its Religion.

In this paper, it will be out of place to enter into a discussion of the origin and development of the poetic art and its manifestations at different levels of culture.

I shall here content myself with briefly noting the salient characteristics of primitive poetry as revealed in the songs of one of our principal aboriginal hill-tribes,—the pre-Aryan and pre-Dravidian Mūṇḍās of Chōṭā-Nāgpur. The comparatively peaceful life of agriculturists with its intervals of leisure has enabled the Mūṇḍās to build up a poetic technique of their own, which serves to give outer expression, however halting and imperfect, to their inner emotions.

The primitive Mūṇḍā seeks to make up for the deficiencies of his language by various simple expedients of which the following are the most marked: Repetition of the same concept in synonymous or almost synonymous words and expressions in successive lines or stanzas so as to present a vivid and complete picture of the object or idea sought to be portrayed ; the employment of quaint circumlocutions and concrete words to express abstract ideas for which he has no words in his language ; the employment of terms expressive of individual and concrete objects to express generic or collective and class names for which he has few terms in his native vocabulary ; the use of obsolete or foreign (Hindi) words to add force and emphasis to synonymous words in his own tongue ; the employment of parallels and contrasts, synonyms and antonyms, metaphors and allegories to add vividness and emphasis to an idea or picture ; the reduplication of words or syllables and the use of onomatopoetic words and jingles and sonorous compound-words, the lengthening of vowel-sounds for the sake of euphony or emphasis ; the infixing of short vowels in the middle of words and suffixing of such vowels at the end of words for the sake of melody ; the use of an initial liquid *n*-sound before words beginning with a vowel, and the omission of an aspirate *h* at the beginning of a word, to secure a smooth flowing sound.

As Mūṇḍā poems are mostly songs meant to be sung and not recited, the beauty of rhymes does not appear to have particularly impressed the Mūṇḍā poet. Such rhymes as occur here and there in Mūṇḍā poetry are more accidental than deliberate ; the same or similar grammatical suffixes (*tānā, kānā, etc.*) would account for most of them.

Although the Mūṇḍā poet appears to appreciate the beauty of symmetry and proportion and the desirability of having a uniform number of syllables in each line of a poem or song, he more often fails than succeeds in securing such uniformity. The length of the line, however, is sought to be accommodated to the length of the melody by the repetition of words or syllables, by the insertion of expletives such as *go, ogo, ho, do, he, re, ge,* and by the addition of terms of endearment like *dādā, māi, miru, mainā,* besides the lengthening of vowel-sounds and the infixing and suffixing of redundant vowels to which I have already referred.

With devices like these, the humble Mūṇḍā singer manages to give in such rhythmical language as his own ideas of harmony dictate and the resources of his speech permit, concrete artistic expression to the emotional reactions produced in his mind by the stimuli of the outer world around him.

Deficiencies in the rhythmic flow of words in his songs the Mūṇḍā singer further seeks to eke out in part by the rhythmic movements of his feet in dance,—for the bulk of the Mūṇḍā's poetic productions is in the form of songs meant to accompany his seasonal dances. In fact, there are reasons to believe that rhythm and metre in poetry, the varying cadences of sound in song and the regular intervals of time represented by the line, the half-line, the couplet and the stanza in poetry, originally reflected the varying steps of the dance ; that dance and song, if not related to each other as elder and younger sisters, are, at any rate, the twin-daughters of Emotion. And instrumental Music was devised quite early as a helpful handmaid.

Mūṇḍā youths of both sexes sing these dancing songs together, the young men playing upon musical instruments and standing a little apart from the girls. The young men begin a song, and when they have sung a distich the girls take it up and repeat it or the last lines of it in chorus with generally slight variations towards the end, and dance to the tune of the song.

Although the bulk of Mūṇḍāri songs, are, as I have stated, meant to be sung at the seasonal dances, it may be noted, however, that there are some songs which may not be accompanied by dance. Some such are specially sung at weddings with or without dances, a few are composed by magicians and sung, unaccompanied by dances, at their incantations and seances, a few are sung by children at certain singing games, and a fewer still are narrative songs inserted in some of their folk-stories known as 'Durāng-kāhāni' or 'song-stories.'

However halting and imperfect, in many respects, the manner of his poetic expression may be, the matter of the Mūṇḍā's poetry is mostly concerned with some of those elemental and permanent affections common to humanity. The joys and sorrows of youthful love are portrayed by the Mūṇḍā poet with sincerity and depth of feeling in a large number of songs. The affections and anxieties of parents for their children, and the anguish of bereavement through death are expressed in a few songs of simple pathos. The hilarious enjoyment of work in his fields, the joyful anticipation of a good harvest, the keen excitement and gusto of hunting and war, the exhilarating pleasures of dancing and singing, music and merry-making, the pleasurable excitement of youth in attending a periodical fair or festival,—all these find vivid expression in many a Mūṇḍāri song.

In a considerable number of dainty little songs, the Mūṇḍā poet expresses his joyous appreciation of the beauty of natural objects in his fields and groves, hills and valleys, streams and woods. A lovely landscape, the green and yellow crops waving in the breeze, the lovely flowers of various forms and hues in jungle and grove, the silvery white fishes sparkling in the sun as they glide in wavy movements in the limpid waters of his native hill-streams or ensconce themselves in their silvery sand-beds, the pretty birds of his fields and woods, bushes and briars, hopping about and chirping, and singing in joyful or plaintive notes, around him and above him, the manifold sights and sounds of the inanimate and animate worlds that surround him,—these feed his imagination and gladden his heart or move him to tenderness and sympathy. And he is stimulated to artistic creation of beauty in song.

Nor is he altogether insensible to the sublimer aspects of Nature. The violent summer storms that sometimes tear down the giant trees of his forests and despoil the birds of their nests and men of their huts, the sudden floods of his narrow native hill-streams that carry away man and beast and tree in their mad vehemence, the dangers from venomous serpents and beasts of prey that lurk in hill and forest,—these make a deep impression on his mind and form the themes of some of his songs.

Some of his songs, again, though not directly didactical, indirectly tend to emphasise the customary moral code of the tribe. These either hold up to ridicule or brand with infamy or depict in lurid colours the unenviable fate of rebels against time-honoured tribal regulations in matters regarded by the tribe as of vital moment to society, such as restrictions relating to love and marriage, touch-taboos and food-taboos, and the like.

Lastly, in a few of his songs the Mūṇḍā poet rises to the dignity of a primitive philosopher. And we hear the Mūṇḍā singer bewailing the decay of youth and beauty, the uncertainty of life, and the impermanence of earthly pleasures.

Owing to the limited space accorded to a contributor to this volume, I regret I cannot in this paper give illustrations of the various characteristics of Mūṇḍāri poetry noted above. I shall content myself with merely citing two or three examples of the Mūṇḍā's love-songs.

In the following simple song, the Mūṇḍā singer expresses the anguish of a lover at the absence of his sweet-heart, his ardent longing for her return, and his joy at reunion.

Youth: *Hijume rē, gāting, mōntāing dō gōsō jān,*
Hō rē gāting, chiulārē gāting nelṛuāṛmē?
Hōrāging nelā, piṛiging āridā.
Hō rē gāting, chiulārē gāting nelṛuāṛmē?

Hijulenāng, gāting, montāing dō sukujānā
Hō rē gāting chiulārē, gāting, kāing bāgimā.
Hōrāging nelā piṛiging āridā
"Hō rē, gāting, chiulārē, gāting, nelṛuāṛmē?"

Maiden: *Hōrārē bāgṛibā bākṛirē chāmpā bāhā*
Chāmpā bāhārē gāting gūtū tūkāingme.
Hōrāgingō nelā piṛigingō āridā,
"Hō rē gāting, chiulārē gāting, nelṛuāṛmē?"

[*Translation*]

Youth: Come, my love, to my heart withered like a dried-up flower,
O, my beloved, when shall I find thee again?
I have been watching [longingly] the road, I have been watching [fondly] the fields [for thee]:
Alas, my dear, when shall I find thee again?

Now that thou art back, my love, my heart is glad;
Never again, my love, shall I suffer thee to leave me;
I have kept watching the roads, I have watched the fields,
[Saying—] "O sweet, when shall I find thee again?"

Maiden: There blooms on the road the *gulaichi*, in the garden the *chāmpā*;
With *chāmpā* flowers, my love, do thou weave a wreath for me.
I, too, have watched the roads, I have watched [fondly] the fields,
[Saying—] "O, my love, when shall I find thee again?"

In the following song the Mūṇḍā lover expresses his yearning to meet the maiden of his choice, and his fruitless search from field to field for her :—

Mōdē piṛi lelemerē gāting.
Kām lelō lelōā gāting!
Bārēpiṛi chināmerē, sāngāing,
Kām chināo chināo!

Hūṇḍi-bā-ing gūtūlēdā, gāting,
Kām lelō lelōā, gāting,
Bākāṛi-bā-ing gālāng-ledā, sangaing,
Kām chināo chināo!

Hūṇḍi-bā-ing gūtūlēdā, gāting,
Sutāmregē gōsō-jān!
Sutāmregē gōsō-jānā, gāting,
Sutāmregē gōsō jān!

Bākāṛi-bā-ing gālāngledā, sāngāing,
Chāriregē gōsō jānā!
Chārireing gālāng ledā, sāngāing,
Chāriregē mailā jānā!
Hiatingē moningā, re gāting,
Chākātingē moningā!

Sūtāmregē gōsōjānā, gāting,
Chāriregē mailājānā!

[*Translation*]

In one field I looked [for thee], my dear,
[But] I did not—did not—meet thee, dear!
A second field I searched [for thee], my love,
[There, too] I did not—did not—find thee,

With *hūṇḍi*-flowers, garlands [for thee] I wove, my dear,
[But] did not meet thee—meet thee, dear,
Bākāṛi-flowers I wove into garlands, my love,
[But] did not find thee—find thee.

The *hūṇḍi*-flowers that I wove into wreaths, my dear,
On their threads, did they shrivel up.
They dried up on their threads, my dear,
They shrivelled up on their reeds,

On the reeds on which I strung them, love,
On those same reeds, did they wither.
My heart was sore, my dear,
Full heavy was my heart.

On their threads, the flowers faded, my dear,
On their reeds, did they wither.

In connection with Mūṇḍā love songs, it is worth noting that although there are very few Mūṇḍās who have any knowledge of the Hindu legends of Rādhā and Krishṇa, or indeed have any idea that they belong to Hindu mythology, the love songs of Rādhā-Krishṇa, once sung by Vaishṇava preachers among them and still sung by their Hindu neighbours must have made a deep impression on the Hindi-knowing Mūṇḍā's mind ; and the Mūṇḍās readily borrowed and assimilated such elements from them as appeared to fit in with their own ideal of human love, and incorporated them with suitable modifications in Mūṇḍāri love-songs. Here is an instance of such a song, which its Mūṇḍā singers regard as depicting the love of a youth and maiden of their own tribe :—

Gāṛā jāpā kadamb-sūbā, hendē hendē duti-tādāe,
'Rādhā Rādhā' mente rutui ōṛōng-kenā, nurigāi gō gūpitānā.
Jūi chāmeli gūtū-tānā, nōkōrē tāingā gāting dūbā kānā?
Bā'-tādae bhālā bhālā : supidātadāe hālā hālā,
Kāingleltē med-dā jōrō-tānā
Ōkōrē tāingā gāting dūbā kānā?
Tesan med-dā jōrō-tānā, jesan gāṛā-dā lingitānā,
Ichā-bā'-rē rāsi jōrōtānā,
Ōkōrē tāing gāting dūbākānā?

[*Translation*]

By river's side, under *kadamb* tree, with black-bordered *dhoti* on
Piping the tune of 'Rādhā, Rādhā,' he [my beloved] tends his oxen and kine.
Wreaths of *jūi* and *chāmeli* I weave ; Oh, where doth my beloved tarry ?
[For him] I have decked my hair with flowers choice and sweet,
and woven my braids in pattern fine,
Without sight of him, tears stream down my eyes,
Oh ! where doth my sweetheart tarry ?
Tears trill down my eyes [even] as water flows down the stream,
Or as sweet juice (honey) trickles down an *ichā* flower,
O, where doth my beloved stay away ?

RANCHI, CHOTA NAGPUR, INDIA

SARAT CHANDRA ROY

RABINDRANATH AND WORLD-FORCES

ON the occasion of Rabindranath's seventieth birthday it has occurred to me to read once more some of the verses composed by him in his earlier years. Some three and forty years ago, in 1888, when he was a young man of twenty-seven, the poet wrote *Duranta Āśā* (Unruly Hope). The obstinate hope or rather turbulent wish of this brilliant artistic junior is in part worded as follows:

Ucchwasita rakta āsi *vakṣa-tal pheliche grāsi,* *Prakāś-hīn cintā-rāśi* *kariche hānāhāni.*	Blood enthused comes in a rush and swallows the breast full, And swarms of thoughts unexprest are moving to and fro.
Kothāo yadi chuṭite pāi— *bāñciyā jāi tabe,* *Bhavyatār gaṇḍi-mājhe* *śānti nāhi māni.*	Oh, could I run to somewhere, how alive I would be! Within the bounds of fettered life No peace can I find.

This full-blooded quest of movements, of richness of life, of the peace of unrest with which the poetry of young Rabi greets us, is Whitmanesque in its stir and turmoil. Here we encounter the spirit of "Pioneers, O Pioneers!" in the American *Leaves of Grass*. This is but a phase indeed of the *Sturm und Drang*, of storm and stress, in the life and art of Young India. One is likewise easily reminded of *David Singing Before Saul* in Robert Browning's lines:

"Oh, the wild joys of living! the leaping from rock up to rock,
The strong rending of boughs from the fir tree, the cool silver shock
Of the plunge in a pool's living water, * * * *
And the sleep in the dried river-channel where bulrushes tell
That the water was wont to go warbling so softly and well."

There are very few human beings, especially among poets, painters and other artists whose thoughts have found so ample and so varied expression, and whose career, both artistic and personal or social, has been so full of holidayings from the *bhavyatār gaṇḍi-mājh*, from the fetters of forms formulæ and systems, and punctuated with so many excursions "to somewhere" as Rabindranath Tagore. Neither that great encyclopaedist of the middle ages, the cavalier-mystic-Ghibelline-exile, the author of *Divina Commedia*, nor that "pagan humanist, *der göttliche* Goethe," the poet-scientist-statesman, the father of romanticism in modern literature, would appear to have experienced such fullness, such diversity, such movements as have been lived and sung or painted by Rabindranath.

Several years later, while he was running his thirtieth year, the poet published *Viśva-Nṛtya* (World-Dance). In 1892 his heart aches to find that

Saṁsār-srōt jāhnavī-sama	World-currents like the river Jāhnavī
bahu dūre geche sariyā,	have moved far far away,
E śudhu uṣar bālukā-dhūsar	This land is barren and sandy-grey
maru-rūpe āche mariyā.	and lies like desert dead.

And what are the marks of *maru-rūpe āche mariyā,* of lying "dead as desert?" There are to be found

"No motion's trace and no song,
No work, no inspiration."

But what is his own heart's desire? Says he:

Hṛday āmār krandan kare	My heart is longing and crying
mānav-hṛdaye miśite,	to mix with human hearts,
Nikhiler sāthe mahā rāja-pathe	With the world on the great highways
calite divas-niśīthe.	to travel day and night.

Nay, more. Rabi would not be content if this heart-to-heart world-intercourse, this pilgrimage among human beings, is enjoyed by himself alone. This enrichment of life, these "wild joys of living," this greatening of the soul, he longs at the same time for the people of his land too. He asks—

Jagat-mātāno saṅgīt-tāne	With the world-maddening music
ke dibe eder nācāye?	who is there to make them dance?
Jagater prāṇ karāiyā pān	By making them drink of the world's life
ke dibe eder bāñcāye?	who is there to enliven them?

Tagore here yearns after a state of things such as is in a certain measure depicted in the following words, again, of Browning's ***David***:

"Oh, our manhood's prime vigour! No spirit feels waste,
Not a muscle is stopped in its playing nor sinew unbraced.
How good is man's life, the mere living! how fit to employ
All the heart and the soul and the senses for ever in joy!"

All these longings after "great highways," night and day travels, world-dance, and so forth were more than a dozen years before the "event of 1905," when Bengal and along with Bengal the whole of India started dancing with the "world-maddening music" of Asian unrest. To-day in 1931 it is but a bare fact of literary biography to record that Rabi's life and art did not cease to flow with merely declaring the "unruly hope" of abandon and unrest or with simply posing the question as to who was to make his countrymen "drink of world's life." Rabi has ever been a going concern, always on the world's highways, perpetually on the move.

Rabi has been on the move from the city to the village, from the plains to the hills, from the forests to the rivulets, from the jasmine to the stars. He has been on the move from the peasants to the princes, from the masses to the classes, from the warriors and statesmen to the folk-minstrels, from the moderns to the mediævals, from the past to the present, from the Hindu to the Musalman and from them both to the Christian and the Jew. He has been on the move from district to district, from province to province, from continent to continent, from India to Japan and China, to Europe, to the New Hemisphere and back again to India, from the East to the West and from the West to the East.

The limits of conventions and the bounds of controlled life he has transcended, he has drunk and drunk deep of the world's living springs, the world-maddening music of the varied races and regions he has made his own. He has danced with the *Bāul* singers of Bengal, the *Abhañg*-poets of the Marathas, and the *Cārans* of the Rajputs. He has danced with the street-processionists of the *Swadeshi* epoch, with the boys and girls of his own Santiniketan, with the young men and women of the four quarters of the globe. Like Naṭarāja he has participated in the dance of the universe. This characteristic *élan vital* has rendered the Rabindric literary and artistic creations so many moments in the continuous expression of the dynamic spirit itself,—of the yearning to move, to break, to grow, of the heart's keen solicitude to experience the contacts of other hearts, of the all-absorbing passion to cultivate the intimacy of world-forces.

I remember once again some of the lines written by Rabindranath in 1888 at the age of twenty-seven. An important landmark of his artistic career is embodied in the poem entitled *Parityakta* (Forsaken). We encounter him in the act of dedicating himself to the motherland, in the following lines:

Dāṇḍāye viśāl dharaṇīr tale
ghuce gela bhay lāj,
Bujhite pārinu e jagat mājhe
āmāro rayeche kāj.

As I stood on the wide Earth,
disappeared all fear and shame:
I could feel that in this world
even for me there was some work.

Swadeśer kāche dāṇḍāye prabhāte
kahilām joḍ kare—
'Ei laha, mātaḥ, e cira jīvan
sonpinu tomāri tare.'

So I stood by my country one morn
and prayed with folded hands:
"Accept, O Mother, all my life,
this I consecrate to Thee."

This is a noble dedication of self to the Motherland.

It is to be observed, however, that with one breath Rabi's blood was longing for excursions into the universe, but with another it was seeking self-realization in the country's service. Has it been possible to construct a bridge between the country and the universe, the home and the world, the known and the unknown, the near and the far?

The activities, restlessnesses, travels of Rabindranath,—these world-contacts or minglings with the world-forces, these pilgrimages among mankind known and unknown, these experiences of shoulder-rubbings with "strange faces, other minds" have not turned out to be the idle luxuries of a Bohemian aesthete. Asia, Europe, Africa, America, all have realized that this restless globe-trotter from Bengal, this unruly Indian vagabond has by his gentle pilgrim's staff succeeded in engineering the "world-currents" back to the land of his birth and in transporting his people into the whirlpool of the world-forces. In regard to the emergence of the "Indian question" as an important item of international politics, economics and culture, not the least powerful formative agency have been these hemispheroidal "day and night travels" of this indefatigable *avatar* of *Wanderlust.*

The last quarter of a century has been one of the most momentous epochs in the creative activities of the Indian people. As some of the loftiest and noblest specimens of these creations the personality, poetry, prose and paintings of Rabindranath have contributed enormously to the possibility of the Indian people utilizing the international forces, political, economic and cultural, in the interest of its own expansion. Tagore, the singer of "unruly hope," the poet of "world-maddening dance-music," the romantic wanderer among human hearts, requires thus to be appraised also as an architect of the India of "entangling alliances," of an India which by constant association with the powers great, medium and small, Asian and Eur-American, seeks to "drink of the world's life" and acquire a fresh lease of existence, free and unfettered, mighty and prosperous. Not many Indians have served their motherland as effectively and substantially as this poet of the hemispheres, the artist of the world-forces.

Well has Rabindranath served his country as well as mankind. So on the occasion of his seventieth birth festival let me offer for him my prayer in the words of Dante:

"Here kneeleth one,
Who of all spirits hath reviewed the state,
From the world's lowest gap unto this height.
Suppliant to thee he kneels, imploring grace
For virtue yet more high, to lift his ken
Toward the bliss supreme."

May the *Mānasa-Sundarī,* the Inspiration-Deity, the "Beatrice" of Rabindranath, lead him on to "virtue yet more high," until he possesses for himself and for us the "bliss supreme."

THE UNIVERSITY, CALCUTTA

BENOY KUMAR SARKAR

SOME THOUGHTS ON AHIMSA

ONE of the foremost contributions of India to the moral progress of mankind is the idea and ideal of *Ahiṁsā*. It is often translated by 'non-violence,' but the Indian term deserves, like *Karma* and *Nirvāṇa,* to be added to the vocabulary of Western languages. It is not often that the etymology of a word gives so full an explanation of its meaning, as in the case of *Ahiṁsā*. The verb *hiṁs* is a desiderative form of *han,* and therefore means 'to wish to slay, to hurt, to injure, to harm,' and the substantive *a-hiṁsā* means 'not wishing to slay, to hurt, to injure, to harm.' The history of *Ahiṁsā* begins with the Chāndogya-Upaniṣad (III, 17, 4) where the moral conduct of man is summarized in the words: *tapo dānam ārjavam ahiṁsā satya-vacanam* 'austerity, alms-giving, righteousness, *Ahiṁsā* and truthfulness.' According to the Yoga-sūtra (II, 30) *Ahiṁsā* is the first of the eight conditions for Yoga. In the Brahmanical Dharma-śāstras *Ahiṁsā* is prescribed as the first rule of a holy life for the Brahmacārin, the Snātaka, and the Sannyāsin, but it also heads the list of the duties of all castes in Manu's law-book (X, 63). In the Mahābhārata we find the story of the shopkeeper Tulādhāra and the Brahman Jājali. The latter, a great Yogin, was standing in the forest, like a wooden post, without moving. A pair of birds came flying towards him, and built their nest in the dishevelled hair of his head, and he did not move until the she-bird had laid eggs in the nest on his head, the eggs were hatched and the young birds were fledged and had flown away. After this mighty feat of asceticism he called out exultingly: 'I have achieved religious merit!' But he was told by a heavenly voice that he was not even equal to Tulādhāra, an honest shopkeeper in Benares. The great Yogin is quite disheartened, goes to Tulādhāra, and enquires of him as to wherein his renowned religious merit consists. Then Tulādhāra explains to him the eternal law of *Ahiṁsā,* which is known as the old doctrine, beneficial to all, the doctrine of love (*maitra*): 'A manner of life which is combined with complete harmlessness, or only with slight harm, to all beings, that is the highest religion; in accordance with this I live, O Jājali....If one fears no being, and no being fears one, if one has preference for nobody and hates nobody, then he becomes united with Brahman."

It is, however, in Buddhism and especially in Jainism that *Ahiṁsā* as the highest moral law (*ahiṁsā paramo dharmaḥ*) is most strongly emphasized. We read in the Jaina scriptures: 'He should not kill, not cause others to kill, not consent to the killing of others.' 'The Arhats and Bhagavats of the past, present, and future, all say thus, speak thus, declare thus, explain thus: no breathing, existing, living, sentient creatures should ever be slain, or treated with violence, or abused, or tormented, or harassed.' 'All beings hate pain, therefore one should not kill them. This is the quintessence of wisdom: not to kill anything." And in Buddhist Sūtras it is said: 'As I am, so are these, as these are, so am I; identifying himself with others, let him not kill nor cause any one to kill.'

'Putting away the murder of that which lives, he abstains from destroying life. The cudgel and the sword he lays aside ; and, full of modesty and pity, he is compassionate and kind to all creatures that have life.'

From a historical point of view, *Ahiṁsā* was at first, like *tapas,* the virtue of the perfect man, the ascetic, the saint, who had to practise it, in order that his soul may be purified and prepared for final emancipation. In course of time, probably under the indirect influence of Buddhists and Jainas, it came to be a general law of morality for all men, though there were always a great many ifs and buts to this 'general' law. The same law-books which teach *Ahiṁsā* as the first duty of all castes, also teach the *Varnâśrama-Dharma,* according to which it is the Kṣatriya's duty to fight and to kill ; and an ancient Hindu law-book says that the slaughter of beasts for sacrifice 'is no slaughter.' The Buddhist poet Mātṛceta, in his letter to the Mahārāja Kaniṣka, implores his royal friend to give up hunting, with the curious argument that since the king found sufficient practice in the use of arms in battle, why should he do harm to the wild creatures in the forest and at the same time to his own self? And even the Jaina author of Nīti-śāstra says: 'Calmness towards evil-doers is the ornament of ascetics, but not of kings.'

When we remember that, already in the hymns of the Ṛgveda, Indra, the lord of gods, is a great warrior and slayer of foes ; that the Hindu Epics revel in descriptions of battle scenes ; that Bhīṣma is not only a great sage and Yogin, but also a mighty killer of men ; that the Bhagavad-gītā, the most sacred book of the Hindus, teaches a warrior's morality, in which slaughter is justified by God Kṛṣṇa saying that 'the soul never slays and is never slain,'—and when we think of the most recent events in India, we shall hardly be able to agree with the late Deśabandhu C. R. Das who once said that he was opposed to revolutionary methods because 'violence is not part of our being as it is of Europe.'

In fact, violence is part of human nature in India, as it is in the West. Every living creature has a right to live, and no man has a right to destroy life. And yet, life is impossible without destruction of life. Looking at it from man's point of view, there is nothing as cruel and merciless as Nature, as 'God's beautiful creation' (as it is sometimes called), in which life and destruction of life—rarely an euthanasia, a beautiful and speedy passing away, more often a slow decay and destruction with infinite pains and tortures—are eternally interwoven.

And this is the great problem of *Ahiṁsā.* In a Jaina legend, a Śabara chief and his wife meet with a Sādhu who teaches them *Ahiṁsā.* One day the Śabara and his wife encounter a lion in the forest. The Śabara seizes his bow to shoot at the lion, but is reminded by his wife of the Sādhu's teaching. The Śabara chief throws his weapon aside, —and of course the couple are swallowed by the lion, but at the same moment they are reborn in the Saudharma Heaven as long-lived gods. Infidels as we are, we cannot be satisfied with such a solution of the *Ahiṁsā* problem.

Nay, the problem is there, and we have to face it. It is true that it is often necessary to destroy life, in order to save our own lives or a more valuable life, and to do harm and inflict suffering, in order to create some greater good for our people or for mankind. But it is required of us that we should sharpen our consciences, and should not lightly take life or inflict suffering on any living being, but that we should be at greatest pains to consider in every single case whether there is really *an absolute necessity* for killing or injuring. Only in such a case we are allowed to make ourselves guilty. For we are always loading guilt upon us whenever we inflict suffering on any living creature.

It is true that violence and hatred are natural, but it is no less true that love and sympathy are natural. And if we come to think of it, love is wise, and hatred is foolish, love alone is creative and hatred is destructive. It is an eternal truth that violence only creates violence again and can never bring peace. As it is said in the old Buddhist adage: 'Not by hatred is hatred appeased, by not-hatred hatred is appeased.'

Therefore, *Ahiṁsā*, the *not-wishing to harm,* remains a great moral ideal, however difficult it may be to achieve it fully. Though we may have to obey necessity and to make ourselves guilty, we can never cease to strive after this ideal. It may not always be possible to refrain from hurting, but it is possible to foster in us *the will to non-hurting, the will to peace.*

While everywhere in the world the goddess of violence is worshipped, and lives without number are sacrificed to her, there is one man in India, the Mahatma Gandhi who is holding up the old Indian ideal of *Ahiṁsā,* making it his political program. That this program has found so many followers among the masses of India goes far to prove how deeply this ancient moral doctrine has taken root in the soul of a great nation.

The Poet, whom we remember to-day in love and gratitude, has said that *the force of arms only reveals man's weakness,* and he has said again that *peace is true and not conflict, love is true and not hatred.* When people in the West will learn these truths, when they will have learnt that there is not only truth and wisdom but also strength in love and *Ahiṁsā,* then and then only Western civilisation will be rescued from that utter ruin by which, in spite of an unheared of technical progress, it is threatened in our days.

GERMAN UNIVERSITY, PRAGUE, CZECHOSLOVAKIA

M. WINTERNITZ

SELECTED TRANSLATIONS

NIOBE

[Three Fragments of an early Drama by the Author written about his twentieth year, in Rome, during his sojourn at the French school of the Farnese Palace.]

First Fragment

Country round Thebes. At the gates of the town. An autumn evening, shortly before sunset. Singing in the distance. The Niobids appear, young boys and girls, holding one another by the hand.

NIOBIDS

O country of Thebes, soil of our native land, perfumed air that caresses one, how sweet it is to feel thy loving breath! And you Cithæron, ye sacred hills, how I love your rocky heights, when I follow the hunt of the leaping deer over the sharp stones; or when in the solitary purity of the hill-tops the dark azure of the sky is mirrored in my blue eyes, as I watch the golden clouds floating by, whilst the hidden nightingales sigh forth their langorous plaints around me tenderly.

Then in the evening I descend, whilst the shadows mount from the sleeping earth below. The sheep-bells tinkle in the valley. The crickets sound their insistent rattle. The mysterious atmosphere is illumined by a shower of sparks, golden eyes in peaceful flight, with a soft beating of wings. I adorn my fair hair with fireflies, the flowers of night, and we return gaily towards the high shadows of the walls of Thebes, which stand out in the distance against the roseate horizon, holding one another by the hand grouping ourselves in noble dances across the fields, and bathing our white feet in the silvery streams.

NIOBE

O my children, your voices have the freshness of springs; your mouths and arms have the scent of the woods. Deioneus, Iole, Hyacinthus, my sweet hearts, how long you have tarried, this evening! As soon as you appear, I feel that I was without life, when I was without you. And thou, Deidamia, dreamer with the languid steps, why dost thou come alone, my daughter, lagging behind the others? Thy fine pale hair veils thy milk-white forehead; what hast thou done to-day, afar from me? Come, tell me. . . . .

DEIDAMIA

Under the trembling leaves of the aspen, by the side of the clear stream, listening to the ripple of the water flowing between the stones, with silent voice and closed eyes, without moving, as if in sleep,—I heard the sighs of the wind in the reeds, and the vivid breath of the zephyr, which refreshed my brow, without soothing my trouble.

NIOBE

What is the matter with you?

DEIDAMIA

I know not. Methinks my heart beats too fast. Methinks . . . all the shivers of the wind pass through me ; and my breast is too small to feel all that I feel.

NIOBE

Scan thy brow against my knees. Thy illness is not an ill, O my Deidamia, it is the approach of a delicious well-being. (How intoxicatingly sweet it is to feel the blossoming of these flowers of my blood, so chaste and so voluptuous!)

And thou, Callirhoe, thou little leaping fawn, thou art not sad, art thou? Thou hast no torments, O youngest of the Niobids?

How thou hast run! The brambles have marked thy brown calves with their claws. The nape of thy neck is sunburnt. And thy lips are reddened with the pulp of strawberries. What does it matter to thee? Dost thou but know that thou art beautiful? Thou laughest . . . Ah! when love seeks to possess her, how she will fly, my little swallow!

My heart is pierced with a proud tenderness. My children!

Ye Olympians, look upon us! Apollo, ocean of light, Artemis, calm lake wherein the day is mirrored,—which of you, O Immortals, is more beautiful than my sons? Which of you, O goddesses, is happier than I?

THE POPULACE

Niobe, fearest thou not the jealousy of the gods?

NIOBE

It is better to excite envy than pity!

POPULACE

O my daughter, the one is often very near to the other.

The night falls suddenly. Heavy clouds cover the sky.

[The scene following during a night of storm sees the passing of Atreus, king of Argos and brother of Niobe, who is pursued by the vengeance of the Olympians.]

Second Fragment

The dark veil of the sky has slowly lifted. Light is reborn. It is a day like twilight, soft and sad. The sun sinks behind the hills.

AT PARIS, 1926

After a drawing by Mr. K. Matsuhara.

POPULACE

The night grows gently clearer. Her long veils fall back with peaceful majesty. O day! I shall again see thy beautiful body shine forth! Friend, mine eyes kiss thee most lovingly.

NIOBE

O Gods, may everything be effaced,—and all that I have said! . . . Yes, the tender light . . . . A fresh breath bathes my burning brow. Zeus smiles. Zeus forgives . . . (*Music of distant flutes*). What is this plaintive song?

POPULACE

It is the procession of the Great Goddess. Demeter has lost her daughter, the fair Proserpine. She wanders through the meadows, and calls to her with loud cries. Nature is in mourning ; she sleeps beneath the earth, fair Proserpine, and for long months Demeter will groan.

NIOBE

Poor unfortunate . . . My heart is stirred with pity! Ah! how much I feel it, the weight of thy grief.

THE NIOBIDS

The gentle autumn is ended. The languishing light smiles mournfully. The woods of reddish gold extinguish their splendour. Nature sleeps the long sleep of winter . . . O flowers, shut your eyes. The hungry earth devours you. You are going to disappear within her bosom, in the night, and you will deck the fields of Hades for the charming feet of the young goddess, whilst our hearts will sigh for you . . . . Little fragrant souls, you are going to console the pale brows of the spirits, who have not forgotten . . . . Their exhausted lips, which will drink in your breath, will seek on your lips the traces of the kisses of bygone days. . . . .

But we shall meet again, dear little flowers! And you also, birds that sing of the spring! We shall rejoice together over the return of the sun, the young shoots that pierce through the prison of the bark, the amorous thrill of awakening life, the breath of the earth and the streaming of the waves of light . . . Why am I not already in the midst of those happy days . . . . Lovely daughter of the august Ceres, be thou not too faithful a spouse! Come back to us, young friend, we pine for thee! Come, we love laughter, dancing and love. Are we not more pleasant companions than the gloomy Pluto? Come back, dear friend, come back to join in our choruses! There is always time to sleep beneath the sod!

NIOBE

My heart is filled with a profound sweetness. The music of your voices, O my children, effaces the dream which oppressed me. I breathe again. The light lengthens. The gold of your hair is kindled with its reflections. I see your innocent faces near me. The blue sky blossoms forth again amidst the rosy clouds. And rending the last veils with his arrows, Apollo reappears.

Whilst Niobe speaks, the light actually increases, and takes on an intense brilliance. And when Niobe pronounces the name of Apollo, the apotheosis of the setting sun sets fire to the horizon. On this red sky appears Apollo, marble-like, dazzling, impassive, with arm outstretched, bow in hand.

POPULACE

(*seized with fright*)

Apollo!

(*Niobe turns round, utters a stifled cry, can neither speak nor move.*)

THE NIOBIDS

(*flee in disorder, like a flight of birds.*)

Ah! . . . .

[The scene which follows the second fragment describes the chasing of the Niobids by the Divine Archer.]

Third Fragment

The sun has disappeared behind the hills. It has left behind on the sky, large trails of golden dust and orange-red reflections, which gradually die out during the following scene.

NIOBE

O beloved ones, beloved ones!

POPULACE

O queen, I reply with sobs.

NIOBE

I cannot bear any more . . . . I fall . . . . .

POPULACE

Friends, let us support her. Unhappy woman! My eyes are flooded with tears!

NIOBE

Weep for me! I cannot weep . . . . . .

POPULACE

You see I weep and tear my hair.

NIOBE

My children! My love, my pride and my life!

POPULACE

They sleep amidst the flowers, which they were singing in praise of, but now.

NIOBE

Ah! thy pity is cruel! 'But now' . . . . But thou, what hast thou done, traitor, to defend them? Shouldst thou not have protected them with thy body? Thou hast only thought of thyself, of saving thy miserable life!

POPULACE

Niobe, life is sweet, even to those who suffer.

NIOBE

Coward, then take my life, my horrible life! Ah! take it, murderer, thou blood-stained god with the fierce bright eyes, Apollo! Just judge, that takest upon thyself the charge of punishing crimes, who will punish thine? What had these innocents done to thee? I alone scorned thee, and I scorn thee still! Executioner, I scorn thee! Thou god who slayest children, strike me! Art thou afraid?

POPULACE

Be silent, I pray thee.

NIOBE

What! should I not hate the monster that rends me?

POPULACE

Alas! they are the gods; they can do with us what they will . . . . . .

NIOBE

It is because they can do everything, that I want to hate them. Against their atrocious power, I have only my contempt; but my contempt alone is beyond their blows.

POPULACE

Take care lest their vengeance be not exhausted!

NIOBE

What can their vengeance do to me? There is nothing more that I love!

POPULACE

Grief is like a vast ocean. Who knows all its waves? Grief is like the unfathomable sky. Who has seen its depths?

NIOBE

Grief is limited by the limits of our life. I can die. Therefore I have nothing more to fear.

POPULACE

Unhappy woman, speak not of the worst misfortune!

NIOBE

I have touched the bottom of the abyss. My soul has descended into infinite night. Never again will it see the light that is lost. The void envelops me. I fall. There is nothing more . . . . . .

Night falls gently, the beautiful luminous night. The pale green sky is tender like a flower. The notes of a flute are heard again in the distance.

POPULACE

In the shades of the forest, the wandering Demeter carries on her inconsolable song for ever.

NIOBE

Alas!

POPULACE

(*looking at Niobe*)

The kindly music has made the tears well forth from her heavy heart.

NIOBE

O sweet and sad lament, which mingles itself with mine! Demeter, have pity! Thou knowest my grief, I suffer like thee.

POPULACE

Thou seest, my daughter, the gods are subject to the universal sorrow.

NIOBE

Thinkest thou my heart is so vile as to find solace in the unhappiness of others? Leave me! Get thee gone! . . . . . (*more gently*) Friend, I thank thee. Thy heart is good and simple. But leave me, I would weep alone.

The populace retire silently. The music of the flutes continues very softly in the distance.

NIOBE

She is seated, leaning on a mound of grass in the middle of the scene.

Demeter, how much we both are suffering! Immortal, thou bearest an immortal grief, and thy grief blossoms forth, eternally renewed. Unfortunate one, thou canst not die! But thou, thou wilt see thy daughter again! And I,—they will never return, my beloved ones. . . . O Demeter, thou knowest not the horror of 'Never!' Thy heart is resigned, and thy calm sorrow breathes forth in solemn laments, filled with pity! . . . . . But thou knowest not what means this 'Never!' . . . . Save me! I ask not of thee the lives of my children. Alas! thou weepest for thine! But death, ... O goddess . . . . . grant me death! The only grace which is left me, and which the lowest of wretches has the right to hope for . . . . Thy tears fall on me with the evening dew. I feel thy tender compassion floating in the air . . . . What a sudden peace! Behold! cruel life is leaving me at last. Light, thou art so beautiful! . . . . And yet, to the unhappy one who suffers, how sweet it is to lose thee!

HERMES

(*appears behind Niobe*)

Niobe, I am Hermes, messenger of death. Mine is a helping hand. It guides desolate souls to eternal oblivion. Come, lean on it. Do not accuse the gods. The gods have pity for thy tears.

NIOBE

(sighs sorrowfully)

Alas! could they not have let them live again? . . . . .
O my beloved sons!

HERMES

Whilst he is speaking, one sees on the face of Niobe sorrow succeeded by resignation, calm, a melancholy peace, and finally a weary smile. Dying, she gazes up at the sky, with head thrown back.

Zeus has delivered them. He has saved their souls from the destiny of thy race. Their arms were broken before being sullied by the heritage of pride and of insane power. Accuse not the gods, O daughter of Tantalus! Think of the reprobate laid low by thunderbolt! Think of thy brother Atreus, the madman who is carried off by the hurricane, that howling wolf who bequeathes to his descendants his torments and his crimes . . . . . Thy sons are asleep in the divine smile of nature. They are filled with the unalterable peace of the Infinite. Their breath is mingled with the serene torrent of light. Their souls are united with our immortal soul. He who has once tasted the waters of the eternal spring, will never again approach with his lips the troubled waters in which thy tears mingle . . . . . Woman, weep no more! The divine Olympians smile tenderly when they see thee shed so many tears for the sake of living. . . . Soothe thy wounded heart! Thy grief is ended. I pour upon thy brow the long sleep that knows no dream. Under its beneficent balm, pain disappears; all that which one suffered is no more. Sleep, Niobe, in the tender arms of the Good Nurse. August Demeter rocks thee gently. Here comes the fragrant evening; like a purple river, the light overflows. The soul that is wearied with the hard labour of the long day sees with joy the approach of the great night of Peace. The affectionate breath of the deep earth rises and kisses thy heavy drooping head. The all-powerful sun extinguishes its golden gaze. The grave melancholy of the music dies on the listless air. Everything lapses into silence. Everything stops. Everything dreams. . . . Everything is dream. . . . . . .

Very soft music accompanies his voice, and fades away, at the end. It is the soft dull light that follows the day and precedes the night. The moon has not yet risen. Stars blossom in the pale-green sky. Finally one of them shoots forth. It traces a luminous furrow on the sky, and dies out.

Niobe is seen from the front. At the appearance of Hermes, she has not turned at all, nor made the slightest movement to see him; she looks straight before her, and sees him, at is were, within herself.

To the magic bird of India I offer this youthful song of a little blackbird of France, who was trying his wings, on leaving the nest.

To Rabindranath Tagore, with my affection and respect.

VILLENEUVE, SWITZERLAND — ROMAIN ROLLAND

To

RABINDRANATH TAGORE

Many years have passed since the day
when I heard Rabindranath Tagore deliver his speech of thanks for the Noble Prize ;
but I still bear in mind the memory of a stately figure,
clad in loose, flowing robes of grey silk,
and of a countenance of rare nobility.
When one compared it with the other faces there,
it seemed to be modelled with far greater care and skill.
A spirit gifted with a keener thirst for beauty,
or perhaps with a clearer recollection of its heavenly origin
than is commonly vouchsafed to us,
had formed this head and body for its earthly dwelling-place.

I saw him stand at a desk in an ordinary lecture room.
Men and women in evening attire filled it to the last place.
Everywhere one met familiar faces ;
not for a moment could one forget
that one was in Stockholm, in 'Old Sweden.'
The lecturer spoke in English—clear and easily comprehensible English.
Not for a moment could one forget
that one was in Europe, and in the West.

But the foreign bard began to speak to us,
and, in a few simple words,
transported us to a far off, magic land.
I dare not say that it was precisely India,
but it was a land which he bore in his heart ;
a land without unrest, a land of peace,
where no jealous strivings, no harassing lust for power had place.

A heavenly peace enveloped us,
we wandered, as it were, along the banks of slowly gliding streams ;
under the summer stars we listened to the gentle words of wisdom ;
and life was shaped anew by fair and happy people
into poetry and good-will.

When it shall dawn—that day, so distant, so ardently longed for,
when life has reached its goal, when the final harmony is attained,
and the old dream of Paradise has become a reality ;
then will the men of that time remember the Indian seer

as one among those who prepared the happy future,
as one among those who, with invincible hope,
uprooted the poison-plants of hatred,
to sow in their stead the apples of love, and the roses of peace.

STOCKHOLM SELMA LAGERLOF

I shall never forget the day when my husband gave me *Gitanjali* and we began to read those beautiful hymns together. It was like coming home,—I know no better word for that blissful feeling when the soul finds its resting place. From that day Rabindranath Tagore has been the light of our home and the treasure of our hearts. Other wonderful books followed—the *Gardener*—the *Crescent Moon*—and then, during the time of the war, those unique lectures, full of wisdom: *Nationalism* and *Sadhana*. It was then that Rabindranath Tagore actually became the centre of my life, that I laid down my school work and entirely devoted myself to the translation and propagation of my Poet's work. For in his books, I firmly believe, the deepest longing of the human soul finds its fulfilment.

Rabindranath Tagore, Thou Golden Book of Wisdom and Beauty, Thou blessed Messenger of God, My heart bows to Thee!

WANDSBEK HELENE MEYER-FRANCK

What message can mighty India give us?

There is no higher message, than that of her renunciation of every force other than that of spirit.

And what spiritual lesson can India give us, of the preaching of which we stand in need?

There is none more impressive, than the song of freedom, in sonorous strophes, with which the Poet charmed us when he was a guest in our country and we came to see him.

We shall remember his tall figure and his radiant visage.

For we are come out of the power of dispensation and the infinite might of the same Creator.

FRANKFORT-ON-MAIN ALFONS PACQUET

TO RABINDRANATH TAGORE

FROM SERGEY VASILENKO, MOSCOW

Сергей Василенко

Рабиндранат Тагору

Гениальному поэту и мыслителю
Рабиндранат Тагору
в семидесятилетие его славной
жизни от заслуженного
деятеля искусства, профессора
Московской Консерватории
Сергея Василенко

С. Василенко

12/IV 1931 г.

С. Василенко
S. Wassilenko
Moderato ♩=63.
p
poco rall.
a tempo.
p
cresc. e accel.
a tempo
ff
affrettando
p

Agitato.
accel. molto
cresc.
rall.
Luminoso con esaltazione. ♩ = 88
ff
con Ped.
Ped.
Ped.
Ped.

Calando
rall. e dim.
Sostenuto ♩=69.
pp dolcissimo
Ped.
rit. molto
Ped.

Tempo I° (Moderato)
Ped.
rall.
a tempo.
p
rit.
p
a tempo.
poco accel.
sosten.
pp
rit. molto
dolce
pp
pp
Ped.
Ped.
29/III 1931.

قونسلگری دولت شاهنشاهی ایران
بمبئی

در این هنگام که آن دانشمند معظم از عمر شریف بمرحلهٔ هفتاد رسیده و دل و دیدهٔ
عموم دوستان خود و هواخواهان عالم انسانیت را روشنی تمام بخشیده اند مراتب
قدردانی اعلیحضرت اقدس همایون شاهنشاه پهلوی را بآن جناب ابلاغ و موقع را
مغتنم شمرده احساسات صمیمانهٔ شخص خود را نیز با ادعیهٔ خالصانه برای دوام
ایام فیروز و طالع بخش آن وجود محترم تقدیم مینماید. وزیر امور خارجه
فروغی

[TRANSLATION]

ON this happy occasion of the revered Sage's noble life reaching its seventieth birthday—of the Sage who has so fully illumined and enlightened the eyes and the hearts of all his friends and the well-wishers of the world of humanity—I tender to your noble self my Sovereign His Imperial Majesty Reza Shah Pehlevi's high regards for and appreciation of your life and work.

At the same time, I take the opportunity to offer you personally my most cordial sentiments on the occasion, and my sincerest wishes and benedictions for your long and prosperous life,—a life fraught with happiness to others.

TEHRAN, PERSIA

FOROUGHI,
Minister of Foreign Affairs

FROM THE CONSUL-GENERAL OF THE REPUBLIC OF CHINA FOR INDIA

如月之恒如日之升如南山之
壽如松柏之茂此詩人頌祝
之辭吾藉其辭以頌
太戈爾詩人
中華民國二十年十二月十八日
國民政府記名公使駐印度總領事張銘

May your life be as perpetual as the
movements of the Moon and the Sun ;
Equivalent to the longevity of the
Southern Mountain ;
And as flourishing as the Pine and the Cypress.

CALCUTTA

CHANG MING

GREETINGS FROM THE FIRST PIONEERS' COMMUNE

(TRANSLATION AT PAGE 265)

Поэту Рабиндранат Тагору.

Дорогой поэт.

В день вашего семидесятилетнего юбилея 1ая Пионер-Коммуна шлет Вам свой горячий коммунарский привет. Коммунары еще и сейчас помнят тот вечер который провели вместе с вами.

Мы хорошо помним песню индского народа, которую вы нам пели. После вашего отъезда жизнь далеко бросила нас вперед. За этот маленький промежуток времени страна сделала несколько гиганских шагов к социализму.

Каждый день приносит все новые и новые фабрики, заводы, которые досрочно выполняют пятилетний план, того самого плана, выполнение которого не так давно все наши враги считали фантазией. Энтузиазм народа творит чудеса. В строительстве участвуют не только взрослые, но и четыре миллиона ребят пионеров, которые заявили, что они строители не только будущего, но и настоящего. Наши коммунары вместе со всеми дерутся на трудовом фронте страны. Мы ведем работу на заводе металлоизделий „Серп и Молот". Этот завод раньше принадлежал французскому копиталисту Гужону. На заводе еще есть остатки старого. Есть несознательные рабочие которые часто прогуливают, пьянствуют. Вот с этими рабочими мы ведем большую воспитательную работу. Мы применяем самый мощный рычаг нашей стройки — это соц-соревнование берем с них обязательство не прогуливать и сами в свою очередь обязуемся хорошо учиться в школе. 20 прогульщиков дали слово — больше не срывать стройку, а принять в ней активную работу. Есть еще страшное наследие старого — это неграмотность. В стране еще сотни тысяч неграмотных людей и мы тоже включились в работу по борьбе с неграмотностью. Мы обучаем 50 человек. Кроме этого мы ведем работу культурную в красном уголке, в библиотеке. Ведем работу по внедрению техники в рабочие массы (распространение техники, проведение читок, помощь в организации тех кружков и т. д.)

Мы на своей общественной работе политически воспитываем себя и в условиях коммуны готовим коммунаров для великой стройки.

Желаем Вам много счастья и надеемся встретится еще раз с Вами в нашей свободной социалистической стране

С приветом коммунары.

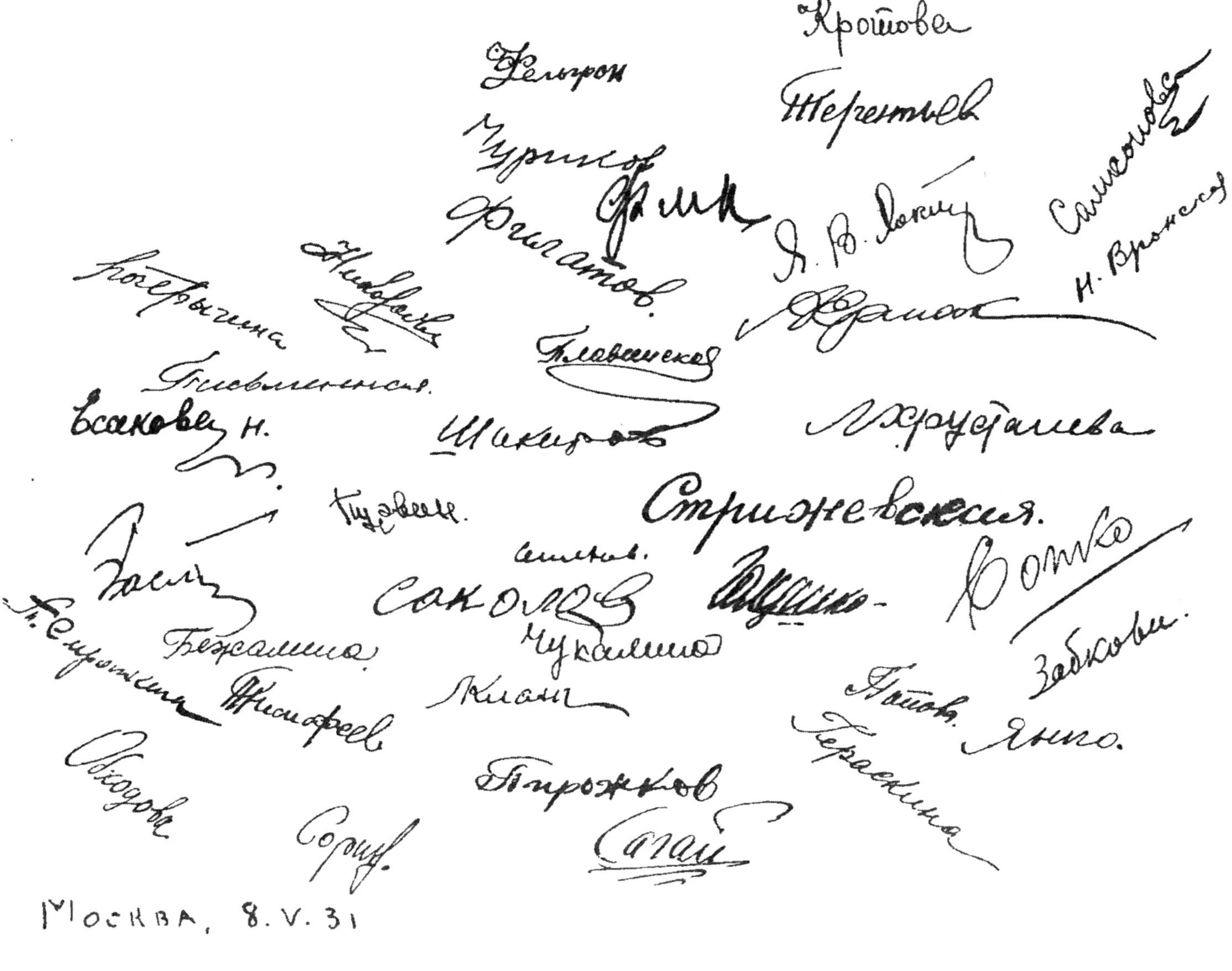

Москва, 8.V.31

GREETINGS FROM HIS MAJESTY THE KING OF SIAM

HIS Majesty the King has been pleased to command me to convey his felicitations on the occasion of the Seventieth Birthday Anniversary of Rabindranath Tagore.

I wish moreover to record my great pleasure (in complying with the request of the Golden Book of Tagore Committee) in writing something on this occasion. As an Asiatic and a Buddhist, I cannot but admire the cultured expressions and sympathies of the great Poet. As a worker in the field of education I wish to put on record my appreciation of the clear-sighted and sound theory maintained by Rabindranath Tagore. As a personal acquaintance, having had the pleasure of receiving him a few years ago in this country, I have been charmed by the magnetic personality of the poet and philosopher.

BANGKOK

DHANI

FROM PRINCE DAMRONG RAJANUBHAB OF SIAM

It was during his visit to Siam in 1927 that I had the pleasure of meeting Dr. Rabindranath Tagore, whose conversation and speeches left on me a most favourable impression. I knew of his reputation as a poet, and had seen some of his books in translation; but it was personal contact which enhanced the opinion I had formed of his great qualities.

I am glad to take this opportunity to congratulate Dr. Tagore on the approaching Anniversary of his Birthday, the Seventieth year of a long and useful life. By the power of the Three Gems, may he be blessed with health and strength, long to continue to guide the mission of his life.

VARADIS PALACE, BANGKOK

DAMRONG

It gives me great pleasure to express my tribute of respectful affection and profound esteem for the Poet Rabindranath Tagore and to offer him my heartfelt and warmest congratulations upon the completion of the Seventieth year of his noble life. In him I ever rejoice to see a happy and unique blend of purity and simplicity as well as a meeting place of the best in cultures of the East and West. With all the fervour at my command I pray the Almighty Lord to grant a long life of health and happiness as well as many turns of such joyous occasions to Rabindranath Tagore, the shining gem in the intellectual crest of India, our Mother-land.

THE PALACE, BHOR, BHOR STATE

R. S. PANT SACHIV

I am asked by the University to convey the felicitations of the Andhra University on the attainment of the Seventieth Birthday of the Poet. His work for the cultural renaissance of the country is unrivalled. And we are delighted to know that one, who infused the spirit of courage and self-reliance into the minds of our young men at a time when defeatism was invading us, is happily still with us, and we pray that he will live long to enjoy his well-earned rest.

ANDHRA UNIVERSITY,
WALTAIR

S. RADHAKRISHNAN

FIRST PIONEERS' COMMUNE COMPOSING GREETINGS FOR THE POET (MOSCOW, 1930)

ON behalf of the Professors and Lecturers of the Post-Graduate Arts Department of the Calcutta University I offer you our heartiest felicitations on the happy occasion of your Seventieth Birthday. Your life-long devotion to the cause of culture has very largely helped the attainment by our people of the goal for which the Calcutta University stands. You have immensely enriched the literature of Bengal, and have inspired your countrymen with the lofty ideals of nationalism and internationalism. The lustre of your genius has illumined the minds of men in the West as well as in the East, and has spread the name and fame of your dear Motherland. Although to-day you are a world-poet, Bengal claims you as her own and feels a pride in your greatness. May you enjoy health and happiness for many years to come, and may you continue long to render service to your country and to humanity at large.

THE UNIVERSITY,
CALCUTTA

PRAMATHANATH BANERJEA

L' Academie Royale de la Langue et de Litterature Française de Belgiques associe aux manifestations de sympathie et d' admiration en l'honneur du poète Rabindranath Tagore.

BRUXELLES

VAN ZYPE

RABINDRANATH AS CONVERSATIONALIST

Saṁsāra-viṣa-vṛkṣasya dve eva madhure phale:
kāvyâmṛta-rasâsvādaḥ, saṅgamaḥ sajjanāiḥ saha.

'THE poison-tree of Life bears only two sweet fruits: the immortal taste of Poetry, and converse with the great.'

So says the Sanskrit poet.

Anybody who has had the good fortune of hearing the Poet talk has enjoyed the taste of both these fruits.

Those who have not had the privilege of knowing him intimately may form some idea of the wonderfully illuminating character of Rabindranath's conversation from his '*Pancha Bhuter* Diary'—imaginary conversations which are only a transcript of his own talks.

I know nothing in literature which can be compared to them, except some of Plato's earlier dialogues.

CALCUTTA

PRAMATHA CHAUDHURI

BOTH as an economist and as a Zoroastrian it is my pleasant duty to express my admiration of one particular aspect of the many-sided activities of the great Poet of India. It has not always been duly emphasised that the University movement so widely and closely associated with his name has a special aspect as regards moral reconstruction and progress in India. While so many have envisaged the carrying back of industries to the villages, it is he alone who has not only conceived but carried out the idea of taking University education to the very door of the peasant. For half a century this was his dream; but for the last decade it has become a performance and an achievement. For in founding the Sri-Niketan (the abode of Lakshmi) he has taken back, in very truth, not only her but her august sister Saraswati as well, to their rural and natural environment. May they long continue to bless rural India, and may the example thus set by the Poet secure imitation all the world over.

CALCUTTA

J. C. COYAJEE

Love and Grateful Remembrances.

TOTNES, DEVONSHIRE, ENGLAND

LEONARD AND DOROTHY ELMHIRST

IT is given to few men in our generation, or in any generation, so to gain the attention of the youth of our universities that, besides being enlivened in their apprehensions of beauty, their whole spiritual apprehension is kindled. To Rabindranath Tagore belongs this distinction. In Harvard University we have especial reason to remember with gratitude his presence. The great opening discourse on personality, in the book called *Sadhana*, was first delivered there; and we recall still vividly his noble and stirring addresses relating to the modes of meeting of East and West. With full heart, we join in the greeting and recognition of this day.

CALCUTTA

WILLIAM ERNEST HOCKING
(HARVARD UNIVERSITY)

IT is very difficult to write a suitable appreciation of the work of our great poet-philosopher. His beneficent influence has been so manifold and wide-spread that many pages would be necessary for the purpose. I shall confine myself, therefore, to only one aspect which has appealed to me most, and, under the present circumstances of the country, appears to me to be most beneficent. What appeals to me most is the very practical turn that he has given to the abstrusest doctrines of our philosophy, by proving that the salvation, not only of India, but of the whole world, lies not in reforms and in systems of government, but in the change in the innermost recesses of our hearts.

THE UNIVERSITY, ALLAHABAD

GANGANATHA JHA

TAGORE, ARTIST AND INTERNATIONALIST

I happened to be in Italy when the first English translation of *Gitanjali* appeared, and I well remember the impressions of some of my Italian friends. In Italy, as in other Western countries, artists had been exploring the field of sensations, and it seemed to them as if there were no new fields whence to create new masterpieces. A sentiment of staleness was evident in many of them. When, then, Tagore appeared on the scene, it seemed as if once again something of the tender bloom of spring was to be felt in the invisible field of events which is the domain of Art. It was the artlessness and child-like response of Tagore to Life which seemed so deliciously fresh and young. Of course, behind his art, there lay a philosophy that was exquisite to the materialistic mind of the West. But above all things, it was the new glow of youth which charmed all in the West who discovered Tagore.

It is this element which has moved Europe and the two Americas very deeply. Three years ago I spent twelve months in travel in seventeen countries of Latin America. In every one of them all the educated men and women knew of Tagore—whose name, however, they pronounced in the Spanish fashion Tagoré—and through his writings had contracted what was to them the romance of India. Not only had most of them read his writings, but I think there was scarcely a home among them where I was a guest which did not have several of his works in translation.

All those who have had the privilege of knowing Tagore know how one of the most lasting impressions about him is his youthfulness. Who of us who has ever seen him dance will forget the sense of delight at seeing an elderly man throw himself with the abandon of a child into an artistic creation like the dance? The unity of the various aspects of Art is so strong in him that he is not solely a poet, as are so often poets in the West. He is a musician, actor and dancer too, and therefore every song and every play of his has a larger content than is the case with similar creations in the West.

Tagore's work at Santiniketan is now famous, and is a matter of pride for India. His contributions in the domain of education show, particularly to us in India, what is the only way to build the new Indian Nation.

MADRAS — C. JINARAJADASA

London Bengali Literary Society wishes you long life and fulfilment of your Ideals.

LONDON — PRABODH BOSE

RABINDRANATH Tagore has by life-long creative activities proved that the the vast evolution of culture, education, philosophy and art in modern India qualifies ourselves in a special measure to co-operate with other countries and nations on the cause of the development of international spirit and world peace. The cosmopolitan institution established by him at Bolpur which has for its main object the synthesis of the culture of the East and the West is a signal manifestation of his ideals. Our hearty felicitations to the Poet on this auspicious occasion.

DELHI — B. L. MITTER

We convey to you from the Authors' Club of New York our sincere regard and greetings on your birthday.

NEW YORK — MONTROSE J. MOSES
DANIEL HENDERSON

Heartfelt greetings. Praying for India and World Unity.

NEW YORK — HINDUSTAN ASSOCIATION

NEW History Society in memory of your gracious presence offers heartfelt felicitations on your birthday. May you as herald of new age continue shedding spiritual influence over hearts of East and West uniting man in aspirations for universal peace.

NEW YORK CHAIRMAN

Love and best wishes.

TAHITI, OCEANIA M. DUBOIS

Institute Indian Civilisation congratulates on Seventieth Anniversary. Best wishes and love.

PARIS A. FOUCHER, S. LEVI

HOMAGE OF YOUTH

SALUTATIONS to you, Gurudeva, our beloved Master, on completing the seventieth year of your noble and sublime life! It is indeed an occasion of rejoicing and jubilation for your disciples, friends and admirers all over the world, whom have reached your winged words with the subtle message of Light and Beauty, Hope and Harmony. The youths of the world will, I feel, hail this auspicious opportunity by offering thanks to God and profound homage to you.

AHMEDABAD MANILAL PATEL

TO

RABINDRANATH TAGORE

The Oriental Institute in Praha greets you on the threshold of the seventieth year of your fruitful life, wishes you peaceful days for the rest of your journey in this world and thanks you for the work done for your Nation, for Humanity and for drawing the East and the West nearer together.

PRAGUE, CZECHOSLOVAKIA PRESIDENT

Love and gratitude from American Quakers.

PHILADELPHIA, PA., U.S.A. PICKETT

RABINDRANATH represents the ideal of the progressive culture, not only national or international, but of universal humanity (*Visva-manava*).

This has been possible for him, on account of the all-embracing and all-pervading sympathy which his great soul entertains for all the movements throughout the ages, relating to the human as well as the extra-human.

This loving interest has found expression not only in his poetry, painting, dissertations, and other effusions of his soul, but also in the various creative efforts that he has made throughout his life for the advancement of humanitarian interest and humanistic ideals.

From this view-point Science, Philosophy, Poetry, Art and Religion are but different aspects of such culture as is essential to man.

The human race, generally speaking, however, is yet a long way behind the attainment of this life-giving objective. In the present stage of human progress it is only in very rare instances that we notice an earnest pursuit of this ideal by an individual, for less an achievement. The hearts are few that respond with a glowing love to everything that happend in the past, that are happening now in the present, and that will happen in the future in this great dwelling-house of man. The eyes are few that are gifted with the vision of seeing everything, irrespective of the limitations of time and space. The lips are few that can pour into unwilling and sceptical ears the outpourings of a soul that feels and a mind that sees. The personalities are few that bend in a contagiously loving and prayerful reverence before the Supreme Master.

Rabindranath, however, is far ahead of others in his easy progress towards those ideals. It is with a sense of pardonable pride that I congratulate myself in being able to appreciate the supreme beauty of his art, the soul-stirring effect of his poetry, the profoundness of his universal sympathy, the all-comprehensiveness of his vision, and the intensity and loftiness of his religion.

Poet, Seer, Worker, Lover, our divine Rabindranath occupies to-day the tenderest spot in every heart that feels. May his spirit forever illumine the path of humanity through his motherland.

THE UNIVERSITY, CALCUTTA NIL RATAN SIRCAR

South African Indian Congress send you grateful thanks for all you have done for us in sending out Mr. Andrews and giving us your own blessing. May God give you many years of further service for humanity. Please spare us Mr. Andrews again and ask him to come back to us and help us in our trouble.

DURBAN

DR. RABINDRANATH TAGORE

OF the few persons who have made the culture of modern India understood and appreciated by the world at large, Rabindranath is perhaps the most brilliant and outstanding exponent. He has helped to dispel an immense volume of ignorance about our country and our culture, and we cannot adequately express our admiration and feelings of indebtedness to him. India in the imagination of the West was a country disunited by castes and creeds, the home of strange religious rituals and practices. Her culture was considered as a thing of the past. Therefore the translation of Rabindranath's *Gitanjali* evoked admiration mingled with surprise in his readers outside India.

The ideas about India and her civilization began to improve when the West awoke to the consciousness that India was still an intellectual and spiritual force in the world, radiant with beauty and pulsating with life.

On the occasion of the seventieth birthday of the Poet, some of the greatest minds of Europe and Asia have united to pay their tribute of honour and reverence to him, and thus Rabindranath has been instrumental in making the East and West meet on a platform of equality.

We should be grateful to Rabindranath, not only because he has won through his poetry such a splendid recognition for India, but also because of the greater cause of humanity which he has served. He has realised in his soul the unity of man and the harmony of nature. The ideal which he has set up is freedom of the mind and spirit, and universal peace and good-will by true understanding between the peoples of the East and of the world at large.

He has founded a University at Bolpur in Bengal which is a striking piece of original work. He has dissociated himself from the beaten track of university education. He has not founded a denominational institution for the benefit of any one class or section of people, but has set up a seat of learning named *Santi-niketan*—the 'Abode of Peace,' placed amidst nature's own surroundings. Its atmosphere of freedom and simplicity is a stimulating factor in the discipline of the mind and body.

The poet has realised in a way that few people have that a liberal education alone can bridge the gulf of narrow denominational bias and prejudice.

Rabindranath's poetry is marked by a singular freedom from conventionality. His songs speak with a touching sincerity and with the naturalness of his relationship with the Unseen ; his passionate love of nature and his mystic sensitiveness are supreme.

His first spiritual inspiration must have come from his great father, Maharshi Debendranath Tagore. The Maharshi was a passionate admirer of the mystic poetry of Sufiism, and Rabindranath's poetry, too, in its spiritual content is reminiscent of the poems of the immortal Hafiz and other great Sufi or mystic poets of Iran. His external appearance has the stamp of a Persian saint and a Muslim Sufi. The Tagores with their broad spiritual outlook, received the best from Islamic mysticism. In their culture they seem to indicate the best type of Hindu-Muslim Unity.

My thoughts naturally turn to the friendly relations between our national poet and the University of Calcutta. Rabindranath has been associated with the University of Calcutta in setting papers in Bengali and in examining theses for our examinations. His active co-operation was obtained by the late Sir Asutosh Mookerjee in connexion with the scheme of higher studies and research in Indian Vernaculars. His books are studied by our students as text-books. He also delivered a series of readership lectures in the University in the year 1923. The stimulus that Rabindranath gave to a scientific study of the Bengali language and literature has been largely responsible for the collection of about 9,000 manuscripts in the Post-Graduate Department of our University. In 1913, during the Vice-Chancellorship of Sir Asutosh Mookerjee, my great predecessor, our University conferred the degree of D.Litt., *honoris causa,* on the poet, on the eve of the award of the Nobel Prize. To me personally it is a matter of the greatest satisfaction that as the first Muslim custodian of this great Temple of Learning I should be called upon to arrange the University celebrations in connexion with the Seventieth Birthday of the cosmopolitan Rabindranath Tagore—a great embodiment of Hindu-Muslim culture and unity.

THE UNIVERSITY,
CALCUTTA

HASAN SUHRAWARDY

OM !

TO the supremely-gifted Seer, the rightful heir to the heaven-illumined spirit of the Maharshi, is reverently rendered this humble homage, through the devoutest *pranamas,* of a heart that is moved with deep gratitude for the rich inspiration emanating from his sublime teachings. Out of the untold treasures of his golden words the one held most precious by the struggling, foot-sore way-farer is the evangel that God sets up His dear abode where dwell the humble and the lowly, the neglected and the dejected. He who by His breath kindles the quenchless stars, yet seeks delight in the frail earthen lamps of man ; He who passes in His royal progress attended with all the wealth of the worlds, yet pauses to stretch out His hand for the least of the little grains in the scrip of the beggar. Is not he who conveys this exalting message a closer friend, a nearer brother, of humanity than he who brings down wisdom from heaven to earth? For heaven, imagined to be far off, is here brought home to our hearts as enveloping and transfiguring whatever seems of the earth earthy. With all its after abasement, the soul, in essence, is God-born ; and to the pure eye of the All-Holy it is pictured even as the image of His Beauty—a Joy unto Him for ever. God takes joy in His creation, and the spirit of His Paradise pervades the earth everywhere. Here is the perfect presentation of the God of Love (*Anandam*), and here the sure ground of faith in Soul's Immortality (*Amritam*). Thus is God 'magnified,' and His *Rishi* 'proved.'

PITHAPURAM,
MADRAS PRESIDENCY, INDIA

R. VENKATARATNAM

Warmest wishes, love and greetings.

WANNSEE, BERLIN

BRUNO & HERTHA MENDEL

Warmest wishes, faithful love.

VILLENEUVE, SWITZERLAND

MADELEINE ROLLAND

Affectionate greetings on your seventieth birthday and best wishes from your Quaker friends.

LONDON

A. T. SILCOCK

ESTEEMED Master, the ancient Charles University at Prague, Czechoslovakia, highly appreciates your great merit, your work, and your influence, both moral and material, for culture and science. All your life you have bestowed gifts upon East and West in the great endeavour to draw them together. We sense the beauty of your work, and recall that our University had the honour of attending your learned address. We wish you, Master, all success as Poet, Teacher of your own people, and Prophet.

LESNY,
Professor of Indology

HUJER,
Dean of the Faculty of Philosophy

FREEDOM IN SPIRIT AND CULTURE

WHEN my people are again in possession of a great and living culture, and can surrender themselves completely to the interests of Humanity, it is then, not national freedom only, that will have put them in a position to do so: but, even as the Greeks had first to surrender their national independance to their conquerors the Romans, before they were in a position to bestow their cultural gifts to the latter, it will be a freedom which Rabindranath Tagore has begged for his own people in his *Gitanjali*.

Long may he be spared us to be the *Guru* for many.

THE HAGUE, HOLLAND

NOTO SOEROTO

Though somewhat late, I cannot hesitate to pay tribute for the great services which Rabindranath Tagore, the famous Poet and Philosopher, has rendered to the world of culture. Therefore, on my behalf and on that of my country, I offer my congratulations to the revered Poet on his Seventieth Anniversary.

KABUL, AFGHANISTAN

ALI MOHD. KHAN
Minister of Education

Canadian Delegation to League of Nations greets you on your Seventieth Birthday and wishes you health and happiness for many years to come.

GENEVA

GUTHRIE

DEAR DR. KALIDAS NAG,

The Academy of Athens has received your invitation with great pleasure. It has specially touched those members of our Academy who are Poets, for they stand closer to the great work of your National Poet and have deeper admiration of his achievements. Rabindranath Tagore's poems, distributed all over the world through various translations ever since the award of the Nobel Prize, have met with students and translators in our country as well. The interest in the work of the celebrated Indian Poet has become more wide-spread now in Greece. We admire profoundly his fertility in all branches of literature, lyrical, narrative, as well as dramatic. Tagore has combined the tradition of the profoundly philosophical speculations of his ancestors with all the elegance of occidental art. We know further that his creative activities go beyond the limits of pure poetical inspiration, that is, the elevation of humanity, the renaissance of his own country, and last, though not least distinguished factor—World Peace.

Hence we participate whole-heartedly in your Tagore Celebration, and we greet, from the historic land of Greece, the living symbol of the hoary wisdom of India. Some specimens of that wisdom reached us eighty years ago through our renowned Athenian writer, Demetrios Galanos, who translated some of your ancient texts from the original Brahmanic language.

May Rabindranath Tagore live long and continue his glorious and creative work for the good of humanity.

THE ACADEMY, ATHENS

PRESIDENT

HOMAGE AND ACKNOWLEDGMENTS

IN closing this *Golden Book* in print, before presenting it to the public I cannot help feeling that I have the privilege of recording only a few of the myriad voices speaking to Rabindranath. And while thanking our contributor-friends for their eloquent tributes to the Master Poet and to India, I cannot but raise my humble voice at the end, to remind the readers of this volume, that the silent love and good-wishes of the countless admirers of the Poet, all over the world, supply the real and permanent *base* of this superb Golden Music composed on this solemn occasion. The Inarticulate collaborate as vigorously as the Articulate with the Spinners of soul-symphonies: else how could we have a Beethoven? So our profound gratitude goes spontaneously to all those lovers of Beauty and Harmony who could not by chance enter formally into the list of contributors to this *Golden Book*, yet who combine to give the golden touch of love to every line of this volume. Those deeper undertones, those subtler upper partials, go to enrich and enliven the chance anthology of Greetings and Appreciations, Offerings and Dedications in the *Golden Book*.

Love alone can evoke love; and Rabindranath, the supreme musician, has unconsciously though inevitably drawn men and women the world over into this cosmic orchestra. He sang to the rivers, and the hills, to the flowers, and the shooting-stars, and they sang back to him, enriching his lyrics with their musical echoes. He sang to men and women, and they responded, as they must, to the exquisite importunities of a lover. He scented like a Seer the epidemic of Greed and Hatred slowly undermining the health of Humanity, and he threw away the flute of poetry for a while, and struck the warning chords of prophecy. In an age of Discord he sang of Harmony—'the august marriage of Love and Hatred,' as sung by his great musical *confrère* Romain Rolland. So his voice is as much of the ageless past as of the limitless future, as should be the voice of all world-poets. After centuries Rabindranath has sent forth a voice—his voice, from India and the renascent East, to every corner of the globe; and that voice has touched sympathetic chords in human hearts from Finland to South Africa and from Russia to Oceania—mystic orchestration of Life and Things—augury of a great future, wherein India and the Orient will co-operate with the rest of the world to bring out a new Era of Peace, Goodness, and Unity, of *Santam, Sivam* and *Advaitam*—basic elements in our Poet's Temple of Harmony. That temple is nowhere, and yet it is everywhere; and Rabindranath's supreme call to "the humblest, the lowliest and the lost" will carve for him a niche in the eternal pantheon of human poetry, and will ever shine as a beacon light to that supreme fruition of human destiny.

* * *

We are now offering the *Golden Book* to Rabindranath. In 1930, when various suggestions were being considered for the celebrations in connexion with the Seventieth Birthday of the Poet, it was felt that a permanent token of the world's appreciation should be presented to him on that occasion. This idea was voiced by M. Romain Rolland in the following Appeal communicated to Mr. Ramananda Chatterjee, our present Chairman, with a covering letter dated 30th Sept., 1930:

Rabindranath Tagore accomplit, en mai prochain, sa soixante-dixième année. Cette date doit rassembler autour de lui ses amis dans le monde, tous ceux dont la vie a été éclairée, élargie, ennoblie par la sienne. Il a été pour nous le symbole vivant de l'Esprit de lumière et d'harmonie, qui plane, grand oiseau libre, au milieu des tempêtes,—le chant d'éternité qu' Ariel fait vibrer sur sa harpe d'or, au dessus de la mer des passions déchaînée.

Mais son art souverain ne s'est jamais désintéressé de l'humaine misère et des luttes héroïques des peuples pour la liberté. Il a été "la grande Sentinelle," comme l'a nommé Gandhi (qui serait le premier parmi nous, pour le fêter, s'il n'était séparé de nous par les murs d'une prison). Il fut, aux heures tragiques, la vigie au regard lucide et intrépide, de son peuple et du monde.

Au nom des milliers, que sa voix mélodieuse a nourris d'espérance de foi et de beauté, nous convions ses amis poètes, artistes et savants à venir lui présenter, pour la fête de mai 1931, une gerbe de leurs fleurs et de leurs fruits spirituels. Il ne s'agit point d'hommages rendus personnellement au Poète—(nous croyons savoir qu'il ne le desire point). Mais, en signe de gratitude, que chacun lui offre une branche de son jardin: un poème, un essai, un chapitre de livre, une recherche scientifique, un dessin, une pensée!

Car tous ce que nous sommes et ce que nous avons créé a ses racines ou ses rameaux baignés dans le grand fleuve Gange de poésie et d'amour.*

---

*In May next Rabindranath Tagore completes his seventieth year. This occasion ought to bring round him his friends all over the world—friends whose lives have been illumined, broadened, ennobled by his own life. He has been for us the living symbol of the spirit of Light and of Harmony,—the great free bird which soars in the midst of tempests,—the song of Eternity which Ariel makes to vibrate on his golden harp, above the sea of unloosened passions.

But his sovereign Art has never remained indifferent to human misery and to the heroic struggles of peoples for freedom. He has been the "Great Sentinel" as he was named by Gandhi (who would be the first amongst us, to greet him, if he is not separated from us by the prison walls). In tragic hours, Tagore is the clear-eyed and undaunted watchman of his own people and of the world.

In the name of thousands whom his melodious voice has nourished with hope, faith and beauty, we invite his friends, poets, artists, scholars, to come forward and present to him on his seventieth birthday celebration, a bunch of their spiritual fruits and flowers. It need not be a personal homage to the Poet (we know that he does not like it). But as a token of gratitude, everyone might offer him a twig from his own garden—a poem, an essay, a chapter of a book, a piece of scientific research, a drawing, a thought.

For, all that we are and all that we have created, have had their roots or their branches bathed in the great Ganges of Poetry and Love.

The idea was taken up in India and abroad, and Mahatma Gandhi, Prof. Albert Einstein, M. Kostes Palamas, and Sir Jagadis Chandra Bose joined M. Romain Rolland in sponsoring *The Golden Book of Tagore* and issued an appeal. The contents of the volume testify to the response which this appeal has received.

A *Golden Book of Tagore* Committee was formed with the following gentlemen as members:

CHARU CHANDRA BHATTACHARYA, M.A., Department of Physics, Presidency College, Calcutta.

NANDALAL BOSE, Director of the Kala-bhavan, Visva-bharati, Santiniketan.

RAJ SEKHAR BOSE, Author, and Manager of the Bengal Chemical and Pharmaceutical Works, Ltd., Calcutta.

AMIYA CHANDRA CHAKRAVARTY, B.A., Lecturer, Visva-bharati, Santiniketan.

KEDAR NATH CHATTERJEE, B.Sc. (London), Manager, *Prabasi* Press, Calcutta.

RAMANANDA CHATTERJEE, M.A., Editor of the *Modern Review* and the *Prabasi*, Calcutta.

SUNITI KUMAR CHATTERJI, M.A. (Calcutta), D.Lit. (London), Khaira Professor of Indian Linguistics and Phonetics, Calcutta University.

NIRAD CHANDRA CHAUDHURI, M.A., Asst. Editor, The *Modern Review*, Calcutta.

O. C. GANGOLY, Solicitor, and Editor, *Rupam*, Calcutta.

AMAL HOME, Editor, *Calcutta Municipal Gazette*.

PRASANTA CHANDRA MAHALANOBIS, B.Sc. (Calcutta), M.A. (Cantab.), I.E.S., Professor of Physics, Presidency College, Calcutta.

KALIDAS NAG, M.A. (Calcutta), D.Litt. (Paris), Department of History, The University, Calcutta.

Mr. Ramananda Chatterjee was requested to act as Chairman and Editor.

I beg to express my best thanks to my colleagues, the Members of the Committee, for all they have done in bringing out the *Golden Book*. Mr. Amal Home and Mr. Amiya Chandra Chakravarty were in charge of the collection of contributions in the early stages. Mr. Raj Sekhar Bose, Mr. Charu Chandra Bhattacharya and Mr. Nirad Chandra Chaudhuri attended to the general work of the Committee and business arrangements. Mr. Nandalal Bose, in addition to his own pictorial contributions, is responsible for the cover design and the decorations for the special copy presented to the Poet. The best thanks of the committee are due to Mr. O. C. Gangoly and Mr. Kedar Nath Chatterjee for their valuable services in connexion with the illustrations. Finally I wish to offer my personal appreciation and thanks to my friends Mr. Suniti Kumar Chatterji and Mr. Prasanta Chandra Mahalanobis for the help they rendered unstintedly in seeing the book through the Press.

I have further to place on record the enthusiastic support rendered by the proprietor of the Art Press, Mr. Narendra Nath Mukherjee, as well as by his entire staff ; and also to Messrs. U. Ray & Sons for the care with which they have reproduced the illustrations.

The *Golden Book of Tagore* Committee places on record its grateful thanks to those whose co-operation alone made the volume possible—*viz.* the Contributors and the Artists, and the owners of the pictures who permitted us to use them for the book.

We regret that it has not been possible to print all the contributions received, as some of them arrived too late for inclusion and some had been already published fully or in substance. Certain contributions had to be edited and condensed mainly owing to reasons of space.

The Committee also has to express its thanks to those ladies and gentlemen including members of the various consular services in Calcutta and Bombay for furnishing translations and in some cases revising proofs of contributions in languages other than English.

Cordial thanks of the Committee are due to the warm support given to it by the Founder-Subscribers, in practically guaranteeing the publication. Without their co-operation it would have been exceedingly difficult to produce the volume.

Any profits accruing from the *Golden Book* will be funded for a *Ravindra-Vijaya,* a Tagore Commemoration of a permanent and international character.

I have also to crave indulgence from the Contributors and the Public for some inaccuracies which have unavoidably crept in the typography, and for the absence of system in arranging the contributions. The actual work of printing could be taken in hand only after the end of the first week of December, and it was completed during the last week of the same month : the task of receiving and marshalling contributions from all over the world was to some extent responsible for this.

This book, however, inspite of all its deficiences in printing and format, is offered to the Poet, and to all who love him and his works, as an embodiment, in its varied contents contributed from all parts of the world, of the guiding principle of Rabindranath's own Visva-Bharati, *viz.* :

यत्र विश्वम् भवत्येकनीडम् ।

Yatra Viśvam bhavaty Eka-nīḍam

'Where the Whole World finds its One Nest.'

CALCUTTA,
27th December, 1931

KALIDAS NAG
Secretary,
Golden Book of Tagore Committee

A TAGORE CHRONICLE: 1861—1931

The following brief chronicle has been compiled to give some idea of important phases of the Poet's career, and his activities mainly in the literary sphere. Dates of works have been selected with this purpose in view, without giving an exhaustive bibliography. Excepting important publications in English, no mention has been made of the large number of translations of the Poet's works into the other languages of the world.

The Poet took a leading part in all the dramatic performances mentioned here, but no attempt has been made to give a complete list of all performances in which he appeared himself. No mention has been made of the performances in the Santiniketan School in which he often takes an active part, nor of the numerous productions of his plays on the public stage in India and abroad. The dates of composition of Songs—about 2000 in number—have also been omitted.

It has not been found feasible to include references to Rabindranath's contact with personalities in India and abroad. Neither has it been possible to indicate his active participation in the educational and cultural, social and religious, and economic and political life of his country, and his untiring efforts to promote international good will and peace. In the case of Lectures and Sermons only a few of outstanding importance have been mentioned.

The date of Bengali publications in book form is given within brackets ; the approximate date of writing outside brackets. In the case of English translations, the dates refer to publication either in journals or in book-form. Most of the publications in Bengali give the Bengali year which begins in April. Owing to this lack of correspondence with the European year, a discrepancy of one year may have occurred in a few cases in which the month of publication could not be traced.

PRASANTA CHANDRA MAHALANOBIS

The following abbreviations have been used :

B.E.	=Bengali Era	L.	=Letters	V.	=Verse
B.M.	=Bengali Monthly	N.	=Novel	V.D.	=Verse Drama
E.	=Essays	P.D.	=Prose Drama	vols.	=volumes
Eng. tr.	=English translation	pub.	=published		

Eng.=Volume(s) partly or wholly written and published in English.

In the Bengali names in *Italics*, it may be noted that *a* is pronounced as in Eng. *all; c* as Eng. *ch.; ś, ṣ, s* all like Eng. *sh;* and *v* as *b* (after a consonant,=*w*).

The Poet's family belongs to the *Śāṇḍilya* clan (*gotra*) of the *Rāḍhīya* branch of *Brāhmaṇas*, and his ancesters are believed to have settled in Rāḍha or West Bengal about the 8th century After Christ. In the 17th century the Poet's family acquired the distinctive appellation *Ṭhākur*, meaning 'Respected Lord' (*Seigneur*), which was Anglicised first as *Tagoure*, and then as *Tagore*.

The Poet's name in Bengali is *Ravīndranāth Ṭhākur*, the *v* in Bengali being pronounced as *b*. The literal meaning of the personal name, *Ravīndranāth* (*Ravīndra-nātha* in the original Sanskrit form, and usually written as *Rabindranath* in English) is 'Sun-Lord'.

1861. Rabindranath Tagore born on Monday, May 6, 1861. (*Vaiśākha* 25, Saka Era 1783, Bengali Era 1268).

1867-74. Irregular attendance at various schools and studies at home with private tutors. First experiments in versification about 1868.

1873-74. *Upanayana* (Initiation) ceremony: first acqaintance with the *Gāyatrī* prayer. First visit to Santiniketan, and the Himalayas, with his father, Maharṣi Debendranath.

Sarada Devi (mother) died March 8, 1874.

1875-76. First publication of writings: Poem composed on the occasion of the Hindu Mela pub. in the *Amrita Bazar Patrika,* Feb. 25, 1875. Also poems, literary essays, and a long poem, *Vana-phul* (V., 1879. Wild Flower) in 8 cantos in *Jñānāṅkur,* a Bengali Monthly (1282-83 B.E.).

1877-78. First appearance in dramatic performance as *Alīk Bābu* in a Bengali Comedy by Jyotirindranath (elder brother). A new B.M., *Bhāratī,* started in *Śrāvaṇa,* 1284 B.E. (July, 1877) under the editorship of Dwijendranath (eldest brother). In 9 months the Poet contributed about 22 poems, (including some of the poems of *Bhānusiṁha Ṭhākur,* 1884), 2 essays, 6 articles of literary criticism, a long story (*Bhikhāriṇī,* the Beggar Maid), an unfinished serial novel (*Karuṇā),* and a long poem, *Kavi-Kāhinī* (V., 1878, A Poet's Story). Sojourn in Ahmedabad, Bombay Presidency, April—September, 1878, First musical compositions.

1878-80. First visit to Europe: left Bombay, September 20, 1878. Joined school in Brighton, then University College, London. Studied European music. Returned to India early in 1880.

Contributed to *Bhāratī* numerous poems and ballads, some of which were collected in *Saiśav Saṅgīt* (V. 1884, Songs of Childhood) ; literary essays (including articles on Anglo-Saxon Literature, Dante, Petrarch, Goethe, Anglo-Norman Literature, Chatterton, etc.), translations from Shakespeare, Burns, Moore, Shelley, Tennyson.

Yurop-pravāsīr Patra (1881, Letters of a Visitor to Europe). *Bhagna-hṛday* (V.D. 1881, The Broken Heart) begun in England. On return composed two musical dramas, *Vālmīki-pratibhā* (1881, The Inspiration of Valmiki) and *Kāl-mṛgayā* (1882, The Fateful Hunt) and took leading part in dramatic performances of both.

1881-83. Poems of *Sandhyā Saṅgīt* (1881, Evening Songs). Active participation in attempts to start a Bengali Literary Academy. *Vividha-prasaṅga* (1883, Miscellaneous Essays) and *Bau-ṭhākuraṇīr Hāṭ* (1884, The Bride-Queen's Market), first completed novel, started *Bhāratī* in 1881. First public lecture in Calcutta on 'Music'. Left for England to join the Bar, but returned from Madras, 1881. *Rudra-caṇḍa* (V.D. 1881) Poems of *Prabhāt Saṅgit,* 1882-83 (V. 1883, Morning Songs). Sojourn in Karwar. *Prakṛtir Pratiśodh* (V.D. 1884, *Eng. tr.* 'Sanyasi,' 1917). Poems of *Chavi O Gān* (1884, Pictures and Songs).

Married Mrinalini Devi, December 9, 1883 (*Agrahāyaṇa* 24, 1290 B.E.).

1884-90. Poems of *Kaḍi O Komal* (V. 1887. Sharps and Flats, includes translations from Shelley, Mrs. Browning, Ernest Myers, Aubrey De Vere, Augusta Webster, P. B.

Marston, Victor Hugo etc.). Prose sketches of *Ālocanā,* 1884-85 (Discussions). Literary studies collected in *Samālocanā* (1887, Criticism). First 2 short stories. *Nalinī* (P.D. 1884). Started new B.M., *Bālak,* from *Vaiśākha,* 1292 B.E. (April, 1885, amalgamated with the *Bhāratī* after 1 year) to which he contributed about 12 poems, 20 articles on various topics, 9 letters on social questions (*Ciṭhi-patra,* 1887), 8 humerous sketches in dramatic form, one prose drama, Mukuṭ (1908, The Crown), and a serial novel, *Rājarṣi* (1887, The Saint-King). Joint-editor, *Pada-ratnāvalī* (1885, anthology of Vaishnava lyrics). Lecture on *Satya* (Truth) 1885. *Ravi-chāyā* (1885, 1st collection of Songs). Secretary, Adi Brahmo Samaj (The Theistic Church of Raja Ram Mohun Roy and Maharshi Debendranath) 1887-1911. Poems of *Mānasī* 1887-90 (V. 1890, The Heart's Desire). Lecture on 'Hindu Marriage,' 1887. *Māyār Khelā* (Musical Drama, 1888. Play of Illusion). Appeared as King *Vikram* in performance of *Rājā O Rāṇī* (V.D. 1889, *Eng. tr.* 'The King and the Queen,' 1917). Appeared as *Raghupati* in *Visarjan* (V.D. 1890, *Eng. tr.* 'Sacrifice,' 1917). Took charge of the management of the Tagore Estates.

1890. Second visit to Europe, August-November, 1890: Italy, France, England.

1891-95. Started new B.M., *Sādhanā,* from *Agrahāyaṇa,* 1298 B.E. (November, 1891) to which he contributed for 4 years numerous poems, stories (collected in *Choṭa Galpa ; Vicitra Galpa* 2 vols. ; *Kathā-catuṣṭaya,* 1894 ; *Galpa-daśak,* 1895) ; literary essays, reviews, political articles and topical notes. Foundation Vice-President, Vangiya Sahitya Parishad (Bengal Academy of Letters), 1894.

Yurop-yātrīr Ḍāyāri (1891-93, Diary of a Traveller to Europe). *Citrāṅgadā* 1891 (V.D. *Eng. tr.* 'Chitra,' 1914). Poems of *Sonār Tarī* (The Golden Barge) 1892-93. Lecture on *Sikṣār Her-pher* (The Tortuosities of Education) 1892. *Pañca-bhūter Ḍāyāri* from 1893 (E. 1897, Diary of the Five Elements). Poems of *Citrā* 1893-95 (V. 1896). *Vidāy-abhiśāp* 1893 (V.D. 1894, *Eng. tr.* 'The Curse at Farewell,' 1924). Lecture on 'Englishmen and Indians,' 1893. Essay on 'Folklore,' 1894. *Mālinī,* 1895 (V.D. *Eng. tr.* 1917), and poems of *Caitāli* (The Last Harvest) 1895-96, published together with the 1st collected Poetical Works (Quarto, 1 vol.) in 1896. *Nadī* (V. 1896, The River).

1897-1902. Appeared as *Kedār* in dramatic performance of *Vaikuṇṭher Khātā* (Prose Comedy, 1897, Vaikuntha's Manuscript). Essays on Ancient India and ideals of civilization. *Kaṇikā* (V. November, 1899, Sparks), *Kathā* (V. January, 1900, Stories), *Kāhinī* (V. March, 1900, Tales), *Kalpanā* (V. May, 1900, Dreams). Editor, *Bhāratī* (1898-99), contributed in 1 year about 15 poems, 7 stories, 6 social and political essays, 4 religious and educational studies, 12 literary essays, and 1 verse drama, *Lakṣmīr Parīkṣā* (The Trial of Lakshmi). Poems of *Kṣaṇikā* (The Fleeting One), 1899-1900. *Cira-kumār Sabhā,* prose comedy, 1900-01 (The Bachelors' Club). Poems of *Naivedya* (V. 1901, Offerings). Essays on the Upanishads (*Brahma-mantra, Aupaniṣad Brahma,* etc.).

Founded the Brahma-Vidyālaya (Santiniketan School), December 22, 1901 (*Pauṣa* 7, 1308 B.E.).

Editor, *Vaṅga-darśan* (B.M., new series) for about 5 years from *Vaiśakha,* 1308 B.E. (April, 1901). *Cokher Bāli,* novel, 1901-02 (N. 1903, *Eng. tr.* 'Eyesore,' 1914). Poems of *Utsarga,* 1901-03 (V. 1914, Dedications). Lecture on *Atyukti* (Exaggerations, with reference to the Delhi Durbar), 1902.

Mrinalini Devi (wife) died November 23, 1902 (*Agrahāyaṇa* 7, 1309 B.E.).

1902-05. Poems of *Smaraṇ* (In Memoriam), 1902-03. *Naukā-ḍubi,* novel, 1903-04 (*Eng. tr.* 'The Wreck,' 1921). Poems of *Śiśu* 1902-03 (The Child, partly in *Eng. tr.* 'Crescent Moon,' 1913). Collected Poetical Works in 13 parts, 1903-04. Swadeshi and anti-Partition (of Bengal) movement. Lecture on *Svadeśī Samāj,* 1904. *Śivājī Utsav,* 1904. Swadeshi (patriotic) Songs (collected in *Bāul,* 1905). Political essays (collected in *Ātma-Śakti* and *Bhārata-varṣa,* 1905).

Maharshi Debendranath (father) died January 19, 1905 (*Māgha* 6, 1311 B.E.).

1905-10. Editor, *Bhāṇḍār* (B.M., political and economic) for 2 years from *Vaiśākha,* 1312 B.E. (April, 1905). Active participation in the National Council of Education, 1905-06. *Rākhī-bandhan* ceremony, October 16, 1905. Lecture on *Vijayā-sammilan,* 1905. Poems of *Kheyā,* 1904-06 (V. 1906, Crossing). Prose Works (exclusive of novels and short stories) in 16 vols. (comprising literary studies, 5 vols. ; social and political, 4 vols. ; educational 1 vol. ; linguistic 1 vol. ; and religious 1 vol.), 1907-08. *Gorā,* novel, 1907-10 (N. 1910, *Eng. tr.* 1924). President, First Bengali Literary Conference, 1907. President, Provincial Conference, Pabna, 1908. Lecture on 'East and West,' 1908. *Śāradotsav* (P.D. 1908, *Eng. tr.* 'Autumn Festival,' 1919). *Prāyaścitta* (P.D. 1909, Atonement). Sermons and religions discourses (1908-14) collected in *Śānti-niketan* (17 parts, 1909-16). Most of the poems of *Gītāñjali* written 1909-10. *Rājā* (P.D. 1910, *Eng. tr.* 'The King of the Dark Chamber,' 1914).

1911. Fiftieth Birthday Celebrations ; Poet as *Ṭhākur-dādā* in performance of *Rājā* at Santiniketan, May, 1911 ; Celebration in Calcutta 1911-12: Address presented by the Vangiya Sahitya Parishad.

1911-12. *Acalāyatan* (P.D. 1911, The Immovable Monastery). Lecture on 'Hindu University,' 1911. First publication of translations into English by the Poet, 1911-12. Attempts at reconstruction of Adi Brahmo Samaj. Editor, *Tattvabodhinī Patrikā,* 4 years, (1911-15). Lecture on *Dharmer Adhikār* (The Right to Religion, 1912). *Jīvan-smṛti* 1910-12 (1912, *Eng. tr.* 'My Reminiscences,' 1917). *Chinna-patra* (1912, Letters written 1885-1895. *Eng. tr.* 'Glimpses of Bengal,' 1921). Lecture on *'Bhāratavarṣer Itihāser Dhārā* (Main Currents of Indian History), 1912. *Ḍāk-ghar* (P.D. 1912. *Eng. tr.* 'The Post Office,' 1914). Projected visit to Europe postponed owing to illness, March, 1913. Translations of *Gītāñjali* poems into English during convalescence.

1912. Third Foreign Tour (May, 1912—September, 1913). English 'Gitanjali' published in England, 1912. Lecture tour in U.S.A., winter, 1912-13.

1913. Lecture on 'The Realization of Life', London (published in *Eng.* 'Sadhana'). Returned to India, September, 1913. *Eng.* 'Gardener' and 'Crescent Moon.'

Nobel Prize in Literature. Public reception at Santiniketan. D. Litt. (*Honoris Causa*), Calcutta University.

1914-16. Started village welfare work at Surul. Chief contributor to new B.M., *Sabuj-patra* (mainly literary) from *Vaiśākha,* 1321 B.E. (April, 1914) for about 3 years. *Gīti-mālya* (V. 1914, Garland of Songs) poems written mainly 1912-14. *Gītāli* (V. 1914) poems written in 1914. Recepient of Knighthood. Poems of *Balākā,* 1914-16 (V. 1916. *French tr.* 'Cygne' 1924). Short stories (collected in *Galpa-Saptak,* 1915). *Caturaṅga,* novel, 1914-15 (N. 1916, *Eng. tr.* 'Broken Ties,' 1925). Mahatma Gandhi and the inmates of his Asram resided temporarily at Santiniketan, 1915. *Phālgunī,* prose drama, 1915 (*Eng. tr.* 'Cycle of Spring,' 1917). Started *Vicitrā,* a literary club, in Calcutta, 1915-20. *Ghare-bāire,* novel, 1915-16 (N. 1916, *Eng. tr.* 'The Home and the World,' 1919). Lecture on *Sikṣār Vāhan* (Vehicle of Instruction) 1915. Performance of *Phālgunī,* January, 1916. *Paricay* and *Sañcay* (2 vols. of collected essays, 1916). Collected Poetical Works in 10 vols. (1915-16). *Eng.* 'Fruit-gathering' and 'Hungry Stones,' 1916.

1916-17. Fourth Foreign Tour (May, 1916—March, 1917). Lectures in Japan (*Eng.* 'Nationalism' 1917). Lectures in U.S.A., 1916-17 (*Eng.* 'Personality,' 1917).

1917-20. *Jāpān-yātrī* (L. 1919, Traveller to Japan). *Eng.* 'Stray-birds,' 1917. Performance of *Ḍāk-ghar* in the Vicitrā. Lecture on *Kartār Icchāy Karma* (As the Master Wills), 1917. Chairman, Reception Committee, Indian National Congress, Calcutta (for a few days only). *Guru* (P.D. 1918). Poems of *Palātakā* 1917-18 (V. 1918, Fugitive). *Gīta-pañcāśikā* and other collections of songs, 1918-20. Lecture on 'The Centre of Indian Culture,' 1918. *Eng.* 'Lover's Gift and Crossing,' 'Mashi and Other Stories,' 1918. Renounced Knighthood in protest against the Jalianwalla Bagh incident at Amritsar, 1919. Lecture on 'The Message of the Forest,' 1919. Prose sketches of *Lipikā* (1922) written mostly in 1919. Chief contributor to new B.M., '*Sānti-niketan* (*Patrikā*),' school magazine published from Santiniketan from April, 1919. *Arūp-ratan* (P.D. 1920).

1920-21. Fifth Foreign Tour (May, 1920—July, 1921). England, France, Holland, U. S. A., Switzerland, Germany, Denmark, Sweden, Austria, Czecho-slovakia. Lectures on 'East and West,' 'An International University,' etc.

1921. Returned to India, July, 1921. Lecture on *Sikṣār Milan* (Meeting of Cultures) and *Satyer Āhvān* (The Call of Truth). *Eng.* 'The Fugitive.' *Varṣā-maṅgal* (Music Festival of the Rainy Season).

Sixtieth Birthday Celebrations: Address presented by the Vangiya Sahitya Parishad.

Inaugural Ceremony of the Visva-bharati at Santiniketan, December 22, 1921 (*Pauṣa* 8, 1328 B. E.).

1922-24. Foundation of Sriniketan (Department of Rural Reconstruction, Visva-bharati) February, 1922. *Mukta-dhārā* 1922 (P. D. 1922. *Eng. tr.* 'The Waterfall' 1922). *Siśu Bholānāth* (V. 1922, Child Poems). *Eng.* 'Creative Unity' 1922. Visva-bharati Sammilani, literary club, started in Calcutta, 1922. Presided over Shelley Centenary, 1922. *Varṣā-maṅgal* (Rain-Festival), and *Sārodotsav* (Autumn Festival) 1922, *Vasanta-utsav* (Spring Festival), 1923. Started new English Journal, 'Visva-bharati Quarterly' (Editor, 1st quarter, April, 1923). Appeared as *Jay Siṁha* in performance of *Visarjan* 1923. *Ratha-yātrā,* 1923. (P. D., *Eng. tr.* 'The Car of Time,' 1924).

1924-25. Sixth Foreign Tour (March—July, 1924): Burma, Malaya, China, Japan. *Eng.* 'Talks in China', 1925. *Rakta-Karavī*, 1924 (P. D. *Eng. tr.* 'Red Oleanders', 1924).

Seventh Foreign Tour (September, 1924—February, 1925): invited to attend Peru Centenary, but returned from Beunos Aires (Argentine Republic) owing to illness; visited Italy in January.

1925-26. Most of the poems of *Pūrabī* (V. 1925) written during the South American tour. Performance of *Śeṣ-varṣaṇ* (Last Rains, musical drama) 1925. *Pravāhinī* (V. 1925. Collection of Songs). *Gṛha-praveś* (P. D. 1925. The House-Entry). *Śodh-bodh* (P. D. 1925. The Reckoning). First President, Indian Philosophical Congress, December, 1925. *Naṭīr Pūjā* (P. D. 1926. *Eng. tr.* 'The Worship of the Dancing Girl,' 1927). *Ṛtu-utsav* (P. D. Collection of 5 Season Festivals).

1926. Eighth Foreign Tour (May—December, 1926): Italy, Switzerland, Austria, France, England, Norway, Sweden, Denmark, Germany, Czecho-slovakia, Hungary, Jugoslavia, Bulgaria, Rumania, Turkey, Greece and Egypt.

1927. Ninth Foreign Tour (July—October, 1927): Malaya, Java, Bali, and Siam.

1927-29. Performance of *Naṭīr Pūjā* in January, and *Ṛtu-raṅga* (Cycle of Seasons) in December, 1927. *Naṭa-rāj*, verse drama, 1927. *Yogāyog* (Cross Currents), novel, 1927-28, (N. 1929). *Śeṣer Kavitā* (The Last Poem) 1928. (N. 1929). Poems of *Mahuā* (V. 1929) mostly written in 1928. Sermon on 'The Message of Ram Mohun Roy,' *Bhādra* 6, 1335 B.E. (August 22, 1928) in commemoration of the Centenary of the Brahmo Samaj (Theistic Church of India). *Eng.* 'Fireflies,' and 'Letters to a Friend,' 1928. *Lekhan* (Writing), composed at various times, published in 1928.

1929. Tenth Foreign Tour (February—July, 1929): Malaya, China, Japan; attended the Triennial Conference of the National Council of Education, Canada; U. S. A.; Indo-China.

1929-30. Message to the Parliament of Religions, Calcutta, 1929. *Yātrī* (Letters, 1929. Traveller). *Paritrāṇ* (P. D. 1929, Redemption). *Tapatī* (P. D. 1929). Performance of *Tapatī*, 1929. *Bhānusiṁher Patrāvalī* (Letters, 1930). Various Educational Primers.

1930-31. Eleventh Foreign Tour (February, 1930—January, 1931): France, England, Denmark, Germany, Russia, U. S. A. Hibbert Lectures in England in 1930 on 'The Religion of Man' (1931). Exhibition of Drawings in Europe and U. S. A.

1931. *Rāśiyār Ciṭhi* (Letters from Russia, 1931). Performance of *Navīn* (musical drama) in March, *Gīta-utsav* (Music Festival) in August, *Naṭīr Pūjā* and *Śāp-mocan* (Dance; Expiration) in December. *Vana-vāṇī* (V. 1931. Forest-message). *Gīta-vitān* (Collection of Songs, 1931).

Seventieth Birthday Celebration at Santiniketan, May, 1931. Civic, National and International Celebrations in Calcutta, 25th—31st December, 1931.

Presentation of *THE GOLDEN BOOK OF TAGORE*, on the 27th December, 1931.

FOUNDER-SUBSCRIBERS

MISS MAY ARATHOON, Villa Primrose, Monte Carlo, Monaco.

RISHIKUMAR PANDIT RAMDAS BADUNI, Ghari Pauri, Garhwal, U.P., India.
KUMAR PRAMATHESH BARUA, GAURIPUR RAJ, Gauripur, Assam.
BIRENDRA KUMAR BASU, I.C.S., District Judge, Bankura.
SRIMATI KANAK PRABHA BASU, 11, Mahendra Goswami Lane, Calcutta.
JEHANGIR FRAMJI BATLIBOI, 48, Ridge Road, Malabar Hill, Bombay.
E. C. BENTHALL, 37, Baliganj Park, Calcutta.
PROF. PANDIT BASANTA KUMAR BHATTACHARYYA, JYOTIRBHUSHAN, 105, Grey Street, Calcutta.
SHEOKISSENDAS BHATTAR, President of Indian Chamber of Commerce, 30, Clive Street, Calcutta.
GUSTADJI D. BILLIMORIA, Bombay.
BRIJMOHAN BIRLA, 8, Royal Exchange Place, Calcutta.
LAKSHMINIVAS BIRLA, 8, Royal Exchange Place, Calcutta.
KARUNABINDU BISWAS, 117/1, Bowbazar Street, Calcutta.
DR. AJIT MOHAN BOSE, 5/1, Swinhoe Street, Calcutta.
HIMANSU MOHAN BOSE, Bar-at-Law, 25/1, Rowland Road, Calcutta.
DR. KARTICK CHANDRA BOSE, M.B., Dr. Bose's Laboratory, 45, Amherst Street, Calcutta.
MRS. NALINI BOSE, C/o. DR. DEVENDRA MOHAN BOSE, 92, Upper Circular Road, Calcutta.
NONIGOPAL BOSE, B.S. (COM.), "Foxchase," 18, Los Angles Avenue, Hollywood, Philadelphia, U.S.A.
RAJ SEKHAR BOSE, 14, Parsibagan Lane, Calcutta.
SARAT CHANDRA BOSE, 17, Woodburn Park, Calcutta.
RAS BIHARI BOSE, 79, Onden, Aoyama, Tokyo.
J. M. BOTTOMLEY, B.A. (OXON.), I.E.S., Director of Public Instruction, Bengal.

AMIYA C. CHAKRAVARTY, Santiniketan, Bengal.
MATHURAMOHAN CHAKRAVARTI, Sakti Aushadhalay, Dacca.
MRS. ARUNDHATI CHATTERJEE, C/o. KEDAR NATH CHATTERJEE, 2/1, Townshend Road, Calcutta.
ASOKA CHATTERJEE, B.A. (CANTAB.), 2/1, Townshend Road, Calcutta.
BIJAY CHANDRA CHATTERJEE, Bar-at-Law, 21, Baliganj Circular Road, Calcutta.
MRS. KAMALA CHATTERJEE, C/o. ASOKA CHATTERJEE, 2/1, Townshend Road, Calcutta.
KEDAR NATH CHATTERJEE, B.SC. (LONDON), 2/1, Townshend Road, Calcutta.
RAMANANDA CHATTERJEE, M.A., Editor, *The Modern Review*, Calcutta.
SUBIMAL CHANDRA CHATTERJEE, 33, Linton Street, Calcutta.
SUNITI KUMAR CHATTERJI, Professor, the University, Calcutta.
SARAT CHANDRA CHATTOPADHYAYA, Santaber, Panitras, Howrah, Bengal.
AMIYA NATH CHAUDHURI, Bar-at-Law, 42, Jhautala Road, Baliganj, Calcutta.

MRS. B. L. CHAUDHURI, 9A, New Park Street, Calcutta.
MRS. MIRA CHAUDHURI, C/o PRAPHULLA CHAUDHURI, 4, Sambhunath Pandit Street, Calcutta.
KUMAR J. K. ACHARYYA CHAUDHURY, Muktagacha, Mymensingh, Bengal.
SAJAN KUMAR CHAUDHURI, M.L.C., 21, Belvedere Road, Alipur, Calcutta.
MRS. SITA CHAUDHURI, C/o. SUDHIR KUMAR CHAUDHURI, 283, Park Circus, Calcutta.
SHETH JIVANLAL CHOONILAL CHINAI, 79, Masjid Bunder Road, Mandvi, Bombay.
GULZARSINGH CHOBE, Bakuba, Tanganyika Territory, East Africa.
LAURA W. COLE, 570, South Greenwood Ave., Pasadena, California, U.S.A.
NORMAN FRANK COLEMAN, A.M., LL.D., Reed College, Portland, Oregon, U.S.A.
JAMES H. COUSINS, Theosophical Society, Adyar, Madras, India.

SETH DINSHAW F. DABOO, B.A., Park View, Lunsikui, Navsari, Bombay Presy.
S. N. DALMIA, 70, Cotton Street, Calcutta.
RAI BAHADUR GIRISH CHANDRA DAS, 35/1A, Badur Bagan Street, Calcutta.
NALINI NATH DAS GUPTA, Bengal Civil Service, Noakhali.
BHULABHAI J. DESAI, Advocate, Bombay.
MRS. INDIRA DEVI, C/o. PRAMATHA CHAUDHURI, 20, Mayfair, Baliganj, Calcutta.
MUKUL CHANDRA DEY, A.R.C.A., Principal, Government School of Arts, Calcutta.
SIR HORMUSJEE COWASJEE DINSHAW, KT., M.V.O., O.B.E., 121, Meadows Street, Fort, Bombay.

MRS. M. VAN EEGHEN-BOISREVAIN, Meentweg 5, Naarden, Holland.

BRUCE M. FALCONN, 26, East 63rd Street, New York, U.S.A.
F. J. FIELDEN, M.A. (LOND.), M.A. (CANTAB.), Principal, Agra College, Agra.

H. H. GENERAL SIR KAISAR SHAMSHER, J.B.R., K.B.E., Kaisar Mahal, Kathmandu, Nepal.
JUSTICE BIPIN BIHARI GHOSE (retired), Dover Lane, Calcutta,
THE HON'BLE JUSTICE SIR CHARU CHANDRA GHOSE, KT., 10, Debendra Ghose Road, Calcutta.
K. B. GHOSE, Solicitor, 6, Old Post Office Street, Calcutta.
ANU GHOSH, 19, Dumdum Road, Calcutta.
M. GHOSH, M.A., B.L., 39, Russa Road, Calcutta.
RAI BADRIDAS GOENKA BAHADUR, C.I.E., M.L.C., 145, Muktaram Babu Street, Calcutta.
TULSI CHARAN GOSWAMI, Serampore, Bengal.
SISIR KUMAR GUPTA, 55, Canal East Road, Calcutta.
S. K. GUPTA, B.A., 41, Girish Park North, P.O. Beadon Street, Calcutta.
DR. BHAGWAN SINGH GYANEE, Kansas City, U.S.A.

SUDHINDRA KUMAR HALDAR, I.C.S., Calcutta Club, Calcutta.
W. W. HAWKINS, 230, Park Avenue, New York City, U.S.A.

PRABHUDAYAL HIMATSINGKA, M.A., B.L., P1, Chittaranjan Avenue, Calcutta.
CARL ADALRIK HOGMAN, Publications *Chitra*, Paris.
MRS. ILA HOME, C/o. AMAL HOME, 99/1N, Cornwallis Street, Calcutta.
ARTHUR HUGHES, Chinsurah, Bengal.
DR. L. K. HYDER, B.A. (CANTAB.), PH.D. (Heidelberg), Aligarh University, Aligarh, U.P.
MRS. STEPHANIE HYDER, Doctor of Philosophy (Berlin), Aligarh University, Aligarh, U.P.

D. J. IRANI, B.A., LL.B., 49, Esplande Road, Fort, Bombay.

CURRIMJEE JEEWANJEE, Port Louis, Mauritius.
PROF. AMARANATH JHA, English Department, Allahabad University, Allahabad.

BHAGIRATH KANORIYA, 8, Royal Exchange Place, Calcutta.
A. P. KAPUR, 177, Khetwadi Balk Road, Bombay.
DEVIPRASAD KHAITAN, M.A., B.L., 8, Royal Exchange Place, Calcutta.
DURGAPRASAD KHAITAN, M.A., B.L., 43, Zakaria Street, Calcutta.
KALIPRASAD KHAITAN, M.A., B.L., Barrister-at-Law, 43, Zakaria Street, Calcutta.
LAKSHMI NARAYAN KHETTRY, 44, Maniktala Street, Calcutta.
MISS ADAH L. KIEFFER, B.A., 76, Linden Avenue, Engle Wood, New Jersey, U.S.A.
KUMAR KRISHNA KUMAR, M.A., B.L., M.R.A.S., 31, Burtola Street, Calcutta.

SHETH KASTURBHAI LALBHAI, Pankore's Naka, Ahmedabad.
NARENDRANATH LAW, M.A., B.L., P.R.S., PH.D., 96, Amherst Street, Calcutta.
ANIEKA YAN LEGGETT, Villa Star-Poggiochiaro, Castello, Florence, Italy.
VINCO LESNY, Professor, Czech University, Prague, Czechoslovakia.
MISS ALMA L. LISSBERGER, 302 West 86th Street, New York, U.S.A.
J. J. LYNN, 6440, Brooklyn Avenue, Kansas City, Missouri, U.S.A.

MRS. NIRMAL KUMARI MAHALANOBIS, C/o. PRASANTA CHANDRA MAHALANOBIS, 210, Cornwallis Street, Calcutta.
PRASANTA CHANDRA MAHALANOBIS, Professor, Presidency College, Calcutta.
K. C. MAHINDRA, 12, Mission Row, Calcutta.
MAHARAJA KUMAR UDAYCHAND MAHTAB, B.A., the Palace, Burdwan, Bengal.
SISIR KUMAR MAITRA, M.A., PH.D., Hindu University, Benares.
JOHN I. B. MCCULLOCH, New College, Oxford, England.
THE HON'BLE MR. JUSTICE SATYENDRA CHANDRA MALLIK, B.A. (CANTAB.) M.A. (CAL.), I.C.S., 7/3, Burdwan Road, Calcutta.
RAGHUNATH MALLIK, M.A., 237, Maniktala Main Road, Calcutta.
H. H. PANGERAN ARIO ADHIPATI MANGKOENEGORO VII, Mangkoenegoran, Soerakarta, Java.
MRS. B. R. MEHTA, Palmlands, Nepean Road, Malabar Hill, Bombay.
SISIR KUMAR MITRA, Professor, University College of Science, Calcutta.
THE HON'BLE SIR BROJENDRA LAL MITTER, KT., Member, Executive Council, Government of India, Delhi.

Rai Bahadur Khagendra Nath Mitter, M.A., 10, Dover Lane, Calcutta.
Prof. Sushil Chandra Mitter, M.A., D.LITT. (Paris), No. 4, The Mall, Dum Dum.
Sir Rajendra Nath Mookerjee, K.C.I.E., K.C.V.O., 7, Harington Street, Calcutta.
Birendranath Mookerjee, M.A. (Cantab.), 12, Mission Row, Calcutta.
The Hon'ble Mr. Justice Manmatha Nath Mukherjee, M.A., B.L., 8/1, Harsi Street, Calcutta.
Narendranath Mukherjee, 31, Central Avenue, Calcutta.
Maharani Lila Devi of Mymensingh, 74, Lower Circular Road, Calcutta.

Kumari Santisri Nag, C/o. Dr. Kalidas Nag, 283, Park Circus, Calcutta.
Soorajmull Nagarmull, 61, Harrison Road, Calcutta.
Prithwisingh Nahar, B.A., 38, Indian Mirror Street, Calcutta.
Mrs. Henry Necaisulmer, 225, West 86th Street, New York, U.S.A.
Major Fred J. Ney, M.C., Secretary, National Council of Education, Winnipeg, Canada.

K. M. Panikkar, Secretary, Chamber of Princes, Bhopal.
Sree Raja Rao Venkata Kumara Mahipati Surya Rao Bahadur, O.B.E., Maharaja of Pithapuram, Madras Presidency, India.
Seth Hanuman Prasad Poddar, M.L.C., 10/A, Chittaranjan Avenue South, Calcutta.
Lakshman Prasad Poddar, 2, Hastings Park Road, Alipur, Calcutta.
Rustom Sorabjee Powvala, Homecroft, The Ridge, Malabar Hills, Bombay.

Rao Bahadur S. E. Ranganadhan, M.A., Vice-Chancellor, Annamalai University, Chidambaram.
C. S. Rangaswami, Editor, *Indian Finance*, Calcutta.
Sir Sarvapalli Radhakrishnan, KT., Vice-Chancellor, Andhra University, Waltair, Madras.
Sir Chandrasekhara Venkata Raman, KT., M.A., PH.D., D.SC., LL.D., F.R.S., Professor, the University, Calcutta.
Sardarsinhji R. Rana, 56, Rue Lafayette, Paris.
M. V. V. Rau, Bengal Nagpur Railway Audit Department, Calcutta.
Dr. S. C. Ray, Editor, *Industrial & Finance Review*, 14, Clive Street, Calcutta.
Bezawada Gopala Reddi, Buchireddipalem, Nellore Dist., Madras Pres., India.
Asoka K. Roy, Bar-at-Law, Calcutta.
Basanta Kumar Roy, New York, U.S.A.
Bhupendranath Roy, Behala, 24-Perganas, Bengal.
Devi Prasad Roy Choudhury, Principal, Government School of Arts, Madras.
Dharani Mohun Roy, 85, Amherst Street, Calcutta.
Manindra Nath Roy, Behala, 24-Perganas, Bengal.
Sudhir Kumar Rudra, M.A. (Cantab.), Reader in Economics, the University, Allahabad.

JOSEPH A. SADONY, Valley of the Pines, Montague, Michigan, U.S.A.
PRINCESS SAVITRIBAI SAHIBA, C/o. B. T. DHAVALE, B.A., L.D.M., Snehalataganj, Indore.
MRS. AMIYA SANTRA, c/o. Kishori Mohan Santra, Budge Budge.
KUMAR AMIYA NARAYAN SANYAL OF PUTHIA RAJ, Rajshahi, Bengal.
KUMAR SACHINDRA NARAYAN SANYAL OF PUTHIA RAJ, Rajshahi, Bengal.
MRS. AMBALAL SARABHAI, Shahibagh, Ahmedabad.
NALINI RANJAN SARKAR, 6A, Corporation Street, Calcutta.
LAKSHMAN SARUP, Professor, Oriental College, Lahore.
BINAY RANJAN SEN, Indian Civil Service, Noakhali.
RAS BIHARI SEN, Delhi.
BHUPATI MOHAN SEN, Principal, Presidency College, Calcutta.
I. B. SEN, Bar-at-Law, 57/1, Harish Mukherjee Road, Bhowanipur, Calcutta.
MRS. MIRA SEN, C/o. SUDHIR KUMAR SEN, 32, Ghughu Danga Lane, Baliganj, Calcutta.
DR. S. N. SEN, Meteorologist, Alipore Observatory, Calcutta.
ACHALANANDA SEN GUPTA, "Ramkali Bhaban," Bankipore P.O., Patna Junction.
P. SESHADRI, Principal, Sanatan Dharma College, Cawnpur.
VENKATARAO C. SETALVAD, B.A., LL.B., Setalvad Road, Napean Sea, Bombay.
ARTHUR MAYCE SEYMORE, Florida State College for Women, Tallahassee, Florida, U.S.A.
PANDIT RAJGURU HEMRAJ SHARMA, C.I.E., Dhokatol, Nepal.
LORD AROON SINHA, 7, Lord Sinha Road, Calcutta.
BAHADUR SINGH SINGHI, 116, Lower Circular Road, Calcutta.
THE HON'BLE LIEUT.-COL. BIJAY PRASAD SINGH, M.A., M.L.C., Minister, Government of Bengal, Calcutta.
SUHRID CHANDRA SINHA, Susang, Mymensingh, Bengal.
MRS. SIMANTI SINHA, C/o Suhrid Chandra Sinha, Susang, Mymensingh.
THE HON'BLE MR. SUSIL K. SINHA, I.C.S., Chief Presidency Magistrate, Calcutta.
HIS HIGHNESS MAHARANA SHRI DAULAT SINHJI, K.C.S.I., K.C.I.E., Thakore Saheb of Limbdi, Kathiawar.
REV. J. T. SUNDERLAND, 1510, Cambridge Road, Ann Arbor, Michigan, U.S.A
THE HON'BLE SIR NRIPENDRA NATH SIRCAR, KT., Bar-at-Law, Advocate General, Calcutta.
LT.-COL. DR. HASAN SUHRAWARDY, O.B.E., M.D., F.R.C.S.I., D.P.H., Vice-Chancellor, University of Calcutta.

PRAPHULLA NATH TAGORE, Sheriff of Calcutta.
H. H. THE RAJA OF TEHRI-GARHWAL STATE, Narendranagar, U.P., India

VIKRAMADEO VARMA, RAJA SAHIB, Jeypore, Vizagapatam District, Madras Presy.

THOS. J. WATSON, 270, Broadway, New York City, U.S.A.
MRS. ANNIE BEARD WOODHOUSE, 25, Broadway, Withington, Manchester.
WILLIAM H. WOODIN, 30, Church Street, New York City, U.S.A.